CHAUCER'S

Canterbury Tales

(SELECTED)

AN INTERLINEAR TRANSLATION

BY

VINCENT F. HOPPER

PROFESSOR OF ENGLISH
NEW YORK UNIVERSITY

REVISED
EDITION

BARRON'S EDUCATIONAL SERIES, INC.

All inquiries should be addressed to:
Barron's Educational Series, Inc.
250 Wireless Boulevard
Hauppauge, NY 11788
www.barronseduc.com

Library of Congress Catalog Card No. 70-99791

ISBN-13: 978-0-8120-0039-9
ISBN-10: 0-8120-0039-0

PRINTED IN THE UNITED STATES OF AMERICA
39 38 37 36 35 34

Table of Contents

Preface to the New Enlarged Edition

The original interlinear translation of the general prologue and some of the best of *The Canterbury Tales* has been so well received since its initial publication in 1948 that I have been encouraged to enlarge it. The ideal enlargement, I suppose, would be to add everything else that Chaucer wrote as part of his ambitious design. But this kind of interlinear translation is so lavish in its physical demands on space that such a project would have resulted in a volume high in price and bulky in size.

With the idea, then, of keeping the amount of additional material within reasonable bounds, I considered each of the remaining untranslated tales and concluded that the Miller's and the Reeve's stories were most worthy of inclusion. But a tally of the number of lines in each made it obvious that for the amount of space to be consumed even by the single story of Patient Griselda, I could add two typical shorter Chaucerian tales together with their prologues and simultaneously allow the reader to see Chaucer's original plan completely carried out from the opening of the general prologue through the conclusion of the Reeve's Tale. "Shortly for to seyn," this was the exact reason for my selection of this additional material.

A Note on the Translation

The attempt to translate poetry from one language to another has always been a somewhat futile procedure. Since the art of the poet depends so much on his phrase-making ability, there is no way of transposing exactly the effect of the original to a different language. In no two languages are meanings and associations the same for any but the commonest words; consequently the particular effect of any group of words in one language can never be reproduced in another.

The translator is therefore faced with a painful choice. He may strive to obtain a close approximation of the meaning of each individual word by giving what is known as a "literal" translation, and in so doing sacrifice the poet by representing him in wooden and uninspired prose; or he may attempt to recreate the spirit of the original by a "free" translation, the success of which depends on the poetic flair of the translator himself. But however admirable in itself the result of either kind of translation may be, it never speaks with the voice of the original poet.

Translating Chaucer poses a very special problem in that Chaucer wrote in a language which is very close to modern English but not quite close enough to be readily comprehensible. A literal translation does not, therefore, do as much violence to Chaucer's language as would be the case if he had written in an entirely foreign tongue. At the same time, the difference between Chaucer's and modern English is sufficiently pronounced so that phrases that were apt and fluid in Chaucer's language appear clumsy and inept in modern speech. This difficulty can be avoided by a free translation; yet it seems unreasonable to be forced to rely upon a modernized version of Chaucer, which inevitably loses much of the poet's individuality, when Chaucer himself is by no means inaccessible.

The following interlinear translation is therefore offered as a method of reading Chaucer in the original without the annoying necessity of constant interruption for consultation of a glossary or dictionary. It should be easy for the eye and ear to follow the original while translation of difficult words and phrases in the interlineation will suggest to the mind a close approximation of the meanings intended.

With the deliberate intent of allowing Chaucer to speak for himself, this translation makes no claim to recapture anything of the poet's charm or verbal music. The modern English follows the original, word for word, as closely as possible, deviating from this rule only when a freer rendering clarifies what might otherwise be obscure to a modern reader. Chaucer's English is not so remote that he cannot be read with ease after a little practice. The running translation is intended to make the process of familiarizaton as painless as possible, and also to give needed assistance over the more difficult passages; thus restoring Chaucer's original intention of being completely intelligible and providing his reader with unalloyed pleasure.

New York University, N.Y.   VINCENT F. HOPPER
August, 1969

Introduction

"THE POET'S EYE, in a fine frenzy rolling" has little or no connection with the first great English poet. Chaucer was an eminently sane and well-balanced man of affairs, who was derived from a family of business men and who appears to have discharged equally well, during his lifetime, the functions of diplomacy and the supervision of public works. His claim to literary preëminence rests on his possession of an alert imagination, a vital and active mentality, a keen interest in humanity, an observant eye, and a wonderfully sensitive ear. Although he had nothing of Shakespeare's sweep and intensity, he is closer to Shakespeare than any other English poet in his absorbed interest in the fascinating spectacle of humanity. His is also the special distinction of having taken the crude and uncertain accents of a language and a metric which were still very much in the process of formation and, by study of French and Italian models, of having fashioned from his native Middle English a highly fluid and mellifluous verse; wherefore he is sometimes referred to as "the father of English poetry."

Geoffrey Chaucer was born in London around 1340. As the son of a prosperous wine merchant who had also held various government posts, he was undoubtedly given a respectable schooling. How far his formal education continued cannot be ascertained, but men then relied less than at present on the classroom as a source of knowledge. Chaucer's writings offer ample testimony that he was an avid reader, interested in the science of the day, particularly astrology, and in religious and secular literature and learning, both ancient and contemporary. Something of the range of his reading may be gathered from his very considerable familiarity with the Roman authors, Seneca, Ovid, and Horace; the medieval Boëthius, Macrobius, and Alanus de Insulis; the contemporary French Machaut, Froissart, and Deschamps; and the Italian Dante, Petrarch, and Boccaccio.

Chaucer's connection with government first appears in his

employment, at the age of seventeen, possibly as a page, in the household of Elizabeth, Countess of Ulster and wife of Prince Lionel, third son of Edward III. Two years later he was with the English army in France where he was taken prisoner. His ransom, to which the king contributed, allowed him to return to the service of Prince Lionel who apparently used him to carry dispatches across the English Channel during the subsequent peace negotiations in France. In 1366 he married Philippa Roet who was in the service of the queen and whose sister became the third wife of the powerful John of Gaunt. In 1367 he was in the service of the king as a gentleman in waiting, from which position he rose, in 1368, to that of esquire, which entailed the responsibility of helping to arrange court functions and entertain guests. During the next ten years he was engaged in a series of diplomatic missions to the continent where his reading of French poetry acted as a powerful stimulus to his own early attempts at versification, as it was to remain the strongest literary influence of his life. During these years he also found a patron in John of Gaunt who, in 1374, granted him an annual pension.

His diversified career at this time is revealed in the record that, in 1369, he was again in military service in France, and that, in the same year, the death of John of Gaunt's first wife was the occasion for the composition of a poem in her memory. From December 1, 1372 to May 23, 1373 he was engaged in a diplomatic mission which took him to Italy, where Petrarch and Boccaccio were the leaders of a flourishing literary renaissance. He may actually have met Petrarch, and his reading of Dante, Petrarch, and Boccaccio provided him with subject matter as well as inspiration for later writings.

In 1374 he was given a lease by the corporation of London on a house of his own at Aldgate on the sole condition that he keep it in repair. In the same year he was appointed Comptroller of the Customs and Subsidy of Wool, Skins, and Hides in the port of London. In 1375 he obtained the lucrative wardship of the heir and lands of Edward Staplegate in Kent. Being engaged in several foreign missions between 1376 and 1381, he was permitted to employ a deputy for his post as Comptroller. He met the French king in Flanders during the peace negotiations of 1377 and, later in the year, went to

France as a member of a commission to arrange a marriage between the newly enthroned Richard II and a French princess.

After 1378 there is only one record of a foreign mission, but in 1382 he received the appointment of Comptroller of the Petty Customs of the port of London, and in 1385 was permitted to have a permanent deputy for that post. In 1386 he resigned from his positions in the custom house, gave up his house in London, and retired to Kent, to which county he had been appointed Justice of the Peace in 1385. In the summer of 1386 he was elected Knight of the Shire (like the Franklin in *The Canterbury Tales*).

When Richard II came of age in 1389, Chaucer was made Clerk of the King's Works. In 1390 he was given a special appointment to attend to repairs to St. George's Chapel, Windsor. In the same year, he supervised the construction of scaffolds for two tournaments (which were probably not as elaborate as those described in *The Knight's Tale*), and he was also a member of a commission to look after the walls, bridges, sewers, and ditches along the Thames. In 1391 he resigned from the important and probably strenuous Clerkship of the Works and took his last regular office as Deputy Forester of a royal forest in Somerset.

He continued to receive various temporary appointments, and remained in the royal service after the coronation of Henry IV in 1399. In that same year, he took the lease of a house in the garden of Westminster Abbey, but died soon thereafter, on October 25, 1400. He is buried in Poet's Corner of the Abbey, where a monument to him was erected by Nicholas Brigham, a minor poet of the sixteenth century.

This record of his manifold activities and his connections with English nobility, continental diplomats and rulers, with men of learning and men of trade, explains the breadth of knowledge and the kind of temperament which made Chaucer one of the best recorders of the medieval world. His literary career, which was rather late in flowering, probably began during his early connections with courtly society in the composition of brief love lyrics which have not survived but which he mentions in *The Legend of Good Women*. His models were undoubtedly French as was the basis of his first ambitious literary undertaking, the translation of the long but extremely popular French *Roman de la Rose.* Although it is certain that he undertook this task, the date and the extent of his translation are unknown; only fragments remain, and there is doubt of Chaucer's authorship of all of these. In 1369 he wrote *The Book of the Duchess,* an allegory in the form of a dream, to commemorate the death of Lady Blanche, wife of John of Gaunt. Using Ovid's story of Ceyx and Halcyon, Chaucer in his skillful use of dialogue and graceful treatment of nature gave promise of later talents, although metrically the poem is often uncertain. A few minor poems complete the extant productions of what is commonly referred to as his French period, ending around 1372.

Inspired by the superiority of the Italian literature which he had come to know through his diplomatic missions, Chaucer, during his so-called Italian period, was extremely productive between 1375 and 1385. He translated *The Consolation of Philosophy* by the early Christian philosopher, Boëthius (c. 480-524), which was to influence his own thinking, and wrote a number of major poems. *The House of Fame,* influenced by Dante's *Divine Comedy,* is another dream-allegory concerning earthly glory and its value, a favorite theme of Chaucer's time which reappears in *The Canterbury Tales.* His finest work during this period, and second only to *The Canterbury Tales,* was *Troilus and Creseyde,* a long narrative poem derived from Boccaccio's *Il Filostrato.* Abjuring the sentimentality of his model, Chaucer makes this very beautifully phrased and cadenced work a masterpiece of detached humor and an ironic commentary on human nature. The story is ancient but the characters and their behavior were made contemporary and universal; and Chaucer's deftness in handling both them and their story signalized him as a highly talented and individual poet of humanity. *The Parliament of Fowls* celebrates allegorically the events of Richard's courtship and marriage to Anne of Bohemia in 1382. Using birds in place of humans, Chaucer portrays the eagle (Anne) as being besieged by three male eagles. Birds of prey symbolize the peers, and fowls of lower degree represent the worlds of business and agriculture. The entire graceful and imaginative composition foreshadows the fable of Chanticleer and Pertelote of *The Nun's Priest's Tale.* He also wrote, around this time, the story of Palamon and

Arcite which was later incorporated in *The Canterbury Tales* as *The Knight's Tale.*

Chaucer's maturity as an independent poet and commentator on human nature was reached during the last fifteen years of his life (1385-1400), which comprise what is called, by way of distinction, his third or English period. The writings composed during these years assume a much more realistic and less derivative character. A transitional work, *The Legend of Good Women,* was an ambitious project which was to have consisted of a prologue and legends of nineteen noble women of classical antiquity who faithfully served the god of love. After completing nearly nine of these, including the stories of Cleopatra, Thisbe, Dido, and Medea, he apparently tired of the monotony of the scheme and abandoned it for the more diversified plan of *The Canterbury Tales.* The entire *Legend* was written in heroic couplets, and seems to have made the first use in English of this form of ten-syllable rhyming couplets (with five accents to each line) in which most of *The Canterbury Tales* was written.

Begun soon after 1386, *The Canterbury Tales* presents Chaucer at his richest and his best. Collections of stories were nothing new in the world, harking back as far as *The Arabian Nights.* The best known of such contemporary collections was Boccaccio's *Decameron,* with which Chaucer was apparently unacquainted, in which ten Florentine youths and maidens of noble families leave Florence to escape the plague and, on ten successive evenings, tell a story apiece each evening to pass the time. Chaucer's plan of a pilgrimage to Canterbury made possible a much greater diversity of story tellers and hence of stories, furnished a much more lively background, and presented greater dramatic possibilities in the contrasts among the pilgrims. Taking advantage of the customary springtime pilgrimages to the shrine of Thomas à Becket, on one of which Chaucer may well have gone himself, he planned a *Prologue* which would describe the gathering of the thirty pilgrims at the Tabard Inn in London and the proposal that each pilgrim should tell two tales on the way to Canterbury and two more on the return trip. The *Prologue* was to have been followed by sixty stories connected by remarks made by the listeners, descriptions of their wayfaring, and accounts of chance occurrences along the route. A description of their arrival at Canterbury and their doings there would then have preceded sixty tales more, together with the account of the return journey. A description of the final banquet tendered to whoever had told the best story would have concluded the book. This colossal undertaking was less than a quarter finished before Chaucer's death, so that the work exists in fragments which have been put together by later editors. Besides completing the *Prologue* and a number of the tales, Chaucer fortunately finished some of the transitional sections as well (described as "prologues" and "epilogues") so that the general characteristics of the work as well as its effectiveness are little harmed by its incompleteness.

The poetry of Chaucer owes its appeal to the breadth rather than the depth of his knowledge; to the vitality of his interests rather than to intensity of feeling. Chaucer was a lover of the world of nature and human nature. The freshness and delicacy of his descriptions of natural beauty have seldom been equalled. Concerning humanity, Chaucer had a broad tolerance and understanding which reached down even to the lower classes. Skeptical about human superstitiousness and satirical about human failings, he describes such frailties as they are, but he never forgets that to be foolish or vain or dishonest is to be human, and that the variations of human conduct make up the perpetually fascinating spectacle of life.

In setting down this panorama of reality, Chaucer possessed a rare technical mastery of verse forms. In his use of the French octasyllabic couplet (of *The Romaunt of the Rose, The Book of the Duchess,* and *The House of Fame*), the heroic couplet (of most of *The Canterbury Tales*), and the seven-line stanza known as rime royal (of *Troilus and Creseyde* and *The Prioress's Tale*), he has never been surpassed. His verse is always fluid, diversified, and alive. Particularly remarkable is its finely tuned combination of sounds, rhythms, and cadences.

Extraordinary in their variety, the narratives of Chaucer, particularly in view of the long-winded and digressive tendency of medieval story telling in general, are usually simple, straightforward, and direct, pausing only for vivid descriptions whose sharply selected details suggest a broad picture, or for dramatic moments and situations. Characterization, dialogue, and presentation of a situation comprise Chaucer's greatest art as a narrator. His most obvious fault is the interruption of narrative for a parade of learning or philosophical commentary; yet even this has some excuse. To his contemporary readers, much of the information presented was doubtless novel and interesting; the philosophizing was, in a more obvious form, what all good narrative and dramatic writers attempt to include as a "spire of meaning" to give their accounts of individual lives or events a universal significance.

Such talents as these, however, have been shared by other authors. What one finds in Chaucer that cannot be duplicated elsewhere is the essential good-humored mellowness of his own nature, which has its most individualized expression in the air of casual informality which pervades *The Canterbury Tales*. Where other authors strive painfully for telling effects, Chaucer seems always completely at his ease, writing when he pleases with sharpness, directness, originality, and sure-footed skill; but at other times repeating himself without embarrassment, filling in a line with words which add nothing to the sense, tossing in an all but meaningless phrase to complete a rhyme, promising to end a tale quickly and instantly forgetting his promise. In the mouths of the pilgrims, such deliberate carelessness helps reinforce the informal atmosphere of the journey, keeps the story teller himself before the reader, and personalizes the story according to the character of the narrator. But even in the *Prologue* where Chaucer speaks directly to the reader, the same holiday mood prevails. The descriptions of the various pilgrims turn in rapid sequence from an article of clothing to a point of character and back again with no apparent organization or desire for it. Yet so effective is this artful artlessness that each pilgrim stands out sharply as a type of medieval personality and also as a highly individualized character. Here the very jumbling of details allows the reader to see the picture all at once as a composite unit, rather than as a catalogued series of compartmented aspects. As a result, *The Canterbury Tales* is a vivacious picture of the Middle Ages and an eternally alive gallery of humanity.

The selections in this volume include the best of *The Canterbury Tales,* and also give a clear indication of the variety of the stories and the connecting episodes between them.

CANTERBURY TALES

The Prologue

Whan that Aprille with his shoures sote
When April with his showers sweet

The droghte of Marche hath perced to the rote,
The drought of March has pierced to the root,

And bathed every veyne in swich licour,
And bathed every vein in such liquor,

Of which vertu engendred is the flour;
From whose virtue is engendered the flower;   4

Whan Zephirus eek with his swete breeth
When Zephyr' too with his sweet breath

Inspired hath in every holt and heeth
Has quickened, in every grove and field,

The tendre croppes, and the yonge sonne
The tender sproutings; and the young sun

Hath in the Ram his halfe cours y-ronne,
Has in the Ram his half course run,'   8

And smale fowles maken melodye,
And small birds make melody,

That slepen al the night with open yë
That sleep all the night with open eye

(So priketh hem nature in hir corages):
(So nature goads them in their hearts):

Than longen folk to goon on pilgrimages   12
Then people long to go on pilgrimages

(And palmers for to seken straunge strondes)
(And palmers' to seek strange shores)

To ferne halwes, couthe in sondry londes;
To far-off shrines, known in sundry lands;

And specially, from every shires ende
And especially, from every shire's end

Of Engelond, to Caunterbury they wende,   16
Of England, to Canterbury they wend,

The holy blisful martir for to seke,
The holy blessed martyr to seek,

That hem hath holpen, whan that they were seke.
Who helped them, when they were sick.

   Bifel that, in that seson on a day,
   It happened that, in that season on a day,

In Southwerk, at the Tabard as I lay   20
In Southwark,' at the Tabard' as I lay

Redy to wenden on my pilgrimage
Ready to wend on my pilgrimage

To Caunterbury with ful devout corage,
To Canterbury with a fully devout heart,

At night was come in-to that hostelrye
At night there came into that inn

Wel nyne and twenty in a companye,   24
Full nine and twenty in a company,

Of sondry folk, by aventure y-falle
Of sundry folk, by chance fallen

In felawshipe, and pilgrims were they alle,
Into fellowship, and pilgrims were they all,

That toward Caunterbury wolden ryde;
That toward Canterbury would ride;

The chambres and the stables weren wyde,   28
The chambers and the stables were large,

And wel we weren esed atte beste.
And well we were treated with the best.

And shortly, whan the sonne was to reste,
And briefly, when the sun had gone to rest,

So hadde I spoken with hem everichon,
So had I spoken with them every one,

That I was of hir felawshipe anon,   32
That I was of their fellowship forthwith,

And made forward erly for to ryse,
And made an agreement to rise early,

To take our wey, ther as I yow devyse.
To take our way, as I shall tell you.

But natheles, whyl I have tyme and space,
But nevertheless, while I have time and space,

Er that I ferther in this tale pace,   36
Ere that I further in this tale proceed,

Me thinketh it acordaunt to resoun,
I think it appropriate

To telle yow al the condicioun
To tell you all about the nature

Of ech of hem, so as it semed me,
Of each of them, as they appeared to me,

And whiche they weren, and of what degree;   40
And who they were, and of what station in life;

And eek in what array that they were inne:
And also in what clothes they were garbed:

And at a knight than wol I first biginne.
And with a knight then will I first begin.

A KNIGHT ther was, and that a worthy man,
A KNIGHT there was, and he a worthy man,

That fro the tyme that he first bigan   **44**
That from the time that he first began

To ryden out, he loved chivalrye,
To ride forth, he loved chivalry,

Trouthe and honour, fredom and curteisye.
Truth and honor, generosity and courtesy.

Ful worthy was he in his lordes werre,
Full worthy was he in his lord's war,

And therto hadde he riden (no man ferre)   **48**
And therein had he ridden (no man farther)

As wel in Christendom as hethenesse,
Both in Christian and in heathen lands,

And ever honoured for his worthinesse.
And ever honored for his worthiness.

At Alisaundre he was, whan it was wonne;
At Alexandria he was, when it was won;

Ful ofte tyme he hadde the bord bigonne   **52**
Many a time he had headed the table

Aboven alle naciouns in Pruce.
In international dinners in Prussia.

In Lettow hadde he reysed and in Ruce,
In Lithuania had he fought and in Russia,

No Cristen man so ofte of his degree.
More than any other Christian of his rank.

In Gernade at the sege eek hadde he be   **56**
In Grenada, too, he had been at the siege

Of Algezir, and riden in Belmarye.
Of Algeciras, and ridden in Benmarin.

At Lyeys was he, and at Satalye,
At Ayas was he, and at Adalia,

Whan they were wonne; and in the Grete See
When they were won; and in the Great Sea

At many a noble aryve hadde he be.   60
At many a noble landing had he been.

At mortal batailles hadde he been fiftene,
In fifteen mortal battles had he engaged,

And foughten for our feith at Tramissene
And fought for our faith at Tremeyen

In listes thryes, and ay slayn his fo.
In the lists thrice, and always slain his foe.

This ilke worthy knight had been also   64
This same worthy knight had been also

Somtyme with the lord of Palatye,
Once with the lord of Palatia,

Ageyn another hethen in Turkye:
Against another heathen in Turkey:

And evermore he hadde a sovereyn prys.
And evermore he had a sovereign reputation.

And though that he were worthy, he was wys,   68
And even though he was valiant, he was wise,

And of his port as meke as is a mayde.
And in his manner as meek as a maiden.

He never yet no vileinye ne sayde
He had never uttered any vileness

In al his lyf, un-to no maner wight.
In all his life, to any kind of person.

He was a verray parfit gentil knight.   72
He was a truly perfect gentle knight.

But for to tellen yow of his array,
But to tell you of his dress,

His hors were gode, but he was nat gay.
His horses were good, but he was not gaudy.

Of fustian he wered a gipoun
Of coarse cloth he wore a doublet

Al bismotered with his habergeoun;   76
All rust-spotted by his coat-of-mail;

For he was late y-come from his viage,
For he had lately come from his voyage,

And wente for to doon his pilgrimage.
And went to make his pilgrimage.

With him ther was his sone, a yong SQUYER,
With him there was his son, a young SQUIRE,

A lovyere, and a lusty bacheler,   80
A lover, and a lusty aspirant for knighthood,

With lokkes crulle, as they were leyd in presse.
With locks curled, as if from a curling-iron.

Of twenty yeer of age he was, I gesse.
About twenty years of age he was, I guess.

Of his stature he was of evene lengthe,
In stature he was of average height,

And wonderly deliver, and greet of strengthe.   84
And wonderfully agile, and great of strength.

And he had been somtyme in chivachye,
And he had been once in the cavalry,

In Flaundres, in Artoys, and Picardye,
In Flanders, in Artois, and Picardy,

And born him wel, as of so litel space,
And bore himself well, considering the short time,

In hope to stonden in his lady grace.   88
In hopes of standing in his lady's grace.

Embrouded was he, as it were a mede
Embroidered was he like a meadow

Al ful of fresshe floures, whyte and rede.
All full of fresh flowers, white and red.

Singinge he was, or floytinge, al the day;
Singing he was, or fluting, all the day;

He was as fresh as is the month of May.   92
He was as fresh as is the month of May.

Short was his goune, with sleves longe and wyde.
Short was his gown, with sleeves long and wide.

Wel coude he sitte on hors, and faire ryde.
Well could he sit on horse, and fairly ride.

He coulde songes make and wel endyte,
He could songs make and well compose,

Juste and eek daunce, and wel purtreye and wryte.   96
Joust and also dance, and well draw and write.

So hote he lovede, that by nightertale
So hot he loved, that at night-time

He sleep namore than dooth a nightingale.
He slept no more than does a nightingale.

Curteys he was, lowly, and servisable,
Courteous he was, modest and serviceable,

And carf biforn his fader at the table.   100
And carved before his father at the table.

   A YEMAN hadde he, and servaunts namo
   A YEOMAN had he, and no other servants

At that tyme, for him liste ryde so;
At that time, for he preferred to travel so;

And he was clad in cote and hood of grene;
And he was clad in coat and hood of green;

A sheef of pecok-arwes brighte and kene   104
A sheaf of peacock-arrows bright and sharp

Under his belt he bar ful thriftily;
Under his belt he bore right carefully;

(Wel coude he dresse his takel yemanly:
(Well could he handle his equipment yeoman-like:

His arwes drouped noght with fetheres lowe),
His arrows didn't droop with trailing feathers),

And in his hand he bar a mighty bowe.   *108*
And in his hand he bore a mighty bow.

A not-heed hadde he, with a broun visage.
A cropped head had he, and a brown visage.

Of wode-craft wel coude he al the usage.
The practice of woodcraft he understood thoroughly.

Upon his arm he bar a gay bracer,
Upon his arm he bore a gay arm-guard,

And by his syde a swerd and a bokeler,   *112*
And by his side a sword and a buckler,

And on that other syde a gay daggere,
And on the other side a fine dagger,

Harneised wel, and sharp as point of spere;
Fashioned well, and sharp as a spear-point;

A Cristofre on his brest of silver shene.
A silver Christopher' shone on his breast.

An horn he bar, the bawdrik was of grene;   *116*
A horn he bore, the carrying-strap was green;

A forster was he, soothly, as I gesse.
A forester was he, truly, as I guess.

   Ther was also a Nonne, a PRIORESSE,
   There was also a Nun, a PRIORESS,

That of hir smyling was ful simple and coy;
That in her smiling was simple and sweet;

Hir gretteste ooth was but by sëynt Loy;   *120*
Her greatest oath was but by Saint Loy;'

And she was cleped madame Eglentyne.
And she was called Madame Eglentine.

Ful wel she song the service divyne,
Full well she sang the divine service,

Entuned in hir nose ful semely;
Intoned in her nose full seemly;

And Frensh she spak ful faire and fetisly,   *124*
And French she spoke fluently and elegantly,

After the scole of Stratford atte Bowe,
After the school of Stratford-at-Bow,'

For Frensh of Paris was to hir unknowe.
For Parisian French was to her unknown.

At mete wel y-taught was she with-alle;
At meals well taught was she withal;

She leet no morsel from hir lippes falle,   *128*
She let no morsel from her lips fall,

Ne wette hir fingres in hir sauce depe.
Nor wet her fingers deeply in her sauce.

Wel coude she carie a morsel, and wel kepe,
Well could she handle a morsel, and be careful

That no drope ne fille up-on hir brest.
That no drop ever fell upon her breast.

In curteisye was set ful muche hir lest.   *132*
Courtesy was her particular delight.

Hir over lippe wyped she so clene,
Her upper lip wiped she so clean,

That in hir coppe was no ferthing sene
That in her cup was no trace seen

Of grece, whan she dronken hadde hir draughte.
Of grease, when she had drunk her draught.

Ful semely after hir mete she raughte,   *136*
Becomingly after her food she reached,

And sikerly she was of greet disport,
And indeed she was very diverting,

And ful plesaunt, and amiable of port,
And very pleasant, and amiable of disposition,

And peyned hir to countrefete chere
And she strove to simulate the behavior

Of court, and been estatlich of manere,   140
Of court, and be stately in manner,

And to ben holden digne of reverence.
And to be held worthy of reverence.

But, for to speken of hir conscience,
But, to speak of her inner nature,

She was so charitable and so pitous,
She was so charitable and so piteous,

She wolde wepe, if that she sawe a mous   144
She would weep, if only she saw a mouse

Caught in a trappe, if it were deed or bledde.
Caught in a trap, if it were dead or bleeding.

Of smale houndes had she, that she fedde
Some small dogs had she, that she fed

With rosted flesh, or milk and wastel-breed.
With roasted meat, or milk and finest bread.

But sore weep she if oon of hem were deed,   148
But sorely would she weep if one of them were dead,

Or if men smoot it with a yerde smerte:
Of if men struck it with a stick smartly:

And al was conscience and tendre herte.
She was altogether kind and tender hearted.

Ful semely hir wimpel pinched was;
Most neatly her wimpel [10] *was pleated;*

Her nose tretys; hir eyen greye as glas;   152
Her nose attractive; her eyes grey as glass;

Hir mouth ful smal, and ther-to softe and reed;
Her mouth very small, and therewith soft and red;

But sikerly she hadde a fair forheed;
But certainly she had a fair forehead;

It was almost a spanne brood, I trowe;
It was almost a span broad, I believe;

For, hardily, she was nat undergrowe.   156
For she was not exactly undergrown.

Ful fetis was hir cloke, as I was war.
Very neat was her cloak, as I was aware.

Of smal coral aboute hir arm she bar
Of small coral about her arm she wore

A peire of bedes, gauded al with grene;
A rosary, with the division beads of green;

And ther-on heng a broche of gold ful shene,   160
And thereon hung a brooch of gold full bright,

On which ther was first write a crowned A,
On which there was first written a crowned A,

And after, AMOR VINCIT OMNIA:
And beneath, "Love conquers all."

Another NONNE with hir hadde she,
Another NUN with her had she,

That was hir chapeleyne, and PREESTES THREE.   154
Who was her chaplain, and THREE PRIESTS.

A MONK ther was, a fair for the maistrye,
A MONK there was, a masterful personality,

An out-rydere, that lovede venerye;
An outrider,[11] that loved hunting;

A manly man, to been an abbot able.
A manly man, capable of being an abbot.

Ful many a deyntee hors hadde he in stable: 168
Full many a valuable horse had he in stable:

And, whan he rood, men mighte his brydel here
And, when he rode, men might his bridle hear

Ginglen in a whistling wind as clere,
Jingling in a whistling wind as clear,

And eek as loude as dooth the chapel-belle
And also as loud as doth the chapel bell

Ther as this lord was keper of the celle.   172
Of the convent where this lord was prior.

The reule of seint Maure or of seint Beneit,
The rule of Saint Maur or of Saint Benedict,

By-cause that it was old and som-del streit,
Because it was old and somewhat strict,

This ilke monk leet olde thinges pace,
This same monk let such old things pass,

And held after the newe world the space.   176
And adopted the course of the new world.

He yaf nat of that text a pulled hen,
He valued that text not worth a plucked hen,

That seith, that hunters been nat holy men;
That says, that hunters are not holy men;

Ne that a monk, whan he is cloisterlees,
Nor that a monk, when he is cloisterless,

Is lykned til a fish that is waterlees;   180
Is likened to a fish that is waterless;

This is to seyn, a monk out of his cloister.
That is to say, a monk out of his cloister.

But thilke text held he nat worth an oistre;
But this text he held not worth an oyster;

And I seyde, his opinioun was good.
And I said, his opinion was good.

What sholde he studie, and make himselven wood,   184
Why should he study, and drive himself mad,

Upon a book in cloistre alwey to poure,
Over a book in a cloister always to pour,

Or swinken with his handes, and laboure,
Or work with his hands, and labor,

As Austin bit? How shal the world be served?
As St. Augustine bids? How shall the world be served?

Lat Austin have his swink to him reserved.   *188*
Let Augustine have his work to himself reserved.

Therfore he was a pricasour aright;
Therefore he was a true hard rider;

Grehoundes he hadde, as swifte as fowel in flight;
Greyhounds he had, as swift as birds in flight;

Of priking and of hunting for the hare
In riding and in hunting for the hare

Was al his lust, for no cost wolde he spare.   *192*
Was all his pleasure, for no cost would he spare.

I seigh his sleves purfiled at the hond
I saw his sleeves trimmed at the hand

With grys, and that the fyneste of a lond;
With grey fur, and that the finest in the land;

And, for to festne his hood under his chin,
And, to fasten his hood under his chin,

He hadde of gold y-wroght a curious pin: *196*
He had of wrought gold a curious pin:

A love-knotte in the gretter ende ther was.
A love-knot in the larger end there was.

His heed was balled, that shoon as any glas,
His head was bald, that shone like any glass,

And eek his face, as he had been anoint.
And also his face, as if he had been anointed.

He was a lord ful fat and in good point;   *200*
He was a lord full fat and well fleshed;

His eyen stepe, and rollinge in his heed,
His eyes sharp, and rolling in his head,

That stemed as a forneys of a leed;
That glowed like a fire under a caldron;

His botes souple, his hors in greet estat.
His boots supple, his horse in fine shape.

Now certeinly he was a fair prelat;   204
Now certainly he was a fair prelate;

He was nat pale as a for-pyned goost.
He was not pale like a harried ghost.

A fat swan loved he best of any roost.
A fat swan loved he best of any roast.

His palfrey was as broun as is a beryé.
His palfrey was as brown as is a berry.

A FRERE ther was, a wantown and a merye,   208
A FRIAR there was, a wanton and a merry one,

A limitour, a ful solempne man.
A limiter," a very important man.

In alle the ordres foure is noon that can
In all the four orders" is no one who knows

So muche of daliaunce and fair langage.
So much of gossip and engaging language.

He hadde maad ful many a mariage   212
He had performed many a marriage

Of yonge wommen, at his owne cost.
Of young women, at his own cost.

Un-to his ordre he was a noble post.
In his order he was a noble pillar.

Ful wel biloved and famulier was he
Well loved and familiar was he

With frankeleyns over-al in his contree,   216
With rich farmers all over his country,

And eek with worthy wommen of the toun:
And also with worthy women of the town:

For he had power of confessioun,
For he had authority in confession,

As seyde him-self, more than a curat,
As he said himself, more than a parish-priest,

For of his ordre he was licentiat.   220
For in his order he held a papal license.

Ful swetely herde he confessioun,
Most sweetly heard he confession,

And plesaunt was his absolucioun;
And pleasant was his absolution;

He was an esy man to yeve penaunce
He was an easy man to give penance

Ther as he wiste to han a good pitaunce;   224
Whenever he knew he'd have a good remuneration;

For unto a povre ordre for to yive
For to give to a poor order

Is signe that a man is wel y-shrive.
Is a sign that a man is well shriven.

For if he yaf, he dorste make avaunt,
For if one gave, he dared assert,

He wiste that a man was repentaunt.   228
He knew that man was repentant.

For many a man so hard is of his herte,
For many a man is so hard of heart,

He may nat wepe al-thogh him sore smerte.
He cannot weep even though he suffers sorely.

Therefore, in stede of weping and preyeres,
Therefore, instead of weeping and prayers,

Men moot yeve silver to the povre freres.   232
Men should give silver to the poor friars.

His tipet was ay farsed ful of knyves
His cape was ever stuffed full of knives

And pinnes, for to yeven faire wyves.
And pins, to give to fair women.

And certeinly he hadde a mery note;
And certainly he had a merry note;

Wel coude he singe and pleyen on a rote.   236
Well could he sing and play on the fiddle.

Of yeddinges he bar utterly the prys.
In songs he easily carried off the prize.

His nekke whyt was as the flour-de-lys;
His neck was as white as the fleur-de-lis;

Ther-to he strong was as a champioun.
Yet he was as strong as a champion.

He knew the tavernes wel in every toun,   240
He knew the taverns well in every town,

And everich hostiler and tappestere
And every innkeeper and barmaid

Bet than a lazar or a beggestere;
Better than he did a leper or a beggar-woman;

For un-to swich a worthy man as he
For such a worthy man as he

Acorded nat, as by his facultee,   244
It was not fitting, considering his position,

To have with seke lazars aqueyntaunce.
To be acquainted with sick lepers.

It is nat honest, it may nat avaunce
It is not creditable, it holds no profit

For to delen with no swich poraille,
To deal with any such paupers,

But al with riche and sellers of vitaille.   248
But rather with the rich and sellers of food.

And over-al, ther as profit sholde aryse,
And anywhere, wherever profit might appear,

Curteys he was, and lowly of servyse.
Courteous he was, and lowly of service.

Ther nas no man no-wher so vertuous.
There was no man anywhere so virtuous.

He was the beste beggere in his hous;   252
He was the best beggar in his house;

For thogh a widwe hadde noght a sho,
For though a widow had never a shoe,

So plesaunt was his "IN PRINCIPIO,"
So pleasant was his "In the beginning,"[14]

Yet wolde he have a ferthing, er he wente.
That he would have a farthing, ere he left.

His purchas was wel bettre than his rente.   256
His collections were much better than his property income.

And rage he coude, as it were right a whelpe.
And carry on he could, as if he were a puppy.

In love-dayes ther coude he muchel helpe.
On love-days[15] he was a great help.

For there he was nat lyk a cloisterer,
For there he was not like a recluse,

With a thredbar cope, as is a povre scoler,   260
With threadbare cape, as is a poor scholar,

But he was lyk a maister or a pope.
But he was like a high official or a pope.

Of double worsted was his semi-cope,
Of double worsted was his half-cape,

That rounded as a belle out of the presse.
That stood out like a bell fresh from the clothes-press.

Somewhat he lipsed, for his wantownesse,   264
He lisped a little, it was a whim of his,

To make his English swete up-on his tonge;
To make his English sweet upon his tongue;

And in his harping, whan that he had songe,
And in his harping, after he had sung,

His eyen twinkled in his heed aright,
His eyes twinkled in his head rightly,

As doon the sterres in the frosty night.   *268*
As do the stars in the frosty night.

This worthy limitour was cleped Huberd.
This worthy limiter was called Hubert.

  A MARCHANT was ther with a forked berd,
  A MERCHANT was there with a forked beard,

In mottelee, and hye on horse he sat,
In motley array, and high on horse he sat,

Up-on his heed a Flaundrish bever hat;   *272*
Upon his head a Flemish beaver hat;

His botes clasped faire and fetisly.
His boots fastened tight and elegantly.

His resons he spak ful solempnely,
His ideas he delivered most solemnly,

Souninge always th'encrees of his winning.
Connected always with the increase of his profits.

He wolde the see were kept for any thing   *276*
He wanted the sea safeguarded at any price

Bitwixe Middleburgh and Orewelle.
Between Middleburg and Orwell."

Wel coude he in eschaunge sheeldes selle.
Well could he in exchange sell French crowns.

This worthy man ful wel his wit bisette;
This worthy man kept all his wits about him;

Ther wiste no wight that he was in dette,   *280*
No one knew that he was in debt,

So estatly was he of his governaunce,
So stately was he in his dealings,

With his bargaynes, and with his chevisaunce.
In bargaining, and in borrowing.

For sothe he was a worthy man with-alle,
For truly he was a worthy man withal,

But sooth to seyn, I noot how men him calle.   284
But truth to tell, I don't know his name.

   A CLERK ther was of Oxenford also,
   A CLERK there was of Oxford also,

That un-to logik hadde longe y-go.
Who to logic had long since turned.

As lene was his hors as is a rake,
As lean was his horse as is a rake,

And he nas nat right fat, I undertake;   288
And he wasn't exactly fat, I might add;

But loked holwe, and ther-to soberly.
But looked hollow, and likewise sober.

Ful thredbar was his overest courtepy;
Quite threadbare was his outermost cloak;

For he had geten him yet no benefyce,
For he had not yet gotten himself a benefice,

Ne was so worldy for to have offyce.   292
Nor was worldly enough to seek office.

For him was lever have at his beddes heed
For he would rather have at his bed's head

Twenty bokes, clad in blak or reed,
Twenty books, bound in black or red,

Of Aristotle and his philosophye,
Of Aristotle and his philosophy,

Than robes riche, or fithele, or gay sautrye.   296
Than robes rich, or a fiddle, or a gay harp.

But al be that he was a philosophre,
But although he was a philosopher,

Yet hadde he but litel gold in cofre;
Yet had he but little gold in coffer;[17]

But al that he mighte of his freendes hente,
But all that he might get from his friends,

On bokes and on lerninge he it spente,   *300*
On books and learning he spent,

And bisily gan for the soules preye
And busily prayed for the souls

Of hem that yaf him wher-with to scoleye.
Of those that gave him the wherewithal to study.

Of studie took he most cure and most hede.
Of study took he most care and most heéd.

Noght o word spak he more than was nede,   *304*
Not a word spoke he more than was needed,

And that was seyd in forme and reverence,
And that was said with care and respect,

And short and quik, and ful of hy sentence.
And short and quick, and full of high meaning.

Souninge in moral vertu was his speche,
Resonant with moral virtue was his speech,

And gladly wolde he lerne, and gladly teche.   *308*
And gladly would he learn, and gladly teach.

A SERGEANT OF THE LAWE, war and wys,
A SERGEANT-OF-LAW, wary and wise,

That often hadde been at the parvys,
Who often had been at the church-porch,[18]

Ther was also, ful riche of excellence.
There was also, rich in excellence.

Discreet he was, and of greet reverence: *312*
Discreet he was, and of great reverence:

He semed swich, his wordes weren so wyse.
He seemed so, his words were so wise.

Justyce he was ful often in assyse,
A justice he was often in session,

By patente, and by pleyn commissioun;
By patent, and by full commission;

For his science, and for his heigh renoun   316
For his learning, and for his high renown

Of fees and robes hadde he many oon.
Fees and robes had he many.

So greet a purchasour was no-wher noon.
So great a maker of deeds was nowhere to be found.

Al was fee simple to him in effect,
All was fee simple to him in effect,

His purchasing mighte nat been infect.   320
His deeds might not be contested.

No-wher so bisy a man as he ther nas,
Nowhere so busy a man as he existed,

And yet he semed bisier than he was.
And yet he seemed busier than he was.

In termes hadde he caas and domes alle,
Verbatim he knew all the cases and judgments,

That from the tyme of king William were falle.   324
That from the time of King William had occurred.

Therto he coude endyte, and make a thing,
So well he could draw up and make an instrument,

Ther coude no wight pinche at his wryting;
That no man could find a flaw in his writing;

And every statut coude he pleyn by rote.
And every statute could he recite by rote.

He rood but hoomly in a medlee cote   328
He rode but homely in a motley coat

Girt with a ceint of silk, with barres smale;
Belted with a girdle of silk, with stripes small;

Of his array telle I no lenger tale.
Of his dress tell I no longer tale.

A FRANKELEYN was in his companye;
A FRANKLIN[19] was in his company;

Whyt was his berd, as is the dayesye.   332
White was his beard, as is the daisy.

Of his complexioun he was sangwyn.
Of his complexion he was ruddy.

Wel loved he by the morwe a sop in wyn.
Well loved he in the morning a sop in wine.

To liven in delyt was ever his wone,
To live in delight was ever his wont,

For he was Epicurus owne sone,   336
For he was Epicurus' own son,

That heeld opinioun, that pleyn delyt
Who held the theory, that complete delight

Was verraily felicitee parfyt.
Was verily perfect felicity.

An housholdere, and that a greet, was he;
A householder, and a great one, was he;

Seint Julian he was in his contree.   340
Saint Julian[20] he was in his country.

His breed, his ale, was alwey after oon;
His bread, his ale, were always equally good;

A bettre envyned man was no-wher noon.
A man with a better wine cellar did not exist.

With-oute bake mete was never his hous,
Without meat pie was never his house,

Of fish and flesh, and that so plentevous,   344
Of fish and flesh, and that so plenteous,

It snewed in his hous of mete and drinke,
It snowed in his house of meat and drink,

Of alle deyntees that men coude thinke.
Of all dainties that one could think of.

After the sondry sesons of the yeer,
According to the various seasons of the year,

So chaunged he his mete and his soper.   348
He varied his meat and his supper.

Ful many a fat partrich hadde he in mewe,
Full many a fat partridge had he in coop,

And many a breem and many a luce in stewe.
And many a bream and many a pike in his pond.

Wo was his cook, but-if his sauce were
Woe to his cook, unless his sauces were

Poynaunt and sharp, and redy al his gere.   352
Poignant and sharp, and ready all his carvers.

His table dormant in his halle alway
His table stationed in his hall always

Stood redy covered al the longe day.
Stood ready set all the day long.

At sessiouns ther was he lord and sire;
At court sessions was he lord and sire;

Ful ofte tyme he was knight of the shire.   356
Often he attended parliament as knight of the shire.

An anlas and a gipser al of silk
A dagger and a pouch all of silk

Heng at his girdel, whyt as morne milk.
Hung at his girdle, white as morning milk.

A shirreve hadde he been, and a countour;
A sheriff had he been, and a treasurer;

Was no-wher such a worthy vavasour.   360
There was nowhere such a worthy vassal.

An HABERDASSHER and a CARPENTER,
A HABERDASHER and a CARPENTER,

A WEBBE, a DYERE, and a TAPICER,
A WEAVER, a DYER, and an UPHOLSTERER,

Were with us eek, clothed in o liveree,
Were with us too, clothed in one livery,

Of a solempne and greet fraternitee.   *364*
Of a solemn and great guild.

Ful fresh and newe hir gere apyked was;
Full fresh and new their clothes were trimmed;

Hir knyves were y-chaped noght with bras,
Their knives were mounted not with brass,

But al with silver, wroght ful clene and weel,
But all with silver, wrought full clean and well,

Hir girdles and hir pouches every-deel.   *368*
Their girdles and their money-bags in keeping.

Wel semed ech of hem a fair burgeys,
Each of them seemed a sufficiently good citizen,

To sitten in a yeldhalle on a deys.
To sit in a guildhall on a dais.

Everich, for the wisdom that he can,
Each one, for the wisdom that he knew,

Was shaply for to been an alderman.   *372*
Was fit to be the head of a guild.

For catel hadde they y-nogh and rente,
For possessions had they enough and income,

And eek hir wyves wolde it wel assente;
And also their wives would agree to it;

And elles certein were they to blame.
And otherwise certainly were they to blame.

It is ful fair to been y-clept "ma dame,"   *376*
It is right pleasant to be called "madam,"

And goon to vigilyës al bifore,
And go to vigils before everyone,

And have a mantel royalliche y-bore.
And have a mantle royally carried.

 A COOK they hadde with hem for the nones,
 A COOK they had with them for the occasion,

To boille the chiknes with the mary-bones,   380
To boil the chickens with the marrow-bones,

And po idre-marchant tart, and galingale.
And tart flavoring, and spice.

Wel coude he knowe a draughte of London ale.
Well could he appreciate a draught of London ale.

He coude roste, and sethe, and broille, and frye,
He could roast, and boil, and broil, and fry,

Maken mortreux, and wel bake a pye.   384
Make stew, and well bake a pie.

But greet harm was it, as it thoughte me,
But a great pity was it, as I thought,

That on his shine a mormal hadde he;
That on his shin a bad sore had he;

For blankmanger, that made he with the beste.
As for spiced chicken, that made he with the best.

 A SHIPMAN was ther, woning fer by weste: 388
 A SAILOR was there, hailing from the west:

For aught I woot, he was of Dertemouthe.
For aught I know, he was from Dartmouth.

He rood up-on a rouncy, as he couthe,
He rode upon a nag, as well as he could,

In a gowne of falding to the knee.
In a gown of coarse cloth to the knee.

A daggere hanging on a laas hadde he   392
A dagger hanging on a cord had he

Aboute his nekke under his arm adoun.
About his neck, extending under his arm.

The hote somer had maad his hewe all broun;
The hot summer had made his hue all brown;

And, certeinly, he was a good felawe.
And, certainly, he was a good fellow.

Ful many a draughte of wyn had he y-drawe   396
Full many a draught of wine had he drawn

From Burdeux-ward, whyl that the chapman sleep.
On trips from Bordeaux, while the importer slept.

Of nyce conscience took he no keep.
Of delicate conscience took he no heed.

If that he faught, and hadde the hyer hond,
If he fought, and had the upper hand,

By water he sente hem hoom to every lond.   400
By water he sent them home to every land."

But of his craft to rekene wel his tydes,
But concerning his skill to reckon his tides,

His stremes and his daungers him bisydes,
His currents and the dangers that beset him,

His herberwe and his mone, his lode-menage,
His harbor and his moon, his pilotage,

Ther nas noon swich from Hulle to Cartage.   404
There was none such from Hull to Carthage.

Hardy he was, and wys to undertake;
Hardy he was, and shrewd in his ventures;

With many a tempest hadde his berd been shake.
With many a tempest had his beard been shaken.

He knew wel alle the havenes, as they were,
He knew well all the havens, exactly as they were,

From Gootlond to the cape of Finistere,   408
From Gottland to the Cape of Finisterre,

And every cryke in Britayne and in Spayne;
And every creek in Brittany and in Spain;

His barge y-cleped was the Maudelayne.
His ship was named The Madeleine.

With us ther was a DOCTOUR OF PHISYK,
With us there was a PHYSICIAN,

In al this world ne was ther noon him lyk   412
In all this world never was there his like

To speke of phisik and of surgerye;
To speak of medicine and of surgery;

For he was grounded in astronomye.
For he was grounded in astrology.

He kepte his pacient a ful greet del
He kept his patient fully attuned

In houres, by his magik naturel.   416
To the stars, by his natural magic.

Wel coude he fortunen the ascendent
Well could he make fortuitous the rise

Of his images for his pacient.
Of the stars connected with his patient.

He knew the cause of everich maladye,
He knew the cause of every malady,

Were it of hoot or cold, or moiste, or drye,   420
Were it of hot or cold, or moist, or dry,

And where engendred, and of what humour;
And where engendered, and of which humor;[20]

He was a verrey parfit practisour.
He was a very perfect practicioner.

The cause y-knowe, and of his harm the rote,
The cause known, and of his disease the root,

Anon he yaf the seke man his bote.   424
At once he gave the sick man his remedy.

Ful redy hadde he his apothecaries,
All ready had he his apothecaries,

To sende him drogges and his letuaries,
To send him drugs and his syrups,

For ech of hem made other for to winne;
For each of them made profit for the other;

Hir frendschipe nas nat newe to biginne.   *428*
Their friendship had not just begun.

Wel knew he th'oldo Esculaplus,
Well knew he the old Aesculapius,

And Deiscorides, and eek Rufus,
And Dioscorides, and also Rufus,

Old Ypocras, Haly, and Galien;
Old Hippocrates, Haly, and Galen;

Serapion, Razis, and Avicen;   *432*
Serapion, Rhasis, and Avicenna;

Averrois, Demascien, and Constantyn;
Averroes, Damascene, and Constantine;

Bernard, and Gatesden, and Gilbertyn.
Bernard, and Gatisden, and Gilbertine.[23]

Of his diete mesurable was he,
Of his diet moderate was he,

For it was of no superfluitee,   *436*
For it was of no superfluity,

But of greet norissing and digestible.
But of great nourishment and digestible.

His studie was but litel on the Bible.
His study was but little in the Bible.

In sangwin and in pers he clad was al,
In blood-red and in sky-blue he was clad,

Lyned with taffata and with sendal;   *440*
Lined with taffeta and with thin silk;

And yet he was but esy of dispence;
And yet he was careful in spending;

He kepte that he wan in pestilence.
He kept what he earned during plague-time.

For gold in phisik is a cordial,
For gold in medicine is a cordial,

Therfore he lovede gold in special.   *444*
Therefore he loved gold especially.

   A good WYF was ther OF bisyde BATHE,
   A good WIFE was there OF around BATH,

But she was som-del deef, and that was scathe.
But she was somewhat deaf, and that was a pity.

Of clooth-making she hadde swiche an haunt,
Of cloth-making she had such a knack,

She passed hem of Ypres and of Gaunt.   *448*
She surpassed them of Ypres and of Ghent.

In al the parisshe wyf ne was ther noon
In all the parish, woman was there none

That to th'offring bifore hir sholde goon;
That to the collection box before her should go;

And if ther dide, certeyn, so wrooth was she,
And if any did, certainly, so angry was she,

That she was out of alle charitee.   *452*
That she was completely out of patience.

Hir coverchiefs ful fyne were of ground;
Her kerchiefs were finely woven,

I dorste swere they weyeden ten pound
(I would swear they weighed ten pounds)

That on a Sonday were upon hir heed.
That on a Sunday were on her head.

Hir hosen weren of fyn scarlet reed,   *456*
Her hose were of fine scarlet red,

Ful streite y-teyd, and shoos ful moiste and newe.
Tightly secured, and shoes all soft and new.

Bold was hir face, and fair, and reed of hewe.
Bold was her face, and fair, and red of hue.

She was a worthy womman al hir lyve,
She was a worthy woman all her life,

Housbondes at chirche-dore she hadde fyve,   460
Husbands at church door she'd had five,

Withouten other companye in youthe;
Not to mention other company in youth;

But thereof nedeth nat to speke as nouthe.
But there is no need to discuss that now.

And thryes hadde she been at Jerusalem;
And thrice had she been at Jerusalem;

She hadde passed many a straunge streem;   464
She had crossed many a strange stream;

At Rome she hadde been, and at Boloigne,
At Rome she had been, and at Boulogne,

In Galice at seint Jame, and at Coloigne.
In Spain at Santiago, and at Cologne.

She coude muche of wandring by the weye:
She knew much of wayfaring:

Gat-tothed was she, soothly for to seye.   468
Her teeth were widely spread, to speak truth.

Up-on an amblere esily she sat,
Upon an ambling horse easily she sat,

Y-wimpled wel, and on hir heed an hat
Veiled neatly, and on her head a hat

As brood as is a bokeler or a targe;
As broad as is a buckler or a target;

A foot-mantel aboute hir hipes large,   472
A protective skirt about her large hips,

And on hir feet a paire of spores sharpe.
And on her feet a pair of sharp spurs.

In felawschip wel coude she laughe and carpe.
In fellowship well could she laugh and joke.

Of remedyes of love she knew perchaunce,
Remedies of love she doubtless knew about,

For she coude of that art the olde daunce.   *476*
For she knew that art from of old.

  A good man was ther of religioun,
  A good man there was of religion,

And was a povre PERSOUN of a toun;
Who was a poor PARSON of a town;

But riche he was of holy thoght and werk.
But rich he was of holy thought and work.

He was also a lerned man, a clerk,   *480*
He was also a learned man, a clerk,

That Cristes gospel trewely wolde preche;
That Christ's gospel truly would preach;

His parisshens devoutly wolde he teche.
His parishioners devoutly would he teach.

Benigne he was, and wonder diligent,
Benign he was, and wonderfully diligent,

And in adversitee ful pacient;   *484*
And in adversity entirely patient;

And swich he was y-preved ofte sythes.
And so he had proved many times.

Ful looth were him to cursen for his tythes,
Altogether loath was he to threaten for his tithes,

But rather wolde he yeven, out of doute,
But rather would he give, beyond a doubt,

Un-to his povre parisshens aboute   *488*
Unto his various poor parishioners

Of his offring, and eek of his substaunce.
Of his collections, and also of his own.

He coude in litel thing han suffisaunce.
He could with little have sufficient.

Wyd was his parisshe, and houses fer a-sonder,
Large was his parish, with houses far apart,

But he ne lafte nat, for reyn ne thonder,   492
But he did not neglect, because of rain or thunder,

In siknes nor in meschief, to visyte
In sickness or in trouble, to visit

The ferreste in his parisshe, muche and lyte,
The farthest in his parish, great and small,

Up-on his feet, and in his hand a staf.
On foot, with a staff in his hand.

This noble ensample to his sheep he yaf,   496
This noble example to his sheep he gave,

That first he wroghte, and afterward he taughte;
That first he practiced, and afterwards he preached;

Out of the gospel he tho wordes caughte;
From the gospel he took these words;

And this figure he added eek ther-to,
And this simile he added in addition,

That if gold ruste, what shal iren do?   500
That if gold rust, what shall iron do?

For if a preest be foul, on whom we truste,
For if a priest be foul, in whom we trust,

No wonder is a lewed man to ruste;
No wonder that a sinful man will rust;

And shame it is, if a preest take keep,
And shameful it is, let priests take notice,

A shiten shepherde and a clene sheep.   504
A befouled shepherd and a clean sheep.

Wel oghte a preest ensample for to yive,
Well ought a priest set the example,

By his clennesse, how that his sheep shold live.
By his cleanness, how his sheep should live.

He sette nat his benefice to hyre,
He didn't hire out his benefice,

And leet his sheep encombred in the myre,   508
And leave his sheep stuck in the mire,

And ran to London, un-to sëynt Poules,
And run to London, to Saint Paul's,

To seken him a chaunterie for soules,
To apply for a place as a chanter for souls,

Or with a bretherhed to been withholde;
Or to be retained by a guild;

But dwelte at hoom, and kepte wel his folde,   512
But dwelt at home, and guarded well his fold,

So that the wolf ne made it nat miscarie;
So that the wolf would not do it mischief;

He was a shepherde and no mercenarie.
He was a shepherd, not a business man.

And though he holy were, and vertuous,
And although he was holy and virtuous,

He was to sinful man nat despitous,   516
He was to sinners not merciless,

Ne of his speche daungerous ne digne,
Nor of his speech disdainful or haughty,

But in his teching discreet and benigne.
But in his teaching quiet and kindly.

To drawen folk to heven by fairnesse
To lead people to heaven by honorableness

By good ensample, was his bisinesse: 520
And good example was his ambition:

But it were any persone obstinat,
But were any person obstinate,

What-so he were, of heigh or lowe estat,
Whoever he were, of high or low degree,

Him wolde he snibben sharply for the nones.
He would reprove him sharply for it.

A bettre preest, I trowe that nowher noon is.   524
A better priest, I believe, does not exist.

He wayted after no pompe and reverence,
He yearned after no pomp and reverence,

Ne maked him a spyced conscience,
Nor considered himself above reproach,

But Cristes lore, and his apostles twelve,
But Christ's lore, and that of His apostles twelve,

He taughte, and first he folwed it himselve.   528
He taught, and first he followed it himself.

   With him ther was a PLOWMAN, was his brother,
   With him there was a PLOWMAN, his brother,

That hadde y-lad of dong ful many a fother,
Who had carted many a load of dung,

A trewe swinker and a good was he,
A true worker and good was he,

Livinge in pees and parfit charitee.   532
Living in peace and perfect charity.

God loved he best with al his hole herte
God loved he best with all his whole heart

At alle tymes, thogh him gamed or smerte,
At all times, whether he prospered or suffered,

And thanne his neighebour right as himselve.
And then his neighbour exactly as himself.

He wolde thresshe, and ther-to dyke and delve,   536
He would thrash, and likewise ditch and dig,

For Cristes sake, for every povre wight,
For Christ's sake, for every poor person,

Withouten hyre, if it lay in his might.
Without pay, if it lay in his might.

His tythes payed he ful faire and wel,
His tithes paid he fairly and squarely,

Bothe of his propre swink and his catel.   540
Both on his own work and his property.

In a tabard he rood upon a mere.
In working clothes he rode upon a mare.

Ther was also a Reve and a Millere,
There were also a Reve"⁴ and a Miller,

A Somnour and a Pardoner also,
A Summoner²⁵ and a Pardoner²⁶ also,

A Maunciple, and my-self: ther were namo.   544
A Manciple,²⁷ and myself, there were no more.

The MILLER was a stout carl, for the nones,
The MILLER was a stout fellow (to begin with him),

Ful big he was of braun, and eek of bones;
Large of muscle, and of bones too;

That proved wel, for over-al ther he cam,
That had been fully proved, for wherever he went,

At wrastling he wolde have alwey the ram.   548
At wrestling he would always win the prize.

He was short-sholdred, brood, a thikke knarre,
He was short-shouldered, broad, chunkily built,

Ther nas no dore that he nolde heve of harre,
There was no door he couldn't heave off its hinges,

Or breke it, at a renning, with his heed.
Or break it, by running at it with his head.

His berd as any sowe or fox was reed,   552
His beard was as red as any sow or fox,

And ther-to brood, as though it were a spade.
And as broad as if it were a spade.

Up-on the cop right of his nose he hade
Right on the tip of his nose he had

A werte, and ther-on stood a tuft of heres,
A wart, and from it sprang a tuft of hair,

Reed as the bristles of a sowes eres;   556
Red as the bristles of a sow's ears;

His nose-thirles blake were and wyde.
His nostrils were black and large.

A swerd and bokeler bar he by his syde;
A sword and buckler bore he by his side;

His mouth as greet was as a greet forneys.
His mouth was as large as a large furnace.

He was a janglere and a goliardeys,   560
He was a loose talker and a ribald joker,

And that was most of sinne and harlotryes.
Mostly on subjects of sin and immorality.

Wel coude he stelen corn, and tollen thryes;
Well could he steal corn, and charge triple;

And yet he hadde a thombe of gold, pardee.
And yet he had a thumb of gold,[28] by heaven.

A whyt cote and a blew hood wered he.   564
A white coat and a blue hood wore he.

A baggepype wel coude he blowe and sowne,
He could play a bagpipe splendidly,

And ther-with-al he broghte us out of towne.
And with this music he brought us out of town.

   A gentil MAUNCIPLE was ther of a temple,
   A gentle MANCIPLE was there of an Inn of Court,

Of which achatours mighte take exemple   568
From whom buyers might take example

For to be wyse in bying of vitaille.
To learn wisdom in purchasing provisions.

For whether that he payde, or took by taille,
For whether he paid cash, or took on credit,

Algate he wayted so in his achat,
Always he marketed so carefully

That he was ay biforn and in good stat.   572
That he was ever ahead and in good shape.

Now is nat that of God a ful fair grace,
Now is that not a fair mercy of God,

That swich a lewed mannes wit shal pace
That such a common man's knowledge shall exceed

The wisdom of an heep of lerned men?
The wisdom of a heap of learned men?

Of maistres hadde he mo than thryes ten,   576
Of masters had he more than thrice ten,

That were of lawe expert and curious;
Who were in law expert and skillful;

Of which ther were a doseyn in that hous
Of whom there were a dozen in that house

Worthy to been stiwardes of rent and lond
Capable of being stewards of buildings and grounds

Of any lord that is in Engelond,   580
Of any lord in England,

To make him live by his propre good,
To enable him to live on his income,

In honour dettelees, but he were wood,
Honorably and debtless, unless he were crazy,

Or live as scarsly as him list desire;
Or live as frugally as he might desire;

And able for to helpen al a shire   584
And able to help a whole shire

In any cas that mighte falle or happe;
In any mischance that might occur;

And yit this maunciple sette hir aller cappe.
And yet this manciple could outwit them all.

The REVE was a sclendre colerik man,
The REVE was a slender, choleric man,

His berd was shave as ny as ever he can.   588
His beard was shaven as close as possible

His heer was by his eres round y-shorn.
His hair was cut high around his ears.

His top was dokked lyk a preest biforn.
And clipped short in front like a priest's.

Ful longe were his legges, and ful lene,
His legs were very long and lean,

Y-lyk a staf, ther was no calf y-sene.   592
Like a stick; no calf was visible.

Wel coude he kepe a gerner and a binne;
Well could he maintain a granary and bin;

Ther was noon auditour coude on him winne.
No inspector could get the better of him.

Wel wiste he, by the droghte, and by the reyn,
He could predict, regardless of drought or rain,

The yelding of his seed, and of his greyn.   596
The yield of his seed and grain.

His lordes sheep, his neet, his dayerye,
His lord's sheep, his cattle, his dairy,

His swyn, his hors, his stoor, and his pultrye,
His swine, his horses, his stock, and his poultry,

Was hoolly in this reves governing,
Were wholly in this reve's care,

And by his covenaunt yaf the rekening,   600
And by agreement he had submitted his accounts,

Sin that his lord was twenty year of age;
Ever since his lord was twenty years old;

Ther coude no man bringe him in arrerage.
No man could find him in arrears.

Ther nas baillif, ne herde, ne other hyne,
There was no supervisor, herdsman, nor other servant,

That he ne knew his sleighte and his covyne;   604
Whose cunning and trickery he didn't know;

They were adrad of him, as of the deeth.
They were as afraid of him as of the plague.

His woning was ful fair up-on an heeth,
His home was in a fair countryside,

With grene treës shadwed was his place,
With green trees shading the place,

He coude bettre than his lord purchase.   608
He was a better buyer than his lord.

Ful riche he was astored prively,
He had accumulated private wealth,

His lord wel coude he plesen subtilly,
He knew subtle ways of pleasing his lord,

To yeve and lene him of his owne good,
Giving and loaning him his own goods,

And have a thank, and yet a cote and hood.   612
And receiving thanks, and also a coat and hood.

In youthe he lerned hadde a good mister;
In youth he had learned a good trade;

He was a wel good wrighte, a carpenter.
He was a right good worker, a carpenter.

This reve sat up-on a ful good stot,
This reve sat on a very good steed,

That was al pomely grey, and highte Scot.   616
That was all dapple grey, and named Scot.

A long surcote of pers up-on he hade,
A long upper-coat of Persian blue he wore,

And by his syde he bar a rusty blade.
And at his side he bore a rusty blade.

Of Northfolk was this reve, of which I telle,
From Norfolk was this reve, of whom I speak,

Bisyde a toun men clepen Baldeswelle.   620
Near a town men call Baldeswell.

Tukked he was, as is a frere, aboute,
He was girdled up like a friar,

And ever he rood the hindreste of our route.
And always he rode last in our group.

   A SOMNOUR was ther with us in that place,
*   There was a SUMMONER with us in that place,*

That hadde a fyr-reed cherubinnes face,   624
Who had a fire-red cherubim's face,

For sawcefleem he was, with eyen narwe.
For pimpled he was, with narrow eyes.

As hoot he was, and lecherous, as a sparwe;
As hot he was, and lecherous, as a sparrow;

With scalled browes blake, and piled berd;
With scabby black brows, and scraggly beard;

Of his visage children were aferd.   628
Of his visage children were afraid.

Ther nas quik-silver, litarge, ne brimstoon,
There was no quick-silver, lead oxide, nor brimstone,

Boras, ceruce, ne oille of tartre noon,
Borax, white lead, nor cream of tartar,

Ne oynement that wolde clense and byte,
Nor cleansing and caustic ointment,

That him mighte helpen of his whelkes whyte,   632
That could cure him of his white pimples,

Nor of the knobbes sittinge on his chekes.
Or of the lumps sitting on his cheeks.

Wel loved he garleek, oynons, and eek lekes,
Well loved he garlic, onions, and also leeks,

And for to drinken strong wyn, reed as blood.
And to drink strong wine, red as blood.

Than wolde he speke, and crye as he were wood.   636
Then would he talk and shout as if he were mad.

And whan that he wel dronken hadde the wyn,
And when he had drunk wine heavily,

Than wolde he speke no word but Latyn.
Then would he speak no word but Latin.

A few termes hadde he, two or three,
He knew a few terms, two or three,

That he had lerned out of som decree;   640
Which he had learned from some decree;

No wonder is, he herde it al the day;
No wonder at that, he heard it all day long;

And eek ye knowen wel, how that a jay
And you yourself know how a jay

Can clepen "Watte," as well as can the pope.
Can say "Walter" as well as the pope can.

But who-so coude in other thing him grope,   644
But if anyone questioned him on anything else,

Thanne hadde he spent al his philosophye;
Then he had exhausted all his learning;

Ay "QUESTIO QUID JURIS" wolde he crye.
Constantly, "QUESTIO QUID JURIS"[29] would he cry.

He was a gentil harlot and a kinde;
He was a gentle scoundrel and a kind one;

A bettre felawe sholde men noght finde.   648
A better companion couldn't be found.

He wolde suffre, for a quart of wyn,
For a quart of wine, he would allow

A good felawe to have his concubyn
A good fellow to have his mistress

A twelf-month, and excuse him atte fulle:
For a year, and call it even:

Ful prively a finch eek coude he pulle.   652
But he could also take advantage of a simpleton.

And if he fond o-wher a good felawe,
And if he found anywhere a good fellow,

He wolde techen him to have non awe,
He would teach him to have no fear,

In swich cas, of the erchedeknes curs,
In such an affair, of excommunication,

But-if a mannes soule were in his purs;   656
Unless a man's soul were in his purse;

For in his purs he sholde y-punisshed be.
In that case his purse should be punished.

"Purs is the erchedeknes helle," seyde he.
"The purse is the archdeacon's hell," said he.

But wel I woot he lyed right in dede;
But well I know he most certainly lied;

Of cursing oghte ech gilty man him drede—   660
Excommunication should be the dread of guilty men—

For curs wol slee, right as assoilling saveth—
For excommunication will kill, as absolution saves—

And also war him of a *significavit.*
And also let him beware of a Church prison-sentence.

In daunger hadde he at his owne gyse
In his own way he had control

The yonge girles of the diocyse,   664
Over the young people of the diocese,

And knew hir counseil, and was al hir reed.
And knew their secrets, and was their adviser.

A gerland hadde he set up-on his heed,
A garland he wore on his head,

As greet as it were for an ale-stake;
As large as an alehouse sign;

A bokeler hadde he maad him of a cake.   668
A round loaf of bread was his buckler.

   With him ther rood a gentil PARDONER
   With him there rode a gentle PARDONER

Of Rouncival, his freend and his compeer,
Of Rouncivalle, his friend and comrade,

That streight was comen fro the court of Rome.
Who had come straight from the court of Rome.

Ful loude he song, "Com hider, love, to me."   672
Full loudly he sang, "Come hither, love, to me."

This somnour bar to him a stif burdoun,
The summoner joined him with a stiff bass,

Was never trompe of half so greet a soun.
Never was there trumpet half so powerful.

This pardoner hadde heer as yelow as wex
This pardoner had hair as yellow as wax

But smothe it heng, as dooth a strike of flex;   676
But smooth it hung, as does a hank of flax,

By ounces henge his lokkes that he hadde,
Such locks as he had hung down thinly,

And ther-with he his shuldres overspradde;
And with them he covered his shoulders;

But thinne it lay, by colpons oon and oon;
But sparsely it lay, by shreds here and there;

But hood, for jolitee, ne wered he noon,   680
Yet, for amusement, he wore no hood,

For it was trussed up in his walet.
For it was packed in his bag.

Him thoughte, he rood al of the newe jet;
He thought he rode in the latest style;

Dischevele, save his cappe, he rood al bare.
Dishevelled and bareheaded except for his cap.

Swiche glariuge eyen hadde he as an hare.   684
He had glistening eyes like a hare's.

A vernicle hadde he sowed on his cappe.
He had a veronica³⁰ sewed on his cap.

His walet lay biforn him in his lappe,
His bag lay before him on his lap,

Bret-ful of pardoun come from Rome al hoot.
Cram.ned with pardons brought from Rome all hot.

A voys he hadde as smal as hath a goot.   688
A voice he had as tiny as a goat's.

No berd hadde he, ne never sholde have,
No beard had he, nor ever would have,

As smothe it was as it were late y-shave;
As smooth he was as if he'd just shaved;

I trowe he were a gelding or a mare.
I believe he was a gelding or a mare.

But of his craft, fro Berwik into Ware,   692
But in his occupation, from Berwick to Ware,

Ne was there swich another pardoner.
There was not another such pardoner.

For in his male he hadde a pilwe-beer,
For in his bag he had a pillowcase,

Which that, he seyde, was our lady veyl:
Which he said was Our Lady's veil:

He seyde, he hadde a gobet of the seyl   696
He said he had a small piece of the sail

That Seynt Peter hadde, whan that he wente
That Saint Peter had, when he walked

Up-on the see, til Jesu Crist him hente.
Upon the sea, until Jesus Christ rescued him.

He hadde a croys of latoun, ful of stones,
He had a cross of brass, full of gems,

And in a glas he hadde pigges bones.   700
And in a glass he had pig's bones.

But with thise relikes, whan that he fond
But with these relics, whenever he found

A povre person dwelling up-on lond,
A poor parson living in the country,

Up-on a day he gat him more moneye
Within a day he took in more money

Than that the person gat in monthes tweye.   704
Than the parson got in two months.

And thus, with feyned flaterye and japes,
And thus, with feigned sincerity and tricks,

He made the person and the peple his apes.
He made monkeys out of the parson and the people.

But trewely to tellen, atte laste,
But to tell the truth, all in all,

He was in chirche a noble ecclesiaste.   708
He was in church a noble ecclesiastic.

Wel coude he rede a lessoun or a storie,
Well could he read a lesson or a story,

But alderbest he song an offertorie;
But best of all he sang an offertory;

For wel he wiste, whan that song was songe,
For well he knew, when that song was sung,

He moste preche, and wel affyle his tonge,   712
He must preach, and sharpen his tongue,

To winne silver, as he ful wel coude;
To win silver, as he well knew how;

Therefore he song so meriely and loude.
Therefore he sang so merrily and loud.

Now have I told you shortly, in a clause,
Now have I told you briefly, in a sentence,

Th'estat, th'array, the nombre, and eek the cause   716
The status, the clothes, the number, and also the cause

Why that assembled was this companye
Of the gathering of this company

In Southwerk, at this gentil hostelrye,
In Southwark, at this fine hotel,

That highte the Tabard, faste by the Belle.
Named the Tabard, close to the Bell Inn.

But now is tyme to yow for to telle   720
But now it is time to tell you

How that we baren us that ilke night,
What we did that same night,

Whan we were in that hostelrye alight.
On which we arrived at that hotel.

And after wol I telle of our viage,
And afterwards I will tell of our journey,

And al the remenaunt of our pilgrimage.   724
And everything else about our pilgrimage.

But first I pray yow, of your curteisye,
But first I beg you, out of your courtesy,

That ye n'arette it nat my vileinye,
That you ascribe it not to my crudeness,

Thogh that I pleynly speke in this matere,
Even though I speak plainly in this narration,

To telle yow hir wordes and hir chere;   728
To tell you their words and their behavior;

Ne thogh I speke hir wordes properly.
Even if I repeat their exact words.

For this ye knowen al-so wel as I,
For this you know as well as I,

Who-so shal telle a tale after a man,
Whoever tells another man's story,

He moot reherce, as ny as ever he can,   732
Must reproduce, as exactly as he can,

Everich a word, if it be in his charge,
Every word, if his memory serves,

Al speke he never so rudeliche and large;
However vulgar and broad his language;

Or elles he moot telle his tale untrewe,
Or else he must falsify his tale,

Or feyne thing, or finde wordes newe.   736
Or invent things, or find new words.

He may nat spare, al-thogh he were his brother;
He may spare no one, not even his brother;

He moot as wel seye o word as another.
He might as well speak one word as another.

Crist spak him-self ful brode in holy writ,
Christ Himself spoke broadly enough in Holy Writ,

And wel ye woot, no vileinye is it.   740
And well you know that isn't wrong.

Eek Plato seith, who-so that can him rede,
Besides, Plato says, whoever can read him,

The wordes mote be cosin to the dede.
The words should be cousin to the deed.

Also I prey yow to foryeve it me,
Also I beg you to forgive me

Al have I nat set folk in hir degree,   744
If I have not placed people in their rank,

Here in this tale, as that they sholde stonde;
Here in this tale, in the order that they should be;

My wit is short, ye may wel understonde.
My brains are weak, you can well understand.

Greet chere made our hoste us everichon,
Our host gave each of us a great welcome,

And to the soper sette us anon;   748
And set us down to supper forthwith;

And served us with vitaille at the beste.
And served us with the best of food.

Strong was the wyn, and wel to drinke us leste.
Strong was the wine, and we were in a mood to drink.

A semely man our hoste was with-alle
Our host was a man altogether fit

For to han been a marshal in an halle;   752
To have been a marshall in a dining-hall;

A large man he was with eyen stepe,
A large man he was with bright eyes,

A fairer burgeys is ther noon in Chepe:
There isn't a finer citizen in Cheapside:

Bold of his speche, and wys, and wel y-taught,
Bold of speech, sensible, and well educated,

And of manhod him lakkede right naught.   756
And lacking nothing at all of manhood.

Eek therto he was right a mery man,
Along with this, he was a merry man,

And after soper pleyen he bigan,
And after supper he began to fool,

And spak of mirthe amonges othere thinges,
And spoke of amusement among other things,

Whan that we hadde maad our rekeninges;   760
After we had settled our reckonings;

And seyde thus: "Now, lordinges, trewely,
And spoke thus: "Now, gentlemen, truly,

Ye been to me right welcome hertely:
You are heartily welcome here:

For by my trouthe, if that I shal nat lye,
For by my troth, if I don't tell a lie,

I ne saugh this yeer so mery a companye
I haven't seen this year so merry a company

764

At ones in this herberwe as is now.
At once in this inn as at present.

Fáyn wolde I doon yow mirthe, wiste I how.
I'd like to give you pleasure, if I knew how.

And of a mirthe I am right now bithoght,
And a pastime has just occurred to me,

To doon yow ese, and it shal coste noght.
To give you pleasure, and it will cost nothing.

768

"Ye goon to Caunterbury; God yow spede,
"You go to Canterbury; God speed you,

The blisful martir quyte yow your mede.
May the blessed martyr reward you.

And wel I woot, as ye goon by the weye
And well I know, as you go along

Ye shapen yow to talen and to pleye;
You plan to tell tales and amuse yourselves;

772

For trewely, confort ne mirthe is noon
For truly, there is no comfort nor mirth

To ryde by the weye doumb as a stoon;
In riding along the way silent as a stone;

And therfore wol I maken yow disport,
And therefore will I create a diversion,

As I seyde erst, and doon yow som confort.
As I said before, and give you some comfort.

776

And if yow lyketh alle, by oon assent,
And if you all agree, by common consent,

Now for to stonden at my jugement,
To be ruled now by my judgment,

And for to werken as I shal yow seye,
And to proceed as I shall explain,

To-morwe, whan ye ryden by the weye,   780
Tomorrow, when you go on your way,

Now, by my fader soule, that is deed,
Now, by my father's soul, who is dead,

But ye be merye, I wol yeve yow myn heed.
If you are not merry, I will give you my head.

Hold up your hond, withouten more speche."
Hold up your hands, without further discussion."

Our counseil was nat longe for to seche;   784
Our decision was not hard to find;

Us thoughte it was noght worth to make it wys,
We thought it hardly worth making an issue of it,

And graunted him withouten more avys,
And agreed with him without further consideration,

And bad him seye his verdit, as him leste.
And bade him give his verdict, as he pleased.

"Lordinges," quod he, "now herkneth for the beste;   788
"Gentlemen," he said, "now listen with good will;

But tak it not, I prey yow, in desdeyn;
And take it not, I beg you, disdainfully;

This is the poynt, to speken short and pleyn,
This is the point, to speak briefly and plainly,

That ech of yow, to shorte with your weye,
That each of you, to shorten the journey,

In this viage, shal telle tales tweye,   792
On this trip, shall tell two tales.

To Caunterbury-ward, I mene it so,
En route to Canterbury, I mean what I say,

And hom-ward he shal tellen othere two,
And two more on the return trip home,

Of aventures that whylom han bifalle.
Of adventures that have once happened.

And which of yow that bereth him best of alle,   796
And whichever of you does the best of all,

That is to seyn, that telleth in this cas
That is to say, that tells in this contest

Tales of best sentence and most solas,
The most meaningful and amusing tales,

Shal have a soper at our aller cost
Shall be given a dinner at the expense of all

Here in this place, sitting by this post,   800
Here in this place, sitting by this post,

Whan that we come agayn fro Caunterbury.
When we return from Canterbury.

And for to make yow the more mery,
And to make you more merry,

I wol my-selven gladly with yow ryde,
I will myself gladly ride with you,

Right at myn owne cost, and be your gyde.   804
Even at my own expense, and be your guide.

And who-so wol my jugement withseye
And whoever opposes my judgment

Shal paye al that we spenden by the weye.
Shall pay all that we spend along the way.

And if ye vouche-sauf that it be so,
And if you pledge that it be so,

Tel me anon, with outen wordes mo,   808
Tell me immediately, without more words,

And I wol erly shape me therfore."
And I will make plans accordingly."

This thing was graunted, and our othes swore
This thing was granted, and our oaths sworn

With ful glad herte, and preyden him also
With entirely glad hearts, and we begged him too

That he wolde vouche-sauf for to do so,   812
That he would agree to do his part,

And that he wolde been our governour,
And that he would be our director,

And of our tales juge and reportour,
And remember and judge our tales,

And sette a soper at a certeyn prys;
And plan a dinner at a certain price;

And we wold reuled been at his devys,   816
And we would be ruled at his direction,

In heigh and lowe; and thus, by oon assent,
In great and small; and thus, by general consent,

We been accorded to his jugement.
We were in accord with his plan.

And ther-up-on the wyn was fet anon;
And thereupon the wine was quickly served;

We dronken, and to reste wente echon,   820
We drank, and each of us went to bed

With-outen any lenger taryinge.
Without any further tarrying.

A-morwe, whan that day bigan to springe,
Next morning, when the day began to dawn,

Up roos our host, and was our aller cok,
Up rose our host, and was rooster for us all,

And gadrede us togidre, alle in a flok,   824
And gathered us together, all in a flock,

And forth we riden, a litel more than pas,
And forth we rode, slightly faster than a walk,

Un-to the watering of seint Thomas.
Up to the watering-place of Saint Thomas.

And there our host bigan his hors areste,
And there our host slowed down his horse,

And seyde: "Lordinges, herkneth, if yow leste.   828
And said: "Gentlemen, listen, if you please.

Ye woot your forward, and I it yow recorde.
You know your agreement, and I remind you of it.

If even-song and morwe-song acorde,
If evening and morning are in agreement,

Lat see now who shal telle the firste tale.
Let us see now who shall tell the first tale.

As ever mote I drinke wyn or ale,   832
If ever again I drink wine or ale,

Who-so be rebel to my jugement
Whoever rebels at my decision

Shal paye for al that by the weye is spent.
Shall pay for all that by the way is spent.

Now draweth cut, er that we ferrer twinne;
Now draw lots, before we proceed farther;

He which that hath the shortest shal biginne.   836
Whoever draws the shortest shall begin.

Sire knight," quod he, "my maister and my lord,
Sir knight," said he, "my master and my lord,

Now draweth cut, for that is myn acord.
Now draw your lot, for that is my order.

Cometh neer," quod he, "my lady prioresse;
Come closer," said he, "my lady prioress;

And ye, sir clerk, lat be your shamfastnesse,   840
And you, sir clerk, forget your bashfulness,

Ne studieth noght; ley hond to, every man."
Don't think it over; lay hand to, every man."

Anon to drawen every wight bigan,
And so every one began to draw,

And shortly for to tellen, as it was,
And to speak briefly, as it came out,

Were it by aventure, or sort, or cas,   *844*
Whether by accident, luck, or chance,

The sothe is this, the cut fil to the knight,
The fact is this, the lot fell to the knight,

Of which ful blythe and glad was every wight;
Which was entirely pleasing to everyone;

And telle he moste his tale, as was resoun,
And tell his tale he must, as was right,

By forward and by composicioun,   *848*
By agreement and according to plan,

As ye han herd; what nedeth wordes mo?
As you have heard; why waste more words?

And whan this gode man saugh it was so,
And when this good man saw that it was so,

As he that wys was and obedient
Since he was wise and willing

To keep his forward by his free assent,   *852*
To keep his agreement by free consent,

He seyde: "Sin I shal beginne the game,
He said: "Since I am to begin the game,

What, welcome be the cut, a Goddes name!
Why, welcome be the lot, in God's name!

Now lat us ryde, and herkneth what I seye."
Now let us ride along, and listen to what I say."

And with that word we riden forth our weye;   *856*
And with that word we rode forth on our way;

And he bigan with right a mery chere
And he began in high good spirits

His tale anon, and seyde in this manere
His tale forthwith, and spoke in this manner.

The Knight's Tale

IAMQUE DOMOS PATRIAS, SCITHICE POST ASPERA

GENTIS PRELIA, LAURIGERO, &C.[1]

Part One

Whylom, as olde stories tellen us,
Once, as old histories tell us,

Ther was a duk that highte Theseus;
There was a duke named Theseus;

Of Athenes he was lord and governour,
He was lord and ruler of Athens,

And in his tyme swich a conquerour,   4
And in his time such a conqueror,

That gretter was ther noon under the sonne.
That there was no greater under the sun.

Ful many a riche contree hadde he wonne;
Many a rich country had he won;

What with his wisdom and his chivalrye,
What with his wisdom and his skill at arms,

He conquered al the regne of Femenye,   8
He conquered all the realm of the Amazons,

That whylom was y-cleped Scithia;
Which was formerly named Scythia;

And weddede the quene Ipolita,
And married the queen Hippolyta,

And broghte hir hoom with him in his coutree
And brought her home with him to his country

With muchel glorie and greet solempnitee,   *12*
With much pomp and circumstance,

And eek hir yonge suster Emelye.
And also her young sister Emily.

And thus with victorie and with melodye
And thus in triumph and with melody

Lete I this noble duk to Athenes ryde,
I leave this noble duke riding to Athens,

And al his hoost, in armes, him bisyde.   *16*
And all his host, in arms, with him.

And certes, if it nere to long to here,
And indeed, were it not too long to listen to,

I wolde han told yow fully the manere,
I would have told you in full the details,

How wonnen was the regne of Femenye
How the realm of the Amazons was conquered

By Theseus, and by his chivalrye;   *20*
By Theseus, and by his knights;

And of the grete bataille for the nones
And of the great battle

Bitwixen Athenës and Amazones;
Between the Athenians and Amazons;

And how asseged was Ipolita,
And of the besieging of Hippolyta,

The faire hardy quene of Scithia;   *24*
The fair sturdy queen of Scythia;

And of the feste that was at hir weddinge,
And of the feast there was at her wedding,

And of the tempest at hir hoom-cominge;
And of the tempest at her home-coming;

But al that thing I moot as now forbere.
But all of that I must omit for the present.

I have, God woot, a large feeld to ere,   28
I have, God knows, a large field to cover,

And wayke been the oxen in my plough.
And weak are the oxen in my plough.

The remenant of the tale is long y-nough.
The rest of the tale is long enough.

I wol nat letten eek noon of this route;
Besides, I won't handicap any other of this group;

Lat every felawe telle his tale aboute,   32
Let every person tell his tale in turn,

And lat see now who shal the soper winne;
And let us see who will win the dinner.

And ther I lefte, I wol ageyn biginne.
And where I left off, I will begin again.

This duk, of whom I make mencioun,
This duke, whom I have mentioned,

When he was come almost unto the toun,   36
When he had almost reached the town,

In al his wele and in his moste pryde,
In all his glory and greatest pride,

He was war, as he caste his eye asyde,
Became aware, as he glanced sideways,

Wher that ther kneled in the hye weye
That there was kneeling in the highway

A companye of ladies, tweye and tweye,   40
A company of ladies, two by two,

Ech after other, clad in clothes blake;
One after the other, dressed in black clothes;

But swich a cry and swich a wo they make,
But such a cry and such a wail they made,

That in this world nis creature livinge,
That in this world no living creature

That herde swich another weymentinge;   **44**
Ever heard another such lamentation;

And of this cry they nolde never stenten,
And this crying they would never abate,

Til they the reynes of his brydel henten.
Until they had seized the reins of his bridle.

   "What folk ben ye, that at myn hoom-cominge
   "What people are you, that at my home-coming

Perturben so my feste with cryinge?"   **48**
Disturb my celebration so with crying?"

Quod Theseus, "have ye so greet envye
Asked Theseus, "Have you such envy

Of myn honour, that thus compleyne and crye?
Of my fame that thus you lament and cry?

Or who hath yow misboden, or offended;
Or who hath wronged you, or offended;

And telleth me if it may been amended;   **52**
And tell me if it can be remedied;

And why that ye ben clothed thus in blak?"
And why you are dressed this way in black?"

   The eldest lady of hem alle spak,
   The oldest lady of them all spoke,

When she hadde swowned with a deedly chere,
After she had swooned with a deathly pallor,

That it was routhe for to seen and here,   **56**
That it was pitiable to see and hear,

And seyde: "Lord, to whom Fortune hath yiven
And said: "Lord, to whom Fortune has given

Victorie, and as a conquerour to liven,
Victory, and to live as a conqueror,

Noght greveth us your glorie and your honour;
Your glory and your fame grieve us not at all;

But we biseken mercy and socour.   60
But we beg mercy and assistance.

Have mercy on our wo and our distresse.
Have mercy on our woe and our distress.

Som drope of pitee, thurgh thy gentilesse,
One drop of pity, by your nobility,

Up-on us wrecched wommen lat thou falle.
Upon us wretched women deign to let fall.

For certes, lord, ther nis noon of us alle,   64
For truly, lord, there is not one of us

That she nath been a duchesse or a quene;
Who has not been a duchess or a queen;

Now be we caitifs, as it is wel sene:
Now are we captives, as is clearly seen:

Thanked be Fortune, and hir false wheel,
Thanks be to Fortune, and her false wheel,

That noon estat assureth to be weel.   68
That gives assurance to no one's welfare.

And certes, lord, t'abyden your presence,
And indeed, lord, to abide your coming,

Here in the temple of the goddesse Clemence
Here in the temple of the goddess Clemency

We han ben waytinge al this fourtenight;
We have been waiting all this fortnight;

Now help us, lord, sith it is in thy might.   72
Now help us, lord, since it is in your power.

"I wrecche, which that wepe and waille thus,
"I, now weeping and wailing in my wretchedness,

Was whylom wyf to king Capaneus,
Was formerly wife to King Capaneus,

That starf at Thebes, cursed be that day!
Who died at Thebes, cursed be that day!

And alle we, that been in this array,   70
And all of us who are dressed like this,

And maken al this lamentacioun,
And make all this lamentation,

We losten alle our housbondes at that toun,
We all lost our husbands at that town,

Whyl that the sege ther-aboute lay.
While the siege was laid about it.

And yet now th'olde Creon, weylaway!   80
And now old Creon, alas!

The lord is now of Thebes the citee,
Who is now lord of the city of Thebes,

Fulfild of ire and of iniquitee,
Filled with anger and evil,

He, for despyt, and for his tirannye,
For the sake of revenge, and to play the tyrant,

To do the dede bodyes vileinye,   84
To disgrace the dead bodies

Of alle our lordes, whiche that ben slawe,
Of all our lords, who have been slain,

Hath alle the bodyes on an heep y-drawe,
Had all the bodies piled in a heap,

And wol nat suffren hem, by noon assent,
And will not permit them, under any circumstances,

Neither to been y-buried nor y-brent,   88
Either to be buried or burned,

But maketh houndes ete hem in despyt."
But has set hounds to eat them out of spite."

And with that word, with-outen more respyt,
And with that word, without further respite,

They fillen gruf, and cryden pitously,
They fell face downward and wept piteously,

"Have on us wrecched wommen som mercy,   92
"Have mercy on us wretched women,

And lat our sorwe sinken in thyn herte."
And let our sorrow sink into your heart."

This gentil duk doun from his courser sterte
This noble duke leaped down from his horse

With herte pitous, whan he herde hem speke.
With pitying heart, when he heard them speak.

Him thoughte that his herte wolde breke,   96
He thought that his heart would break,

Whan he saugh hem so pitous and so mat,
When he saw them so pathetic and dejected,

That whylom weren of so greet estat.
Who formerly were of so high a rank.

And in his armes he hem alle up hente,
And in his arms he gathered them all

And hem conforteth in ful good entente;   100
And comforted them with good intent;

And swoor his ooth, as he was trewe knight,
And swore his oath, as he was a true knight,

He wolde doon so ferforthly his might
That he would wreak so thoroughly his might

Up-on the tyraunt Creon hem to wreke,
Upon the tyrant Creon, to destroy him,

That al the peple of Grece sholde speke   104
That all the people of Greece would tell

How Creon was of Theseus y-served,
How Creon was treated by Theseus,

As he that hadde his deeth ful wel deserved.
As one who had full well deserved his death.

And right anoon, with-outen more abood,
And immediately, without further delay,

His baner he desplayeth, and forth rood   108
His banner he unfurled, and rode forth

To Thebes-ward, and al his host bisyde;
Toward Thebes, and all his host with him;

No neer Athenës wolde he go ne ryde,
No nearer Athens would he walk or ride,

Ne take his ese fully half a day,
Nor take his ease even half a day,

But onward on his wey that night he lay;   112
But was well on his way before he slept that night;

And sente anoon Ipolita the quene,
And straightway sent Hippolyta the queen,

And Emelye hir yonge suster shene,
And Emily her beautiful young sister,

Un-to the toun of Athenës to dwelle;
To live in the town of Athens;

And forth he rit, ther nis namore to telle.   116
And forth he rode, there is no more to tell.

The rede statue of Mars, with spere and targe,
The red figure of Mars, with spear and shield,

So shyneth in his whyte baner large,
So shone upon his large white banner,

That alle the feeldes gliteren up and doun;
That all the fields glittered up and down;

And by his baner born is his penoun   120
And next to his banner was borne his pennant

Of gold ful riche, in which ther was y-bete
Of gold full rich, on which was depicted

The Minotaur, which that he slough in Crete.
The Minotaur, which he had slain in Crete.

Thus rit this duk, thus rit this conquerour,
Thus rode this duke, thus rode this conqueror,

And in his host of chivalrye the flour,   *124*
And in his host the flower of chivalry,

Til that he cam to Thebes, and alighte
Until he came to Thebes, and alighted

Faire in a feeld, ther as he thoughte fighte.
Fairly in a field, where he planned to battle.

But shortly for to speken of this thing,
But to speak of this affair briefly,

With Creon, which that was of Thebes king,   *128*
With Creon, who was King of Thebes,

He faught, and slough him manly as a knight
He fought, and slew him manfully as a knight

In pleyn bataille, and putte the folk to flight;
In open battle, and put his followers to flight;

And by assaut he wan the citee after,
And afterwards he won the city by assault,

And rente adoun bothe wal, and sparre, and rafter;   *132*
And razed walls and beams and rafters;

And to the ladyes he restored agayn
And to the ladies he restored again

The bones of hir housbondes that were slayn,
The bones of their husbands who were slain,

To doon obsequies as was tho the gyse.
To perform the obsequies which were then customary.

But it were al to long for to devyse   *136*
But it would take too long to describe

The grete clamour and the waymentinge
The great weeping and wailing

That the ladyes made at the brenninge
That the ladies made at the cremation

Of the bodyes, and the grete honour
Of the bodies, and the great honor

That Theseus, the noble conquerour,   *140*
That Theseus, the noble conqueror,

Doth to the ladyes, whan they from him wente;
Did to the ladies, when they departed from him;

But shortly for to telle is myn entente.
For to speak briefly is my intention.

Whan that this worthy duk, this Theseus
When this worthy duke, this Theseus,

Hath Creon slayn, and wonne Thebes thus,   *144*
Had slain Creon, and so won Thebes,

Stille in that feeld he took al night his reste
In that same field he rested all night

And dide with al the contree as him leste.
And did with all the country as he pleased.

  To ransake in the tas of bodyes dede,
  To ransack the heap of dead bodies,

Hem for to strepe of harneys and of wede,   *148*
To strip them of arms and clothing,

The pilours diden businesse and cure,
The pillagers worked busily and diligently

After the bataille and disconfiture.
After the battle and defeat.

And so bifel, that in the tas they founde,
And it so happened, that in the heap they found,

Thurgh-girt with many a grevous blody wounde,   *152*
Stabbed through with many a grievous bloody wound,

Two yonge knightes ligging by and by,
Two young knights lying side by side,

Bothe in oon armes, wroght ful richely,
Both with the same coat of arms, richly wrought,

Of whiche two, Arcita hight that oon,
Of which two, Arcite was the name of one,

And that other knight hight Palamon.   156
And the other knight was called Palamon.

Nat fully quike, ne fully dede they were,
Neither fully alive nor fully dead were they,

But by hir cote-armures, and by hir gere,
But by their coats of arms and their armor,

The heraudes knewe hem best in special,
The heralds recognized them as highest born,

As they that weren of the blood royal   160
As being of the royal blood

Of Thebes, and of sustren two y-born.
Of Thebes, and born of two sisters.

Out of the tas the pilours han hem torn,
Out of the heap the pillagers tore them,

And han hem caried softe un-to the tente
And carried them gently to the tent

Of Theseus, and he ful son hem sente   164
Of Theseus, who quickly sent them

To Athenës, to dwellen in prisoun
To Athens, to be placed in prison

Perpetuelly, he nolde no raunsoun.
For life, he would not hear of ransom.

And whan this worthy duk hath thus y-don,
And when this worthy duke had done this,

He took his host, and hoom he rood anon   168
He assembled his host, and home he rode forthwith

With laurer crowned as a conquerour;
With laurel crowned like a conqueror;

And there he liveth, in joye and in honour,
And there he lived, in happiness and honor,

Terme of his lyf; what nedeth wordes mo?
To the end of his life; what more need be said?

And in a tour, in angwish and in wo,   *172*
And in a tower, in anguish and woe,

Dwellen this Palamoun and eek Arcite,
Languished this Palamon and Arcite,

For evermore, ther may no gold hem quyte.
For evermore, no gold could ransom them.

This passeth yeer by yeer, and day by day,
This continued year after year, and day after day,

Til it fil ones, in a morwe of May,   *176*
Until it once happened, on a May morning,

That Emelye, that fairer was to sene
That Emily, who was fairer to behold

Than is the lilie upon his stalke grene,
Than is the lily on its green stalk,

And fressher than the May with floures newe—
And fresher than May with its new flowers—

For with the rose colour stroof hir hewe,   *180*
For her complexion vied with the color of roses,

I noot which was the fairer of hem two—
I know not which was the fairer of the two—

Er it were day, as was hir wone to do,
Before daybreak, as was her usual practice,

She was arisen, and al redy dight;
She had risen, and was already dressed;

For May wol have no slogardye a-night.   *184*
For May will have no slug-abeds.

The sesoun priketh every gentil herte,
That season rouses every gentle heart,

And maketh him out of his sleep to sterte,
And makes it startle from its sleep,

And seith, "Arys, and do thyn observaunce."
And says, "Arise, and do your homage."

This maked Emelye have remembraunce   188
This caused Emily to remember

To doon honour to May, and for to ryse.
To do honor to May, and to arise.

Y-clothed was she fresh, for to devyse;
Fresh clothed was she, to describe her appearance;

Hir yelow heer was broyded in a tresse,
Her yellow hair was braided in a tress,

Bihinde hir bak, a yerde long, I gesse.   192
Behind her back, a yard long, I imagine.

And in the gardin, at the sonne up-riste,
And in the garden, as the sun rose,

She walketh up and doun, and as hir liste
She walked up and down, and for her pleasure

She gadereth floures, party whyte and rede,
She gathered flowers, some white and some red,

To make a sotil gerland for hir hede,   196
To make a dainty garland for her head,

And as an aungel hevenly she song.
And like an angel from heaven she sang.

The grete tour, that was so thikke and strong,
The great tower, that was so thick and strong,

Which of the castel was the chief dongeoun,
Being the principal dungeon of the castle

(Ther-as the knightes weren in prisoun,   200
(Where the knights were in prison,

Of whiche I tolde yow, and tellen shal)
Of whom I told you, and shall tell more),

Was evene joynant to the gardin-wal
Was exactly adjacent to the garden wall

Ther as this Emelye hadde hir pleyinge.
Where this Emily was amusing herself.

Bright was the sonne, and cleer that morweninge,   204
Bright was the sun, and clear the morning,

And Palamou, this woful prisoner,
And Palamon, this woeful prisoner,

As was his wone, by leve of his gayler,
As was his wont, by leave of his jailer,

Was risen, and romed in a chambre on heigh,
Had arisen, and roamed in a chamber on high,

In which he al the noble citee seigh,   208
From which he viewed all the noble city.

And eek the gardin, ful of braunches grene,
And also the garden, full of green branches,

Ther-as this fresshe Emelye the shene
Where this fresh, glittering Emily

Was in hir walk, and romed up and doun.
Was walking, and strolled up and down.

This sorweful prisoner, this Palamoun,   212
This sorrowful prisoner, this Palamon,

Goth in the chambre, roming to and fro,
Walked in the chamber, pacing back and forth,

And to him-self compleyning of his wo;
And complaining to himself about his woe;

That he was born, ful ofte he seyde, "alas!"
That ever he was born, often he said, "Alas!"

And so bifel, by aventure or cas,   216
And it so happened, by coincidence or chance,

That thurgh a window, thikke of many a barre
That through a window, guarded by many a bar

Of yren greet, and square as any sparre,
Of heavy iron, and square as any beam,

He caste his eye upon Emelya,
He cast his eye upon Emily,

And ther-with-al he bleynte, and cryde "a!"   220
And thereupon he blanched, and cried, "Ah!"

As though he stongen were un-to the herte.
As though he were smitten to the heart.

And with that cry Arcite anon up-sterte,
And with that cry Arcite at once jumped up,

And seyde, "Cosin myn, what eyleth thee,
And said, "Cousin mine, what ails you,

That art so pale and deedly on to see?   224
That you look so pale and deathly?

Why crydestow? Who hath thee doon offence?
Why did you cry? Who has done you harm?

For Goddes love, tak all in pacience
For the love of God, endure in patience

Our prisoun, for it may non other be;
Our imprisonment, for it may not be otherwise;

Fortune hath yeven us this adversitee.   228
Fortune has given us this adversity.

Some wikke aspect or disposicioun
Some evil aspect or disposition

Of Saturne, by sum constellacioun,
Of Saturn, by some constellation,

Hath yeven us this, al-though we hadde it sworn;
Has given us this, though we had sworn it should not be;

So stood the heven whan that we were born;   232
So the heavens decreed when we were born;

We moste endure it: this is the short and pleyn."
We must endure it: this is the long and short of it."

This Palamon answerde, and seyde ageyn,
This Palamon answered, and spoke again,

"Cosyn, for sothe, of this opinioun
"Cousin, truly, in giving this opinion

Thou haste a veyn imaginacioun.   236
You suffer from a false conception.

This prison caused me nat for to crye.
This prison did not cause my outcry.

But I was hurt right now thurgh-out myn yë
But I was just now wounded through my eyes

In-to myn herte, that wol my bane be.
Right to the heart, enough to cause my death.

The fairnesse of that lady that I see   240
The beauty of that lady whom I see

Yond in the gardin romen to and fro,
Yonder in the garden strolling to and fro,

Is cause of al my crying and my wo.
Is the cause of all my outcries and my woe.

I noot wher she be womman or goddesse;
I know not whether she be woman or goddess;

But Venus is it, soothly, as I gesse."   244
But it must be Venus, I truly believe."

And ther-with-al on kneës doun he fil,
And instantly he fell upon his knees,

And sayde: "Venus, if it be thy wil
And said: "Venus, if it be thy will

You in this gardin thus to transfigure
To appear in this garden thus

Bifore me, sorweful wrecche creature,   248
Before me, a sorrowful wretched creature,

Out of this prisoun help that we may scapen.
Help us to escape from this prison.

Or if so be my destinee be shapen
Or if it be that my destiny is decreed

By eterne word to dyen in prisoun,
By eternal word to die in prison,

Of our linage have som compassioun,   252
Have some compassion on our lineage,

That is so lowe y-broght by tirannye."
That is brought so low by tyranny."

And with that word Arcite gan espye
And with that word Arcite saw

Wher-as this lady romed to and fro.
Where this lady walked to and fro.

And with that sighte hir beautee hurte him so,   256
And with the sight her beauty smote him so,

That, if that Palamon was wounded sore,
That, if Palamon was sorely wounded,

Arcite is hurte as muche as he, or more.
Arcite is hurt as much as he, or more.

And with a sigh he seyde pitously:
And with a sigh he said piteously:

"The fresshe beautee sleeth me sodeynly   260
"The untarnished beauty slays me suddenly

Of hir that rometh in the yonder place;
Of her who is wandering out there;

And, but I have hir mercy and hir grace,
And, unless I win her mercy and her grace,

That I may seen hir atte leest weye,
That I may at least look upon her,

I nam but deed; ther nis namore to seye."   264
I am but dead; there is no more to say."

This Palamon, whan he tho wordes herde,
This Palamon, when he heard these words,

Dispitously he loked, and answerde:
Looked savagely, and answered:

"Whether seistow this in ernest or in pley?"
"Do you say this in earnest or in fun?"

"Nay," quod Arcite, "in ernest, by my fey!   268
"No," said Arcite, "in earnest, by my faith!

God help me so, me list ful yvele pleye."
God help me if I joke about this."

This Palamon gan kitte his browes tweye:
This Palamon knitted his brows:

"It nere," quod he, "to thee no greet honour
"It does you no great honor," he said,

For to be fals, ne for to be traytour   272
"To be false, or to be a traitor

To me, that am thy cosin and thy brother
To me, your cousin and brother-in-arms

Y-sworn ful depe, and ech of us til other,
Most deeply sworn, and each of us to the other,

That never, for to dyen in the peyne,
That never, though we should die by torture,

Til that the deeth departe shal us tweyne,   276
Until death part us two,

Neither of us in love to hindren other,
Would either of us hinder the other in love,

Ne in non other cas, my leve brother;
Or in any other affair, my dear brother;

But that thou sholdest trewely forthren me
But that you would faithfully assist me

In every cas, and I shal forthren thee.   280
In every event, and that I should assist you.

This was thyn ooth, and myn also, certeyn;
This was your certain oath, and mine as well;

I wot right wel, thou darst it nat withseyn.
I know right well you dare not contraaict me.

Thus artow of my conseil, out of doute.
Consequently, you are on my side, beyond a doubt.

And now thou woldest falsly been aboute   284
And now in bad faith you were about

To love my lady, whom I love and serve,
To love my lady, whom I love and serve,

And ever shal, til that myn herte sterve.
And ever shall, until my heart dies.

Now certes, fals Arcite, thou shalt nat so.
Now certainly, false Arcite, you shall not persevere.

I loved hir first, and tolde thee my wo   288
I loved her first, and told you of my woe

As to my counseil, and my brother sworn
As to my adviser and my brother sworn

To forthre me, as I have told biforn.
To assist me, as I said before.

For which thou art y-bounden as a knight
Therefore you are bound as a knight

To helpen me, if it lay in thy might,   292
To help me, if it lies in your power,

Or elles artow fals, I dar wel seyn."
Or else are you false, I dare declare."

This Arcitë ful proudly spak ageyn,
This Arcite full proudly spoke again,

"Thou shalt," quod he, "be rather fals than I;
"You shall," said he, "more likely be false than I;

But thou art fals, I telle thee utterly;   296
But you are false, I tell you bluntly;

For *par amour* I loved hir first er thow.
Since I loved her as a lover before you did.

What wiltow seyn? Thou wistest nat yet now
What will you say? You don't know even now

Whether she be a womman or goddesse!
Whether she is a woman or a goddess!

Thyn is affeccioun of holinesse,   30J
Yours is adoration of holiness,

And myn is love, as to a creature;
And mine is love as of a mortal;

For which I tolde thee myn aventure
Wherefore I told you my situation

As to my cosin, and my brother sworn.
As to my cousin and my sworn brother.

I pose, that thou lovedest hir beforn;   304
Even assuming that you loved her first;

Wostow nat wel the olde clerkes sawe,
Do you not know the old clerk's proverb,

That 'who shal yeve a lover any lawe?'
Which says, 'Who shall make laws for lovers?'

Love is a gretter lawe, by my pan,
Love is a greater law, by my head,

Than may be yeve to any erthly man.   308
Than can be given to any earthly man.

And therefore positif lawe and swich decree
And therefore precise laws and such decrees

Is broke al-day for love, in ech degree.
Are daily broken for love by all classes.

A man moot nedes love, maugree his heed.
A man can't control love in spite of his reason.

He may nat fleen it, thogh he sholde be deed,   312
He cannot escape it, though he should die for it,

Al be she mayde, or widwe, or elles wyf.
Whether she be maid, widow, or even a wife.

And eek it is nat lykly, al thy lyf,
And besides you are not likely, in all your life,

To stonden in hir grace; namore shal I;
To win her favor; and neither shall I;

For wel thou woost thy-selven, verraily,   *316*
For well you know yourself, of a truth,

That thou and I be dampned to prisoun
That you and I are condemned to prison

Perpetuelly; us gayneth no raunsoun.
Perpetually, no ransom can help us.

We stryve as dide the houndes for the boon,
We struggle as did the hounds for the bone,

They foughte al day, and yet hir part was noon;   *320*
They fought all day, and neither had gotten any;

Ther cam a kyte, whyl that they were wrothe,
Along came a kite, while they were contending,

And bar awey the boon bitwixe hem bothe.
And snatched away the bone from between them.

And therfore, at the kinges court, my brother,
And therefore, at the king's court, my brother,

Ech man for him-self, ther is non other.   *324*
It's each man for himself, there is no alternative.

Love if thee list; for I love and ay shal;
Love if you please; for I love and ever shall;

And soothly, leve brother, this is al.
And truly, dear brother, that is all.

Here in this prisoun mote we endure,
Here in this prison we must suffer,

And everich of us take his aventure."   *328*
And each of us accept whatever befalls."

   Greet was the stryf and long bitwixe hem tweye,
   Great was the strife and long beween the two,

If that I hadde leyser for to seye;
If I had the leisure to describe it;

But to th' effect. It happed on a day,
But to the outcome. It happened one day,

(To telle it yow as shortly as I may)   332
(To speak as briefly as I can)

A worthy duk that highte Perotheus,
A worthy duke named Pirothous,

That felawe was un-to duk Theseus
Who had been a friend of Duke Theseus

Sin thilke day that they were children lyte,
Since the time that they were little children,

Was come to Athenes, his felawe to visyte,   336
Had come to Athens to visit his friend,

And for to pleye, as he was wont to do,
And to find pastime, as he was accustomed to do,

For in this world he loved no man so:
For he loved no other man in the world so much:

And he loved him as tendrely ageyn.
And Theseus returned his love as tenderly.

So wel they loved, as olde bokes seyn,   340
So well they loved, as ancient writers tell,

That whan that oon was deed, sothly to telle,
That when one of them died, to say the truth,

His felawe wente and soghte him doun in helle;
His friend went and sought him down in hell;

But of that story list me nat to wryte.
But that story I am not disposed to write.

Duk Perotheus loved wel Arcite,   344
Duke Pirothous loved Arcite fondly,

And hadde him knowe at Thebes yeer by yere;
And had known him at Thebes for many years;

And fynally, at requeste and preyere
And finally, at the request and entreaties

Of Perotheus, with-oute any ransoun,
Of Pirothous, without any ransom,

Duk Theseus him leet out of prisoun,   *348*
Duke Theseus let him out of prison,

Freely to goon, wher that him liste over-al,
Free to go anywhere that he pleased,

In swich a gyse, as I you tellen shal.
On such conditions as I shall tell you.

This was the forward, pleynly for t'endyte,
This was the agreement, to put it simply,

Bitwixen Theseus and him Arcite: *352*
Between Theseus and Arcite:

That if so were that Arcite were y-founde
That if it happened that Arcite were found

Ever in his lyf, by day or night or stounde
Ever in his life at any hour, day or night,

In any contree of this Theseus,
In any realm of this Theseus

And he were caught, it was accorded thus,   *356*
And if he were caught, it was so agreed,

That with a swerd he sholde lese his heed;
That by a sword he would lose his head;

Ther nas non other remedye ne reed,
There was no remedy nor help for it,

But taketh his leve, and homward he him spedde;
So he took his leave, and sped homeward;

Let him be war, his nekke lyth to wedde!   *360*
Let him beware, his neck is pledged as security!

How great a sorwe suffreth now Arcite!
How great a grief Arcite suffers now!

The deeth he feleth thurgh his herte smyte;
He feels death clutching at his heart;

He wepeth, wayleth, cryeth pitously;
He weeps, wails and groans pitifully;

To sleen him-self he wayteth prively.　　　　364
He plans secretly to kill himself.

He sayde, "Allas that day that I was born!
He said, "Alas, the day that I was born!

Now is my prison worse than biforn;
Now is my prison worse than before;

Now is me shape eternally to dwelle
Now am I doomed eternally to dwell

Noght in purgatorie, but in helle,　　　　368
Not in purgatory, but in hell,

Allas! that ever knew I Perotheus!
Alas! that I ever knew Pirothous!

For elles hadde I dwelled with Theseus
For otherwise I would have remained with Theseus

Y-fetered in his prisoun ever-mo.
Chained in his prison for evermore.

Than hadde I been in blisse, and nat in wo.　　　　372
Then I would have been in bliss, not woe.

Only the sighte of hir, whom that I serve,
Only the sight of her, whom I serve,

Though that I never hir grace may deserve,
Though I never may deserve her grace,

Wolde han suffised right y-nough for me.
Would have been entirely enough for me.

O dere cosin Palamon," quod he,　　　　376
O dear cousin Palamon," said he,

"Thyn is the victorie of this aventure,
"Yours is the victory of this situation,

Ful blisfully in prison maistow dure;
Full blissfully in prison may you endure;

In prison? Certes nay, but in paradys!
In prison? Quite the contrary, in paradise!

Wel hath Fortune y-turned thee the dys,   380
Well has Fortune cast the dice for you,

That hast the sighte of hir, and I th' abscence,
That you have the sight of her, and I the absence,

For possible is, sin thou hast hir presence,
For it is possible, since you have her presence,

And art a knight, a worthy and an able,
And are a knight, worthy and able,

That by som cas, sin Fortune is chaungeable,   384
It may bechance, since Fortune is changeable,

Thou mayst to thy desyr som-tyme atteyne.
That you may sometime attain your desire.

But I, that am exyled, and bareyne
But I, who am exiled, and barren

Of alle grace, and in so greet despeir,
Of all grace, and in so great despair,

That ther nis erthe, water, fyr, ne eir,   388
That neither earth, water, fire, nor air,

Ne creature, that of hem maked is,
Nor any creature composed of them,

That may me helpe or doon confort in this:
Can help me or bring comfort in this:

Wel oughte I sterve in wanhope and distresse;
Well may I die in hopelessness and distress;

Farwel my lyf, my lust, and my gladnesse!   392
Farewell my life, my joy, and my happiness!

"Allas, why pleynen folk so in commune
"Alas, why do people so constantly complain

Of purveyaunce of God, or of Fortune,
Of the provisions of God, or of Fate,

That yeveth hem ful ofte in many a gyse
That often gives them in many respects

Wel bettre than they can hem-self devyse?   *396*
Much better lots than they could plan for themselves?

Som man desyreth for to han richesse,
One man desires to have wealth,

That cause is of his mordre or greet siknesse.
Which becomes the cause of his murder or illness.

And som man wolde out of his prison fayn,
And another wants to escape from prison,

That in his hous is of his meynee slayn.   *400*
Only to be slain in his house by his servants.

Infinite harmes been in this matere;
Infinite are the evils of this earth;

We witen nat what thing we preyen here.
We know not what thing we pray for here.

We faren as he that dronke is as a mous;
We fare as one who is as drunk as a mouse;

A dronke man wot wel he hath an hous,   *404*
A drunken man knows well that he has a house,

But he noot which the righte wey is thider;
But he doesn't know how to get to it;

And to a dronke man the wey is slider.
And to a drunken man the way is slippery.

And certes, in this world so faren we;
And truly, in this world so fare we;

We seken faste after felicitee,   *408*
We search diligently for happiness,

But we goon wrong ful often, trewely.
But we very often go wrong, without doubt.

Thus may we seyen alle, and namely I
Thus may we all say, and especially I

That wende and hadde a greet opinioun,
Who believed and had a firm notion,

That, if I mighte escapen from prisoun,   412
That, if I could escape from prison,

Than hadde I been in joye and perfit hele,
Then would I be in joy and perfect contentment,

Ther now I am exyled fro my wele.
Whereas now I am exiled from my happiness.

Sin that I may nat seen yow, Emelye,
Since I cannot see you, Emily,

I nam but deed; ther nis no remedye."   416
I am but dead; there is no remedy."

    Up-on that other syde Palamon,
    On the other hand, Palamon,

Whan that he wiste Arcite was agon,
When he knew Arcite had departed,

Swich sorwe he maketh, that the grete tour
Made such sorrow, that the great tower

Resouneth of his youling and clamour.   420
Resounded with his outcries and wailing.

The pure fettres on his shines grete
Even the fetters on his great shins

Weren of his bittre salte teres wete.
Were wet from his bitter salt tears.

"Allas!" quod he, "Arcita, cosin myn,
"Alas!" said he, "Arcite, cousin mine,

Of al our stryf, God woot, the fruyt is thyn.   424
Of all our strife, God knows, the fruit is yours.

Thow walkest now in Thebes at thy large,
You walk at large now in Thebes,

And of my wo thou yevest litel charge.
And to my woe you give little heed.

Thou mayst, sin thou hast wisdom and manhede,
You may, since you have wisdom and manhood,

Assemblen alle the folk of our kinrede,   428
Assemble all the people of our kindred,

And make a werre so sharp on this citee,
And wage so fierce a war on this city,

That by some aventure, or some tretee,
That by some chance, or kind of treaty,

Thou mayst have hir to lady and to wyf,
You may have her as your lady and wife,

For whom that I mot nedes lese my lyf.   432
For whom I must needs lose my life.

For, as by wey of possibilitee,
Since (considering the possibilities)

Sith thou art at thy large, of prison free,
You are at large, free from prison,

And art a lord, greet is thyn avauntage,
And are a lord, great is your advantage,

More than is myn, that sterve here in a cage.   436
Greater than mine, who am dying here in a cage.

For I mot wepe and wayle, whyl I live,
For I must weep and wail, as long as I live,

With al the wo that prison may me yive,
Because of all the misery that prison brings,

And eek with peyne that love me yiveth also,
And in addition the pain that love gives me,

That doubleth al my torment and my wo."   440
Which doubles all my torment and my woe."

Ther-with the fyr of jelousye up-sterte
Thereat the fire of jealousy leaped up

With-inne his brest, and hente him by the herte
Within his breast, and pierced him to the heart

So woodly, that he lyk was to biholde
So madly, that his appearance was like

The box-tree, or the asshen dede and colde.   444
A box-tree, or ashes dead and cold.

Tho seyde he, "O cruel goddes, that governe
Then said he, "O cruel gods, who govern

This world with binding of your worde eterne,
This world under constraint of your eternal word,

And wryten in the table of athamaunt,
And write in adamantine tables

Your parlement, and your eterne graunt,   448
Your decisions, and your eternal decree,

What is mankinde more un-to yow holde
How is mankind more beholden to you

Than is the sheep, that rouketh in the folde?
Than the sheep that huddles in the fold?

For slayn is man right as another beste,
For man is slain like any other beast.

And dwelleth eek in prison and areste,   452
And also dwells in prison and detention,

And hath siknesse, and greet adversitee,
And suffers sickness and great adversity,

And ofte tymes giltelees, pardee!
And many times guiltless, God knows!

   "What governaunce is in this prescience,
   "What justice is in this Omniscience,

That giltelees tormenteth innocence?   456
That torments guiltless innocence?

And yet encreseth this al my penaunce,
And yet this increases all my torture,

That man is bounden to his observaunce,
That man is bound by his obedience,

For Goddes sake, to letten of his wille,
For God's sake, to restrain his desires,

Ther as a beest may al his lust fulfille.   460
Whereas a beast may fulfill all its appetites.

And whan a beest is deed, he hath no peyne;
And when a beast is dead, it endures no pain;

But man after his deeth moot wepe and pleyne,
But man after his death must weep and wail,

Though in this world he have care and wo:
Even though in this world he had care and woe:

With-outen doute it may stonden so.   464
Without doubt it may well be so.

Th' answere of this I lete to divynis,
The answer to this I leave to the divines,

But wel I woot, that in this world great pyne is.
But well I know that in this world is great misery.

Allas! I see a serpent or a theef,
Alas! I see a viper or a thief,

That many a trewe man hath doon mescheef,   468
That has done mischief to many a true man,

Goon at his large, and wher him list may turne.
Go at large, and take any direction he pleases.

But I mot been in prison thurgh Saturne,
But I am doomed to prison through Saturn,

And eek thurgh Juno, jalous and eek wood,
And through Juno too, jealous and mad as well,

That hath destroyed wel ny al the blood   472
Who has destroyed very nearly all the blood

Of Thebes, with his waste walles wyde.
Of Thebes, with its broad walls razed.

And Venus sleeth me on that other syde
And on the other hand, Venus slays me

For jelousye, and fere of him Arcite."
With jealousy and fear of Arcite."

   Now wol I stinte of Palamon a lyte,   476
   Now will I ignore Palamon a little,

And lete him in his prison stille dwelle,
And leave him locked up in his prison,

And of Arcita forth I wol yow telle.
And I will tell you now about Arcite.

   The somer passeth, and the nightes longe
   The summer passed, and the long nights

Encresen double wyse the peynes stronge   480
Increased doubly the strong pains

Bothe of the lovere and the prisoner.
Of both the lover and the prisoner.

I noot which hath the wofullere mester.
I don't know which has the sadder plight.

For shortly for to seyn, this Palamoun
For, to speak briefly, this Palamon

Perpetuelly is dampned to prisoun,   484
Is doomed perpetually to prison,

In cheynes and in fettres to ben deed;
To die in chains and fetters;

And Arcite is exyled upon his heed
And Arcite is exiled at the price of his head

For ever-mo as out of that contree,
Forevermore away from that country,

Ne never-mo he shal his lady see.   488
Nor ever again shall he see his lady.

   Yow loveres axe I now this questioun,
   You lovers, I ask now this question:

Who hath the worse, Arcite or Palamoun?
Who has the worse, Arcite or Palamon?

That oon may seen his lady day by day,
The one may see his lady every day,

But in prison he moot dwelle alway.   492
But he must always remain in prison.

That other wher him list may ryde or go,
The other may ride or walk where he pleases,

But seen his lady shal he never-mo.
But nevermore will he see his lady.

Now demeth as yow liste, ye that can,
Now conclude however you please, if you can,

For I wol telle forth as I bigan.   496
For I will continue the story I began.

Part Two

Whan that Arcite to Thebes comen was,
When Arcite had arrived at Thebes,

Ful ofte a day he swelte and seyde "allas,"
Many a day he fainted and said, "Alas!"

For seen his lady shal he never-mo.
Because he would nevermore see his lady.

And shortly to concluden al his wo,   500
And to describe all his woe briefly,

So muche sorwe had never creature
So much sorrow never befell any creature

That is, or shal, whyl that the world may dure.
That is, or shall be, while the world endures.

His sleep, his mete, his drink is him biraft,
Sleep, food, and drink deserted him,

That lene he wex, and drye as is a shaft.   *504*
So that he became thin and dry as a stick.

His eyen holwe, and grisly to biholde;
His eyes hollow, and gruesome to behold;

His hewe falwe, and pale as asshen colde,
His complexion yellow, and pale as cold ashes,

And solitarie he was, and ever allone,
And he was solitary, and always alone,

And wailling al the night. making his mone.   *508*
And wailing all the night, making his moan.

And if he herde song or instrument,
And if he heard songs or instruments,

Then wolde he wepe, he mighte nat be stent;
Then he would weep, he could not be comforted;

So feeble eek were his spirits, and so lowe,
Besides, his spirits were so weak and low,

And chaunged so, that no man coude knowe   *512*
And so changed, that no one could recognize

His speche nor his vois, though men it herde.
His speech or his voice when people heard it.

And in his gere, for al the world he ferde
And in his behavior he acted, for all the world,

Nat oonly lyk the loveres maladye
Not only as if he had the lover's disease

Of Hereos, but rather lyk manye   *516*
Of Cupid, but more as if he had a mania

Engendred of humour malencolyk
Engendered of the melancholy humor

Biforen, in his celle fantastyk.
In the imagination cells of his brains.

And shortly, turned was al up-so-doun
And briefly, everything was turned upside down,

Bothe habit and eek disposicioun 520
Both the behavior and the disposition

Of him, this woful lovere daun Arcite.
Of this woeful lover, Sir Arcite.

What sholde I al-day of his wo endyte?
Why should I write all day about his woe?

Whan he endured hadde a yeer or two
When he had endured a year or two

This cruel torment, and this peyne and wo, 524
This cruel torment, and this pain and woe,

At Thebes, in his contree, as I seyde,
At Thebes, in his country, as I said,

Up-on a night, in sleep as he him leyde,
One night, as he lay asleep,

Him thoughte how that the winged god Mercurie
It seemed to him that the winged god Mercury

Biforn him stood, and bad him to be murye. 528
Stood before him, and bade him to rejoice.

His slepy yerde in hond he bar uprighte;
His sleeping wand he held upright in his hand;

An hat he werede up-on his heres brighte.
A hat he wore upon his bright hair.

Arrayed was this god (as he took keepe)
Arrayed was this god (as Arcite noticed)

As he was whan that Argus took his sleep; 532
As he was when he lulled Argus to sleep;[2]

And seyde him thus: "To Athenës shaltou wende;
And he spoke thus: "To Athens shall you go;

Ther is thee shapen of thy wo an ende."
An end to your woe is there arranged."

And with that word Arcite wook and sterte.
And with that word Arcite woke and leaped up.

"Now trewely, how sore that me smerte," *536*
"Now indeed, however much I suffer,"

Quod he, "to Athenës right now wol I fare;
Said he, "to Athens will I go right now;

Ne for the drede of deeth shal I nat spare
Nor out of dread of death shall I fail

To see my lady, that I love and serve;
To see my lady, whom I love and serve;

In hir presence I recche nat to sterve." *540*
In her presence I do not fear to die."

And with that word he caughte a greet mirour,
And with that word he seized a great mirror

And saugh that chaunged was al his colour,
And saw that his complexion was entirely changed,

And saugh his visage al in another kinde.
And saw that his face was very different.

And right anoon it ran him in his minde, *544*
And instantly it ran through his mind

That, sith his face was so disfigured
That, since his face was so disfigured

Of maladye, the which he hadde endured,
By the illness which he had endured,

He mighte wel, if that he bar him lowe,
He well might, if he went as a common man,

Live in Athenes ever-more unknowe, *548*
Live in Athens unknown evermore,

And seen his lady wel ny day by day.
And see his lady nearly every day.

And right anon he chaunged his array,
And instantly he changed his clothes,

And cladde him as a povre laborer,
And dressed himself as a poor laborer,

And al allone, save oonly a squyer, 552
And all alone, except for a squire,

That knew his privetee and al his cas,
Who knew his secret and the entire situation,

Which was disgysed povrely, as he was,
And was dressed as poorly as he was,

To Athenes is he goon the nexte way.
To Athens he went by the shortest road.

And to the court he wente up-on a day, 556
And to the court he went one day,

And at the gate he profreth his servyse,
And at the gate he offered his services,

To drugge and drawe, what so men wol devyse.
To work and carry, or do whatever was necessary.

And shortly of this matere for to seyn,
And to speak briefly of this matter,

He fil in office with a chamberleyn, 560
He found employment with a chamberlain

The which that dwelling was with Emelye;
Who was in service with Emily;

For he was wys, and coude soon aspye
For he was shrewd, and quickly found out

Of every servaunt, which that serveth here.
About every servant who served her.

Wel coude he hewen wode, and water bere, 564
Well could he hew wood and carry water,

For he was yong and mighty for the nones,
For he was young and sturdy at that time,

And ther-to he was strong and big of bones
And he was sufficiently strong and big-boned

To doon that any wight can him devyse.
To do whatever anyone might order.

A yeer or two he was in this servyse,   568
A year or two he was in this service,

Page of the chambre of Emelye the brighte;
Page of the chamber of Emily the bright;

And "Philostrate" he seide that he highte.
And he said his name was Philostrate.

But half so wel biloved a man as he
One half so well beloved a man as he

Ne was ther never in court, of his degree;   572
Was there never in court, of his rank;

He was so gentil of condicioun,
He was so much a gentleman in bearing,

That thurghout al the court was his renoun.
That his renown spread through all the court.

They seyden, that it were a charitee
They said that it would be a good deed

That Theseus wolde enhauncen his degree,   576
If Theseus would raise his rank,

And putten him in worshipful servyse,
And put him in gentlemanly service,

Ther as he mighte his vertu excercyse.
Where he might use his talents.

And thus, with-inne a whyle, his name is spronge
And thus, in a short time, he was so talked about

Bothe of his dedes, and his goode tonge,   580
Because of his actions and his good sayings,

That Theseus hath taken him so neer
That Theseus brought him so close

That of his chambre he made him a squyer,
That he made him a squire of his chamber,

And yaf him gold to mayntene his degree;
And gave him gold to maintain his rank;

And eek men broghte him out of his contree   584
And, besides, men brought him from his country

From yeer to yeer, ful prively, his rente;
From year to year, in utmost secrecy, his revenue;

But honestly and slyly he it spente,
But he spent it so carefully and quietly

That no man wondred how that he it hadde
That no one wondered where it came from.

And three yeer in this wyse his lyf he ladde,   588
And three years he led his life in this manner,

And bar him so in pees and eek in werre,
And so comported himself in peace and war,

Ther nas no man that Theseus hath derre.
That Theseus held no other man so dear.

And in this blisse lete I now Arcite,
And in this bliss I now leave Arcite,

And speke I wol of Palamon a lyte.   592
And will talk of Palamon a little.

In derknesse and horrible and strong prisoun
In darkness and horrible and strong prison

This seven yeer hath seten Palamoun,
For seven years Palamon has sat,

Forpyned, what for wo and for distresse;
Tormented by his woe and his distress.

Who feleth double soor and hevinesse   596
Who feels double hurt and heaviness

But Palamon? that love destreyneth so,
But Palamon, whom love so tortures

That wood out of his wit he gooth for wo;
That he is driven out of his mind by woe?

And eek therto he is a prisoner
And, besides this, he is a prisoner

THE KNIGHT'S TALE

Perpetuelly, noght oonly for a yeer.   600
Perpetually, not for just a year.

Who coude ryme in English proprely
Who could rhyme properly in English

His martirdom? For sothe, it am nat I;
His martyrdom? Indeed, it is not I;

Therefore I passe as lightly as I may.
Therefore I pass over it as lightly as I can.

It fel that in the seventhe yeer, in May,   604
It happened in the seventh year, in May,

The thridde night, (as olde bokes seyn
The third night (as the old books say

That al this storie tellen more pleyn,)
Which tell all this story more completely)

Were it by aventure or destinee.
Whether by chance or destiny,

(As, whan a thing is shapen, it shal be,)   608
(Meaning that when a thing is fated, it shall be)

That, sone after the midnight, Palamoun,
That, soon after midnight, Palamon,

By helping of a freend, brak his prisoun,
By the aid of a friend, broke out of prison,

And fleeth the citee, faste as he may go;
And fled from the city as fast as he could;

For he had yive his gayler drinke so   612
For he had given his jailer such a drink

Of a claree, maad of a certeyn wyn,
Of a cordial, made of a certain wine

With nercotikes and opie of Thebes fyn,
Mixed with narcotics and opium from Thebes,

That al that night, thogh that men wolde him shake,
That all night, even though men should shake him,

The gayler sleep, he mighte nat awake;   *616*
The jailer slept, he couldn't wake up;

And thus he fleeth as faste as ever he may.
And so he fled as fast as ever he could.

The night was short, and faste by the day,
The night was short and it was nearly day,

That nedes-cost he moste him-selven hyde,
So that he needs must hide himself,

And til a grove, faste ther besyde,   *620*
And to a grove, not far away,

With dredful foot than stalketh Palamoun.
With fearful foot then crept Palamon.

For shortly, this was his opinioun,
For, briefly, this was his plan:

That in that grove he wolde him hyde al day,
That in that grove he would hide himself all day,

And in the night than wolde he take his way   *624*
And in the night then would he make his way

To Thebes-ward, his freendes for to preye
Toward Thebes, to beg his friends

On Theseus to helpe him to werreye;
To help him wage war on Theseus;

And shortly, outher he wolde lese his lyf,
And in brief, either he would lose his life

Or winnen Emelye un-to his wyf;   *628*
Or win Emily to be his wife;

This is th'effect and his entente pleyn.
This was the idea and his entire plan.

   Now wol I torne un-to Arcite ageyn,
   Now will I turn back to Arcite again,

That litel wiste how ny that was his care,
Who little knew how close trouble was

Til that Fortune had broght him in the snare. 632
Until Fortune had placed him in the trap.

The bisy larke, messager of day,
The busy lark, messenger of day,

Saluëth in hir song the morwe gray;
Saluted in its song the grey dawn;

And fyry Phebus ryseth up so brighte,
And fiery Phoebus rose up so bright

That al the orient laugheth of the lighte, 636
That all the east laughed with light,

And with his stremes dryeth in the greves
And with his beams dried in the branches

The silver dropes, hanging on the leves.
The silver drops hanging on the leaves.

And Arcite, that is in the court royal
And Arcite, who was in the royal court

With Theseus, his squyer principal, 640
With Theseus, as his chief squire,

Is risen, and loketh on the myrie day.
Had risen, and was looking on the merry day.

And, for to doon his observaunce to May,
And, in order to pay his respects to May,

Remembring on the poynt of his desyr,
Bearing in mind the day he fell in love,

He on a courser, startlynge as the fyr, 644
He on a courser, skittish as fire,

Is riden in-to the feeldes, him to pleye,
Rode out to the fields to disport himself,

Out of the court, were it a myle or tweye;
Away from the court, perhaps a mile or two;

And to the grove, of which that I yow tolde,
And to the very grove I told you of,

By aventure, his wey he gan to holde,   *648*
By chance, he began to take his way,

To maken him a gerland of the greves,
To make himself a garland of boughs

Were it of wodebinde or hawethorn-leves,
Either of woodbine or hawthorn leaves,

And loude he song ageyn the sonne shene:
And loudly he sang in the bright sun:

"May, with alle thy floures and thy grene,   *652*
"May, with all your flowers and greenery,

Wel-come be thou, faire fresshe May,
Welcome to you, fair fresh May,

I hope that I som grene gete may."
I hope that I may get some greenery."

And from his courser, with a lusty herte,
And from his courser, with a lusty heart,

In-to the grove ful hastily he sterte,   *656*
He leaped quickly into the grove,

And in a path he rometh up and doun,
And on a path he roamed up and down,

Ther-as, by aventure, this Palamoun
Near which, by chance, Palamon

Was in a bush, that no man mighte him see,
Was behind a bush so that no one could see him,

For sore afered of his deeth was he.   *660*
For sore afraid of death was he.

No-thing ne knew he that it was Arcite:
He didn't realize at all that it was Arcite:

God wot he wolde have trowed it ful lyte.
God knows he would hardly have suspected it.

But sooth is seyd, gon sithen many yeres,
But a truth was spoken, now many years ago,

That "feeld hath eyen, and the wode hath eres."   664
That "fields have eyes and woods have ears."

It is ful fair to a man to bere him evene,
It pays a man to comport himself carefully,

For al-day meteth men at unset stevene.
For unexpected meetings take place every day.

Ful litel woot Arcite of his felawe,
Arcite was all too little aware of his friend

That was so ny to herknen al his sawe,   668
Who was near enough to hear his every word,

For in the bush he sitteth now ful stille.
For behind the bush he now sat very quietly.

Whan that Arcite had romed al his fille,
When Arcite had had his fill of wandering,

And songen al the roundel lustily,
And had sung his song lustily,

In-to a studie he fil sodeynly,   672
He fell suddenly into a study,

As doon thise lovers in hir queynte geres,
As lovers do in their changeful ways,

Now in the croppe, now doun in the breres,
Now in the treetops, now down in the briars,

Now up, now doun, as boket in a welle,
Now up, now down, like a bucket in a well,

Right as the Friday, soothly for to tellle,   676
Just as on Friday, to state a fact,

Now it shyneth, now it reyneth faste,
Sometimes it shines, sometimes it pours,

Right so can gery Venus overcaste
Just so can fickle Venus overcast

The hertes of hir folk; right as hir day
The hearts of her people; just as her day

Is gerful, right so chaungeth she array.   680
Is changeable, so her appearance changes.

Selde is the Friday al the wyke y-lyke.
Seldom is Friday like the rest of the week.

  Whan that Arcite had songe, he gan to syke,
  After Arcite had sung, he begun to sigh.

And sette him doun with-outen any more:
And sat down without more ado:

"Alas!" quod he, "that day that I was bore!   684
"Alas!" said he, "the day that I was born!

How longe, Juno, thurgh thy crueltee
How long, Juno, through thy cruelty

Woltow werreyen Thebes the citee?
Wilt thou persecute the city of Thebes?

Allas! y-broght is to confusioun
Alas! to confusion is brought

The blood royal of Cadme and Amiphioun;   688
The royal blood of Cadmus and Amphion;

Of Cadmus, which that was the firste man
Of Cadmus, who was the first man

That Thebes bulte, or first the toun bigan,
Who built Thebes, or first founded the town,

And of the citee first was crouned king,
And was first crowned king of the city,

Of his linage am I, and his of-spring   692
Of his lineage am I, and his descendant

By verray ligne, as of the stok royal:
By direct line, as of the royal stock:

And now I am so caitif and so thral,
And now I am so defeated and brought so low

That he, that is my mortal enemy,
That him, who is my mortal enemy,

I serve him as his squyer povrely.   696
I humbly serve as his squire.

And yet doth Juno me wel more shame,
And yet Juno does me this shame besides,

For I dar noght biknowe myn owne name;
That I dare not acknowledge my own name;

But ther-as I was wont to highte Arcite,
But whereas I used to be called Arcite,

Now highte I Philostrate, noght worth a myte.   700
Now I am named Philostrate, not worth a penny.

Allas! thou felle Mars, allas! Juno,
Alas, cruel Mars! Alas, Juno!

Thus hath your ire our kinrede al fordo,
Thus your anger has ruined our kindred,

Save only me, and wrecched Palamoun,
All except me and wretched Palamon,

That Theseus martyreth in prisoun.   704
Whom Theseus makes a martyr of in prison.

And over al this, to sleen me utterly,
And besides all this, to slay me utterly,

Love hath his fyry dart so brenningly
Love so burningly his fiery dart has

Y-stiked thurgh my trewe careful herte,
Pierced through my true careworn heart,

That shapen was my deeth erst than my sherte.   708
That death was tailored for me before my shirt.

Ye sleen me with your eyen, Emelye;
You slay me with your eyes, Emily;

Ye been the cause wherfor that I dye.
You are the reason why I die.

Of al the remenant of myn other care
All the remainder of my other cares

Ne sette I nat the mountaunce of a tare 712
Concern me no more than a weed

So that I coude don aught to your plesaunce!"
If only I could do anything for your pleasure!"

And with that word he fil doun in a traunce
And with that word he fell down in a trance

A longe tyme; and after he up-sterte.
A long time; and later he jumped up.

   This Palamoun, that thoughte that thurgh his herte 716
   This Palamon, who thought that through his heart

He felte a cold swerd sodeynliche glyde,
He felt a cold sword suddenly glide,

For ire he quook, no lenger wolde he byde.
Shook with anger, no longer would he remain quiet.

And whan that he had herd Arcites tale,
And when he had listened to Arcite's harangue,

As he were wood, with face deed and pale, 720
As if he were mad, with face deathly and pale,

He sterte him up out of the buskes thikke,
He jumped up out of the thick bushes,

And seyde: "Arcite, false traitour wikke,
And said: "Arcite, false wicked traitor,

Now artow hent, that lovest my lady so,
Now are you caught, who love my lady so,

For whom that I have al this peyne and wo, 724
For whom I have all this grief and woe,

And art my blood, and to my counseil sworn,
And are of my blood, and sworn to my secrets,

As I ful ofte have told thee heer-biforn,
As I have told you often enough before,

And hast by-japed here duk Theseus,
And you have here tricked Duke Theseus,

And falsly chaunged hast thy name thus;   728
And have falsely changed your name;

I wol be deed, or elles thou shalt dye.
Either I will be dead or else you shall die.

Thou shalt nat love my lady Emelye,
You shall not love my lady Emily,

But I wol love hir only, and namo;
But I alone will love her, and no one else;

For I am Palamoun, thy mortal fo.   732
For I am Palamon, your mortal foe.

And though that I no wepne have in this place,
And though I have no weapon in this place,

But out of prison am astert by grace,
But out of prison have escaped by luck,

I drede noght that outher thou shalt dye,
I do not doubt that either you shall die,

Or thou ne shalt nat loven Emelye.   736
Or else you shall not love Emily.

Chees which thou wilt, for thou shalt nat asterte."
Choose as you please, for you shall not escape."

   This Arcite, with ful despitous herte,
   This Arcite, with heart full of rage,

Whan he him knew, and hadde his tale herd,
When he recognized him and had heard his story,

As fiers as leoun, pulled out a swerd,   740
Fierce as a lion, pulled out a sword,

And seyde thus: "By God that sit above,
And spoke thus: "By God Who sits above,

Nere it that thou art sik, and wood for love,
Were it not that you are sick and mad for love,

And eek that thou no wepne hast in this place,
And also that you have no weapon in this place,

Thou sholdest never out of this grove pace,   744
You would never walk out of this grove

That thou ne sholdest dyen of myn hond.
Without dying by my hand.

For I defye the seurtee and the bond
For I defy the agreement and the bond

Which that thou seyst that I have maad to thee.
Which you say I have made to you.

What, verray fool, think wel that love is free,   748
Why, utter fool, realize that love is free,

And I wol love hir, maugre al thy might!
And I will love her despite all your power!

But, for as muche thou art a worthy knight,
But, inasmuch as you are a worthy knight,

And wilnest to darreyne hir by batayle,
And are willing to fight for her in battle,

Have heer my trouthe, to-morwe I wol nat fayle,   752
Take here my pledge, tomorrow I will not fail,

With-outen witing of any other wight,
Without the knowledge of another soul,

That here I wol be founden as a knight,
To be here, as I am a knight,

And bringen harneys right y-nough for thee;
And bring sufficient armor for you;

And chees the beste, and leve the worste for me.   756
And let you choose the best and leave the worst for me.

And mete and drinke this night wol I bringe
And this night I will bring food and drink

Y-nough for thee, and clothes for thy beddinge.
Enough for you, and covers for your bedding.

And, if so be that thou my lady winne,
And, if it happens that you win my lady,

And slee me in this wode ther I am inne,   760
And slay me in this wood where I am,

Thou mayst wel have thy lady, as for me."
You may well have your lady, for all of me."

This Palamon answerede: "I graunte it thee."
This Palamon answered: "I grant it to you."

And thus they been departed til a-morwe,
And so they parted until the morrow,

When ech of hem had leyd his feith to borwe.   764
When each of them had put his faith in pledge.

   O Cupide, out of alle charitee!
   O Cupid, devoid of generosity!

O regne, that wolt no felawe have with thee!
O ruler, who will not abide a companion!

Ful sooth is seyd, that love ne lordshipe
Truly it is said, that neither love nor lordship

Wol noght, his thankes, have no felaweshipe;   768
Will willingly endure fellowship;

Wel finden that Arcite and Palamoun.
Arcite and Palamon thoroughly found that out..

Arcite is riden anon un-to the toun,
Arcite rode immediately to the town,

And on the morwe, er it were dayes light,
And on the morrow, before it was daylight,

Ful prively two harneys hath he dight,   772
In secrecy he procured two sets of arms,

Bothe suffisaunt and mete to darreyne
Both sufficient and fitting to decide

The bataille in the feeld bitwix hem tweyne.
The battle in the field between the two of them.

And on his hors, allone as he was born,
And on his horse, solitary as he was born,

He carieth al this harneys him biforn;   776
He carried all this equipment before him;

And in the grove, at tyme and place y-set,
And in the grove, at the appointed time and place,

This Arcite and this Palamon ben met.
This Arcite and this Palamon met.

Tho chaungen gan the colour in hir face;
Then the color in their faces began to change;

Right as the hunter in the regne of Trace,   780
Just as the hunter in the realm of Thrace,

That stondeth at the gappe with a spere,
Who stands at the gap with a spear,

Whan hunted is the leoun or the bere,
When the lion or bear is hunted,

And hereth him come russhing in the greves,
And hears him come rushing through the woods,

And breketh bothe bowes and the leves,   784
And breaking both branches and leaves,

And thinketh, "Heer cometh my mortel enemy,
And thinks, "Here comes my mortal enemy,

With-oute faile, he moot be deed, or I;
Inevitably, he must die or I;

For outher I mot sleen him at the gappe,
For either I must slay him at the gap,

Or he mot sleen me, if that me mishappe:"   788
Or he must slay me, if I am so unlucky:"

So ferden they, in chaunging of hir hewe,
So acted they in the changing of color,

As fer as everich of hem other knewe.
As soon as each one recognized the other.

Ther nas no good day, ne no saluing;
There was no "Good-day," and no saluting;

But streight, with-outen word or rehersing,   792
But straightway, without words or rehearsal,

Everich of hem halp for to armen other,
Each of them helped the other to arm,

As freendly as he were his owne brother;
As cordially as if it were his own brother;

And after that, with sharpe speres stronge
And after that, with sharp strong spears

They foynen ech at other wonder longe.   796
They thrust at each other wondrous long.

Thou mightest wene that this Palamoun
You might think that this Palamon

In his fighting were a wood leoun,
Were a wild lion in his fighting,

And as a cruel tygre was Arcite:
And Arcite a cruel tiger:

As wilde bores gonne they to smyte,   800
They began to smite like wild boars

That frothen whyte as foom for ire wood.
That froth white as foam in mad fury.

Up to the ancle foghte they in hir blood.
Up to the ankle in their blood they fought.

And in this wyse I lete hem fighting dwelle;
And in this fashion I leave them fighting;

And forth I wol of Theseus yow telle.   804
And straightway I will tell you of Theseus.

   The destinee, ministre general,
   Destiny, minister general,

That executeth in the world over-al
That executes throughout the entire world

The purveyaunce, that God hath seyn biforn,
The plan which God has foreseen,

So strong it is, that, though the world had sworn   *808*
So strong it is, that, though the world had sworn

The contrarie of a thing, by ye or nay,
The contrary of a thing, by yes or nay,

Yet somtyme it shall fallen on a day
Yet sometimes there will happen on a day

That falleth nat eft with-inne a thousand yere.
That which doesn't occur again in a thousand years.

For certeinly, our appetytes here,   *812*
For certainly, our earthly desires,

Be it of werre, or pees, or hate, or love,
Whether of war or peace, or hate or love,

Al is this reuled by the sighte above.
Are all ruled by heaven's sight.

This mene I now by mighty Theseus,
I mean this in connection with mighty Theseus,

That for to honten is so desirous,   *816*
Who is so eager for the hunt,

And namely at the grete hert in May,
And especially for the great hart in May,

That in his bed ther daweth him no day,
That no day dawns upon him in bed,

That he nis clad, and redy for to ryde
But finds him clothed and ready to ride

With hunte and horn, and houndes him bisyde.   *820*
With huntsmen and horn and hounds beside him.

For in his hunting hath he swich delyt,
For in hunting he has such delight

That it is al his joye and appetyt
That it is all his joy and appetite

To been him-self the grete hertes bane:
To be the bane of the great hart:

For after Mars he serveth now Diane.   824
For after Mars he now serves Diana.

Cleer was the day, as I have told er this,
Clear was the day, as I mentioned formerly,

And Theseus, with alle joye and blis,
And Theseus, filled with joy and happiness,

With his Ipolita, the fayre quene,
With his Hippolyta, the fair queen,

And Emelye, clothed al in grene,   828
And Emily, dressed all in green,

On hunting be they riden royally.
A-hunting went they riding royally.

And to the grove, that stood ful faste by,
And to the grove, that stood quite near by,

In which ther was an hert, as men him tolde,
In which there was a hart, as people told him,

Duk Theseus the streighte wey hath holde.   832
Duke Theseus held a straight course.

And to the launde he rydeth him ful right,
And to the glade he rode directly,

For thider was the hert wont have his flight,
For there the hart was accustomed to run,

And over a brook, and so forth on his weye.
And over a brook, and then on his way.

This duk wol han a cours at him, or tweye,   836
This duke would have a run or two at him

With houndes, swiche as that him list comaunde.
With hounds, such as he pleased to command.

And whan this duk was come un-to the launde,
And when this duke had come to the glade,

Under the sonne he loketh, and anon
He looked away from the sun, and instantly

He was war of Arcite and Palamon,   840
He became aware of Arcite and Palamon,

That foughten breme, as it were bores two;
Who fought furiously like two boars;

The brighte swerdes wenten to and fro
The bright swords flashed to and fro

So hidously, that with the leeste.strook
So hideously, that with the least stroke

It seemed as it wolde felle an ook;   844
It seemed as if an oak would fall;

But what they were, no-thing he ne woot.
But who they were, he had no idea.

This duk his courser with his spores smoot,
This duke goaded his courser with his spurs,

And at a stert he was bitwix hem two,
And with a leap he was between the two,

And pulled out a swerd and cryed, "Ho!   848
And pulled out a sword and cried, "Ho!

Namore, up peyne of lesing of your heed.
No more, on pain of losing your heads!

By mighty Mars, he shal anon be deed
By mighty Mars, he shall instantly be dead

That smyteth any strook that I may seen!
That strikes any blow that I see!

But telleth me what mister men ye been,   852
But tell me what manner of men you are,

That been so hardy for to fighten here
That are so hardy as to fight here

With-outen juge or other officere,
Without judge or other official,

As it were in a listes royally?"
As if you were in the royal lists?"

This Palamon answerede hastily 856
This Palamon answered hastily

And seyde: "Sire, what nedeth wordes mo?
And said: "Sire, what need of more words?

We have the deeth deserved both two.
Both of us have deserved death.

Two woful wrecches been we, two caytyves,
Two woeful wretches are we, two captives,

That been encombred of our owne lyves; 860
Who are encumbered by our own lives;

And as thou art a rightful lord and juge,
And as you are a rightful lord and judge,

Ne yeve us neither mercy ne refuge;
Give us neither mercy nor escape;

But slee me first, for seynte charitee;
But slay me first, for holy charity;

But slee my felawe eek as wel as me. 864
But slay my fellow too as well as me.

Or slee him first; for, though thou knowe it lyte,
Or slay him first; for, though you little suspect it,

This is thy mortal fo, this is Arcite,
This is your mortal foe, this is Arcite,

That fro thy lond is banished on his heed,
Who is banished from your land at the price of his head,

For which he hath deserved to be deed. 868
For which he is deserving of death.

For this is he that cam un-to thy gate,
For this is he who came to your gate,

And seyde, that he highte Philostrate.
And said that he was called Philostrate.

Thus has he japed thee ful many a yeer,
Thus has he tricked you for many a year,

And thou has maked him thy chief squyer: 872
And you have made him your chief squire:

And this is he that loveth Emelye.
And this is he that loves Emily.

For sith the day is come that I shal dye,
For since the day has come when I shall die,

I make pleynly my confessioun,
I make my full confession,

That I am thilke woful Palamoun,   876
That I am that woeful Palamon

That hath thy prison broken wikkedly.
Who escaped from your prison wickedly.

I am thy mortal fo, and it am I
I am your mortal foe, and it is I

That loveth so hote Emelye the brighte,
Who love so ardently Emily the bright

That I wol dye present in hir sighte.   880
That I will die in her presence.

Therfore I axe deeth and my juwyse;
Therefore I ask death and my judgment;

But slee my felawe in the same wyse,
But slay my fellow in the same way,

For bothe han we deserved to be slayn."
For both of us deserve to be slain."

This worthy duk answerde anon agayn,   884
This worthy duke immediately replied,

And seyde, "This is a short conclusioun:
And said, "This is a rapid decision:

Youre owne mouth, by your confessioun,
Your own mouth, by your confession,

Hath dampned you, and I wol it recorde,
Has doomed you, and I will witness it,

It nedeth noght to pyne yow with the corde.　　888
There is no need to torture you on the rack.

Ye shul be deed, by mighty Mars the rede!"
You shall die, by mighty Mars the red!"

The quene anon, for verray wommanhede,
The queen at once, for very womanhood,

Gan for to wepe, and so dide Emelye,
Began to weep, and so did Emily,

And alle the ladies in the companye.　　892
And all the ladies in the company.

Gret pitee was it, as it thoughte hem alle,
Great pity was it, as they all thought,

That ever swich a chaunce sholde falle;
That ever such mischance should occur;

For gentil men they were, of great estat,
For noblemen they were, of high estate,

And no-thing but for love was this debat;　　896
And for nothing but love was this conflict;

And sawe hir blody woundes wyde and sore;
And they saw their bloody wounds long and sore;

And alle cryden, bothe lasse and more,
And all cried, from lowest to highest,

"Have mercy, lord, up-on us wommen alle!"
"Have mercy, lord, upon all us women!"

And on hir bare knees adoun they falle,　　900
And on their bare knees they fell down,

And wolde have kist his feet ther-as he stood,
And would have kissed his feet right where he stood,

Til at the laste aslaked was his mood;
Until at last his mood was assuaged;

For pitee renneth sone in gentil herte.
For pity runs easily into a noble heart.

And though he first for ire quook and sterte,   904
And though at first he quaked and shook with rage,

He hath considered shortly, in a clause,
He reconsidered briefly, in a sentence,

The trespas of hem bothe, and eek the cause:
The crime of them both, and also the cause:

And al-though that his ire hir gilt accused,
And although his anger accused them of guilt,

Yet in his reson he hem bothe excused;   908
Yet in his reason he excused them both

As thus: he thoghte wel, that every man
In this fashion: he reasoned that every man

Wol helpe him-self in love, if that he can,
Will help himself in love, if he can,

And eek delivere him-self out of prisoun;
And also deliver himself out of prison;

And eek his herte had compassioun   912
And, besides, his heart had compassion

Of wommen, for they wepen ever in oon;
On women, for they continued to weep;

And in his gentil herte he thoghte anoon,
And in his noble heart his thoughts changed,

And softe un-to himself he seyde: "Fy
And softly to himself he said, "Fie

Up-on a lord that wol have no mercy,   916
Upon a lord who will have no mercy,

But been a leoun, bothe in word and dede,
But acts like a lion, both in word and deed,

To hem that been in repentaunce and drede
To those who are repentant and respectful

As wel as to a proud despitous man
Just as he does to a proud disdainful man

That wol maynteyne that he first bigan!   920
Who insists on continuing what he started!

That lord hath litel of discrecioun,
That lord is one of little discretion

That in swich cas can no divisioun,
Who can not distinguish in such a situation,

But weyeth pryde and humblesse after oon."
But weighs pride and humility equally."

And shortly, whan his ire is thus agoon,   924
And in brief, when his anger had thus departed,

He gan to loken up with eyen lighte,
He looked up with a light in his eyes,

And spak thise same wordes al on highte:—
And spoke these words as a promise:—

"The god of love, *a! benedicite,*
"The god of love, ah, bless us!

How mighty and how greet a lord is he!   928
How mighty and how great a lord is he!

Ayeins his might ther gayneth none obstacles,
Against his might no barriers prevail,

He may be cleped a god for his miracles;
He may be called a god because of his miracles;

For he can maken at his owne gyse
For he can make, at his own whim,

Of everich herte, as that him list devyse.   932
Whatever he pleases of every heart.

Lo heer, this Arcite and this Palamoun,
See here, this Arcite and this Palamon,

That quitly weren out of my prisoun,
Who were completely out of my prison,

And mighte han lived in Thebes royally,
And might have lived royally in Thebes,

And witen I am hir mortal enemy,   936
And knew that I am their mortal enemy,

And that hir deeth lyth in my might also;
And that their death also lies in my power;

And yet hath love, maugree hir eyen two,
And yet has love, in spite of their two eyes,

Y-brught hem hider bothe for to dye!
Brought both of them hither to die!

Now loketh, is nat that an heigh folye?   940
Consider, is that not the height of folly?

Who may been a fool, but-if he love?
Who can be a fool if not one in love?

Bihold, for Goddes sake that sit above,
Behold, for God's sake Who sits above,

Se how they blede! be they noght wel arrayed?
See how they bleed! Aren't they a splendid sight?

Thus hath hir lord, the god of love, y-payed   944
Thus has their lord, the god of love, paid

Hir wages and hir fees for hir servyse!
Their wages and their fees for their service!

And yet they wenen for to been ful wyse
And yet they consider themselves very wise

That serven love, for aught that may bifalle!
Who serve love, no matter what may happen!

But this is yet the beste game of alle,   948
But this is still the best joke of all,

That she, for whom they han this jolitee,
That she, for whose sake they have this pleasure,

Can hem ther-for as muche thank as me;
Can thank them as much as me for it;

She woot namore of al this hote fare,
She knew no more of all this heated affair,

By God, than woot a cokkow or an hare! 952
By God, than did a cuckoo or a hare!

But al mot been assayed, hoot and cold;
But everything must be tried, hot and cold;

A man mot been a fool, or yong or old;
A man must be a fool in youth or old age;

I woot it by my-self ful yore agoon:
I have experienced that myself years ago:

For in my tyme a servant was I oon. 956
For in my time I was love's servant too.

And therfore, sin I knowe of loves peyne,
And therefore, since I know about love's pain,

And woot how sore it can a man distreyne,
And know how sorely it can hurt a man,

As he that hath ben caught ofte in his las,
As one who has been often caught in his trap,

I yow foryeve al hoolly this trespas, 960
I forgive you altogether for this crime,

At requeste of the quene that kneleth here,
At the request of the queen who kneels here,

And eek Emelye, my suster dere.
And also Emily, my dear sister.

And ye shul bothe anon un-to me swere,
And you shall both swear to me at once,

That never-mo ye shul my contree dere, 964
That you shall nevermore injure my country

Ne make werre up-on me night ne day,
Nor make war upon me night or day,

But been my freendes in al that ye may;
But be my friends in every possible way;

I yow foryeve this trespas every del."
I forgive you this trespass completely."

And they him swore his axing fayre and wel,   *968*
And they swore to his request fairly and well,

And him of lordshipe and of mercy preyde,
And bowed to his authority and his mercy,

And he hem graunteth grace, and thus he seyde:
And he granted them grace, and spoke thus:

"To spεke of royal linage and richesse,
"To speak of royal lineage and wealth,

Though that she were a quene or a princesse,   *972*
Even though she were a queen or a princess,

Ech of yow bothe is worthy, doutelees,
Each of you is worthy, without doubt,

To wedden whan tyme is, but nathelees
To marry when the time comes, but nevertheless

I speke as for my suster Emelye,
In speaking of my sister Emily,

For whom ye have this stryf and jelousye;   *976*
For whom you have this strife and jealousy;

Ye woot your-self, she may not wedden two
You know yourselves she cannot marry two

At ones, though ye fighten ever-mo:
At once, even though you fight forever:

That oon of yow, al be him looth or leef,
So one of you, whether he likes it or not,

He moot go pypen in an ivy-leef;   *980*
Must go whistle in an ivy leaf;

This is to seyn, she may nat now han bothe,
That is to say, she cannot have both of you,

Al be ye never so jelous, ne so wrothe.
No matter how jealous or violent you are.

And for-thy I yow putte in this degree,
And therefore I put you on these terms,

That ech of yow shal have his destinee   *984*
That each of you shall have his fate

As him is shape; and herkneth in what wyse;
As is planned for him; and hear how it shall be;

Lo, heer your ende of that I shal devyse.
Now, here is your part of what I plan.

  "My wil is this, for plat conclusioun,
  "My will is this, for certain conclusion,

With-outen any replicacioun,   *988*
Without any rebuttal,

If that yow lyketh, tak it for the beste,
If it appeals to you, take it in good faith,

That everich of yow shal gon wher him leste
That each of you shall go where he pleases

Frely, with-outen raunson or daunger;
Freely, without ransom or liability;

And this day fifty wykes, fer ne ner,   *992*
And exactly fifty weeks from this day,

Everich of yow shal bringe an hundred knightes,
Each of you shall bring a hundred knights,

Armed for listes up at alle rightes,
Armed to perfection for the lists,

Al redy to darreyne hir by bataille.
Ready to contend for her by battle.

And this bihote I yow, with-outen faille,   *996*
And this I pledge you, without fail,

Up-on my trouthe, and as I am a knight,
On my honor, and as I am a knight,

That whether of yow bothe that hath might,
That whichever of you has the ability,

That is to seyn, that whether he or thou
That is to say, that whether he or you

May with his hundred, as I spak of now, 1000
Can with his hundred, that I just mentioned,

Sleen his contrarie, or out of listes dryve,
Slay his adversary or drive him from the lists,

Him shal I yeve Emelye to wyve,
To him shall I give Emily for wife,

To whom that Fortune yeveth so fair a grace.
Whom Fortune favors so fairly.

The listes shal I maken in this place, 1004
The lists I shall make in this place,

And God so wisly on my soule rewe,
And may God as wisely have pity on my soul

As I shal even juge been and trewe.
As I shall be a fair and upright judge.

Ye shul non other ende with me maken,
You shall make no other agreement with me,

That oon of yow ne shal be deed or taken. 1008
Except that one of you shall die or be vanquished.

And if yow thinketh this is wel y-sayd,
And if you think that this is well said,

Seyeth your avys, and holdeth yow apayd.
Speak your conclusion, and hold yourselves satisfied.

This is your ende and your conclusioun."
This is the last and final conclusion for you."

Who loketh lightly now but Palamoun? 1012
Who looks happy now but Palamon?

Who springeth up for joye but Arcite
Who jumps for joy but Arcite?

Who couthe telle, or who couthe it endyte,
Who could tell, or who could describe

The joye that is maked in the place
The joy that sprang up in that place

Whan Theseus hath doon so fair a grace? 1016
When Theseus had done so fair a favor?

But doun on knees went every maner wight,
But on his knees fell every kind of person,

And thanked him with al her herte and might,
And thanked him with all his heart and strength,

And namely the Thebans ofte sythe.
And especially the Thebans many times.

And thus with good hope and with herte blythe 1020
And thus with good hope and blithe hearts

They take hir leve, and hom-ward gonne they ryde
They took their leave, and began their homeward journey

To Thebes, with his olde walles wyde.
To Thebes, with its thick old walls.

Part Three

I trowe men wolde deme it necligence,
I think that men would consider it negligence,

If I foryete to tellen the dispence 1024
If I forgot to tell of the expenditure

Of Theseus, that goth so bisily
Of Theseus, who proceeded so busily

To maken up the listes royally;
To construct the lists in royal fashion;

That swich a noble theatre as it was,
That such a noble theater as it was,

I dar wel seyn that in this world ther nas. 1028
I dare assert that never in this world was its like.

The circuit a myle was aboute,
The circumference was a mile around,

Walled of stoon, and diched al with-oute.
Walled of stone, and ditched on the outside.

Round was the shap, in maner of compas,
Its shape was round, as if drawn by a compass,

Ful of degrees, the heighte of sixty pas,   *1032*
Full of steps, sixty paces high,

That, whan a man was set on o degree,
So that, when a man sat on one step

He letted nat his felawe for to see.
He did not obstruct the vision of another.

   Est-ward ther stood a gate of marbel whyte,
   Toward the east there stood a gate of white marble;

West-ward, right swich another in the opposit.   *1036*
Toward the west, another like it opposite.

And shortly to concluden, swich a place
And to sum up briefly, such a place

Was noon in erthe, as in so litel space;
Was never on earth, as in so short a time;

For in the lond ther nas no crafty man,
For in the land there was no crafty man,

That geometrie or ars-metrik can,   *1040*
Who knew geometry or arithmetic,

No purtreyour, ne kerver of images,
Nor artist, nor carver of statues,

That Theseus ne yaf him mete and wages
To whom Theseus didn't give food and wages

The theatre for to maken and devyse.
To plan and make the theater.

And for to doon his ryte and sacrifyse,   *1044*
And in order to do his rites and sacrifice,

He est-ward hath, up-on the gate above,
On the east side, up over the gate,

In worship of Venus, goddesse of love,
In honor of Venus, goddess of love,

Don make an auter and an oratorie;
He had made an altar and an oratory;

And west-ward, in the minde and in memorie   1048
And at the west, in remembrance and in memory

Of Mars, he maked hath right swich another,
Of Mars, he had made another one just like it,

That coste largely of gold a fother.
That cost a vast amount of gold.

And north-ward, in a touret on the wal,
And northward, in a turret on the wall,

Of alabastre whyt and reed coral   1052
Of white alabaster and red coral

An oratorie riche for to see,
An oratory rich to behold,

In worship of Dyane of chastitee,
In honor of Diana, goddess of chastity,

Hath Theseus don wroght in noble wyse.
Theseus had built in noble fashion.

But yet hadde I foryeten to devyse   1056
But I nearly forgot to describe

The noble kerving, and the portreitures,
The noble carvings, and the portraitures,

To shap, the countenaunce, and the figures,
The designs, the images, and the figures

That weren in thise oratories three.
That were in these three oratories.

First in the temple of Venus maystow see   1060
First in the temple of Venus might be seen

Wroght on the wal, ful pitous to biholde,
Wrought on the wall, most pathetic to behold,

The broken slepes, and the sykes colde;
The broken sleeps, and the cold sighs;

The sacred teres, and the waymenting;
The sacred tears, and the lamentings;

The fyry strokes of the desiring   1064
The fiery stabs of desire

That loveu servaunts in this lyf enduren;
Which love's servants endure in this life;

The othes, that hir covenants assuren;
The oaths which bind their pledges;

Pleasaunce and Hope, Desyr, Fool-hardinesse,
Pleasure and Hope, Desire, Foolhardiness,

Beautee and Youthe, Bauderie, Richesse,   1068
Beauty and Youth, Lust, Wealth,

Charmes and Force, Lesinges, Flaterye,
Charms and Violence, Lies, Flattery,

Dispense, Bisynesse, and Jelousye,
Expense, Effort, and Jealousy,

That wered of yelwe goldes a gerland,
Who wore a garland of marigolds,

And a cokkow sitting on hir hand;   1072
And a cuckoo sitting on her hand;

Festes, instruments, caroles, daunces,
Feasts, musical instruments, songs, dances,

Lust and Array, and alle the circumstaunces
Pleasure and Clothes, and all the paraphernalia

Of love, whiche that I rekne and rekne shal,
Of love, which I have reckoned and shall reckon,

By ordre weren peynted on the wal,   1076
By order were painted on the wall,

And mo than I can make of mencioun.
And more than I can make mention of.

For soothly, al the mount of Citheroun,
For truly, the entire mount of Citheron,

Ther Venus hath hir principal dwelling,
Where Venus has her principal dwelling,

Was shewed on the wal in portreying,   *1080*
Was depicted on the wall graphically,

With al the gardin, and the lustinesse.
With all the garden, and the liveliness.

Nat was foryeten the porter Ydelnesse,
The porter Idleness was not forgotten,

Ne Narcisus the faire of yore agon,
Nor the fair Narcissus of long ago.

Ne yet the folye of king Solomon,   *1084*
Nor yet the folly of King Solomon,

Ne ye the grete strengthe of Hercules—
Nor yet the great strength of Hercules—

Th' enchauntements of Medea and Circes—
The enchantments of Medea and Circe—

Ne of Turnus, with the hardy fiers corage,
Nor of Turnus of the hardy fierce heart,

The riche Cresus, caytif in servage.   *1088*
The rich Croesus, crestfallen in servitude,

Thus may ye seen that wisdom ne richesse,
Thus you may see that neither wisdom nor wealth,

Beautee ne sleighte, strengthe, ne hardinesse,
Beauty nor cunning, strength nor hardihood,

Ne may with Venus holde champartye;
Can with Venus hold rivalry;

For as hir list the world than may she gye.   *1092*
For she can govern the world as she pleases.

Lo, alle thise folk so caught were in hir las,
Behold, all these people were so caught in her trap,

Til they for wo ful ofte seyde "allas!"
Until for woe they full often said, "Alas!"

Suffyceth heer ensamples oon or two,
One or two examples are here sufficient,

And though I coude rekne a thousand mo.   1096
Although I could compute a thousand more.

   The statue of Venus, glorious for to see,
   The statue of Venus, glorious to see,

Was naked fleting in the large see,
Was naked, floating in the great sea,

And fro the navele doun all covered was
And downward from the navel was entirely covered

With wawes grene, and brighte as any glas.   1100
With waves green and bright as any glass.

A citole in hir right hand hadde she,
She held a zither in her right hand,

And on hir heed, ful semely for to see,
And on her head, most seemly to behold,

A rose gerland, fresh and wel smellinge;
A rose garland, fresh and fragrant;

Above hir heed hir dowves flikeringe.   1104
Above her head her doves were fluttering.

Biforn hir stood hir sone Cupido,
Before her stood her son Cupid,

Up-on his shuldres winges hadde he two;
With two wings on his shoulders;

And blind he was, as it is ofte sene;
And blind he was, as is often evidenced;

A bowe he bar and arwes brighte and kene.   1108
A bow he bore and arrows bright and sharp.

   Why sholde I noght as wel eek telle yow al
   Why should I not as well tell you also

The portreiture, that was up-on the wal
About the representations on the wall

With-inne the temple of mighty Mars the rede
Within the temple of mighty Mars the red?

Al peynted was the wal, in lengthe and brede,   *1112*
Entirely painted was the wall, in length and breadth,

Lyk to the estres of the grisly place
Like the interior of the ghastly place

That highte the grete temple of Mars in Trace,
Which is called the great temple of Mars in Thrace,

In thilke colde frosty regioun,
In that cold, frosty region,

There-as Mars hath his sovereyn mansioun.   *1116*
Where Mars has his sovereign mansion.

First on the wal was peynted a foreste,
First on the wall a forest was painted,

In which ther dwelleth neither man ne beste,
Inhabited by neither man nor beast,

With knotty knarry bareyn treës olde
With knotty gnarled barren old trees

Of stubbes sharpe and hidous to biholde;   *1120*
And stumps sharp and hideous to behold;

In which ther ran a rumbel and a swough,
In which was heard a rumbling and a soughing

As though a storm sholde bresten every bough:
As if a storm would break every bough:

And downward from an hille, under a bente,
And down beneath a hill, under a slope,

Ther stood the temple of Mars armipotente,   *1124*
There stood the temple of armor-mighty Mars,

Wroght al of burned steel, of which th'entree
Made entirely of burnished steel, the entrance to which

Was long and streit, and gastly for to see.
Was long and narrow, and ghastly to behold.

And ther-out cam a rage and such a vese,
And from it came a roar and such a blast

That it made al the gates for to rese.   1128
That it made all the gates tremble.

The northren light in at the dores shoon,
The north light shone in at the doors,

For windowe on the wal ne was ther noon,
For on the wall there was no window

Thurgh which men mighten any light discerne.
Through which men might discern any light.

The dores were alle of adamant eterne,   1132
The doors were all of everlasting adamant,

Y-clenched overthwart and endelong
Barred up and down and sideways

With iren tough; and for to make it strong,
With tough iron; and to give it strength,

Every piler, the temple to sustene,
Every pillar which sustained the temple

Was tonne-greet, of iron bright and shene.   1136
Was barrel-thick of iron bright and shiny.

Ther saugh I first the derke imagining
There saw I first the dark planning

Of felonye, and al the compassing;
Of felony, and all its accomplishment;

The cruel Ire, reed as any glede;
Cruel Anger, red as any ember;

The pykepurs, and eek the pale Drede;   1140
The pickpocket, and also pale Dread;

The smyler with the knyf under the cloke;
The smiler with the knife under his cloak;

The shepne brenning with the blake smoke;
The barn burning with black smoke;

The treson of the mordring in the bedde;
The treachery of murder in bed;

The open werre, with woundes al bibledde;　　　　　*1144*
The open war, with wounds all bleeding;

Contek, with blody knyf and sharp manace;
Conflict, with bloody knife and sharp menace;

Al ful of chirking was that sory place.
Full of grating noises was that sorry place.

The sleere of him-self yet saugh I ther,
The slayer of himself I saw there too,

His herte-blood hath bathed al his heer;　　　　　*1148*
His heart's blood had bathed all his hair;

The nayl y-driven in the shode a-night;
The nail driven in the head by night;

The colde deeth, with mouth gaping up-right.
The cold death with mouth gaping open.

Amiddes of the temple sat Meschaunce,
In the midst of the temple sat Mischance

With disconfort and sory contenaunce.　　　　　*1152*
With grief and a sorrowful countenance.

Yet saugh I Woodnesse laughing in his rage;
Besides, I saw Madness laughing in his rage;

Armed Compleint, Out-hees, and fiers Outrage.
Armed Complaint, Alarm, and fierce Outrage.

The careyne in the bush, with throte y-corve:
The carrion in the bush, with throat cut:

A thousand slayn, and nat of qualm y-storve;　　　　　*1156*
A thousand slain, and not dead of the plague;

The tiraunt, with the prey by force y-raft;
The tyrant, with his prey snatched by force;

The toun destroyed, ther was no-thing laft.
The town destroyed, there was nothing left.

Yet saugh I brent the shippes hoppesteres;
Yet more, I saw the dancing ships burned;

The hunte strangled with the wilde beres;   *1160*
The hunter strangled by wild bears;

The sowe freten the child right in the cradel;
The sow devouring the child right in the cradle;

The cook y-scalded, for al his longe ladel.
The cook scalded in spite of his long ladle.

Noght was foryeten by th' infortune of Marte;
Nothing was forgotten of the misfortunes of Mars;

The carter over-riden with his carte,   *1164*
The carter run over by his cart

Under the wheel ful lowe he lay adoun.
Lay low down under the wheel.

Ther were also, of Martes divisioun,
There were also, under the rule of Mars,

The barbour, and the bocher, and the smith
The barber, and the butcher, and the smith

That forgeth sharpe swerdes on his stith.   *1168*
Who forges sharp swords on his anvil.

And al above, depeynted in a tour,
And above all, depicted in a tower,

Saw I Conquest sittinge in greet honour,
I saw Conquest sitting in great honor,

With the sharpe swerde over his heed
With the sharp sword over his head

Hanginge by a sotil twynes threed.   *1172*
Hanging by a frail twisted thread.

Depeynted was the slaughtre of Julius,
Represented was the slaughter of Caesar,

Of grete Nero, and of Antonius;
Of great Nero, and of Antony;

Al be that thilke tyme they were unborn,
Even though they were unborn at that time,

Yet was hir deeth depeynted ther-biforn,   1176
Yet their deaths were depicted there beforehand,

By manasinge of Mars, right by figure;
Through the menace of Mars, exactly portrayed;

So was it shewed in that portreiture
Exactly was it shown in that portraiture

As is depeynted in the sterres above,
As it is mirrored in the stars above,

Who shal be slayn or elles deed for love.   1180
Who shall be killed or else die for love.

Suffyceth oon ensample in stories olde,
One example from old histories is sufficient,

I may not rekne hem alle, thogh I wolde.
I cannot recollect them all, even if I wanted to.

  The statue of Mars up-on a carte stood,
  The statue of Mars stood on a chariot,

Armed, and loked grim as he were wood;   1184
Armed, and looking as fierce as if he were mad;

And over his heed ther shynen two figures
And over his head there shone two figures

Of sterres, that been cleped in scriptures
Of stars, which have been called in writings

That oon Puella, that other Rubeus.
The one Puella, the other Rubeus.[3]

This god of armes was arrayed thus:—   1188
This god of arms was presented thus:—

A wolf ther stood biforn him at his feet
A wolf stood before him at his feet

With eyen rede, and of a man he eet;
With eyes red, and devouring a man;

With sotil pencel was depeynt this storie,
With skillful pencil was depicted this story,

In redoutinge of Mars and of his glorie.   1192
In honor of Mars and his glory.

Now to the temple of Diane the chaste
Now to the temple of the chaste Diana

As shortly as I can I wol me haste,
As quickly as I can I will hasten,

To telle yow al the descripcioun.
To give you a full description.

Depeynted been the walles up and doun   1196
The walls were covered up and down with scenes

Of hunting and of shamfast chastitee.
Of hunting and modest chastity.

Ther saugh I how woful Calistopee,
There I saw how woeful Callisto,

Whan that Diane agreved was with here,
When Diana became angry with her,

Was turned from a womman til a bere,   1200
Was changed from a woman into a bear,

And after was she maad the lode-sterre;
And afterwards she was made the polar star;

Thus was it peynt, I can say yow no ferre;
Thus was it painted, I can tell you no more;

Hir sone is eek a sterre, as men may see.
Her son is also a star, as men can see.

There saugh I Dane, y-turned til a tree,   1204
There saw I Daphne, turned to a tree,

I mene nat the goddesse Diane,
I don't mean the goddess Diana,

But Penneus doughter, which that highte Dane.
But Peneus' daughter, who was called Daphne.

Ther saugh I Attheon an hert y-maked,
There saw I Actaeon made into a hart,

For vengeaunce that he saugh Diane al naked;   1208
For vengeance for having seen Diana naked;

I saugh how that his houndes have him caught,
I saw how his hounds caught him

And freten him, for that they knewe him naught.
And devoured him because they didn't know him.

Yet peynted was a litel forther-moor,
Still more, a little further on was painted

How Atthalante hunted the wilde boor,   1212
How Atalanta hunted the wild boar,

And Meleagre, and many another mo,
And Meleager, and many others besides,

For which Diane wroghte him care and wo.
For which Diana brought him care and woe.

Ther saugh I many another wonder storie,
There saw I many another wondrous story,

The whiche me list nat drawen to memorie.   1216
Which I am not inclined to call to mind.

This goddesse on an hert ful hye seet,
This goddess sat up high on a hart,

With smale houndes al aboute hir feet;
With small hounds all about her feet;

And undernethe hir feet she hadde a mone,
And underneath her feet she had a moon,

Wexing it was, and sholde wanie sone.   1220
Waxing it was, and would wane soon.

In gaude grene hir statue clothed was,
In yellowish green her statue was clothed,

With bowe in honde, and arwes in a cas.
With bow in hand and arrows in a quiver.

Hir eyen caste she ful lowe adoun,
Her eyes she cast down very low

Ther Pluto hath his derke regioun.   *1224*
Where Pluto has his dark realm.

A womman travailinge was hir biforn,
A woman in labor was before her,

But, for hir child so longe was unborn,
But, because her child was so long unborn,

Ful pitously Lucyna gan she calle,
Most piteously she began to call on Diana,

And seyde, "Help, for thou mayst best of alle."   *1228*
And said, "Help, for thou canst best of all."

Wel couthe he peynten lyfly that it wroghte,
The artist well knew how to paint in lifelike fashion,

With many a florin he the hewes boghte.
With many a florin he had bought his colors.

   Now been thise listes maad, and Theseus,
   Now these lists have been completed, and Theseus,

That at his grete cost arrayed thus   *1232*
Who at great cost had so decorated

The temples and the theatre every del,
The temples and the theater completely,

Whan it was doon, him lyked wonder wel.
When it was done, liked it wondrous well.

But stinte I wol of Theseus a lyte,
But I will ignore Theseus a little,

And speke of Palamon and of Arcite.   *1236*
And speak of Palamon and of Arcite.

   The day approcheth of hir retourninge,
   The day approached of their return,

That everich sholde an hundred knightes bringe,
When each should bring a hundred knights,

The bataille to darreyne, as I yow tolde;
To contest the battle, as I told you;

And til Athenes, hir covenant for to holde,   *1240*
And to Athens, to keep the agreement,

Hath everich of hem broght an hundred knightes
Had each of them brought a hundred knights

Wel armed for the werre at alle rightes.
Well armed for the war at every point.

And sikerly, ther trowed many a man
And truly, many a man believed

That never, sithen that the world bigan,   *1244*
That never, since the world began,

As for to speke of knighthod of hir hond,
Speaking of the prowess of knighthood,

As fer as God hath maked see or lond,
As far as God created sea or land,

Nas, of so fewe, so noble a companye.
Was there, for so few, so noble a company.

For every wight that lovede chivalrye,   *1248*
For every man who loved chivalry,

And wolde, his thankes, han a passant name,
And was ambitious to have a renowned name,

Hath preyed that he mighte ben of that game;
Had begged that he might join the adventure;

And wel was him, that ther-to chosen was.
And fortunate was he who was chosen.

For if ther fille to-morwe swich a cas,   *1252*
For if such a situation occurred tomorrow,

Ye knowen wel, that every lusty knight,
You well know that every lusty knight

That loveth paramours, and hath his might,
Who loves devotedly, and has his strength,

Were it in Englelond, or elles-where,
Whether in England, or elsewhere,

They wolde, hir thankes, wilnen to be there,   *1253*
Would desire most eagerly to be there,

To fighte for a lady—*benedicite!*
To fight for a lady—God bless us!

It were a lusty sighte for to see.
It would be a lusty sight to see.

   And right so ferden they with Palamon.
   And so it was with Palamon's followers.

With him ther wenten knightes many oon;   *1260*
With him there rode many a knight;

Som wol ben armed in an habergeoun,
Some would be armed in a coat of mail,

In a brest-plat and in a light gipoun;
In a breast-plate and a light jacket;

And somme woln have a peyre plates large;
And some would have large plates front and back;

And somme woln have a Pruce sheld, or a targe;   *1264*
And some would have a Prussian shield, or a target;

Somme woln ben armed on hir legges weel,
Some would be well armed on their legs,

And have an ax, and somme a mace of steel.
And have an axe, and some a mace of steel.

Ther nis no newe gyse that it nas old.
There is no new equipment that is not old.

Armed were they, as I have you told,   *1268*
Armed were they, as I have told you,

Everich after his opinioun.
Each according to his own ideas.

Ther maistow seen coming with Palamoun
There you might have seen coming with Palamon

Ligurge him-self, the grete king of Trace;
Lycurgus himself, the great king of Thrace;

Blak was his berd, and manly was his face.   *1272*
Black was his beard, and manly was his face.

The cercles of his eyen in his heed,
The circles of his eyes in his head

They gloweden bitwixe yelow and reed:
Burned in a glow between yellow and red:

And lyk a griffon loked he aboute,
And like a griffin he looked about,

With kempe heres on his browes stoute;   *1276*
With shaggy hairs on his heavy brows;

His limes grete, his braunes harde and stronge,
His limbs massive, his muscles hard and strong,

His shuldres brode, his armes rounde and longe.
His shoulders broad, his arms heavy and long.

And as the gyse was in his contree,
And as the custom was in his country,

Ful hye up-on a char of gold stood he,   *1280*
High up on a golden chariot he stood,

With foure whyte boles in the trays.
With four white bulls in the traces.

In-stede of cote-armure over his harnays,
Instead of a coat of arms over his armor,

With nayles yelwe and brighte as any gold,
With its nails yellow and bright as any gold,

He hadde a beres skin, col-blak, for-old,   *1284*
He had a coal black bearskin, very old,

His longe heer was kembd bihinde his bak,
His long hair was combed behind his back,

As any ravenes fether it shoon for-blak:
Like any raven's feather it shone pitch black:

A wrethe of gold arm-greet, of huge wighte,
A wreath of gold arm-size, of great weight,

Upon his heed, set full of stones brighte,   1288
Was on his head, set full of precious stones,

Of fyne rubies and of dyamaunts.
Of fine rubies and of diamonds.

Aboute his char ther wenten whyte alaunts,
About his chariot there coursed white wolf-hounds,

Twenty and mo, as grete as any steer,
Twenty or more, as large as any steer,

To hunten at the leoun or the deer,   1292
To hunt the lion or the deer,

And folwed him, with mosel faste y-bounde,
And followed him, tightly muzzled,

Colers of gold, and torets fyled rounde.
With collars of gold and filed leash-rings.

An hundred lordes hadde he in his route
A hundred lords he had in his company

Armed ful wel, with hertes sterne and stoute.   1296
Finely armed, with hearts firm and strong.

   With Arcite, in stories as men finde,
   With Arcite, as it is recounted in histories,

The grete Emetreus, the king of Inde,
The great Emetreus, the king of India,

Up-on a stede bay, trapped in steel,
Upon a bay steed, harnessed in steel,

Covered in cloth of gold diapred weel,   1300
Covered with cloth of gold well patterned,

Cam ryding lyk the god of armes, Mars.
Came riding like the god of arms, Mars.

His cote-armure was of cloth of Tars,
His coat of arms was of cloth of Tartary,

Couched with perles whyte and rounde and grete.
Decorated with pearls white and round and large.

His sadel was of brend gold newe y-bete;　　1304
His saddle was of burnished gold newly beaten;

A mantelet upon his shuldre hanginge
A small mantle hung upon his shoulders

Bret-ful of rubies rede, as fyr sparklinge.
Crusted with red rubies, sparkling like fire.

His crispe heer lyk ringes was y-ronne,
His curly hair ran into rings,

And that was yelow, and glitered as the sonne.　　1308
And that was yellow, and glittered like the sun.

His nose was heigh, his eyen bright citryn,
His nose was prominent, his eyes bright green-yellow,

His lippes rounde, his colour was sangwyn,
His lips full, his color was ruddy,

A fewe fraknes in his face y-spreynd,
A few freckles spotted his face,

Bitwixen yelow and somdel blak y-meynd,　　1312
Colored somewhere between yellow and black,

And as a leoun he his loking caste.
And like a lion he cast his looks.

Of fyve and twenty yeer his age I caste.
I estimate his age at about twenty-five.

His berd was wel bigonne for to springe;
His beard was well along in its growth;

His voys was as a trompe thunderinge.　　1316
His voice was like a thundering trumpet.

Up-on his heed he wered of laurer grene
Upon his head he wore, of green laurel,

A gerland fresh and lusty for to sene.
A garland fresh and beautiful to see.

Up-on his hand he bar, for his deduyt,
On his hand he bore, for his pleasure,

An egle tame, as eny lilie whyt.   1320
A tame eagle, white as any lily.

An hundred lordes hadde he with him there.
A hundred lords he had there with him,

Al armed, sauf hir heddes, in al hir gere,
Armed, except for their heads, in complete array.

Ful richely in alle maner thinges.
Most rich in every respect.

For trusteth wel, that dukes, erles, kinges,   1324
For be assured that dukes, earls, kings,

Were gadered in this noble companye,
Were gathered in this noble company,

For love and for encrees of chivalrye.
For love and for the advancement of chivalry.

Aboute this king ther ran on every part
About this king there ran on every side

Ful many a tame leoun and lepart.   1328
Many a tame lion and leopard.

And in this wyse thise lordes, alle and some,
And in this manner these lords, one and all,

Ben on the Sonday to the citee come
Came to the city on a Sunday

Aboute pryme, and in the toun alight.
Early in the morning, and alighted in the town.

This Theseus, this duk, this worthy knight,   1332
This Theseus, this duke, this worthy knight,

Whan he had broght hem in-to his citee,
When he had brought them into his city,

And inned hem, everich in his degree,
And lodged them, each according to his rank,

He festeth hem, and dooth so greet labour
Feasted them, and took such great pains

To esen hem, and doon hem al honour,   1336
To please them, and do them all honor,

That yet men weneth that no mannes wit
That still men believe that no man's ingenuity

Of noon estat ne coude amenden it.
Of whatever rank could outdo it.

The minstralcye, the service at the feste,
The minstrelsy, the service at the feast,

The grete yiftes to the moste and leste,   1340
The great gifts to the highest and the lowest,

The riche array of Theseus paleys,
The rich furnishings of Theseus' palace,

Ne who sat first ne last up-on the deys,
Or who sat first or last upon the dais,

What ladies fairest been or best daunsinge,
Which ladies were fairest or danced the best,

Or which of hem can dauncen best and singe,   1344
Or which of them could dance and sing best,

Ne who most felingly speketh of love:
Or who most feelingly spoke of love:

What haukes sitten on the perche above,
What hawks sat on the perch above,

What houndes liggen on the floor adoun:
What hounds lay on the floor below:

Of al this make I now no mencioun;   1348
Of all this I make now no mention;

But al th'effect, that thinketh me the beste;
But concentrate on the outcome, I think that best;

Now comth the poynt, and herkneth if yow leste.
Now comes the point, and listen if you care to.

The Sonday night, er day bigan to springe,
That Sunday night, before day began to dawn,

When Palamon the larke herde singe,   1352
When Palamon heard the lark singing,

Although it nere nat day by houres two,
Although it was not day by two hours,

Yet song the larke, and Palamon also.
Yet sang the lark, and Palamon, too.

With holy herte, and with an heigh corage
With holy heart, and with high spirits

He roos, to wenden on his pilgrimage   1356
He arose, to go on his pilgrimage

Un-to the blisful Citherea benigne
To the blessed benign Cytherea,

I mene Venus, honurable and digne.
I mean Venus, honored and revered.

And in hir houre he walketh forth a pas
And in her hour he walked forth a step

Un-to the listes, ther hir temple was,   1360
To the lists, where her temple was,

And doun he kneleth, and with humble chere
And down he knelt, and with humble countenance

And herte soor, he seyde as ye shul here.
And troubled heart, he spoke as you shall hear.

"Faireste of faire, O lady myn, Venus,
"Fairest of the fair, O lady mine, Venus

Doughter to Jove and spouse of Vulcanus,   1364
Daughter to Jove and spouse of Vulcan,

Thou glader of the mount of Citheroun,
Thou joy of the mount of Citheron,

For thilke love thou haddest to Adoun,
For that love thou hadst for Adonis,

Have pitee of my bittre teres smerte,
Have pity on my bitter painful tears,

And tak myn humble preyer at thyn herte.   *1368*
And take my humble prayer to thy heart.

Allas! I ne have no langage to telle
Alas! I have no language to describe

Th'effectes ne the torments of myn helle;
The effects or the torments of my hell;

Myn herte may myne harmes nat biwreye;
My heart can not reveal my ills;

I am so confus, that I can noght seye.   *1372*
I am so distracted, that I can say nothing.

But mercy, lady bright, that knowest weel
But mercy, lady bright, who knowest well

My thought, and seest what harmes that I feel,
My thoughts, and seest the woes that I feel,

Considere al this, and rewe up-on my sore,
Consider all this, and have pity on my pain,

As wisly as I shal for evermore,   *1376*
As surely as I shall for evermore,

Emforth my might, thy trewe servant be,
To the extent of my power, thy true servant be,

And holden werre alwey with chastitee;
And wage war always against chastity;

That make I myn avow, so ye me helpe.
That I make my vow, if thou wilt aid me.

I kepe noght of armes for to yelpe,   *1380*
I am not concerned with boast of arms,

Ne I ne axe nat to-morowe to have victorie,
Nor do I ask to have victory tomorrow,

Ne renoun in this cas, ne veyne glorie
Nor renown in this adventure, nor vain glory

Of pris of armes blowen up and doun,
Of fame in arms trumpeted up and down,

But I wolde have fully posessioun   *1384*
But I would completely have possession

Of Emelye, and dye in thy servyse;
Of Emily, and die in thy service;

Find thou the maner how, and in what wyse.
Find thou the means, and by what method.

I recche nat, but it may bettre be,
I care not, whether it is better

To have victorie of hem or they of me,   *1388*
To have victory of them or they of me,

So that I have my lady in myne armes.
If only I have my lady in my arms.

For though so be that Mars is god of armes,
For though it be that Mars is god of arms,

Your vertu is so greet in hevene above,
Thy virtue is so great in heaven above,

That, if yow list, I shal wel have my love.   *1392*
That, if thou desirest, I shall surely have my love.

Thy temple wol I worshipe evermo,
Thy temple will I worship evermore,

And on thyn auter, wher I ryde or go,
And on thine altar, wherever I ride or roam,

I wol don sacrifice, and fyres bete.
I will do sacrifice, and kindle fires.

And if ye wol nat so, my lady swete,   *1396*
And if thou wilt not so, my lady sweet,

Than preye I thee, to-morwe with a spere
Then I beseech thee, tomorrow with a spear

That Arcita me thurgh the herte here.
May Arcite pierce me through the heart.

Thanne rekke I noght, whan I have lost my lyf,
Then care I not, when I have lost my life,

Though that Arcita winne hir to his wyf.   *1400*
If Arcite wins her to be his wife.

This is th'effect and ende of my preyere,
This is the substance and end of my prayer,

Yif me my love, thou blisful lady dere."
Give me my love, thou blessed lady dear."

Whan th'orisoun was doon of Palamon,
When Palamon's orison was completed,

His sacrifice he dide, and that anon   *1404*
His sacrifice he made, and that at once

Ful pitously, with alle circumstaunces,
Most piteously, with full ceremony,

Al telle I noght as now his observaunces.
Although I shall not describe his observances.

But atte laste the statue of Venus shook
But at last the statue of Venus shook,

And made a signe, wher-by that he took   *1408*
And made a sign, whereby he took assurance

That his preyere accepted was that day.
That his prayer was accepted that day.

For thogh the signe shewed a delay,
For though the sign was delayed,

Yet wiste he wel that graunted was his bone;
Yet he well knew that his prayer was granted;

And with glad herte he wente him hoom ful sone.   *1412*
And glad at heart he soon went home.

The thridde houre inequal that Palamon
About three hours after Palamon

Bigan to Venus temple for to goon,
Had set out for the temple of Venus,

Up roos the sonne, and up roos Emelye,
Up rose the sun, and up rose Emily,

And to the temple of Diane gan hye.   1416
And made her way to the temple of Diana.

Hir maydens, that she thider with hir ladde,
Her maidens, whom she took thither with her,

Ful redily with hem the fyr they hadde,
Fully prepared, had the fire with them,

Th'encens, the clothes, and the remenant al
The incense, the clothes, and all the other properties

That to the sacrifyce longen shal;   1420
Which are connected with sacrifice;

The hornes fulle of meth, as was the gyse;
The horns full of mead, as was the custom;

Ther lakked noght to doon hir sacrifyse.
Nothing was lacking to make her sacrifice.

Smoking the temple, ful of clothes faire.
The temple smoking, full of fair hangings,

This Emelye, with herte debonaire,   1424
This Emily, with gentle heart,

Hir body wessh with water of a welle;
Her body washed with water from a well;

But how she dide hir ryte I dar nat telle,
But how she performed her rites, I dare not tell,

But it be any thing in general;
Except in general terms;

And yet it were a game to heren al;   1428
And yet it would be a pleasure to hear all;

To him that meneth wel, it were no charge:
To him who means well, it would be no harm:

But it is good a man ben at his large.
But it is good for one to use his own discretion.

Hir brighte heer was kempt, untressed al;
Her bright hair was combed, all unbraided;

A coroune of a grene ook cerial   *1432*
A crown of an evergreen oak

Up-on hir heed was set ful fair and mete.
Was set fairly and fittingly on her head.

Two fyres on the auter gan she bete,
Two fires on the altar she tended,

And dide hir thinges, as men may biholde
And performed her ceremonies, as men may read

In Stace of Thebes, and thise bokes olde.   *1436*
In Statius' THEBAIAD, *and those old books.*

Whan kindled was the fyr, with pitous chere
When the fire was kindled, with piteous mien

Un-to Diane she spak, as ye may here.
Unto Diana she spoke, as you shall hear.

"O chaste goddesse of the wodes grene,
"O chaste goddess of the green woods,

To whom bothe heven and earthe and see is sene,   *1440*
To whom heaven, earth, and sea are visible,

Quene of the regne of Pluto derk and lowe,
Queen of the dark and low realm of Pluto,

Goddesse of maydens, that myn herte hast knowe
Goddess of maidens, who hast known my heart

Ful many a yeer, and woost what I desire,
Many a long year, and knowest what I desire,

As kepe me fro thy vengeaunce and thyn ire,   *1444*
Preserve me from thy vengeance and thy wrath,

That Attheon aboughte cruelly.
Which Actaeon purchased cruelly.[4]

Chaste goddesse, wel wostow that I
Chaste goddess, well knowest thou that I

Desire to been a mayden al my lyf,
Desire to remain a maiden all my life,

Ne never wol I be no love ne wyf.   1448
Nor would I ever be paramour or wife.

I am, thou woost, yet of thy companye,
I am, thou knowest, still of thy company,

A mayde, and love hunting and venerye,
A maid, and love the pursuit and the kill,

And for to walken in the wodes wilde,
And to walk in the wild woods,

And noght to been a wyf, and be with childe.   1452
And not to be a wife, and be with child.

Noght wol I knowe companye of man.
Never will I know man's company.

Now help me lady, sith ye may and can,
Now help me, lady, since thou canst if thou wilt,

For tho thre formes that thou hast in thee.
Through the three forms⁵ possessed by thee.

And Palamon, that hath swich love to me,   1456
And Palamon, who has such love for me,

And eek Arcite, that loveth me so sore,
And Arcite too, who loves me so desperately,

This grace I preye thee with-oute more,
This only grace I beg of thee,

As sende love and pees bitwixe hem two;
That thou wilt send love and peace between them;

And fro me turne awey hir hertes so,   1460
And so turn their hearts away from me

That al hir hote love, and hir desyr,
That all their hot love, and their desire,

And al hir bisy torment, and hir fyr
And all their constant torment, and their fire

Be queynt, or turned in another place;
May be quenched, or turned to another object;

And if so be thou wolt not do me grace,   *1464*
And if it be that thou wilt not do me grace,

Or if my destinee be shapen so,
Or if my fate is so ordained

That I shal nedes have oon of hem two,
That I needs must have one of them,

As sende me him that most desireth me.
Then send me him that most desires me.

Bihold, goddesse of clene chastitee,   *1468*
Behold, goddess of pure chastity,

The bittre teres that on my chekes falle.
The bitter tears that fall on my cheeks.

Sin thou are mayde, and keper of us alle,
Since thou art a maid, and guardian of us all,

My maydenhede thou kepe and wel conserve,
Guard and preserve my maidenhood,

And whyl I live a mayde, I wol thee serve."   *1472*
And while I live as a maid, I will serve thee."

   The fyres brenne up-on the auter clere,
   The fires burned bright upon the altar

Whyl Emelye was thus in hir preyere;
While Emily was thus engaged in prayer;

But sodeinly she saugh a sighte queynte,
But suddenly she saw a strange sight,

For right anon oon of the fyres queynte,   *1476*
For instantly one of the fires went out,

And quiked agayn, and after that anon
And revived again, and immediately after that

That other fyr was queynt, and al agon;
The other fire was quenched, and went out;

And as it queynte, it made a whistelinge,
And as it died, it made a whistling,

As doon thise wete brondes in hir brenning,   1480
As wet logs do when they burn,

And at the brondes ende out-ran anoon
And at the ends of the wood there run out

As it were blody dropes many oon;
Many drops that looked like blood;

For which so sore agast was Emelye,
At which Emily was so sorely frightened

That she was wel ny mad, and gan to crye,   1484
That she was near hysteria, and began to cry,

For she ne wiste what it signifyed;
For she knew not what it signified;

But only for the fere thus hath she cryed,
But only from fear she cried so,

And weep, that it was pitee for to here.
And wept, that it was pitiful to hear.

And ther-with-al Diane gan appere,   1488
And thereupon Diana made her appearance,

With bowe in hond, right as an hunteresse,
With bow in hand, exactly like a huntress,

And seyde: "Doghter, stint thyn hevinesse.
And said: "Daughter, leave off thy grief.

Among the goddes hye it is affermed,
Among the high gods it is affirmed,

And by eterne word write and confermed,   1492
And written by eternal word, and decreed

Thou shalt ben wedded un-to oon of tho
That thou shalt be wedded to one of those

That han for thee so muchel care and wo;
Who have suffered for you so much care and woe;

But un-to which of hem I may nat telle.
But to which of them I may not tell.

Farwel, for I ne may no lenger dwelle.   *1496*
Farewell, for I may no longer tarry.

The fyres which that on myn auter brenne
The fires which burn on my altar

Shul thee declaren, er that thou go henne,
Shall declare to thee, ere thou goest hence,

Thyn adventure of love, as in this cas."
Thy fortunes in this love affair."

And with that word, the arwes in the cas   *1500*
And with that word, the arrows in the quiver

Of the goddesse clateren faste and ringe,
Of the goddess clattered together and rang,

And forth she wente, and made a vanisshinge;
And forth she went, and vanished;

For which this Emelye astoned was,
Wherefore this Emily was astounded,

And seyde, "What amounteth this, allas!   *1504*
And said, "What means this, alas!

I putte me in thy proteccioun,
I place myself under thy protection,

Diane, and in thy dispisicioun."
Diana, and at thy disposal."

And hoom she gooth anon the nexte weye.
And home she went at once the nearest way.

This is th'effect, ther is namore to seye.   *1508*
This is the substance, there is no more to say.

    The nexte houre of Mars folwinge this,
    In the next hour of Mars after this,

Arcite un-to the temple walked is
Arcite walked to the temple

Of fierse Mars, to doon his sacrifyse,
Of fierce Mars, to make his sacrifice,

With alle the rytes of his payen wyse.   *1512*
With all the rites of his pagan wisdom.

With pitous herte and heigh devocioun,
With humble heart and high devotion,

Right thus to Mars he seyde his orisoun:
He made his prayer to Mars even so:

"O stronge god, that in the regnes colde
"O mighty god, that in the cold realms

Of Trace honoured art, and lord y-holde,   *1516*
Of Thrace art honored and held as lord,

And hast in every regne and every lond
And hast in every realm and every land

Of armes al the brydel in thyn hond,
All the direction of arms in thy hand,

And hem fortunest as thee list devyse,
And favorest those as it pleaseth thee,

Accept of me my pitous sacrifyse.   *1520*
Accept of me my humble sacrifice.

If so be that my youthe may deserve,
If it so be that my youth may deserve,

And that my might be worthy for to serve
And my prowess be worthy to serve

Thy godhede, that I may been oon of thyne,
Thy godhead, so that I may be one of thine,

Than preye I thee to rewe up-on my pyne.   *1524*
Then I beseech thee to have mercy on my ills.

For thilke peyne, and thilke hote fyr,
For this pain, and this hot fire,

In which thou whylom brendest for desyr,
In which thou once hast burned for desire,

Whan that thou usedest the grete beautee
When thou didst use the great beauty

Of fayre younge fresshe Venus free,   1528
Of fair young fresh Venus freely,

And haddest hir in armes at thy wille,
And hadst her in thine arms at thy will,

Al-though thee ones on a tyme misfille
Although once upon a time trouble struck thee

Whan Vulcanus had caught thee in his las,
When Vulcan caught thee in his net

And fond thee ligging by his wyf, allas!   1532
And found thee lying with his wife, alas!

For thilke sorwe that was in thyn herte,
For this sorrow which was in thy heart,

Have routhe as wel up-on my peynes smerte.
Have mercy as well upon my sharp pains.

I am yong and unkonning, as thou wost,
I am young and unsophisticated, as thou knowest,

And, as I trowe, with love offended most,   1536
And, as I believe, more tortured by love

That ever was any lyves creature;
Than ever was any living creature;

For she, that dooth me al this wo endure,
For she, who causes me to endure all this woe,

Ne reccheth never wher I sinke or flete.
Cares not at all whether I sink or float.

And wel I woot, er she me mercy hete,   1540
And well I know, before she will grant me mercy,

I moot with strengthe winne hir in the place;
I must win her in the lists by might of arms;

And wel I woot, withouten help or grace
And well I know, without aid or grace

Of thee, ne may my strengthe noght availle.
From thee, my strength will avail naught.

Than help me, lord, to-morwe in my bataille,   *1544*
Then help me, lord, tomorrow in my battle,

For thilke fyr that whylom brente thee,
By that fire that once consumed thee,

As wel as thilke fyr now brenneth me;
As well as this fire now consuming me;

And do that I to-morwe have victorie.
And grant that I have victory tomorrow.

Myn be the travaille, and thyn be the glorie!   1548
Mine be the struggle, and thine be the glory!

Thy soverein temple wol I most honouren
Thy sovereign temple will I honor most

Of any place, and alwey most labouren
Of any place, and will forever labor most

In thy plesaunce and in thy craftes stronge,
To do thy pleasure and study thy strong crafts,

And in thy temple I wol my baner honge,   1552
And in thy temple I will hang my banner

And alle the armes of my companye;
And all the arms of my company;

And ever-mo, un-to that day I dye,
And evermore, until my dying day,

Eterne fyr I wol biforn thee finde.
An eternal fire I will maintain before thee.

And eek to this avow I wol me binde: *1556*
And, in addition, I will bind myself to this vow:

My berd, myn heer that hongeth long adoun,
My beard, my long hair hanging down,

That never yet ne felte offensioun
Which never yet felt the offence

Of rasour nor of shere, I wol thee yive,
Of razor or of shears, I will give thee,

And been thy trewe servant whyl I live.   1560
And be thy true servant while I live.

Now lord, have routhe up-on my sorwes sore,
Now lord, have pity on my painful sorrow,

Yif me victorie, I aske thee namore."
Grant me victory, I ask no more of thee."

   The preyere stinte of Arcita the stronge,
   The prayer of mighty Arcite ceased,

The ringes on the temple-dore that honge,   1564
The rings that hung on the temple door,

And eek the dores, clatereden ful faste,
And the doors themselves, clattered violently,

Of which Arcita som-what him agaste.
At which Arcite was somewhat aghast.

The fyres brende up-on the auter brighte,
The fires flared up brightly on the altar

That it gan al the temple for to lighte;   1568
So that the entire temple was lighted;

And swete smel the ground anon up-yaf,
And simultaneously the ground emitted sweet odors,

And Arcita anon his hand up-haf,
And Arcite at once raised up his hand,

And more encens in-to the fyr he caste,
And cast more incense into the fire,

With othere rytes mo; and atte laste   1572
Together with other rites, and at last

The statue of Mars bigan his hauberk ringe.
The armor of the statue of Mars began to ring.

And with that soun he herde a murmuringe
And with that sound he heard a murmuring

Ful lowe and dim, that sayde thus, "Victorie:"
Very low and hushed, that said thus, "Victory:"

For which he yaf to Mars honour and glorie.   1576
For which he gave to Mars honor and glory.

And thus with joye, and hope wel to fare,
And so with joy, and hope of faring well,

Arcite anon un-to his inne is fare,
Arcite at once went to his inn,

As fayn as fowel is of the brighte sonne.
As confident as a bird is of the bright sun.

And right anon swich stryf ther is bigonne   1580
And immediately such strife broke out

For thilke graunting, in the hevene above,
For granting these requests, in heaven above,

Bitwixe Venus, the goddesse of love,
Between Venus, the goddess of love,

And Mars, the sterne god armipotente,
And Mars, the stern god of power in arms,

That Jupiter was bisy it to stente;   1584
That Jupiter taxed his powers to stop it;

Til that the pale Saturnus the colde,
Until pale cold Saturn,

That knew so manye of aventures olde,
Who knew so many happenings from of old,

Fond in his olde experience an art,
Drew from his long experience a device

That he ful sone hath plesed every part.   1588
By which he quickly pleased both sides.

As sooth is sayd, elde hath greet avantage;
As is truly said, age has a great advantage;

In elde is bothe wisdom and usage;
In old age is both knowledge and experience;

Men may the olde at-renne, and noght at-rede.
Men may outrun the old, but not outwit them.

Saturne anon, to stinten stryf and drede,   *1592*
Saturn at once, to end strife and doubt,

Al be it that it is agayn his kynde,
Although that is against his nature,

Of al this stryf he gan remedie fynde.
Discovered a solution for all the conflict.

  "My dere doghter Venus," quod Saturne,
  "My dear daughter Venus," said Saturn,

"My cours, that hath so wyde for to turne,   *1596*
"My celestial course with its great orbit

Hath more power than wot any man.
Has more power than any man knows.

Myn is the drenching in the see so wan;
Mine is the drowning in the sea so wan;

Myn is the prison in the derke cote;
Mine is the prison in the dark hut;

Myn is the strangling and hanging by the throte;   *1600*
Mine is the strangling and hanging by the throat;

The murmure, and the cherles rebelling,
The muttering and rebelling of the peasants,

The groyning, and the pryvee empoysoning:
The grumbling, and the secret poisoning:

I do vengeance and pleyn correccioun
I perform vengeance and full punishment

Whyl I dwelle in the signe of the Leoun.   *1604*
When I pass through the zodiac sign of the Lion.

Myn is the ruine of the hye halles,
Mine is the ruin of the high halls,

The falling of the toures and of the walles
The falling of the towers and the walls

Up-on the mynour or the carpenter.
Upon the miner or the carpenter.

I slow Sampsoun in shaking the piler;   1608
I slew Sampson when he shook the pillar;

And myne be the maladyes colde,
And mine are the sinister maladies,

The derke tresons, and the castes olde;
The dark treasons, and ancient treacheries;

My loking is the fader of pestilence.
My gaze is the father of the plague.

Now weep namore, I shal doon diligence   1612
Now weep no more, I shall work it diligently

That Palamon, that is thyn owne knight,
That Palamon, who is your own knight,

Shal have his lady, as thou hast him hight.
Shall have his lady, as you have promised him.

Though Mars shal helpe his knight, yet nathelees
Though Mars aids his knight, nevertheless

Bitwixe yow ther moot be som tyme pees,   1616
Between you there must be eventual peace,

Al be ye noght of o complexioun,
Although you are alike in disposition,

That causeth al day swich divisioun.
Which causes such conflict constantly.

I am thin ayel, redy at thy wille;
I am your grandfather, ready to do your bidding;

Weep thou namore, I wol thy list fulfille."   1620
Weep no more, I will fulfill your desire."

Now wol I stinten of the goddes above,
Now will I stop speaking of the gods above,

Of Mars, and Venus, goddesse of love,
Of Mars, and of Venus, goddess of love,

And telle yow, as pleynly as I can,
And tell you, as fully as I can,

The grete effect, for which that I bigan.   *1624*
The final outcome, for which I started.

Part Four

Greet was the feste in Athenes that day,
Great was the feast in Athens that day,

And eek the lusty seson of that May
And besides, the lively weather of that May

Made every wight to been in swich plesaunce,
Put everyone in such good spirits

That al that Monday justen they and daunce,   *1628*
That all that Monday they jousted and danced,

And spenden it in Venus heigh servyse.
And spent it in the exalted service of Venus.

But by the cause that they sholde ryse
But because they had to rise

Erly, for to seen the grete fight,
Early, in order to see the great fight,

Unto hir reste wente they at night.   *1632*
To their rest they went at night.

And on the morwe, whan that day gan springe,
And on the morrow, when day began to dawn,

Of hors and harneys, noyse and clateringe
The noise and clattering of horses and armor

Ther was in hostelryes al aboute;
Was heard in lodgings all around;

And to the paleys rood ther many a route   *1636*
And to the palace there rode many a company

Of lordes, up-on stedes and palfreys.
Of lords, on steeds and palfreys.

Ther maystow seen devysing of herneys
There you might have seen varieties of armor

So uncouth and so riche, and wroght so weel
So rare and so rich, and wrought so well

Of goldsmithrie, of browding, and of steel;   *1640*
Of goldsmith work, of embroidery, and of steel;

The sheeldes brighte, testers, and trappures;
The glittering shields, helmets, and trappings;

Gold-hewen helmes, hauberks, cote-armures;
Golden helmets, mail plates, coats of arms;

Lordes in paraments on hir courseres,
Lords in rich robes on their coursers,

Knightes of retenue, and eek squyeres   *1644*
Retinues of knights, and also squires

Nailinge the speres, and helmes bokelinge,
Nailing the spearheads, and buckling helmets,

Gigginge of sheeldes, with layneres lacinge;
Fastening shield straps with thongs;

Ther as need is, they weren no-thing ydel;
Wherever needed, they were never idle;

The fomy stedes on the golden brydel   *1648*
The foaming steeds on golden bridles

Gnawinge, and faste the armurers also
Gnawing, and swiftly the armorers too

With fyle and hamer prikinge to and fro;
Hastening here and there with file and hammer;

Yemen on fote, and communes many oon
Yeomen on foot, and many a townsman

With shorte staves, thikke as they may goon;   *1652*
With short staves, as thick as they could crowd;

Pypes, trompes, nakers, clariounes,
Pipes, horns, kettle drums, trumpets,

That in the bataille blowen blody sounes;
That in the battle make bloody sounds;

The paleys ful of peples up and doun,
The palace full of people up and down,

Heer three, ther ten, holding hir questioun,   *1656*
Here three, there ten, having discussions,

Divyninge of thise Theban knightes two.
Making predictions about these two Theban knights.

Somme seyden thus, somme seyde it shal be so;
Some said thus, some said it shall be so and so;

Somme helden with him with the blake berd,
Some sided with him of the black beard,

Somme with the balled, somme with the thikke-herd;   *1660*
Some with the bald, some with the thick haired;

Somme sayde, he loked grim and he wolde fighte;
Some said that one looked grim and would fight;

He hath a sparth of twenty pound of wighte.
And that another had a twenty-pound battle-axe.

Thus was the halle ful of divyninge,
Thus was the hall full of soothsaying,

Longe after that the sonne gan to springe.   *1664*
Long after the sun had begun to shine.

   The grete Theseus, that of his sleep awaked
   The great Theseus, who was awakened from sleep

With minstralcye and noyse that was maked,
By the minstrelsy and the noise that was made,

Held yet the chambre of his paleys riche,
Remained in the chamber of his rich palace

Til that the Thebane knightes, bothe y-liche   *1668*
Until the Theban knights, both equally

Honoured, were into the paleys fet.
Honored, were brought into the palace.

Duk Theseus was at a window set,
Duke Theseus was sitting at a window,

Arrayed right as he were a god in trone.
Arrayed just as if he were a god enthroned.

The peple preesseth thider-ward ful sone   *1672*
The people pressed quickly thitherward

Him for to seen, and doon heigh reverence,
To see him, and do him high reverence,

And eek to herkne his hest and his sentence.
And also to hear his bidding and his pronouncement.

   An heraud on a scaffold made an ho,
   A herald on a scaffold shouted "Ho!"

Til al the noyse of peple was y-do;   *1676*
Until all the people's noise was quieted;

And whan he saugh the peple of noyse al stille,
And when he saw the people entirely silent,

Tho showed he the mighty dukes wille.
Then he proclaimed the mighty duke's will.

   "The lord hath of his heigh discrecioun
   "The lord has, in his high discretion,

Considered, that it were destruccioun   *1680*
Considered that it would be destruction

To gentil blood, to fighten in the gyse
To noble blood to fight in the fashion

Of mortal bataille now in this empryse;
Of mortal battle now in this contest;

Wherfore, to shapen that they shul not dye,
Wherefore, to insure that they shall not die,

He wol his firste purpos modifye.   1684
He will modify his original purpose.

No man therfor, up peyne of los of lyf,
No man therefore, on pain of loss of life,

No maner shot, ne pollax, ne short knyf
No shooting weapon, pole-axe, nor short knife

Into the listes sende, or thider bringe;
May send into the lists, or bring there;

Ne short swerd for to stoke, with poynt bytinge,   1688
Nor short sword for stabbing, with sharp point,

No man ne drawe, ne bere it by his syde.
May be drawn by any man, or carried at his side.

Ne no man shal un-to his felawe ryde
Nor shall any man ride against his opponent

But o cours, with a sharp y-grounde spere;
More than one course, with sharply ground spear;

Foyne, if him list, on fote, him-self to were.   1692
He may fence, if he pleases, on foot to defend himself.

And he that is at meschief, shal be take,
And he who is downed shall be captured

And noght slayn, but be broght un-to the stake
And not slain, but be brought to the stake

That shal ben ordeyned on either syde;
That shall be ordained on either side;

But thider he shal by force, and ther abyde.   1696
And he will be forced to go and remain there.

And if so falle, the chieftayn be take
And if it befalls that the chieftain is taken

On either syde, or elles slee his make,
On either side, or else slays his rival,

No lenger shal the turneyinge laste.
No longer shall the tourneying last.

God spede yow; goth forth, and ley on faste.   1700
God speed you; go forth, and lay on hard.

With long swerd and with maces fight your fille.
With long sword and with maces fight your fill.

Goth now your wey; this is the lordes wille."
Go now your ways; this is the lord's will."

  The voys of peple touchede the hevene,
  The outcry of the people reached the heaven,

So loude cryden they with mery stevene: 1704
So loud they shouted with joyful din:

"God save swich a lord, that is so good,
"God save such a lord, who is so good

He wilneth no destruccioun of blood!"
He wills no destruction of blood!"

Up goon the trompes and the melodye.
Up went the trumpets and the music.

And to the listes rit the companye   1708
And to the lists rode the company

By ordinaunce, thurgh-out the citee large,
In order, all through the large city,

Hanged with cloth of gold, and nat with sarge.
Hung with cloth of gold, not rough cloth.

Ful lyk a lord this noble duk gan ryde,
Most like a lord this noble duke rode forth,

Thise two Thebanes up-on either syde;   1712
The two Thebans on either side;

And after rood the quene, and Emelye,
And next rode the queen, and Emily,

And after that another companye
And after that another company

Of oon and other, after hir degree.
Of this one and that, according to their ranks.

And thus they passen thurgh-out the citee,   1716
And thus they passed through the whole city,

And to the listes come they by tyme.
And to the lists they came in good time.

It nas not of the day yet fully pryme,
It was not yet the middle of the morning,

Whan set was Theseus ful riche and hye,
When Theseus was stationed richly and high,

Ipolita the quene and Emelye,   1720
Hippolyta the queen, and Emily,

And other ladies in degrees aboute.
And other ladies on neighboring tiers.

Un-to the seetes preesseth al the route.
Into the seats pressed all the crowd.

And west-ward, thurgh the gates under Marte,
And westward, through the gates under Mars,

Arcite, and eek the hundred of his parte,   1724
Arcite, together with the hundred of his party,

With baner reed is entred right anon;
With red banner entered very soon;

And in that selve moment Palamon
And at that very moment Palamon

Is under Venus, est-ward in the place,
Was under Venus, on the eastern side,

With baner whyt, and hardy chere and face.   1728
With white banner, and hardy spirits and looks.

In al the world, to seken up and doun,
In all the world, though searched up and down,

So even with-outen variacioun,
So evenly matched without variation,

Ther nere swiche companyes tweye.
There never were two such companies.

For ther nas noon so wys that coude seye, 1732
For there was no one wise enough to say

That any hadde of other avauntage
That either had advantage of the other

Of worthinesse, ne of estaat, ne age,
In valor, or rank, or age,

So even were they chosen, for to gesse.
So evenly were they chosen, as I imagine.

And in two renges faire they hem dresse. 1736
And they dressed themselves fairly in two ranks.

Whan that hir names rad were everichoon,
When their names had all been read,

That in hir nombre gyle were ther noon,
So that there might be no trickery in their number,

Tho were the gates shet, and cryed was loude:
Then the gates were shut, and it was cried aloud:

"Do now your devoir, yonge knightes proude!" 1740
"Now show your mettle, proud young knights!"

The heraudes lefte hir priking up and doun;
The heralds left off their riding up and down;

Now ringen trompes loude and clarioun;
Then trumpets and clarions rang aloud;

Ther is namore to seyn, but west and est
There is no more to say, except that west and east

In goon the speres ful sadly in arest; 1744
The spears were fixed firmly in their rests;

In goth the sharpe spore in-to the syde.
The sharp spurs were pressed into the flanks.

Ther seen men who can juste, and who can ryde;
There men saw who could joust and ride;

Ther shiveren shaftes up-on sheeldes thikke;
There shivered shafts against stout shields;

He feleth thurgh the herte-spoon the prikke.   *1748*
One felt the stab through the breast-bone.

Up springen speres twenty foot on highte;
Up leaped spears twenty feet on high;

Out goon the swerdes as the silver brighte.
Out darted the swords bright as silver.

The helmes they to-hewen and to-shrede;
The helmets they hewed and split;

Out brest the blood, with sterne stremes rede.   *1752*
Out burst the blood in grim red streams.

With mighty maces the bones they to-breste.
With mighty maces they smashed the bones.

He thurgh the thikkeste of the throng gan threste,
One thrust through the thickest of the throng,

Ther stomblen stedes stronge, and doun goth al.
Strong steeds stumbled, and all went down.

He rolleth under foot as dooth a bal.   *1756*
One rolled under foot like a ball.

He foyneth on his feet with his tronchoun,
One fenced on his feet with his broken shaft,

And he him hurtleth with his hors adoun.
And one was hurled down with his horse.

He thurgh the body is hurt, and sithen y-take,
One was hurt through the body, and then captured,

Maugree his heed, and broght un-to the stake;   *1760*
In spite of himself, and brought to the stake;

As forward was, right ther he moste abyde;
As was agreed, he had to stay right there;

Another lad is on that other syde.
Another knight was at the other stake.

And som tyme dooth hem Theseus to reste,
And sometimes Theseus ordered them to rest,

Hem to refresshe, and drinken if hem leste.   1764
To refresh themselves, and drink if they pleased.

Ful ofte a-day han thise Thebanes two
Very often in the day the two Thebans

Togidre y-met, and wroght his felawe wo;
Clashed together, and wrought each other woe;

Unhorsed hath ech other of hem tweye.
Each one had unhorsed the other.

Ther nas no tygre in the vale of Galgopheye,   1768
There is no tiger in the valley of Gargaphia,

Whan that hir whelp is stole, whan it is lyte,
When her whelp is stolen, when it is little,

So cruel on the hunte, as is Arcite
So cruel to the hunter, as was Arcite

For jelous herte upon this Palamoun:
To Palamon because of his jealous heart:

Ne in Belmarye ther nis so fel leoun,   1772
Nor in Benmarin' is there so fierce a lion,

That hunted is, or for his hunger wood,
That is being hunted, or is mad of hunger,

Ne of his praye desireth so the blood,
Nor so desires the blood of its prey,

As Palamon to sleen his fo Arcite.
As Palamon to slay his foe Arcite.

The jelous strokes on hir helmes byte;   1776
The jealous strokes bit into their helmets;

Out renneth blood on both hir sydes rede.
Blood ran out red on both their sides.

    Som tyme an ende ther is of every dede;
    Some time there is an end of every deed;

For er the sonne un-to the reste wente,
For before the sun went to its rest,

The stronge king Emetreus gan hente   1780
The strong king Emetreus attempted to seize

This Palamon, as he faught with Arcite,
This Palamon, as he fought with Arcite,

And made his swerd depe in his flesh to byte;
And thrust his sword deep in his flesh;

And by the force of twenty is he take
And by the strength of twenty was he captured

Unyolden, and y-drawe unto the stake.   1784
Unyielding, and dragged to the stake.

And in the rescous of this Palamoun
And in the attempt to rescue Palamon

The stronge king Ligurge is born adoun;
The mighty king Lycurgus was borne down;

And king Emetreus, for al his strengthe,
And King Emetreus, for all his strength,

Is born out of his sadel a swerdes lengthe,   1788
Was borne a sword's length out of his saddle,

So hitte him Palamon er he were take,
So Palamon struck him before he was captured;

But al for noght, he was broght to the stake.
But all for nothing, he was brought to the stake.

His hardy herte mighte him helpe naught;
His staunch spirit could not help him;

He moste abyde, whan that he was caught,   1792
He must remain, after he was captured,

By force, and eek by composicioun.
By force, and also by agreement.

Who sorweth now but woful Palamoun,
Who sorrows now but woeful Palamon,

That moot namore goon agayn to fighte?
Who may never again return to the fight?

And whan that Theseus had seyn this sighte,   *1796*
And when Theseus had seen this sight,

Un-to the folk that foghten thus echoon
To those who were fighting in this fashion

He cryde, "Ho! namore, for it is doon!
He cried, "Ho! No more, for it is finished!

I wol be trewe juge, and no partye.
I will be a true and impartial judge.

Arcite of Thebes shal have Emelye,   *1800*
Arcite of Thebes shall have Emily,

That by his fortune hath hir faire y-wonne."
Who by his fortune has won her bravely."

Anon ther is a noyse of peple bigonne
At once there started a shouting of the people

For joye of this, so loude and heigh with-alle,
For joy of this, so loud and high withal,

It semed that the listes sholde falle.   *1804*
It seemed as if the lists would collapse.

    What can now faire Venus doon above?
    What now can fair Venus do above?

What seith she now? what dooth this quene of love?
What says she now? What does this queen of love?

But wepeth so, for wanting of hir wille,
She wept so, for the thwarting of her will,

Til that hir teres in the listes fille;   *1808*
Until her tears fell in the lists;

She seyde: "I am ashamed, doutelees."
She said: "I am put to shame, beyond a doubt."

Saturnus seyde: "Doghter, hold thy pees.
Saturn said: "Daughter, hold thy peace.

Mars hath his wille, his knight al his bone,
Mars hath his will, his knight hath his prayer granted,

And, by myn heed, thou shalt ben esed sone."   *1812*
And, by my head, thou shalt be eased soon."

The trompes, with the loude minstralcye,
The trumpets, with the loud minstrelsy,

The heraudes, that ful loude yolle and crye,
The heralds, that loudly shouted and cried,

Been in hir wele, for joye of daun Arcite.
Were in high spirits for joy of Sir Arcite.

But herkneth me, and stinteth now a lyte,   *1816*
But listen to me, and be quiet for a little,

Which a miracle ther bifel anon.
Because a miracle occurred forthwith.

This fierse Arcite hath of his helm y-don,
This fierce Arcite had taken off his helmet,

And on a courser, for to shewe his face,
And on a courser, to show his face,

He priketh endelong the large place,   *1820*
He spurred the length of the large place,

Loking upward up-on this Emelye;
Looking up to Emily;

And she agayn him caste a freendlich yë,
And she cast him a friendly glance in return,

(For wommen, as to speken in comune,
(For women, generally speaking,

They folwen al the favour of Fortune);   *1824*
Follow always the favor of Fortune);

And was al his in chiere, as in his herte.
And was entirely his in appearance, as in his heart.

Out of the ground a furie infernal sterte,
Out of the ground an infernal fury burst,

From Pluto sent, at requeste of Saturne,
Sent from Pluto, at Saturn's request,

For which his hors for fere gan to turne,   *1828*
For fear of which his horse began to turn

And leep asyde, and foundred as he leep;
And leap aside, and foundered as he leaped;

And, er that Arcite may taken keep,
And, before Arcite could take care,

He pighte him on the pomel of his heed,
Pitched him on the top of his head,

That in the place he lay as he were deed,   *1832*
So that he lay there as if he were dead,

His brest to-brosten with his sadel-bowe.
His breast broken by his saddle-bow.

As blak he lay as any cole or crowe,
As black he lay as any coal or crow,

So was the blood y-ronnen in his face.
So did the blood run into his face.

Anon he was y-born out of the place   *1836*
At once he was carried out of the lists

With herte soor, to Theseus paleys.
With aching heart, to Theseus' palace.

Tho was he corven out of his harneys,
Then was he cut out of his armor,

And in a bed y-brought ful faire and blyve,
And gently and swiftly laid in a bed,

For he was yet in memorie and alyve,   *1840*
For he was still conscious and alive,

And always crying after Emelye.
And ever crying for Emily.

 Duk Theseus, with al his companye,
 Duke Theseus, with all his company,

Is comen hoom to Athenes his citee,
Came home to his city of Athens

With alle blisse and greet solempnitee.   1844
With good cheer and great pomp.

Al be it that this aventure was falle,
Even though this mischance had occurred,

He nolde noght disconforten hem alle.
He would not have them all distressed.

Men seyde eek, that Arcite shal nat dye;
Besides, men said that Arcite would not die,

He shal ben heled of his maladye.   1848
But would be healed of his hurt.

And of another thing they were as fayn,
And they were also glad of another thing,

That of hem alle was ther noon y-slayn,
That of them all none was slain,

Al were they sore y-hurt, and namely oon,
Though they were badly wounded, especially one

That with a spere was thirled his brest-boon.   1852
Whose breastbone was pierced by a spear.

To othere woundes, and to broken armes,
For other wounds and for broken arms,

Some hadden salves, and some hadden charmes;
Some had salves and some had charms;

Fermacies of herbes, and eek save
Prescriptions of herbs, and sage too

They dronken, for they wolde hir limes have.   1856
They drank in order to keep their limbs.

For which this noble duk, as he wel can,
Wherefore this noble duke, as he well knew how,

Conforteth and honoureth every man,
Comforted and honored every man,

And made revel al the longe night,
And made revelry all night long

Un-to the straunge lordes, as was right.   *1860*
For the foreign lords, as was fitting.

Ne ther was holden no disconfitinge,
Nor was there felt any discomfiture

But as a justes or a tourneyinge;
Beyond that expected of joust or tournament,

For soothly ther was no disconfiture,
Indeed, there was no discomfiture at all,

For falling nis nat but an aventure;   *1864*
For falling is nothing but sport;

Ne to be lad with fors un-to the stake
Or to be led by force to the stake

Unyolden, and with twenty knightes take,
Unyielding, and captured by twenty knights,

O persone allone, with-outen mo,
One person alone, without help,

And haried forth by arme, foot, and to,   *1868*
And dragged out by arm, foot, and toe,

And eek his stede driven forth with staves,
And his steed also driven out with sticks

With footmen, bothe yemen and eek knaves,
By men on foot, both yeomen and pages,

It nas aretted him no vileinye,
Imputes no disgrace to anyone,

Ther may no man clepen it cowardye.   *1872*
Nor may any call it cowardice.

   For which anon duk Theseus leet crye,
   Wherefore, immediately, Duke Theseus proclaimed,

To stinten alle rancour and envye,
To end all rancor and envy,

The gree as wel ofo syde as of other,
The valor of one side to be equal to the other,

And either syde y-lyk, as otheres brother;   1876
And both sides alike, as brothers to each other;

And yaf hem yiftes after hir degree,
And gave them gifts according to their ranks,

And fully heeld a feste dayes three;
And held a feast fully three days;

And conveyed the kinges worthily
And worthily escorted the kings

Out of his toun a journee largely.   1880
Out of his town a whole day's ride.

And hoom wente every man the righte way.
And every man went his own way home.

Ther was namore, but "far wel, have good day!"
There was no more but, "Farewell, and good luck!"

Of this bataille I wol namore endyte,
Of this battle I will write no more,

But speke of Palamon and of Arcite.   1884
But speak of Palamon and of Arcite.

Swelleth the brest of Arcite, and the sore
The breast of Arcite swelled, and the hurt

Encreesseth at his herte more and more.
Pressed on his heart more and more.

The clothered blood, for any lechecraft,
The clotted blood, despite medical skill,

Corrupteth, and is in his bouk y-laft,   1888
Corrupted, and remained in his body,

That neither veyne-blood, ne ventusinge,
So that neither blood-letting nor operation,

Ne drinke of herbes may ben his helpinge.
Nor drink of herbs could help him.

The vertu expulsif, or animal,
The expulsive or animal virtue,

Fro thilke vertu cleped natural   1892
Called "natural" because of its function,

Ne may the venim voyden, ne expelle.
Could not void nor expell the poison.

The pypes of his longes gonne to swelle,
The tubes of his lungs became swollen,

And every lacerte in his brest adoun
And every muscle from his breast down

Is shent with venim and corrupcioun.   1896
Was defiled with poison and corruption.

Him gayneth neither, for to gete his lyf,
Neither did it aid him, to save his life,

Vomyt upward, ne dounward laxatif;
To vomit upward or excrete downward;

Al is to-brosten thilke regioun,
That region was completely crushed,

Nature hath now no dominacioun.   1900
The dominion of Nature was over.

And certeinly, ther nature wol nat wirche,
And certainly, where Nature will not work,

Far-wel, phisyk! go ber the man to chirche!
Farewell, medicine! Go carry the man to church!

This al and som, that Arcita mot dye,
This is the conclusion: Arcite had to die,

For which he sendeth after Emelye,   1904
Wherefore he sent for Emily

And Palamon, that was his cosin dere;
And Palamon, who was his cousin dear;

Than seyde he thus, as ye shul after here.
Then he spoke thus, as you shall now hear.

"Naught may the woful spirit in myn herte
"The woeful spirit in my heart cannot

Declare o poynt of alle my sorwes smerte 1908
Express a fraction of all my burning sorrows

To yow, my lady, that I love most;
To you, my lady, whom I love most;

But I biquethe the service of my gost
But I bequeath the service of my spirit

To yow aboven every creature,
To you above all creatures,

Sin that my lyf may no lenger dure. 1912
Since my life can no longer endure.

Allas, the wo! allas, the peynes stronge,
Alas, the woe! Alas, the sharp pains,

That I for yow have suffred, and so longe!
Which I have suffered for you, and so long!

Allas, the deeth! allas, myn Emelye!
Alas, the death! Alas, my Emily!

Allas, departing of our companye! 1916
Alas, the severing of our companionship!

Allas, myn hertes quene! allas, my wyf!
Alas, my heart's queen! Alas, my wife!

Myn hertes lady, endere of my lyf!
My heart's lady, ender of my life!

What is this world? what asketh men to have?
What is this world? What do men ask to have?

Now with his love, now in his colde grave 1920
Now with his love, now in his cold grave

Allone, with-outen any companye.
Alone, without any company.

Far-wel, my swete fo! myn Emelye!
Farewell, my sweet foe, my Emily!

And softe tak me in your armes tweye,
Take me gently in your two arms,

For love of God, and herkneth what I seye.   *1924*
For love of God, and listen to what I say.

"I have heer with my cosin Palamon
"Here with my cousin Palamon I have

Had stryf and rancour, many a day a-gon,
Had strife and rancor, for many a day gone by,

For love of yow, and for my jelousye.
Because of love of you and my jealousy.

And Jupiter so wis my soule gye,   *1928*
As I wish Jupiter to guide my soul,

To speken of a servant proprely,
To speak of a true lover,

With alle circumstaunces trewely,
With all befitting characteristics,

That is to seyn, trouthe, honour, and knighthede,
That is to say, truth, honor, and knighthood,

Wisdom, humblesse, estaat, and heigh kinrede,   *1932*
Wisdom, humility, rank, and exalted kindred,

Fredom, and al that longeth to that art,
Generosity, and all that belongs to the art of love,

So Jupiter have of my soule part,
So may Jupiter have part in my soul,

As in this world right now ne knowe I non
As in this world right now I know no one

So worthy to ben loved as Palamon,   *1936*
So worthy to be loved as Palamon,

That serveth yow, and wol don al his lyf.
Who serves you, and will all his life.

And if that ever ye shul been a wyf,
And if you shall ever be a wife,

Foryet nat Palamon, the gentil man."
Forget not Palamon, the noble man."

And with that word his speche faille gan,   1940
And with that word his speech failed him,

For from his feet up to his brest was come
For from his feet up to his breast had come

The cold of deeth, that hadde him overcome.
The chill of death that had overcome him.

And yet more-over, in his armes two
And then likewise, in his two arms

The vital strengthe is lost, and al ago.   1944
The vital strength was lost, and all was over.

Only the intellect, with-outen more,
Only then, and not before, the spirit

That dwelled in his herte syk and sore,
That dwelt in his sick and sore heart

Gan faillen, when the herte felte deeth,
Failed, when the heart felt death,

Dusked his eyen two, and failled breeth.   1948
His two eyes dimmed, and breath faltered.

But on his lady yet casté he his yë;
But on his lady still he cast his eyes;

His laste word was, "Mercy, Emelye!"
His last word was, "Mercy, Emily!"

His spirit chaunged hous, and wente ther,
His spirit changed homes, and went wherever,

As I cam never, I can nat tellen wher.   1952
Since I was never there, I cannot tell.

Therefor I stinte, I nam no divinistre;
Therefore I cease, I am no soothsayer;

Of soules finde I nat in this registre,
Souls I find not in the original text,

Ne me ne list thilke opiniouns to telle
Nor am I disposed to detail the opinions

Of hem, though that they wryten wher they dwelle.   *1956*
Of those who write about where they dwell.

Arcite is cold, ther Mars his soule gye;
Arcite is cold; now Mars guides his soul;

Now wol I speken forth of Emelye.
Now will I relate more of Emily.

Shrighte Emelye, and howleth Palamon,
Emily shrieked, and Palamon howled,

And Theseus his suster took anon   *1960*
And Theseus took his sister,

Swowninge, and bar hir fro the corps away.
Swooning, and carried her away from the corpse.

What helpeth it to tarien forth the day,
What avails it to continue all day

To tellen how she weep, bothe eve and morwe?
To tell how she wept, both evening and morning?

For in swich cas wommen have swich sorwe,   *1964*
For in such instances women have such grief,

Whan that hir housbonds been from hem ago,
When their husbands have departed from them,

That for the more part they sorwen so,
That for the greater part they sorrow so,

Or elles fallen in swich maladye,
Or else fall into such malady,

That at the laste certeinly they dye.   *1968*
That, at last, certainly they die.

Infinite been the sorwes and the teres
Infinite were the sorrows and the tears

Of olde folk, and folk of tendre yeres,
Of old people, and those of tender years,

In al the toun, for deeth of this Theban;
In all the town, for the death of this Theban;

For him ther wepeth bothe child and man;   1972
For him there wept both child and man;

So greet a weping was ther noon, certayn,
So great a weeping was there not, certainly,

When Ector was y-broght, al fresh y-slayn,
When Hector was brought, newly slain,

To Troye; allas! the pitee that was there,
To Troy; alas! the pathos that was there,

Cracching of chekes, rending eek of heer.   1976
Scratching of cheeks and rending of hair.

"Why woldestow be deed," thise wommen crye,
"Why should you be dead," the women cried,

"And haddest gold y-nough, and Emelye?"
"Who had gold enough, and Emily?"

No man mighte gladen Theseus,
No man could console Theseus

Savinge his olde fader Egeus,   1980
Except his old father Aegeus,

That knew this worldes transmutacioun,
Who knew this world's transformations,

As he had seyn it chaungen up and doun,
Since he had seen it change up and down,

Joye after wo, and wo after gladnesse:
Joy after woe, and woe after gladness:

And shewed hem ensamples and lyknesse.   1984
And showed them examples and similar events.

"Right as ther deyed never man" quod he,
"Just as no man ever died," said he,

"That he ne livede in erthe in som degree,
"Who did not live on earth in some manner,

Right so ther livede never man," he seyde,
So there never lived a man," he said,

"In al this world, that som tyme he ne deyde.   *1988*
"In all this world, who did not sometime die.

This world nis but a thurghfare ful of wo,
This world is but a thoroughfare full of woe,

And we ben pilgrimes, passinge to and fro;
And we are pilgrims, passing to and fro;

Deeth is an ende of every worldly sore."
Death is the end of every worldly pain."

And over al this yet seyde he muchel more   *1992*
And, besides this, he added much more

To this effect, ful wysly to enhorte
To the same effect, wisely to exhort

The peple, that they sholde hem reconforte.
The people to comfort themselves.

   Duk Theseus, with al his bisy cure,
   Duke Theseus, with all his earnest care,

Caste now wher that the sepulture   *1996*
Now wondered where the tomb

Of good Arcite may best y-maked be,
Of good Arcite might best be made,

And eek most honurable in his degree.
And be most honorable to his rank.

And at the laste he took conclusioun,
And at last he came to the conclusion

That ther as first Arcite and Palamoun   *2000*
That there where first Arcite and Palamon

Hadden for love the bataille hem bitwene,
Had fought for love between themselves,

That in that selve grove, swote and grene,
That in that same grove, sweet and green,

Ther as he hadde his amorous desires,
Where he had had his amorous desires,

His compleynt, and for love his hote fires,   2004
His complaining, and his hot flames of love,

He wolde make a fyr, in which th'office
He would build a pyre, on which the rituals

Funeral he mighte al accomplice;
Of burial might be performed;

And leet comaunde anon to hakke and hewe
And gave command forthwith to chop and split

The okes olde, and leye hem on a rewe   2008
The ancient oaks, and lay them in a row

In colpons wel arrayed for to brenne;
In lengths well designed for burning;

His officers with swifte feet they renne
His officers ran with swift feet

And ryde anon at his comaundement.
And rode at once to do his bidding.

And after this, Theseus hath y-sent   2012
And after this, Theseus sent

After a bere, and it al over-spradde
For a bier, and covered it all

With cloth of gold, the richest that he hadde.
With cloth of gold, the richest that he had.

And of the same suyte he cladde Arcite;
And with the same material he clad Arcite;

Upon his hondes hadde he gloves whyte;   2016
Who had white gloves on his hands,

Eek on his heed a croune of laurer grene,
And a crown of green laurel on his head,

And in his hond a swerd ful bright and kene.
And in his hand a sword most bright and sharp.

He leyde him, bare the visage, on the bere,
He laid him, face uncovered, on the bier,

Therewith he weep that pitee was to here.   2020
Whereat he wept so that it was a pity to hear.

And for the peple sholde seen him alle,
And so that all the people could see him,

Whan it was day, he broghte him to the halle,
When it was day, he brought him to the hall

That roreth of the crying and the soun.
Which resounded with the crying and the wails.

Tho cam this woful Theban Palamoun,   2024
Then came this woeful Theban Palamon,

With flotery berd, and ruggy asshy heres,
With unkempt beard, and hair roughened with ashes,

In clothes blake, y-dropped al with teres;
In black clothes, all wet with tears;

And, passing othere of weping, Emelye,
And, passing others in weeping, Emily,

The rewfulleste of al the companye.   2028
The most mournful of all the company.

In as muche as the service sholde be
In order that the service might be

The more noble and riche in his degree,
More noble and richer in its performance,

Duk Theseus leet forth three stedes bringe,
Duke Theseus had three steeds brought forth,

That trapped were in steel al gliteringe,   2032
Which were all harnessed in glittering steel,

And covered with the armes of daun Arcite.
And covered with the arms of Sir Arcite.

Up-on thise stedes, that weren grete and whyte,
Upon these steeds, which were massive and white,

Ther seten folk, of which oon bar his sheeld,
Men were placed, of whom one carried his shield,

Another his spere up in his hondes heeld;   2036
Another held his spear up in his hands;

The thridde bar with him his bowe Turkeys,
The third bore with him his Turkish bow,

Of brend gold was the cas, and eek the harneys;
Of burnished gold was the quiver and the mounting;

And riden forth a pas with sorweful chere
And they rode forth at a walk with sorrowful spirits

Toward the grove, as ye shul after here.   2040
Toward the grove, as you shall soon hear.

The nobleste of the Grekes that ther were
The noblest of the Greeks who were there

Upon hir shuldres carieden the bere,
Carried the bier on their shoulders,

With slakke pas, and eyen rede and wete,
With slow pace, and eyes red and wet,

Thurgh-out the citee, by the maister-strete,   2044
Throughout the city, by the main street,

That sprad was al with blak, and wonder hye
Which was all spread with black, and wondrous high

Right of the same is al the strete y-wrye.
All the street was hung in the same way.

Up-on the right hond wente old Egeus,
On the right hand went old Aegeus,

And on the other syde duk Theseus,   2048
And on the other side, Duke Theseus,

With vessels in hir hand of gold ful fyn,
With vessels of finest gold in their hands,

Al ful of hony, milk, and blood, and wyn;
All full of honey, milk, and blood, and wine;

Eek Palamon, with ful greet companye;
Then can 2 Palamon, with a great company;

And after that cam woful Emelye, 2052
And after that came woeful Emily,

With fyr in honde, as was that tyme the gyse,
With fire in her hand, as was the custom then,

To do th'office of funeral servyse.
To perform the ritual of funeral service.

Heigh labour, and ful greet apparaillinge
Great labor, and most elaborate ceremony

Was at the service and the fyr-makinge 2056
Was at the service and the making of the pyre

That with his grene top the heven raughte,
That reached heaven with its green top,

And twenty fadme of brede the armes straughte;
And twenty fathoms wide the arms stretched;

This is to seyn, the bowes were so brode,
That is to say, the branches were so broad.

Of stree first ther was leyd ful many a lode. 2060
First there was laid many a load of straw.

But how the fyr was maked up on highte,
But how the pyre was built up on high,

And eek the names how the treës highte,
And also the names of the trees,

As ook, firre, birch, asp, alder, holm, popler,
Such as oak, fir, birch, aspen, alder, holm, poplar,

Wilow, elm, plane, ash, box, chasteyn, lind, laurer, 2064
Willow, elm, plane, ash, box, chestnut, linden, laurel,

Mapul, thorn, beech, hasel, ew, whippel-tree,
Maple, thorn, beech, hazel, yew, cornel-tree,

How they weren feld, shal nat be told for me;
How they were felled, shall not be told by me;

Ne how the goddes ronnen up and doun,
Nor how the gods ran up and down,

Disherited of hir habitacioun,   2068
Dispossessed from their dwelling,

In which they woneden in reste and pees,
In which they had lived in rest and peace,

Nymphes, Faunes, and Amadrides;
Nymphs, fauns, and hamadryads;

Ne how the bestes and the briddes alle
Nor how all the beasts and birds

Fledden for fere, whan the wode was falle;   2072
Fled for fear, when the trees were felled;

Ne how the ground agast was of the light,
Nor how the ground was aghast at the light,

That was nat wont to seen the sonne bright;
Not being used to seeing the bright sun;

Ne how the fyr was couched first with stree,
Nor how the fire was laid first with straw,

And than with drye stokkes cloven a three,   2076
And then with dry sticks cleft in thirds,

And than with grene wode and spycerye,
And then with green wood and spices,

And than with cloth of gold and with perrye,
And then with cloth of gold and with jewelry,

And gerlandes hanging with ful many a flour,
And garlands hanging with many a flower,

The mirre, th'encens, with al so greet odour;   2080
The myrrh, the incense, with such strong odors;

Ne how Arcite lay among al this,
Nor how Arcite lay amongst all this,

Ne what richesse aboute his body is;
Nor what wealth was about his body;

Ne how that Emelye, as was the gyse,
Nor how Emily, as was the custom,

Putte in the fyr of funeral servyse; 2084
Placed the sacramental fire at the base;

Ne how she swowned whan men made the fyr,
Nor how she swooned when men built up the fire,

Ne what she spak, ne what was hir desyr;
Nor what she spoke, nor what she felt;

Ne what jeweles men in the fyr tho caste,
Nor what jewels men then cast into the fire

Whan that the fyr was greet and brente faste; 2088
When the flames were high and ·burning fast;

Ne how som caste hir sheeld, and som hir spere,
Nor how some hurled their shields, and some their spears,

And of hir vestiments, whiche that they were,
And parts of their clothes which they were wearing,

And cuppes ful of wyn, and milk, and blood,
And cups full of wine, and milk, and blood,

Into the fyr, that brente as it were wood; 2092
Into the fire that blazed like mad;

Ne how the Grekes with an huge route
Nor how the Greeks in a huge mass

Thryës riden al the fyr aboute
Thrice rode all about the fire

Up-on the left hand, with a loud shoutinge,
Keeping it on the left, with a loud shouting,

And thryës with hir speres clateringe; 2096
And thrice with their spears clattering;

And thryës how the ladies gonne crye;
And how the ladies thrice cried out;

Ne how that lad was hom-ward Emelye;
Nor how Emily was led homeward;

Ne how Arcite is brent to asshen colde;
Nor how Arcite was burned to ashes cold;

Ne how that liche-wake was y-holde   2100
Nor how the wake was held

Al thilke night, ne how the Grekes pleye
All that night, nor how the Greeks performed

The wake-pleyes, ne kepe I nat to seye;
The funeral games, I do not intend to say;

Who wrastleth best naked, with oille enoynt,
Who wrestled best naked, anointed with oil,

Ne who that bar him best, in no disjoynt.   2104
Nor who comported himself best in difficulty.

I wol nat tellen eek how that they goon
Neither will I tell how they went

Hoom til Athenes, whan the pley is doon;
Home to Athens, when the games were done;

But shortly to the poynt than wol I wende,
But instead I will come briefly to the point,

And maken of my longe tale an ende.   2108
And make an end of my long tale.

   By processe and by lengthe of certeyn yeres
   Through the passing and duration of some years

Al stinted is the moorning and the teres.
The mourning and the tears came to an end.

Of Grekes, by oon general assent,
Among the Greeks, by general agreement,

Than semed me ther was a parlement   2112
I understand, there was then a parliament

At Athenes, up-on certeyn poynts and cas;
At Athens, on certain points and matters;

Among the whiche poynts y-spoken was
Among which points it was suggested

To have with certeyn contrees alliaunce,
That alliances be made with certain countries,

And have fully of Thebans obeisaunce. 2116
And that Theban submission be made absolute.

For which this noble Theseus anon
Wherefore this noble Theseus at once

Leet senden after gentil Palamon,
Caused noble Palamon to be sent for,

Unwist of him what was the cause and why;
Without his knowing the why or wherefore;

But in his blake clothes sorwefully 2120
But sorrowfully in his black clothes

He cam at his comaundemente in hye.
He came in haste at his command.

Tho sente Theseus for Emelye.
Then Theseus sent for Emily.

Whan they were set, and hust was al the place,
When they had sat down, and all the place was quiet,

And Theseus abiden hadde a space 2124
And Theseus had waited for a while

Er any word cam from his wyse brest,
Before any word proceeded from his wise breast,

His eyen sette he ther as was his lest,
His eyes he turned where he pleased,

And with a sad visage he syked stille,
And with a sad countenance he sighed quietly,

And after that right thus he seyde his wille. 2128
And after that, exactly thus he spoke his will.

"The firste moevere of the cause above,
"The Prime Mover of the Heavenly Rule,

Whan he first made the faire cheyne of love,
When He first made the fair chain of love,

Greet was th'effect, and heigh was his entente;
Great was the result, and exalted was His intention;

Wel wiste he why, and what ther-of he mente;   *2132*
He well knew why, and what He meant by it;

For with that faire cheyne of love he bond
For with that fair chain of love He bound

The fyr, the eyr, the water, and the lond
The fire, the air, the water, and the land

In certeyn boundes, that they may nat flee:
In fixed bonds which they may not escape:

That same prince and that moevere," quod he,   *2136*
That same Prince and that Mover," said he,

"Hath stablissed, in this wrecched world adoun,
"Has established, in this wretched world below,

Certeyne dayes and duracioun
Certain days and length of time

To al that is engendred in this place,
To everything that is engendered here,

Over the whiche day they may nat pace,   *2140*
Beyond which period they may not pass,

Al mowe they yet tho dayes wel abregge;
Although they may well shorten their days;

Ther needeth non auctoritee allegge,
There is no need to quote any authority,

For it is preved by experience,
For it is proved by experience,

But that me list declaren my sentence.   *2144*
Rather would I declare my thoughts.

Than may men by this ordre wel discerne
Then by this order men can well discern

That thilke moevere stable is and eterne.
That yonder Mover is stable and eternal.

Wel may men knowe, but it be a fool,
Men may well know, unless they are fools,

That every part deryveth from his hool.   2148
That every part is derived from its whole.

For nature hath nat take his beginning
For nature did not take its origin

Of no party ne cantel of a thing,
From any part or fragment of a thing,

But of a thing that parfit is and stable,
But of something that is perfect and stable,

Descending so, til it be corrumpable.   2152
Descending from it until it became corruptible.

And therefore, of his wyse purveyaunce,
And therefore, out of His wise foresight,

He hath so wel biset his ordinaunce,
He has so well arranged His ordering

That speces of thinges and progressiouns
That species of things and progressions

Shullen enduren by successiouns,   2156
Shall endure by succession,

And nat eterne be, with-oute lyë:
And not be eternal, I do not lie:

This maistow understonde and seen at yë.
This you may understand and see with your eyes.

   "Lo the ook, that hath so long a norisshinge
   "Behold the oak, that has so long an infancy

From tyme that it first beginneth springe,   2160
From the time it first begins to sprout,

And hath so long a lyf, as we may see,
And has so long a life, as we may see,

Yet at the laste wasted is the tree.
Yet at length the tree decays.

   "Considereth eek, how that the harde stoon
   "Consider too, how hard the stone is

Under our feet, on which we trede and goon, 2164
Under our feet, on which we tread and walk,

Yit wasteth it, as it lyth by the weye.
Yet it crumbles as it lies by the way.

The brode river somtyme wexeth drye.
The broad river eventually goes dry.

The grete tounes see we wane and wende.
The great towns we see wane and disappear.

Than may ye see that al this thing hath ende. 2168
Thus may you see that all things have an end.

"Of man and womman seen we wel also,
"Concerning man and woman we see well also

That nedeth, in oon of thise termes two,
That it is required, in one of these two times,

This is to seyn, in youthe or elles age,
That is to say, in youth or else in age,

He moot ben deed, the king as shal a page; 2172
That he must die, the king as well as a page;

Som in his bed, som in the depe see,
One in his bed, one in the deep sea,

Som in the large feeld, as men may se;
One in the open field, as men may see;

Ther helpeth noght, al goth that ilke weye.
Nothing avails, all go the same way.

Thanne may I seyn that al this thing moot deye. 2176
Thus I may say that everything must die.

What maketh this but Jupiter the king?
What causes this but Jupiter the King?

The which is prince and cause of alle thing,
He is Prince and Cause of everything,

Converting al un-to his propre welle,
Converting all things to their own sources

From which it is deryved, sooth to telle. 2180
From which they were derived, truly speaking.

And here-agayns no creature on lyve
And against this no creature alive

Of no degree availleth for to stryve.
Of any degree may gain anything by striving.

"Thanne is it wisdom, as it thinketh me,
"Therefore it is wisdom, as it seems to me,

To maken vertu of necessitee, 2184
To make a virtue of necessity,

And take it wel, that we may nat eschue,
And take well whatever we cannot avoid,

And namely that to us alle is due.
And especially that which is due us all.

And who-so gruccheth ought, he dooth folye,
And whoever murmurs at all does foolishly,

And rebel is to him that al may gye. 2188
And is a rebel to Him Who directs all things.

And certeinly a man hath most honour
And certainly a man has most honor

To dyen in his excellence and flour,
To die in his prime and flower,

Whan he is siker of his gode name;
When he is sure of his good name;

Than hath he doon his freend, ne him, no shame. 2192
Then has he done no shame to his friend or himself.

And gladder oghte his freend ben of his deeth,
And his friend ought to be more glad of his death,

Whan with honour up-yolden is his breeth,
When with honor he yielded up his breath,

Than whan his name apalled is for age;
Than when his name had faded with age;

For al forgeten is his vasselage.   2196
For all forgotten are his exploits.

Than is it best, as for a worthy fame,
Thus it is best, for a worthy reputation,

To dyen whan that he is best of name.
To die when one is in the height of fame.

The contrarie of al this is wilfulnesse.
The contrary of all this is willfulness.

Why grucchen we? Why have we hevinesse   2200
Why grumble we? Why are we heavy-hearted

That good Arcite, of chivalrye flour,
That good Arcite, the flower of chivalry,

Departed is, with duetee and honour,
Has departed, in duty and honor,

Out of this foule prison of this lyf?
Out of the foul prison of this life?

Why grucchen heer his cosin and his wyf   2204
Why murmur here his cousin and his wife,

Of his wel-fare that loved hem so weel?
Who loved him so well, about his welfare?

Can he hem thank? nay, God wot, never a deel,
Can he thank them? No, God knows, never a bit,

That bothe his soule and eek hem-self offende,
But they offend his soul and themselves too,

And yet they mowe hir lustes nat amende.   2208
And yet they do not satisfy their own desires.

"What may I conclude of this longe serie,
"What must I conclude from this long argument,

But, after wo, I rede us to be merie
But that, after woe, I advise us to be merry

And thanken Jupiter of al his grace?
And thank Jupiter for all His grace?

And, er that we departen from this place,   *2212*
And, before we depart from this place,

I rede that we make, of sorwes two,
I advise that we make, of two sorrows,

O parfyt joye, lasting ever-mo;
One perfect joy, enduring evermore;

And loketh now, wher most sorwe is her-inne,
So look now for the greatest sorrow here,

Ther wol we first amenden and biginne.   *2216*
There will we first begin to make amends.

"Suster," quod he, "this is my fulle assent,
"Sister," said he, "this is my complete wish,

With al th'avys heer of my parlement,
With the full agreement here of my parliament,

That gentil Palamon, your owne knight,
That noble Palamon, your own knight,

That serveth yow with wille, herte, and might,   *2220*
Who serves you with his will, heart, and strength,

And ever hath doon, sin that ye first him knewe,
And ever has, since you first knew him,

That ye shul, of your grace, up-on him rewe,
That you shall, by your grace, have pity on him,

And taken him for housbonde and for lord:
And take him for husband and for lord:

Leen me your hond, for this is our acord.   *2224*
Give me your hand, for this is our decision.

Lat see now of your wommanly pitee.
Let your womanly pity now be seen.

He is a kinges brother sone, pardee;
He is a king's brother's son, by the Lord;

And, though he were a povre bacheler,
And, though he were a poor aspirant for knighthood,

Sin he hath served yow so many a yeer,   2228
Since he has served you so many a year,

And had for yow so greet adversitee,
And suffered for you such great adversity,

It moste been considered, leveth me;
That should be considered, believe me;

For gentil mercy oghte to passen right."
For gentle mercy ought to surpass justice."

Than seyde he thus to Palamon ful right;   2232
Then he spoke thus to Palamon in turn:

"I trowe ther nedeth litel sermoning
"I believe there is need of little lecturing

To make yow assente to this thing.
To make you agree to this thing.

Com neer, and tak your lady by the hond."
Come near, and take your lady by the hand."

Bitwixen hem was maad anon the bond,   2236
Between them was made at once the bond

That highte matrimoine or mariage,
That is called matrimony or marriage,

By al the conseil and the baronage.
By all the council and the baronage.

And thus with alle blisse and melodye
And thus with perfect bliss and melody

Hath Palamon y-wedded Emelye.   2240
Palamon wedded Emily.

And God, that al this wyde world hath wroght,
And God, Who made all this wide world,

Sende him his love, that hath it dere a-boght.
Send him perfect love, who bought it so dearly.

For now is Palamon in alle wele,
For now Palamon has all good things,

Living in blisse, in richesse, and in hele;   2244
Living in bliss, in wealth, and in health;

And Emelye him loveth so tenderely,
And Emily loves him so tenderly,

And he hir serveth al-so gentilly,
And he too serves her so gently.

That never was ther no word hem bitwene
That there has never been a word between them

Of jelousye, or any other tene.   2248
Of jealousy, or any other trouble.

Thus endeth Palamon and Emelye;
Thus end Palamon and Emily;

And God save al this faire companye!—Amen.
And God save all this fair company!—Amen.

Prologue to the Miller's Tale

Whan that the Knight had thus his tale y-told,
When the Knight had thus told his tale,

In all the route nas ther young ne old
In all the group was there neither young nor old

That he ne seyde it was a noble storie,
Who did not say it was a noble story,

And worthy for to drawen to memorie;   **4**
And worthy to be kept in memory;

And namely the gentils everichoon.
And principally the gentlefolk everyone.

Our Hoste lough and swoor, "so moot I goon,
Our Host laughed and swore, "as I hope to stay alive,

This gooth aright; unbokeled is the male;
This goes properly; unbuckled is the bag;

Lat see now who shal telle another tale: **8**
Let's see now who shall tell another tale:

For trewely, the game is wel bigonne.
For truly, the game is well begun.

Now telleth ye, sir Monk, if that ye conne,
Now you tell, Sir Monk, if you know how,

Sumwhat, to quyte with the Knightes tale."
Something, to match the Knight's tale."

The Miller, that for-dronken was al pale,   12
The Miller, who was pale from drunkenness,

So that unnethe up-on his hors he sat,
So that he could scarcely sit on his horse,

He nolde avalen neither hood ne hat,
He could not doff either his hood or hat,

Ne abyde no man for his curteisye,
Nor courteously give way to anyone,

But in Pilates vois he gan to crye,   16
But in Pilate's voice he began to cry,

And swoor by armes and by blood and bones,
And swore by arms and by blood and bones,[1]

"I can a noble tale for the nones,
"I know a noble tale for this occasion,

With which I wol now quyte the Knightes tale."
With which I will now equal the Knight's tale."

Our Hoste saugh that he was dronke of ale,   20
Our Host saw that he was drunk with ale,

And seyde: "abyd, Robin, my leve brother,
And said: "Hold on, Robin, my dear brother,

Som bettre man shal telle us first another:
Some better man shall tell us another first:

Abyd and lat us werken thriftily."
Be patient and let us work profitably."

"By goddes soul," quod he, "that wol nat I;   24
"By God's soul," said he, "that I will not;

For I wol speke, or elles go my wey."
For I will speak, or else go on my way."

Our Hoste answerde: "tel on, a devel wey!
Our Host answered: "Tell on, devil take you!

Thou art a fool, thy wit is overcome."
You are a fool, your brains are befuddled."

"Now herkneth," quod the Miller, "alle and some!   *28*
"Now listen," said the Miller, "each and all!

But first I make a protestacioun
But first I make a protestation

That I am dronke, I knowe it by my soun;
That I am drunk, I know it by the way I sound;

And therefore, if that I misspeke or seye,
And therefore, if I don't talk straight,

Wyte it the ale of Southwerk, I yow preye;   *32*
Blame it on the Southwerk ale, I beg you;

For I wol telle a legende and a lyf
For I will tell a legend and a life

Bothe of a Carpenter, and of his wyf,
Both of a Carpenter, and of his wife,

How that a clerk hath set the wrightes cappe."
How a clerk got the better of the tradesman."

The Reve answerde and seyde, "stint thy clappe,   *36*
The Reve answered and said, "Stop your chatter,

Lat be thy lewed dronken harlotrye.
Give up your lewd drunken lasciviousness.

It is a sinne and eek a greet folye
It is a sin and a great folly too

To apeiren any man, or him diffame.
To injure any man, or defame him.

And eek to bringen wyves in swich fame.   *40*
And also to besmirch the reputation of wives.

Thou mayst y-nogh of othere thinges seyn."
You may talk enough about other things."

This dronken Miller spak ful sone ageyn,
This drunken Miller spoke again immediately,

And seyde, "leve brother Osewold,
And said, "Dear brother Oswald,

Who hath no wyf, he is no cokewold.   44
Whoever has no wife is not a cuckold.

But I sey nat therfore that thou art oon;
But I don't say therefore that you are one;

Ther been ful gode wyves many oon,
There are plenty of good wives,

And ever a thousand gode ayeyns oon badde,
And ever a thousand good for one bad,

That knowestow wel thy-self, but-if thou madde.   48
You know that well yourself, unless you're out of your mind.

Why artow angry with my tale now?
Why are you angry with my tale now?

I have a wyf, pardee, as well as thou,
I have a wife, by Heaven, as well as you,

Yet nolde I, for the oxen in my plogh,
Yet I wouldn't, for the oxen in my plow,

Taken up-on me more than y-nogh,   52
Take upon myself more than enough,

As demen of my-self that I were oon;
As to believe that I was a cuckold;

I wol beleve wel that I am noon.
I will assure myself that I am not.

An housbond shal nat been inquisitif
A husband should not be inquisitive

Of goddes privetee, nor of his wyf.   56
Of God's privacy, nor of his wife's.

So he may finde goddes foyson there,
As long as he finds God's plenty there,

Of the remenant nedeth nat enquere."
There is no point in asking about anything that's left over."

What sholde I more seyn, but this Millere
What more should I say, but that this Miller

He nolde his wordes for no man forbere,   60
Would not stop his flow of words for anybody,

But tolde his cherles tale in his manere;
But told his churlish tale in his own way;

Methinketh that I shal reherce it here.
I think that I shall repeat it here.

And ther-fore every gentil wight I preye,
And therefore I beg of every genteel person,

For goddes love, demeth nat that I seye   64
For God's love, don't believe that I speak

Of evel entente, but that I moot reherce
With evil intent, but that I must repeat

Hir tales alle, be they bettre or werse,
All their tales, be they better or worse,

Or elles falsen som of my matere.
Or else falsify some of my material.

And therfore, who-so list it nat y-here,   68
And therefore, whoever prefers not to hear it,

Turne over the leef, and chese another tale;
Turn over the page, and choose another tale;

For he shal finde y-nowe, grete and smale,
For he will find enough, large and small,

Of storial thing that toucheth gentillesse,
Of storied things that concern gentility,

And eek moralitee and holinesse;   72
And also morality and holiness;

Blameth nat me if that ye chese amis.
Don't blame me if you choose amiss.

The Miller is a cherl, ye knowe wel this;
The Miller is a churl, you know this well;

So was the Reve, and othere many mo.
So was the Reve, and many more of the others.

And harlotrye they tolden bothe two.   76
And both of them told bawdy tales.

Avyseth yow and putte me out of blame;
Make up your minds and don't put the blame on me;

And eek men shal nat make ernest of game.
And besides people should not take fun seriously.

The Miller's Tale

Whylom ther was dwellinge at Oxenford
Once there was living at Oxford

A riche gnof, that gestes heeld to bord,
A rich scoundrel, who took in paying guests,

And of his craft he was a Carpenter.
And who was a carpenter by trade.

With him ther was dwellinge a povre scoler,   4
With him was living a poor scholar,

Had lerned art, but al his fantasye
Who was learned in the art, but all his desire

Was turned for to lerne astrologye,
Was in the direction of mastering astrology,

And coude a certeyn of conclusiouns
And knew a certain number of answers

To demen by interrogaciouns,   8
To satisfy his questioners,

If that men axed him in certein houres,
If someone asked him in certain astrological hours,

Whan that men sholde have droghte or elles shoures,
When people would have drought or else showers,

Or if men axed him what sholde bifalle
Or if people asked him what the future would be

Of every thing, I may nat rekene hem alle.   *12*
Of everything, I can't describe them all.

   This clerk was cleped hende Nicholas;
   This student was called Slick Nicholas;

Of derne love he coude and of solas;
He knew about secret love and pleasure;

And there-to he was sleigh and ful privee,
And in this he was sly and most discreet,

And lyk a mayden meke for to see.   *16*
And appeared to be as meek as a maid.

A chambre hadde he in that hostelrye
He had a room in that hostelry

Allone, with-outen any companye,
Alone, with no one to share it,

Ful fetisly y-dight with herbes swote;
Most pleasantly supplied with sweet herbs;

And he him-self as swete as is the rote   *20*
And he himself was as sweet as the root

Of licorys, or any cetewale.
Of licorice, or any fragrant East Indian drug.

His Almageste and bokes grete and smale,
His Almagest and other astrological books, large and small,

His astrelabie, longinge for his art,
His astrolabe, connected with his art,

His augrim-stones layen faire a-part   *24*
His calculating counters were well arranged

On shelves couched at his beddes heed:
On shelves placed at the head of his bed:

His presse y-covered with a falding reed.
His clothes-press was covered with a coarse red cloth.

And al above ther lay a gay sautrye,
And on it lay a gay psaltery,

On which he made a nightes melodye   28
On which he played a night-time melody

So swetely, that al the chambre rong;
So sweetly that all the bedroom rang;

And *Angelus ad virginem* he song;
And The Annunciation to the Virgin he sang;

And after that he song the kinges note;
And after that he sang The King's Tune;

Ful often blessed was his mery throte.   32
Very often was his merry throat blessed.

And thus this swete clerk his tyme spente
And thus this sweet student spent his time

After his freendes finding and his rente.
With the help of his friends' donations and his own income.

  This Carpenter had wedded newe a wyf
  This carpenter had newly wedded a wife

Which that he lovede more than his lyf;   36
Whom he loved more than his life;

Of eightetene yeer she was of age.
She was eighteen years old.

Jalous he was, and heeld hir narwe in cage,
Jealous he was, and held her closely caged,

For she was wilde and yong, and he was old
For she was wild and young, and he was old

And demed him-self ben lyk a cokewold.   40
And believed himself likely to become a cuckold.

He knew nat Catoun, for his wit was rude,
He did not know Cato, for his learning was skimpy,

That bad man sholde wedde his similitude.
Who counselled men to wed their likes.

Men sholde wedden after hir estaat,
Men should marry in accordance with their conditions,

For youthe and elde is often at debaat.   44
For youth and old age often disagree.

But sith that he was fallen in the snare,
But since he had fallen into the trap,

He moste endure, as othei folk, his care.
He had to endure his troubles like other people.

  Fair was this yonge wyf, and ther-with-al
  Fair was this young wife, and moreover

As any wesele hir body gent and smal.   48
Her body was as slender and tiny as a weasel.

A ceynt she werede barred al of silk,
She wore a girdle of striped silk,

A barmclooth eek as whyt as morne milk
Also an apron as white as morning milk

Up-on hir lendes, ful of many a gore.
Upon her loins, flaring outward from top to bottom.

Whyt was hir smok and brouded al bifore   52
White was her smock and embroidered both in front

And eek bihinde, on hir color aboute,
And behind, all around her collar,

Of col-blak silk, with-inne and eek withoute.
With coal-black silk, both inside and out.

The tapes of hir whyte voluper
The tapes of her white cap

Were of the same suyte of hir coler;   56
Were of the same pattern as her collar;

Hir filet brood of silk, and set ful hye;
Her headband was made of broad silk, and set quite high;

And sikerly she hadde a likerous yë.
And surely she had a wanton eye.

Ful smale y-pulled were hir browes two,
Finely plucked were her two eyebrows,

And tho were bent, and blake as any sloo.   60
And they were arched, and black as any sloe.

She was ful more blisful on to see
She was much more blissful to look at

Than is the newe pere-jonette tree;
Than is the young early-ripening pear tree;

And softer than the wolle is of a wether.
And softer than the wool of a sheep.

And by hir girdel heeng a purs of lether   64
And from her girdle hung a leather purse

Tasseld with silk, and perled with latoun.
Tasseled with silk and decorated with metal.

In al this world, to seken up and doun,
In all this world, to search up and down,

There nis no man so wys, that coude thenche
There is no man so wise who could imagine

So gay a popelote, or swich a wenche.   68
So delicious a poppet, or such a lass.

Ful brighter was the shyning of hir hewe
Much brighter was the shining of her complexion

Than in the tour the noble y-forged newe.
Than a gold coin newly minted in the Tower.

But of hir song, it was as loude and yerne
But of her singing, it was as loud and lively

As any swalwe sitting on a berne.   72
As any swallow sitting on a barn.

Ther-to she coulde skippe and make game
Besides, she could skip and be as playful

As any kide or calf folwinge his dame.
As any kid or calf pursuing his dam.

Hir mouth was swete as bragot or the meeth,
Her mouth was as sweet as honeyed ale or mead,

Or hord of apples leyd in hey or heeth.   76
Or hord of apples stored in hay or field.

Winsinge she was as is a joly colt
Skittish she was as is a jolly colt

Long as a mast and upright as a bolt.
Tall as a mast and straight as a crossbow-bolt.

A brooch she baar up-on hir lowe coler,
A brooch she wore near the bottom of her collar,

As brood as is the bos of a bocler.   80
As broad as the boss of a buckler.

Hir shoes were laced on hir legges hye;
Her shoes were laced high on her legs;

She was a prymerole, a pigges-nye
She was a primrose, a dainty blossom

For any lord to leggen in his bedde,
For any lord to lay in his bed,

Or yet for any good yeman to wedde.   84
Or else for any good yeoman to wed.

Now sire, and eft, sire, so bifel the cas
Now Sir, and again, Sir, it so happened

That on a day this hende Nicholas
That on a day this slick Nicholas

Fil with this yonge wyf to rage and pleye,
Happened to be toying and playing with this young wife,

Whyl that hir housbond was at Oseneye,   88
While her husband was at Oseney,

As clerkes ben ful subtile and ful queynte;
(Students being most subtle and most devious)

And prively he caughte hir by the queynte,
And slyly he caught her by the cunt,

And seyde, "y-wis, but if ich have my wille,
And said, "Truly, unless I have my will,

For derne love of thee, lemman, I spille."   92
For secret love of you, sweetheart, I'll die."

And heeld hir harde by the haunche-bones,
And held her tight by the thigh-bones,

And seyde, "lemman, love me al at-ones,
And said, "Sweetheart, love me instantly,

Or I wol dyen, also god me save!"
Or I will die, as I hope to be saved!"

And she sprong as a colt doth in the trave,   96
And she sprang as a colt does in a confining stall,

And with hir heed she wryed faste awey,
And turned her head suddenly aside,

And seyde, "I wol nat kisse thee, by my fey,
And said, "I will not kiss you, by my faith,

Why, lat be," quod she, "lat be, Nicholas,
Why, let go," said she, "let go, Nicholas,

Or I wol crye out 'harrow' and 'allas.'   100
Or I will cry out 'help' and 'alas.'

Do wey your handes for your curteisye!"
Take your hands off for the sake of your manners!"

  This Nicholas gan mercy for to crye,
This Nicholas began to beg for mercy,

And spak so faire, and profred hir so faste,
And spoke so well, and propositioned her so eagerly,

That she hir love him graunted atte laste,   104
That she promised him her love at last,

And swoor hir ooth, by seint Thomas of Kent,
And swore her oath, by Saint Thomas of Kent,

That she wol been at his comandement,
That she would be at his bidding

Whan that she may hir leyser wel espye.
When she could find the opportunity.

"Myn housbond is so ful of jalousye, 108
"My husband is so full of jealousy,

That but ye wayte wel and been privee,
That unless you are patient and secretive,

I woot right wel I nam but deed," quod she.
I know very well that I'm a dead one," said she.

"Ye moste been ful derne, as in this case."
"You must be very careful in a situation like this."

"Nay, ther-of care thee noght," quod Nicholas, 112
"No, don't worry about that," said Nicholas,

"A clerk had litherly biset his whyle
"A student has poorly spent his time

But-if he coude a carpenter bigyle."
If he can't fool a carpenter."

And thus they been accorded and y-sworn
And thus they have agreed and sworn

To wayte a tyme, as I have told biforn. 116
To wait for an opportunity, as I have said.

Whan Nicholas had doon thus everydeel
When Nicholas had accomplished all of this

And thakked hir aboute the lendes weel,
And patted her well around her thighs,

He kist hir swete, and taketh his sautrye,
He kissed her sweetly, and took his psaltery,

And pleyeth faste, and maketh melodye. 120
And played a lively melody.

Than fil it thus, that to the parish-chirche,
Then it so happened that to the parish church,

Cristes owne werkes for to wirche,
To perform her devotions to Christ,

This gode wyf went on an haliday;
This good wife went on a holy day;

Hir forheed shoon as bright as any day,   124
Her forehead shone as bright as any day,

So was it wasshen whan she leet hir werk.
So scrubbed it was when she left her work.

  Now was ther of that chirche a parish-clerk,
  Now there was a parish clerk belonging to that church,

The which that was y-cleped Absolon.
Who was named Absolon.

Crul was his heer, and as the gold it shoon,   128
His hair was curled and it shone like gold,

And strouted as a fanne large and brode;
And stuck out like a big broad fan;

Ful streight and even lay his joly shode.
The part in his hair was beautifully straight.

His rode was reed, his eyen grey as goos;
His complexion was red, his eyes gray as a goose's;

With Powles window corven on his shoos,   132
With Paul's Church window carved on his shoes,

In hoses rede he wente fetisly.
In red stockings he walked exquisitely.

Y-clad he was ful smal and proprely
He was dressed neatly and handsomely

Al in a kirtel of a light wachet;
In a long blouse of a light blue color

Ful faire and thikke been the poyntes set.   136
Heavily decorated with beautiful tags.

And ther-up-on he hadde a gay surplys
And over it he had a gay surplice

As whyt as is the blosme up-on the rys.
As white as a blossom on a branch.

A mery child he was, so god me save,
A merry lad he was, as I may be saved,

Wel coude he laten blood and clippe and shave,   140
He knew how to let blood and clip and shave,

And make a chartre of lond or acquitaunce.
And draw up a document of land or release.

In twenty manere coude he trippe and daunce
He knew twenty different dance steps

After the scole of Oxenforde tho,
According to the Oxford fashion at that time,

And with his legges casten to and fro,   144
And with his legs thrown to and fro,

And pleyen songes on a small rubible;
And played songs on a small rebeck;

Ther-to he song som-tyme a loud quinible;
To whose accompaniment he sometimes sang a loud shrill treble;

And as wel coude he pleye on his giterne.
And he also knew how to perform on his guitar.

In al the toun nas brewhous ne taverne   148
In all the town was there no beerhouse nor tavern

That he ne visited with his solas,
That he didn't visit with his entertainment,

Ther any gaylard tappestere was.
Wherever there was a lively barmaid.

But sooth to syen, he was somdel squaymous
But to tell the truth, he was somewhat squeamish

Of farting, and of speche daungerous.   152
About farting, and careful in his talk.

   This Absolon, that jolif was and gay,
   This Absolon, in a gay and jolly mood,

Gooth with a sencer on the haliday,
Went with a censer on the holy day,

Sensinge the wyves of the parish faste;
Thoroughly censing the women of the parish;

And many a lovely look on hem he caste,   *156*
And many a loving look on them he cast,

And namely on this carpenteres wyf.
And especially on the carpenter's wife.

To loke on hir him thoughte a mery lyf,
To gaze on her he considered a merry life,

She was so propre and swete and likerous.
She was so comely and sweet and desirable.

I dar wel seyn, if she had been a mous,   *160*
I well dare say, if she had been a mouse,

And he a cat, he wolde hir hente anon.
And he a cat, he would have caught her quickly.

  This parish-clerk, this joly Absolon,
  This parish clerk, this jolly Absolon,

Hath in his herte swich a love-longinge
Had such a love-longing in his heart

That of no wyf ne took he noon offringe;   *164*
That he collected no offering from any women;

For curteisye, he seyde, he wolde noon.
Out of courtesy, he said, he wanted none.

The moon, whan it was night, ful brighte shoon,
The moon, when it was night, shone full bright,

And Absolon his giterne hath y-take,
And Absolon took his guitar

For paramours he thoghte for to wake.   *168*
For paramours he expected to awake.

And forth he gooth, jolif and amorous,
And forth he went, jolly and amorous,

Til he cam to the carpenteres hous
Until he came to the carpenter's house

A litel after cokkes hadde y-crowe;
A little after the roosters had crowed;

And dressed him up by a shot-windowe   *172*
And established himself by a casement window

That was up-on the carpenteres wal.
That was on the carpenter's wall.

He singeth in his vois gentil and smal,
He sang in a tender, soft voice,

"Now, dere lady, if thy wille be,
"Now, dear lady, if you will,

I preye yow that ye wol rewe on me,"   *176*
I beg you to take pity on me,"

Ful wel acordaunt to his giterninge.
Very well-tuned to his guitar playing.

This carpenter awook, and herde him singe,
The carpenter awoke, and heard him sing,

And spak un-to his wyf, and seyde anon,
And spoke to his wife, and said immediately,

"What! Alison! herestow nat Absolon   *180*
"What! Alison! Don't you hear Absolon

That chaunteth thus under our boures wal?"
Who sings so under our bedroom wall?"

And she answerde hir housbond ther-with-al,
And she answered her husband thereupon,

"Yis, god wot, John, I here it every-del."
"Yes, God knows, John, I hear every bit of it."

This passeth forth; what wol ye bet than wel?   *184*
So things went on; what more need be said?

Fro day to day this joly Absolon
From day to day this jolly Absolon

So woweth hir, that him is wo bigon.
So wooed her that he became woebegone.

He waketh al the night and al the day;
He stayed awake all night and all day;

He kempte hise lokkes brode, and made him gay;   *188*
He combed his heavy locks, and made himself attractive;

He woweth hir by menes and brocage,
He wooed her by go-betweens and mediation,

And swoor he wolde been hir owne page;
And swore he would be her own page;

He singeth, brokkinge as a nightingale;
He sang, warbling like a nightingale;

He sente hir piment, meeth, and spyced ale,   *192*
He sent her sweet wine, mead, and spiced ale,

And wafres, pyping hote out of the glede;
And cookies, piping hot from the oven;

And for she was of toune, he profred mede.
And since she was a townswoman, he offered money.

For som folk wol ben wonnen for richesse,
For some people can be won by wealth,

And som for strokes, and som for gentillesse.   *196*
And some by beatings, and some by gentleness.

Somtyme, to shewe his lightness and maistrye,
Once, to show off his agility and skill,

He pleyeth Herodes on a scaffold hye.
He played the part of Herod on a high scaffold.

But what availleth him as in this cas?
But what good did it do him in this instance?

She loveth so this hende Nicholas,   *200*
She so loved this slick Nicholas,

That Absolon may blowe the bukkes horn;
That Absolon might blow the buck's-horn;

He ne hadde for his labour but a scorn,
All he got from his efforts was scorn,

And thus she maketh Absolon hir ape,
And so she made a monkey out of Absolon,

And al his ernest turneth til a jape.   *204*
And all his seriousness turned to a joke.

Ful sooth is this proverbe, it is no lye,
True enough is this proverb, it is no lie,

Men seyn right thus, "alwey the nyo slye
Folks say rightly thus, "Always the near crafty one

Maketh the ferre leve to be looth."
Insures that the more remote person will be odious."

For though that Absolon be wood or wrooth,   *208*
For although Absolon might be raging or furious,

By-cause that he fer was from hir sighte,
Because he was distant from her sight,

This nye Nicholas stood in his lighte.
The nearby Nicholas stood in his light.

   Now bere thee wel, thou hende Nicholas!
   Now comport yourself well, you slick Nicholas!

For Absolon may waille and singe "allas."   *212*
For Absolon may wail and sing "Alas."

And so bifel it on a Saterday,
And it so happened on a Saturday,

This carpenter was goon til Osenay;
This carpenter had gone to Oseney;

And hende Nicholas and Alisoun
And slick Nicholas and Alison

Accorded been to this conclusioun   *216*
Agreed to the conclusion

That Nicholas shal shapen him a wyle
That Nicholas should invent a trick

This sely jalous housbond to bigyle;
To fool this simple jealous husband;

And if so be the game wente aright,
And if the scheme went all right,

She sholde slepen in his arm al night,   220
She would sleep in his arms all night,

For this was his desyr and hir also.
For this was his desire and hers too.

And right anon, with-outen wordes mo,
And right away, without any more words,

This Nicholas no lenger wolde tarie,
This Nicholas wasted no more time,

But doth ful softe un-to his chambre carie   224
But very quietly carried to his bedroom

Bothe mete and drinke for a day or tweye,
Both meat and drink for a day or two,

And to hir housbonde bad hir for to seye,
And told her to say to her husband,

If that he axed after Nicholas,
If he should ask after Nicholas,

She sholde seye she niste where he was,   228
She should say that she didn't know where he was,

Of al that day she saugh him nat with yë;
That all day she hadn't laid eyes on him;

She trowed that he was in maladye,
She guessed that he was sick,

For, for no cry, hir mayde coude him calle;
Since her maid couldn't get a response, no matter how she called.

He nolde answere, for no-thing that mighte falle.   232
He would not answer, no matter what happened.

This passeth forth al thilke Saterday,
This occurred all that Saturday,

That Nicholas stille in his chambre lay
That Nicholas stayed quietly in his bedroom

And eet and sleep or dide what him leste,
And ate and slept or did as he pleased,

Til Sonday, that the soone gooth to reste.   *236*
Until after sunset on Sunday.

   This sely carpenter hath greet merveyle
   This simple carpenter wondered greatly

Of Nicholas, or what thing mighte him eyle,
About Nicholas, or whatever ailed him,

And seyde, "I am adrad, by seint Thomas,
And said, "I am afraid, by Saint Thomas,

It stondeth nat aright with Nicholas.   *240*
Things are not well with Nicholas.

God shilde that he deyde sodeynly!
God forbid that he died suddenly!

This world is now ful tikel, sikerly;
This world is now very uncertain, surely;

I saugh to-day a cors y-born to chirche
Today I saw a corpse being carried to church

That now, on Monday last, I saugh him wirche.   *244*
That only last Monday I saw at work.

Go up," quod he un-to his knave anoon,
Go up," he said to his servant-boy,

"Clepe at his dore, or knokke with a stoon,
"Call at his door, or bang on it with a stone,

Loke how it is, and tel me boldely."
See what's going on, and tell me straight."

   This knave gooth him up ful sturdily,   *248*
   The lad went bravely upstairs

And at the chambre-dore, whyl that he stood,
And as he stood in front of the bedroom door,

He cryde and knokked as that he were wood:
He shouted and knocked as if he were insane:

"What! how! what do ye, maister Nicholay?
"What! Hey! What are you doing, Master Nicholas?

How may ye slepen al the longe day?"   252
How can you sleep all day long?"

But al for noght, he herde nat a word;
But all for nothing, he heard not a word;

An hole he fond, ful lowe up-on a bord,
He found a hole, in one of the bottom boards,

Ther as the cat was wont in for to crepe;
Which the cat used to creep inside;

And at that hole he looked in ful depe,   256
And at that hole he took a thorough look,

And at the laste he hadde of him a sighte.
And at last he got him in sight.

This Nicholas sat gaping ever up-righte,
This Nicholas sat gaping, stiffly upright,

As he had kyked on the newe mone.
As if he had gazed on the new moon.

Adoun he gooth, and tolde his maister sone   260
Downstairs he went and immediately told his master

In what array he saugh this ilke man.
In what condition he saw this same man.

This carpenter to blessen him bigan
The carpenter began to bless himself

And seyde, "help us, seinte Frideswyde!
And said, "Help us, Saint Frideswide!

A man woot litel what him shal bityde.   264
A man little knows what will happen to him.

This man is falle, with his astromye,
This man is seized, with his astronomy,

In som woodnesse or in som agonye;
With some sort of fit or with some misery;

I thoghte ay wel how that it sholde be!
I knew very well how it would be!

Men sholde nat knowe of goddes privetee.   268
Men should not know about God's secrets.

Ye, blessed be alwey a lewed man,
Yea, blessed be always an ignorant man

That noght but only his biluve can!
Who knows nothing except his Faith!

So ferde another clerk with astromye;
So fared another student with astronomy;

He walked in the feeldes for to prye   272
He walked in the fields in order to pry

Up-on the sterres, what ther sholde bifalle,
Upon the stars, what they would predict,

Til he was in a marle-pit y-falle;
Until he fell into a marl-pit;

He saugh nat that. But yet, by seint Thomas,
He didn't forsee that. But yet, by Saint Thomas,

Me reweth sore of hende Nicholas.   276
I'm very sorry about slick Nicholas.

He shal be rated of his studying,
He shall be scolded for his studying,

If that I may, by Jesus, hevene king!
If I am able, by Jesus, Heaven's King!

Get me a staf, that I may underspore,
Get me a staff, that I may jimmy under,

Whyl that thou, Robin, hevest up the dore.   280
While you, Robin, lift up the door.

He shal out of his studying, as I gesse."
He will be through with studying, I imagine."

And to the chambre-dore he gan him dresse.
And he began to address himself to the bedroom door.

His knave was a strong carl for the nonce,
His boy was a strong laborer for the occasion,

And by the haspe he haf it up atones;   284
And by the hasp he had it off instantly;

In-to the floor the dore fil anon.
The door fell down right on the floor.

This Nicholas sat ay stille as stoon,
This Nicholas remained sitting still as a stone,

And ever gaped upward in-to the eir.
And continued to gape up in the air.

This carpenter wende he were in despeir,   288
The carpenter believed him to be in a state of desperation,

And hente him by the sholdres mightily,
And seized him mightily by the shoulders,

And shook him harde, and cryde spitously,
And shook him hard, and cried vehemently.

"What! Nicholay! what, how! what! loke adoun!
"What! Nicholas! What, how! What! Look down!

Awake, and thenk on Cristes passioun;   292
Wake up, and think about Christ's passion;

I crouche thee from elves and fro wightes!"
I cross you against elves and evil spirits!"

Ther-with the night-spel seyde he anon-rightes
Thereupon he immediately recited the night spell

On foure halves of the hous aboute,
Over the four parts of the house,

And on the threshfold of the dore withoute: 296
And on the threshold of the door outside:

"Jesu Crist and seynt Benedight,
"Jesus Christ and Saint Benedict,

Blesse this hous from every wikked wight,
Protect this house from every wicked being,

For nightes verye, the white *paternoster!*
For night-time goblins, the pure Lord's Prayer!

Where wentestow, seynt Petres soster?"   300
Where did you go, Saint Peter's sister?"

And atte laste this hende Nicholas
And at last this slick Nicholas

Gan for to syke sore, and seyde, "allas!
Began to sigh sorrowfully, and said, "Alas!

Shal al the world be lost eftsones now?"
Will all the world be lost right away?"

This carpenter answerde, "what seystow?   304
The carpenter replied, "What are you saying?

What! thenk on god, as we don, men that swinke."
What! Have faith in God, as we working-men do."

This Nicholas answerde, "fecche me drinke;
This Nicholas replied, "Fetch me a drink;

And after wol I speke in privetee
And then I will tell you in privacy

Of certeyn thing that toucheth me and thee;   308
Of certain things that concern you and me;

I wol telle it non other man, certeyn."
I certainly will not tell it to anyone else."

This carpenter goth doun, and comth ageyn,
The carpenter went down, and then returned,

And broghte of mighty ale a large quart;
And brought a big quart of mighty ale;

And whan that ech of hem had dronke his parte,   312
And when each of them had drunk his share,

This Nicholas his dore faste shette,
This Nicholas shut his door tight,

And doun the carpenter by him he sette.
And sat the carpenter down beside him.

He seyde, "John, myn hoste lief and dere,
He said, "John, my dear and cherished host,

Thou shalt up-on thy trouthe swere me here,   *316*
You shall swear to me here on your honor,

That to no wight thou shalt this conseil wreye;
That you will not betray this secret to anyone;

For it is Cristes conseil that I seye,
For it is Christ's secret that I tell,

And if thou telle it man, thou are forlore;
And if you repeat it to anyone, you are utterly lost;

For this vengaunce thou shalt han therefore,   *320*
For the penalty you will have for it

That if thou wreye me, thou shalt be wood!"
Will be that you will go insane if you betray me!"

"Nay, Crist forbede it, for his holy blood!"
"No, Christ forbid, by his holy blood!"

Quod tho this sely man, "I nam no labbe,
Then said this simple man, "I am no tattle-tale,

Ne, though I seye, I nam nat lief to gabbe.   *324*
No, though I say it myself, I am not given to blabbing.

Sey what thou wold, I shal it never telle
Say what you will, I shall never tell it

To child ne wyf, by him that harwed helle!"
To woman or child, by Him that harrowed hell!"

"Now John," quod Nicholas, "I wol nat lye:
"Now John," said Nicholas, "I will not lie:

I have y-found in myn astrology,   *328*
I have discovered by my astrology,

As I have loked in the mone bright,
As I gazed at the full moon,

That now, a Monday next, at quarter-night,
That on next Monday night, at nine oclock,

Shal falle a reyn and that so wilde and wood
Shall fall a rain so wild and furious

That half so greet was never Noës flood.   *332*
That Noah's flood was never half so great.

This world," he seyde, "in lasse than in an hour
This world," he said, "in less than an hour

Shal al be dreynt, so hidous is the shour;
Shall all be drowned, so hideous will be the downpour;

Thus shal mankynde drenche and lese hir lyf."
So will mankind drown and lose its life."

This carpenter answerde, "allas, my wyf!   *336*
The carpenter replied, "Alas, my wife!

And shal she drenche? allas! myn Alisoun!"
And will she drown? Alas, my Alison!"

For sorwe of this he fil almost adoun,
For grief about this thought he almost fell down,

And seyde, "is ther no remedie in this cas?"
And said, "Is there no remedy for this situation?"

"Why, yis, for gode," quod hende Nicholas,   *340*
"Why yes, before God," said slick Nicholas,

"If thou wolt werken after lore and reed,
"If you will be guided by learning and counsel,

Thou mayst nat werken after thyn owene heed.
Instead of trusting in your own head.

For thus seith Salomon, that was ful trewe,
For truly thus spake Solomon,

'Werk al by conseil, and thou shalt nat rewe.'   *344*
'Always take advice, and you won't regret it.'

And if thou werken wolt by good conseil,
And if you will act on good advice,

I undertake, with-outen mast and seyl,
I'll undertake, without mast and sail,

Yet shal I saven hir and thee and me.
I will save her and you and me.

Hastow nat herd how saved was Noë,   348
Haven't you heard how Noah was saved,

Whan that our lord had warned him biforn
When our Lord had warned him in advance

That al the world with water sholde be lorn?"
That all the world would perish by water?"

"Yis," quod this carpenter, "ful yore ago."
"Yes," said the carpenter, "a long time ago."

"Hastow nat herd," quod Nicholas, "also,   352
"Have you not heard," said Nicholas, "besides,

The sorwe of Noë with his felawshipe
The trouble of Noah and his crew

Er that he mighte gete his wyf to shipe?
Before he could get his wife aboard the ark?

Him had be lever, I dar wel undertake,
He would have preferred, I dare well say,

At thilke tyme, than alle hise wetheres blake,   356
At that time, more than all his black sheep,

That she hadde had a ship hir-self allone.
That she had had an ark all to herself.

And ther-fore, wostou what is best to done?
And therefore, do you know what is best to be done?

This asketh haste, and of an hastif thing
This calls for speed, and concerning a hasty thing

Men may nat preche or maken tarying.   360
Men may not preach or cause delay.

Anon go gete us faste in-to this in
Immediately, bring quickly into this house

A kneding-trogh, or elles a kimelin,
A kneading-trough, or else a large shallow tub,

For ech of us, but loke that they be large,
For each of us, but make sure that they are large,

In whiche we mowe swimme as in a barge. 364
In which we may sail as in a barge.

And han ther-inne vitaille suffisant
And put in them enough food

But for a day; fy on the remenant!
For just one day; don't worry about the rest!

The water shal aslake and goon away
The water will abate and go away

Aboute pryme up-on the nexte day. 368
Around nine o'clock in the morning of the next day.

But Robin may nat wite of this, thy knave,
But your boy Robin musn't know of this,

Ne eek thy mayde Gille I may nat save;
Nor am I able to save your maid Gillian either;

Axe nat why, for though thou aske me,
Don't ask why, for even if you ask me,

I wol nat tellen goddes privetee. 372
I won't reveal God's secrets.

Suffiseth thee, but if thy wittes madde,
Let it suffice you, unless you are out of your mind,

To han as greet a grace as Noë hadde.
To have as much grace as Noah had.

Thy wyf shal I wel saven, out of doute,
I will save your wife, beyond a doubt,

Go now thy wey, and speed thee heer-aboute. 376
Now go on your way, and make the arrangements quickly.

But whan thou hast, for hir and thee and me,
But when you have, for her and you and me,

Y-geten us thise kneding-tubbes three,
Gotten for us these three kneading-tubs,

Than shaltow hange hem in the roof ful hye,
Then hang them high up near the roof,

That no man of our purveyaunce spye.   380
So that nobody will spy out our plan.

And whan thou thus has doon as I have seyd,
And when you have done what I've told you,

And hast our vitaille faire in hem y-leyd,
And have provisioned them with food,

And eek an ax, to smyte the corde atwo
And also an axe, to cut the rope

When that the water comth, that we may go,   384
When the water comes, so that we may leave,

And broke an hole an heigh, up-on the gable,
And when you have broken a hole high up on the gable,

Unto the gardin-ward over the stable,
On the garden side over the stable,

That we may frely passen forth our way
So that we may freely sail away

Whan that the grete shour is goon away—   388
As soon as the huge storm has passed away—

Than shaltow swimme as myrie, I undertake,
Then you will sail as merrily, I guarantee,

As doth the whyte doke after hir drake.
As a white duck after its drake.

Than wol I clepe, "how! Alison! how! John!
Then I will call, "How, Alison! How, John!

Be myrie, for the flood wol passe anon."   392
Be merry, for the flood will subside quickly."

And thou wolt seyn, 'hayl, maister Nicholay!
And you will say, 'Hail Master Nicholas!

Good morwe, I se thee wel, for it is day.'
Good morning, I see you clearly, for it is daylight."

And than shul we be lordes al our lyf
And then all our lives we shall be lords

Of al the world, as Noë and his wyf.   *396*
Of all the world, like Noah and his wife.

But of o thyng I warne thee ful right,
But of one thing I warn you most carefully,

Be wel avysed, on that ilke night
Be most certain, and that same night

That we ben entred in-to shippes bord,
That we embark on our boats,

That noon of us ne speke nat a word,   *400*
That none of us utters a word,

Ne clepe, ne crye, but been in his preyere;
Or calls or cries, but remains wrapped in prayer;

For it is goddes owne heste dere.
For this is God's own command.

Thy wyf and thou mote hange fer a-twynne,
Your wife and you must hang far apart,

For that betwixe yow shal be no sinne   *404*
So that there will be no sin between you

No more in looking than ther shal in dede;
No more in looking than in the act;

This ordinance is seyd, go, god thee spede!
This order is given. Go, God be with you!

Tomorwe at night, whan men ben alle aslepe,
Tomorrow night, when everybody is asleep,

In-to our kneding-tubbes wol we crepe,   *408*
We will creep into our kneading-tubs,

And sitten ther, abyding goddes grace.
And sit there, awaiting God's grace.

Go now thy wey, I have no lenger space
Go on your way, I have no more time

To make of this no lenger sermoning.
To add additional sermonizing to this.

Men seyn thus, 'send the wyse, and sey no-thing';   412
People say, 'Send the wise man, and say nothing';

Thou art so wys, it nedeth thee nat teche;
You are so wise, you don't need to be taught;

Go, save our lyf, and that I thee biseche."
Go, save our lives, and that I beg you."

This sely carpenter goth forth his wey.
This simple carpenter went on his way.

Ful ofte he seith "alas" and "weylawey,"   416
Many times he said, "Alas" and "Woe is me,"

And to his wyf he tolde his privetee;
And took his wife into his confidence;

And she was war, and knew it bet than he,
She was aware, and knew better than he,

What al this queynte cast was for to seye.
What all this curious contrivance was all about.

But natheless she ferde as she wolde deye,   420
But nevertheless, she acted as if she would die,

And seyde, "allas! go forth thy wey anon,
And said, "Alas! Go on your way immediately,

Help us to scape, or we ben lost echon;
Help us to escape, or we will all be lost;

I am thy trewe verray wedded wyf;
I am your own true wedded wife;

Go, dere spouse, and help to save our lyf."   424
Go, dear spouse, and help to save our lives."

Lo! which a greet thyng is affeccioun!
Behold! What a great thing is the fancy!

Men may dye of imaginacioun,
Men can die of imagination,

So depe may impressioun be take.
So deeply may impressions be made.

This sely carpenter beginneth quake;   *428*
This simple carpenter began to tremble;

Him thinketh verraily that he may see
He truly believes that he will see

Noës flood come walwing as the see
Noah's flood come rolling in like the ocean

To drenchen Alisoun, his hony dere.
To drown Alison, his honey dear.

He wepeth, weyleth, maketh sory chere,   *432*
He wept, wailed, looked utterly miserable,

He syketh with ful many a sory swogh.
He sighed with many a sorrowful groan.

He gooth and geteth him a kneding-trogh,
He went and got himself a kneading-trough,

And after that a tubbe and a kimelin,
And then a tub and a large shallow tub,

And prively he sente hem to his in,   *436*
And secretly he sent them to his house,

And heng hem in the roof in privetee.
And hung them in the attic in secrecy.

His owne hand he made laddres three
With his own hand he made three ladders

To climben by the ronges and the stalkes
To climb by the rungs and the uprights

Un-to the tubbes hanginge in the balkes,   *440*
Up to the tubs hanging in the rafters,

And hem vitailled, both trogh and tubbe,
And stocked them, both trough and tubs,

With breed and chese, and good ale in a jubbe,
With bread and cheese, and good ale in a jug,

Suffysinge right y-nogh as for a day.
Provisioned well enough for a day.

But er that he had maad al this array,   *444*
But before he had completed all these arrangements,

He sente his knave and eek his wenche also
He sent his boy and his maid too

Up-on his nede to London for to go.
On a trip to London to do an errand for him.

And on the Monday, whan it drow to night,
And on the Monday, when it drew toward night,

He shette his dore with-oute candel-light   *448*
He shut his door without candle-light

And dressed al thing as it sholde be.
And arranged everything properly.

And shortly, up they clomben alle three;
And soon they all three climbed up;

They sitten stille wel a furlong-way.
They sat stock still for a short time.

"Now, *Pater-noster*, clom!" seyde Nicholay.   *452*
"Now the Lord's Prayer. Quiet!" said Nicholas.

And "clom," quod John, and "clom," seyde Alisoun.
And "Quiet," said John, and "Quiet," said Alison.

This carpenter seyde his devocioun,
The carpenter said his devotion,

And stille he sit, and biddeth his preyere,
And sat still, and made his prayer,

Awaytinge on the reyn, if he it here.   *456*
Waiting for the rain, expecting to hear it.

The dede sleep, for wery bisinesse,
A dead sleep, the result of his hard work,

Fil on this carpenter right, as I gesse,
Fell on this carpenter, I believe, right

Aboute corfew-tyme, or litel more;
About curfew time, or a little later;

For travail of his goost he groneth sore,   460
From the troubling of his spirit he groaned sorely,

And eft he routeth, for his heed mislay.
And soon he snored, because of his head's awkward position.

Doun of the laddre stalketh Nicholuy,
Down from the ladder crept Nicholas,

And Alisoun, ful softe adoun she spedde;
And Alison very quietly slithered down;

With-outen wordes mo, they goon to bedde   464
Without more words, they went to bed

Ther-as the carpenter is wont to lye.
Where the carpenter usually slept.

Ther was the revel and the melodye;
There was the sport and the music;

And thus lyth Alison and Nicholas
And thus lay Alison and Nicholas

In bisinesse of mirthe and of solas   468
In the business of amusement and pleasure

Til that the belle of laudes gan to ringe
Until the bell began to ring for lauds

And freres in the chauncel gonne singe.
And friars began to sing in the chancel.

  This parish-clerk, this amorous Absolon,
  The parish-clerk, this amorous Absolon,

That is for love alwey so wo bigon,   472
Who was always so woebegone for love,

Up-on the Monday was at Oseneye
Was at Oseney on that Monday

With companye, him to disporte and pleye,
With others, for diversion and amusement,

And axed up-on cas a cloisterer
And happened to ask a cloister resident

Ful prively after John the carpenter;   476
Very confidentially about John the carpenter;

And he drough him a-part out of the chirche,
And he drew him apart outside the church,

And seyde, "I noot, I saugh him here nat wirche
And said, "I don't know, I haven't seen him working here

Sin Saterday; I trow that he be went
Since Saturday; I imagine he has gone

For timber; ther our abbot hath him sent;   480
To get some timber, where our abbot has sent him;

For he is wont for timber for to go,
For he is accustomed to go for timber,

And dwellen at the grange a day or two;
And stays at the Grange a day or two;

Or elles he is at his hous, certeyn;
Or else he is at home, certainly;

Wher that he be, I can nat sothly seyn."   484
Exactly where he is I cannot truly say."

  This Absolon ful joly was and light,
  This Absolon was most joyous and cheerful,

And thoghte, "now is tyme wake al night:
And thought, "Now is the time to stay awake all night:

For sikirly I saugh him nat stiringe
For surely I did not see him stirring

Aboute his dore sin day bigan to springe.   488
About his door since day began to dawn.

So moot I thryve, I shal, at cokkes crowe,
As I may thrive, I shall, at cock's crow,

Ful prively knokken at his windowe
Most secretly knock at his window

That stant ful lowe up-on his boures wal.
That is placed quite low upon his bedroom wall.

To Alison now wol I tellen al   492
Now I will tell Alison all

My love-longing, for yet I shal nat misse
My love-longing, for I shall hardly fail

That at the leste wey I shall hir kisse.
To kiss her, at the very least.

Som maner comfort shal I have, parfay,
Some kind of comfort I will have, in faith,

My mouth hath icched al this longe day;   496
My mouth has itched all this long day;

That is a signe of kissing atte leste.
That is a sign of kissing at least.

Al night me mette eek, I was at a feste.
Besides, I dreamed all night I was at a feast.

Therefor I wol gon slepe an houre or tweye,
Therefore I will go to sleep for an hour or two,

And al the night than wol I wake and pleye."   500
And all the rest of the night I will stay awake and have fun."

    Whan that the firste cok hath crowe, anon
    When the first cock crowed, immediately

Up rist this joly lover Absolon
Up rose this jolly lover Absolon

And him arrayeth gay, at point-devys.
And dressed himself handsomely with great care.

But first he cheweth greyn and lycorys   504
But first he chewed cardamon and licorice

To smellen swete, er he had kembed his heer.
To smell sweet, before he combed his hair.

Under his tonge a trewe love he beer,
He put a leaf of true-love under his tongue,

For ther-by wende he to ben gracious.
Believing that it would make him appealing.

He rometh to the carpenteres hous,   508
He roamed to the carpenter's house,

And stille he stant under the shot-windowe;
And stood still under the casement window;

Un-to his brest it raughte, it was so lowe;
It reached to his chest, it was so low;

And softe he cogheth with a semi-soun—
And coughed quietly with a suppressed sound—

"What do ye, hony-comb, swete Alisoun?   512
"What are you doing, honeycomb, sweet Alison?

My faire brid, my swete cinamone,
My pretty bird, my sweet cinnamon,

Awaketh, lemman myn, and speketh to me!
Wake up, sweetheart mine, and speak to me!

Wel litel thenken ye up-on my woe,
Precious little do you think about my woe,

That for your love I swete ther I go.   516
That I sweat for your love wherever I go.

No wonder is thogh that I swelte and swete,
It's no wonder that I languish and sweat;

I moorne as doth a lamb after the tete.
I mourn as a lamb does after the teat.

Y-wis, lemman, I have swich love-longing,
Indeed, sweetheart, I have such love-longing,

That lyk a turtel trewe is my moorninge;   520
That my mourning is like that of a turtle-dove;

I may nat ete na more than a mayde."
I cannot eat any more than a maid."

  "Go fro the window, Jakke fool," she sayde,
  "Get away from the window, Jackanapes," she said,

"As help me god, it wol nat be 'com ba me,'
"So help me God, it will not be 'kiss me quick,'

I love another, and elles I were to blame,   524
I love another, and otherwise I would be to blame,

Wel bet than thee, by Jesu, Absolon!
Much better than you, by Jesus, Absolon!

Go forth thy wey, or I wol caste a ston,
Go on your way, or I will throw a stone,

And lat me slepe, a twenty devel wey!"
And let me sleep, in the way of twenty devils!"

  "Allas," quod Absolon, "and weylawey!   528
  "Alas," said Absolon, "and woe is me!

That trewe love was ever so yvel biset!
That true love was ever so badly bestowed!

Than kisse me, sin it may be no bet,
Then kiss me, since it may be no better,

For Jesus love and for the love of me."
For Jesus' love and for the love of me."

  "Wiltow than go thy wey ther-with?" quod she.   532
  "Will you then go on your way?" said she.

  "Ye, certes, lemman," quod this Absolon.
  "Yes, truly, sweetheart," said this Absolon.

  "Thanne make thee redy," said she, "I come anon";
  "Then get ready," she said, "I'm coming immediately";

And un-to Nicholas she seyde stille,
And she whispered to Nicholas,

"Now hust, and thou shalt laughen al thy fille."   536
"Now hush, and you will have a good laugh."

  This Absolon doun sette him on his knees,
  This Absolon got down on his knees,

And seyde, "I am a lord at alle degrees,
And said, "I am a lord in every way,

For after this I hope ther cometh more."
For after this I hope that more will come."

Lemman, thy grace, and swete brid, thyn ore!"   540
Sweetheart, your favor, and sweet bird, your kindness!"

   The window she undoth, and that in haste,
   She unlatched the window quickly,

"Have do," quod she, "com of and speed thee faste,
"*Go ahead,*" *she said,* "*come on and do it quickly,*

Lest that our neighebores thee espye."
In case our neighbors should see you."

   This Absolon gan wype his mouth ful drye;   544
   This Absolon began to wipe his mouth dry;

Derk was the night as pich, or as the cole,
The night was dark as pitch or coal,

And at the window out she putte hir hole,
And out the window she put her hole,

And Absolon, him fil no bet ne wers,
And as for Absolon, it happened no better nor worse

But with his mouth he kiste hir naked ers   548
But with his mouth he kissed her naked arse

Ful savourly, er he was war of this.
Most enjoyable, before he realized what he was kissing.

   Abak he sterte, and thoghte it was amis,
   Back he started, and thought something was wrong,

For wel he wiste a womman hath no berd;
For he well knew women don't have beards;

He felte a thing al rough and long y-herd,   552
He felt a rough and long-haired thing,

And seyde, "fy! allas; what have I do?"
And said, "*Fie! Alas! What have I done?*"

   "Tehee!" quod she, and clapte the window to,
   "*Tehee!*" *said she, and slammed the window shut,*

And Absolon goth forth a sory pass.
And Absolon went off in a sorry state.

"A berd, a berd!" quod hende Nicholas,
"A beard, a beard!" said slick Nicholas,
556

"By goddes *corpus,* this goth faire and weel!"
"By God's body, this goes wonderfully well!"

This sely Absolon herde every deel,
This simple Absolon heard everything,

And on his lippe he gan for anger byte;
And began to bite his lips from anger;

And to him-self he seyde, "I shall thee quyte!"
And he said to himself, "I'll get even with you!"
560

Who rubbeth now, who froteth now his lippes
Who now rubbed, who now scrubbed his lips

With dust, with sond, with straw, with clooth, with chippes
With dirt, with sand, with straw, with cloth, with chips

But Absolon, that seith ful ofte, "Allas!
But Absolon, who often said, "Alas!

My soule bitake I un-to Sathanas,
I'd give my soul to Satan,
564

But me wer lever than al this toun," quod he,
But I'd rather than all this town," said he,

"Of this despyt awroken for to be!
"To be avenged of this spite!

Allas!" quod he, "allas! I ne hadde y-bleynt!"
Alas!" he said, "Alas! If only I had turned aside!"

His hote love was cold and al y-queynt;
His hot love was cold and entirely quenched;
568

For fro that tyme that he had kiste hir ers,
For immediately after he had kissed her arse,

Of paramours he sette nat a kers,
He couldn't care less about mistresses,

For he was heled of his maladye;
For he was cured of his illness;

Ful ofte paramours he gan deffye,   572
He made frequent pronouncements against lovers,

And weep as dooth a child that is y-bete.
And wept like a beaten child.

A softe paas he wente over the strete
Quietly he went down the street

Un-til a smith men cleped daun Gerveys,
To a smith known as Master Gervase,

That in his forge smithed plough-harneys;   576
Who forged plow parts in his smithy;

He sharpeth shaar and culter bisily.
He was busily sharpening shares and coulters.

This Absolon knokketh al esily,
This Absolon knocked in a casual way,

And seyd, "undo, Gerveys, and that anon."
And said, "Open up, Gervase, and do it quickly."

"What, who artow?" "It am I, Absolon."   580
"What, who are you?" "It is I, Absolon."

"What, Absolon! for Cristes swete tree,
"What, Absolon! by Christ's sweet tree,

Why ryse ye so rathe, ey, ben'cite!
Why are you up so early, eh? Bless you!

What eyleth yow? som gay gerl, god it woot,
What ails you? Some light woman, God knows,

Hath broght yow thus up-on the viritoot;   584
Has made you so lively;

By sëynt Note, ye woot wel what I mene."
By Saint Note, you well know what I mean."

  This Absolon ne roghte nat a bene
  This Absolon didn't care a bean

Of al his pley, no word agayn he yaf;
About all his fooling; he offered no reply;

He hadde more tow on his distaf   588
He had more tow on his distaff

Than Gerveys knew, and seyde, "freend so dere,
Than Gervase knew, and said, "My very dear friend,

That hote culter in the chimenee here,
That hot coulter in the fire here,

As lene it me, I have ther-with to done,
Please lend it to me, I have something to do with it,

And I wol bringe it thee agayn ful sone."   592
And I will return it to you very quickly."

    Gerveys answerde, "certes were it gold,
    Gervase replied, "Surely, even if it were gold,

Or in a poke nobles alle untold,
Or a great quantity of gold coins in a bag,

Thou sholdest have, as I am trewe smith;
You should have it, as I am a true smith;

Ey, Cristes foo! what wol ye do there-with?"   596
But by Christ's foot, what will you do with it?"

    "Ther-of," quod Absolon, "be as be may;
    "Let that be as it may," said Absolon;

I shall wel telle it thee to-morwe day"—
I'll certainly tell you some other day"—

And caughte the culter by the colde stele.
And picked up the coulter by the cool end.

Ful softe out at the dore he gan to stele,   600
Very quietly he stole out the door,

And wente un-to the carpenteres wal.
And went to the carpenter's wall.

He cogheth first, and knokketh ther-with-al
First he coughed, and then knocked

Upon the windowe, right as he dide er.
On the window, just as he had before.

This Alison answerde, "Who is ther   604
This Alison replied, "Who is there

That knokketh so? I warante it a theef."
That knocks so? I bet it is a thief."

"Why, nay," quod he, "god woot, my swete leef,
"Why no," said he, "God knows, my sweet love,

I am thyn Absolon, my dereling!
I am your Absolon, my darling!

Of gold," quod he, "I have thee broght a ring;   608
Said he, "I have brought you a gold ring;

My moder yaf it me, so god me save,
My mother gave it to me, as God may save me,

Ful fyn it is, and ther-to wel y-grave;
It is very fine and nicely engraved;

This wol I yeve thee, if thou me kisse!"
I will give it to you if you will kiss me!"

This Nicholas was risen for to pisse,   612
This Nicholas had gotten up to piss,

And thoghte he wolde amenden al the jape,
And thought he would improve on the joke,

He sholde kisse his ers er that he scape.
He should kiss his arse before he escaped.

And up the windowe dide he hastily,
And he quickly threw open the window,

And out his ers he putteth prively   616
And quietly he stuck out his arse

Over the buttok, to the haunche-bon;
Beyond his buttocks to the thigh-bone;

And ther-with spake this clerk, this Absolon,
And then this clerk, this Absolon, said,

"Speke, swete brid, I noot nat wher thou art."
"Speak, sweet bird, I don't know where you are."

This Nicholas anon leet flee a fart, 620
At that this Nicholas let fly a fart,

As greet as it had been a thonder-dent,
As great as if it had been a thunderclap,

That with the strook he was almost y-blent;
So that he was almost blinded by the blast;

And he was redy with his iren hoot,
And he was ready with his hot iron,

And Nicholas amidde the ers he smoot. 624
And he smote Nicholas in the midst of his arse.

Of gooth the skin an hande-brede aboute,
Off peeled the skin about a hand's breadth,

The hote culter brende so his toute,
The hot coulter so burned his behind,

And for the smert he wende for to dye.
And he thought he would die from the pain.

As he were wood, for wo he gan to crye— 628
He began to cry out in anguish, as if he were mad—

"Help! water! water! help, for goddes herte!"
"Help! Water! Water! Help, for God's sake!"

This carpenter out of his slomber sterte,
The carpenter was startled from his sleep,

And herde oon cryen "water' as he were wood,
And heard somebody crying "water" as if he were mad,

And thoghte, "Allas! now comth Nowélis flood!" 632
And thought, "Alas! Now comes Noel's flood!"

He sit him up with-outen wordes mo,
He sat himself up without any more words,

And with his ax he smoot the corde a-two,
And he cut the rope in two with his axe,

And doun goth al; he fond neither to selle,
*And down went everything; he found nothing to do business
    with en route,*

Ne breed ne ale, til he cam to the selle   636
Neither meat nor ale, until he came to the boards

Up-on the floor; and ther aswowne he lay.
On the floor; and there he lay in a swoon.

   Up sterte hir Alison and Nicholay,
   Up jumped Alison and Nicholas,

And cryden "out" and "harrow" in the strete.
And shouted "Come out" and "Help" in the street.

The neighebores, bothe smale and grete,   640
The neighbors, both small and great,

In ronnen, for to gauren on this man,
Ran in to gaze at this man,

That yet aswowne he lay, bothe pale and wan:
Who still lay in a swoon, both pale and wan:

For with the fal he brosten hadded his arm;
For he had broken his arm in the fall;

But stonde he moste un-to his owne harm.   644
But he was mostly stuck with his own misery.

For whan he spak, he was anon bore doun
For when he spoke, he was immediately borne down

With hende Nicholas and Alisoun.
By slick Nicholas and Alison.

They tolden every man that he was wood,
They told everybody that he was mad,

He was agast so of "Nowélis flood"   648
He was so frightened of "Noel's flood"

Thurgh fantasye, that of his vainitee
Through fantasy, that in his delusion

He hadde y-boght him kneding-tubbes three,
He had bought three kneading-tubs,

And hadde hem hanged in the roof above;
And had them hanged in the roof above;

And that he preyed hem, for goddes love,　　　　652
And that he had begged them, for God's love,

To sitten in the roof, *par companye.*
To sit in the roof to keep him company.

The folk gan laughen at his fantasye;
The people began to laugh at his delusion;

In-to the roof they kyken and they gape,
Up into the roof they stared and gaped,

And turned al his harm un-to a jape.　　　　656
And turned all his misery into a joke.

For what so that this carpenter answerde,
For whatever this carpenter might say,

It was for noght; no man his reson herde;
It was for nought; nobody would listen to him;

With othes grete he was so sworn adoun
With great oaths he was so sworn down

That he was holden wood in al the toun;　　　　660
That he was considered mad by the whole town;

For every clerk anon-right heeld with other.
For every student immediately agreed with each other.

They seyde, "the man is wood, my leve brother";
They said, "The man is mad, my dear brother";

And every wight gan laughen of this stryf.
And everybody began to laugh about the matter.

Thus swyved was the carpenteres wyf,　　　　664
Thus the carpenter's wife was screwed,

For al his keping and his jalousye;
For all his watching and his jealousy;

And Absolon hath kist hir nether yë;
And Absolon has kissed her bottom eye;

And Nicholas is scalded in the toute.
And Nicholas was burned on the behind.

This tale is doon, and god save al the route!   *668*
This tale is ended, and God save all the company!

Prologue to the Reeve's Tale

Whan folk had laughen at this nyce cas
When people had laughed at this absurd affair

Of Absolon and hende Nicholas,
Of Absolon and slick Nicholas,

Diverse folk diversely they seyde;
Different people commented differently;

But, for the more part, they loughe and pleyde,   4
But for the most part they laughed and were amused,

Ne at this tale I saugh no man him greve,
Nor did I see anybody sorrowful about this tale,

But it were only Osewold the Reve
Except only Oswald the Reeve

By-cause he was of carpenteres craft.
Because he was a carpenter by trade.

A litel ire is in his herte y-laft,   8
A little anger was left in his heart,

He gan to grucche and blamed it a lyte.
He began to grumble and criticized it a little.

"So thee'k," quod he, "ful wel coude I yow quyte
"As I may thrive," said he, "I could well repay you

With blering of a proud milleres yë
With the blearing of a proud miller's eye

If that me liste speke of ribaudye. 12
If I were willing to speak of ribaldry.

But ik am old, me list not pley for age;
But I am old, too old for dalliance;

Gras-tyme is doon, my fodder is now forage,
Grass time is over, my food is now hay,

This whyte top wryteth myne olde yeres,
This white top advertises my old age,

Myn herte is al-so mowled as myne heres, 16
My heart is also as decayed as my hair,

But-if I fare as dooth an open-ers;
Unless I fare as a medlar fruit does;

That ilke fruit is ever leng the wers,
That fruit is worse the longer it lasts,

Till it be roten in mullok or in stree.
Until it is rotted in refuse or straw.

We olde men, I drede, so fare we; 20
I'm afraid we old men fare so;

Til we be roten, can we nat be rype;
We can't be ripe until we are rotten;

We hoppen ay, whyl that the world wol pype.
We keep on hopping as long as the world will pipe.

For in oure wil ther stiketh ever a nayl,
For in our desires there always sticks a nail,

To have an hoor heed and a grene tayl, 24
To have a hoary head and a green tail,

As hath a leek, for thogh our might be goon,
As does a leek, for though our strength is gone,

Our will desireth folie ever in oon.
Our will desires folly just the same.

For whan we may nat doon, than wol we speke,
For when we can't perform, we'll talk about it,

Yet in our asshen olde is fyr y-reke.   28
Still in our old ashes some fire is raked together.

   Foure gledes han we, whiche I shal devyse,
   We have four glowing coals, which I shall point out,

Avaunting, lying, anger, covuityse,
Boasting, lying, anger, greed;

Thise foure sparkles longen un-to elde.
These four sparks belong to old age.

Our olde lemes mowe wel been unwelde,   32
Our old limbs can scarcely be controlled,

But wil ne shal nat fallen, that is sooth.
But desire does not falter, that is the truth.

And yet ik have alwey a coltes tooth,
And yet I have always had a colt's tooth,

As many a yeer as it is passed henne
For as many years as have passed away

Sin that my tappe of lyf bigan to renne.   36
Since my tap of life began to run.

For sikerly, whan I was bore, anon
For surely, when I was born, at once

Deeth drogh the tappe of lyf and leet it gon;
Death drew from the tap of life and let it flow;

And ever sith hath so the tappe y-ronne
And ever since the tap has so flowed

Til that almost al empty is the tonne.   40
Until the barrel is almost entirely empty.

The streem of lyf now droppeth on the chimbe;
The stream of life now drips from the barrel rim;

The sely tonge may wel ringe and chimbe
The poor tongue may well ring and chime

Of wrecchednesse that passed is ful yore;
About follies that happened long ago;

With olde folk, save dotage, is namore."   **44**
Except for dotage there is nothing else for old folk."

Whan that our host hadde herd this sermoning,
When our host had listened to this sermonizing,

He gan to speke as lordly as a king;
He began to talk as lordly as a king;

He seide, "what amounteth al this wit?
He said, "What does all this wisdom amount to?

What shul we speke alday of holy writ?   **48**
Why must we spend all day talking of holy writ?

The devel made a reve for to prech,
The devil turned a reeve into a preacher,

And of a souter a shipman or a leche.
And turned a cobbler into a sailor or a doctor.

Sey forth thy tale, and tarie nat the tyme,
Tell your tale, and don't waste time,

Lo, Depeford! and it is half-way pryme.   **52**
Look, there's Depford! and it is half-past seven.

Lo, Grenewich, ther many a shrewe is inne;
Look, there's Greenwich, where there's many a scoundrel;

It were al tyme thy tale to beginne."
It is high time to begin your tale."

"Now, sires," quod this Osewold the Reve,
"Now, sirs," said this Oswald the Reeve,

"I pray yow alle that ye nat yow greve,   **56**
"I beg you all not to be offended,

Thogh I answere and somdel sette his howve,
Though I respond and somewhat set his hood awry,

For leveful is with force force of-showve.
For it's permissable to repel force with force.

This dronke millere hath y-told us heer
This drunken miller has told us here

How that bigyled was a carpenteer,   *60*
How a carpenter was beguiled,

Peraventure in scorn, for I am oon.
Perhaps in scorn, for I am one.

And, by your leve, I shal him quyte anoon;
And, by your leave, I shall repay him at once;

Right in his cherles termes wol I speke.
Exactly in his churlish lingo will I speak.

I pray to god his nekke mote breke;   *64*
I pray to God his neck may break;

He can wel in myn yë seen a stalke,
He can readily see a mote in my eye,

But in his owne he can nat seen a balke."
But he can't see a beam in his own."

The Reeve's Tale

———

At Trumpington, nat fer fro Cantebrigge,
At Trumpington, not far from Cambridge,

Ther goth a brook and over that a brigge,
There runs a brook with a bridge over it,

Up-on the which brook ther stant a melle;
Upon which brook there stands a mill;

And this is verray soth that I yow telle.   4
And this is the absolute truth that I tell you.

A Miller was ther dwelling many a day;
A Miller had lived there many a day;

As eny pecok he was proud and gay.
He was as proud and stylish as a peacock.

Pypen he coude and fisshe, and nettes bete,
He could pipe and fish and mend nets,

And turne coppes, and wel wrastle and shete;   8
And turn cups on a lathe, and wrestle and shoot well;

And by his belt he baar a long panade,
And on his belt he wore a long knife,

And of a swerd ful trenchant was the blade.
And a sword with a very sharp blade.

A joly popper baar he in his pouche;
He carried a neat little dagger in his pouch;

Ther was no man for peril dorste him touche.   12
Nobody dared touch him for fear of his life.

A Sheffeld thwitel baar he in his hose:
He carried a large Sheffield knife in his stocking;

Round was his fauo, and camuse was his nose.
He had a round face and a pug nose.

As piled as an ape was his skulle.
His skull was as bald as an ape's.

He was a market-beter atte fulle.   16
He was a thorough-going market swaggerer.

Ther dorste no wight hand up-on him legge,
Nobody dared lay a hand upon him,

That he ne swoor he sholde anon abegge.
He swore that anyone who did would pay for it instantly.

A theef he was for sothe of corn and mele,
He was indeed a thief of corn and meal,

And that a sly, and usaunt for to stele.   20
And a sly one at that, and accustomed to steal.

His name was hoten dëynous Simkin.
He was commonly known as Scornful Simkin.

A wyf he hadde, y-comen of noble kin;
He had a wife who came from a noble family;

The person of the toun hir fader was.
The town parson was her father.

With hir he yaf ful many a panne of bras,   24
He dowered her with a considerable quantity of brass

For that Simkin sholde in his blood allye.
To persuade Simkin to make the alliance.

She was y-fostred in a nonnerye,
She was brought up in a nunnery,

For Simkin wolde no wyf, as he sayde,
For Simkin would have no wife, as he said,

But she were wel y-norissed and a mayde,　　　　28
Unless she was well brought up and a virgin,

To saven his estaat of yomanrye.
To preserve his status of yeomanry.

And she was proud and pert as is a pye.
And she was proud and pert as a magpie.

A ful fair sighte was it on hem two;
The two of them made a really lovely sight;

On haly-dayes biforn hir wolde he go　　　　32
On holy days he would walk in front of her

With his tipet bounden about his heed,
With the hood of his cape tied on his head,

And she cam after in a gyte of reed,
And she followed in a red gown,

And Simkin hadde hosen of the same.
And Simkin wore hose of the same color.

Ther dorste no wight clepen hir but "dame."　　　　36
Nobody dared call her anything but "Madam."

Was noon so hardy that wente by the weye
No one who walked down the street was so foolhardy

That with hir dorste rage or ones pleye
As to dare once to flirt or fool with her

But-if he wolde be slayn of Simkin
Unless he was willing to be killed by Simkin

With panade, or with knyf, or boydekin.　　　　40
With cutlass, knife, or dagger.

For jalous folk ben perilous evermo;
For jealous people are always dangerous;

Algate they wolde hir wyves wanden so.
At least they want their wives to think so.

And eek, for she was somdel smoterlich,
And besides, since her reputation was a bit shady,

She was a digne as water in a dich,   44
She was as proud as ditchwater,

And ful of hoker and of bisemare.
And full of scorn and contempt.

Hir thoughte that a lady sholde hir spare,
She believed that her ladyship should be venerated,

What for her kinrede and hir nortelrye
In consideration of her lineage and her education

That she had lerned in the nonnerye.   48
Which she had gotten in the nunnery.

A doghter hadde they betwixe hem two
Between them, they had a daughter

Of twenty yeer, with-outen any mo
Of twenty years, no more

Savinge a child that was of half-yeer age;
Except a six-month-old child;

In cradel it lay and was a propre page.   52
A healthy baby lying in its cradle.

This wenche thikke and wel y-growen was,
This girl was plumb and well developed,

With camuse nose and yën greye as glas,
With a snub nose and eyes grey as glass,

With buttokes brode and brestes rounde and hye;
With broad buttocks and breasts round and high;

But right fair was hir heer, I wol nat lye.   56
And her hair was very lovely, I will not lie.

The person of the toun, for she was feir,
The town parson, since she was pretty,

In purpos was to maken hir his heir
Had in mind to make her his heir

Bothe of his catel and his messuage,
Both of his worldly goods and his house,

And straunge he made it of hir mariage.   60
And he made marriage for her difficult.

His purpos was for to bistowe hir hye
His intention was to bestow her highly

In-to som worthy blood of anncetrye;
Upon someone of noble ancestry;

For holy chirches good moot been despended
For the goods of Holy Church should be spent

On holy chirches blood that is descended.   64
On blood descended from Holy Church.

Therefore he wolde his holy blood honoure,
Therefore, he would honor his holy blood,

Though that he holy chirche sholde devoure.
Even though he should devour Holy Church.

   Gret soken hath this miller, out of doute,
   Without a doubt, this miller had taken great toll

With whete and malt of al the land about;   68
Of all the surrounding countryside on wheat and malt;

And nameliche ther was a greet collegge,
And especially there was a great college

Men clepen the Soler-halle at Cantebregge,
Called the Soler Hall at Cambridge,

Ther was hir whete and eek hir malt y-grounde.
Whose wheat and malt were ground there.

And on a day it happed, in a stounde,   72
And one day it happened

Sik lay the maunciple on a malydye;
That the manciple became ill with some disease;

Men wenden wisly that he sholde dye.
People really believed that he would die.

For which this miller stal bothe mele and corn
Wherefore this miller stole both meal and corn

An hundred tyme more than biforn;   76
A hundred times more than before;

For ther-biforn he stal but curteisly,
For hitherto he had stolen only courteously,

But now he was a theef outrageously,
But now he was a thief outrageously,

For which the wardeyn chidde and made fare.
Wherefore the warden scolded and made much ado.

But ther-of sette the miller nat a tare;   80
But the miller cared nothing about that;

He craketh boost, and swoor it was nat so.
He talked noisily and swore it wasn't so.

Than were there yonge povre clerkes two,
Then there were two young poor students,

That dwelten in this halle, of which I seye.
That lived in the hall I mentioned.

Testif they were, and lusty for to pleye,   84
Headstrong they were, and eager for fun,

And, only for hir mirthe and revelrye
And, only for pleasure and entertainment

Up-on the wardeyn bisily they crye
They incessantly plagued the warden

To yeve hem leve but a litel stounde
To give them just a short leave

To goon to mille and seen hir corn y-grounde;   88
To go to the mill and watch their corn being ground;

And hardily, they dorste leye hir nekke,
And scarcely, they dared pledge their necks,

The miller shold nat stele hem half a pekke
The miller would not rob them of half a peck

Of corn by sleighte, ne by force hem reve;
Of corn by trickery, nor rob them by force;

And at the laste the wardeyn yaf hem leve.   92
And finally the warden gave them permission.

John hight that oon, and Aleyn hight that other;
One was named John and the other was named Alan;

Of o toun were they born, that highte Strother,
They were born in the same town, known as Strother,

Fer in the north, I can nat telle where.
Far in the north, I can't say where.

  This Aleyn maketh redy al his gere,   96
  This Alan readied all his gear,

And on an hors the sak he caste anon.
And quickly tossed the sack on a horse.

Forth goth Aleyn the clerk and also John,
Off go Alan the student and also John,

With good swerd and with bokeler by hir syde.
With good swords and bucklers by their sides.

John knew the wey, hem nedede no gyde,   100
John knew the way (no guide was needed),

And at the mille the sak adoun he layth.
And at the mill he laid down the sack.

Aleyn spak first, "al hayl, Symond, y-fayth;
Alan spoke first, "All hail, Simon, in faith;

How fares thy faire doghter and thy wyf?"
How are your fair daughter and your wife?"

  "Aleyn! welcome," quod Simkin, "by my lyf,   104
  "Alan! Welcome," said Simkin, "by my life,

And John also, how now, what do ye heer?"
And John too, how's everything, what are you doing here?"

  "Symond," quod John, "by god, nede has na peer;
  "Simon," said John, "by God, need has no peer;

Him boës serve him-selve that has na swayn,
It behooves him to help himself who has no servant,

Or elles he is a fool, as clerkes sayn.   *108*
Or else he is a fool, as scholars say.

Our manciple, I hope he wil be deed,
Our manciple, I hope he will be dead,

Swa werkes ay the wanges in his heed.
So pain the molar teeth in his head.

And forthy is I come, and eek Alayn,
And I've come out, and Alan too,

To grinde our corn and carie it ham agayn;   *112*
To grind our corn and carry it home again;

I pray yow spede us hethen that ye may."
I beg you to let us get back as soon as you can."

"It shal be doon," quod Simkin, "by my fay;
"It shall be done," said Simkin, "by my faith;

What wol ye doon whyl that it is in hande?"
What will you do while it is in the works?"

"By god, right by the hoper will I stande,"   *116*
"By God, right by the hopper will I stand,"

Quod John, "and se how that the corn gas in;
Said John, "and see how the corn goes in;

Yet saugh I never, by my fader kin,
Never yet have I seen, by my father's folks,

How that the hoper wagges til and fra."
How the hopper wags to and fro."

Aleyn answerde, "John, and wiltow swa,   *120*
Alan replied, "John, and will you do so?

Than wil I be bynethe, by my croun,
Then I will be beneath, by my crown,

And se how that the mele falles doun
And see how the meal falls down

In-to the trough; that sal be my disport.
Into the trough; that will be my amusement.

For John, in faith, I may been of your sort;   124
For John, in faith, I may be of your kind;

I is as ille a miller as are ye."
I am as bad a miller as you are."

 This miller smyled of hir nycetee,
 The miller smiled at their nonsense,

And thoghte, "al this nis doon but for a wyle;
And thought, "All this is done only for a trick;

They wene that no man may hem bigyle;   128
They believe that nobody can fool them;

But, by my thrift, yet shal I blere hir yë
But, by my thrift, I'll still blind them

For al the sleighte in hir philosophye.
For all the ingenuity in their learning.

The more queynte crekes that they make,
The more cute tricks that they make,

The more wol I stele whan I take.   132
The more I'll steal when I get it.

In stede of flour, yet wol I yeve hem bren.
Instead of flour I will give them bran, even so.

'The gretteste clerkes been noght the wysest men.'
'The greatest scholars are not the wisest men.'

As whylom to the wolf thus spak the mare,
As once the mare said to the wolf,

Of al hir art I counte noght a tare."   136
I don't give a tare for all their learning."

 Out at the dore he gooth ful prively,
 Out of the door he went most secretly,

Whan that he saugh his tyme, softely;
When he saw his chance, quietly;

He loketh up and doun til he hath founde
He looked up and down until he found

The clerkes hors, ther as it stood y-bounde 140
The students' horse where it stood tethered

Behinde the mille, under a levesel;
Behind the mill, under an arbour;

And to the hors he gooth him faire and wel;
And he went straight up to the horse

He strepeth of the brydel right anon.
And quickly stripped it of its bridle.

And whan the hors was loos, he ginneth gon 144
And when the horse was loose, he began to go

Toward the fen, ther wilde mares renne,
Toward the fen where wild mares run,

Forth with wehee, thurgh thikke and thurgh thenne.
Off with a whinny through thick and thin.

This miller gooth agayn, no word he seyde,
The miller returned without saying a word,

But dooth his note, and with the clerkes pleyde 148
But did his job and kidded with the students

Til that hir corn was faire and wel y-grounde.
Until their corn was nicely and well ground.

And whan the mele is sakked and y-bounde,
And when the meal was sacked and tied,

This John goth out and fynt his horse away,
This John went out and found his horse gone,

And gan to crye "harrow" and "weylaway! 152
And began to shout "Help!" and "Woe is me!

Our hors is lorn! Alayn, for goddes banes,
Our horse is lost! Alan, for God's bones,

Step on thy feet, com out, man, al at anes!
Step on it, come out, man, pronto!

Allas, our wardeyn has his palfrey lorn."
Alas, our warden has lost his palfrey."

This Aleyn al forgat, bothe mele and corn;   156
This Alan forgot everything, both meal and corn;

Al was out of his mynde his housbondrye.
His careful planning went completely out of his mind.

"What? whilk way is he geen?" he gan to crye.
"What? Which way did he go?" he began to cry.

The wyf cam leping inward with a ren,
The wife came dashing in at a run,

She seyde, "allas! your hors goth to the fen   160
She said, "Allas! Your horse has gone to the fen

With wilde mares, as faste as he may go.
With the wild mares, as fast as he could go.

Unthank come on his hand that bond him so,
No thanks to him that tethered him so,

And he that bettre sholde han knit the reyne."
And the one who should have tied the rein better."

"Allas," quod John, "Aleyn, for Cristes peyne,   164
"Alas," said John, "Alan, for Christ's pain,

Lay doun thy swerd, and I wil myn alswa;
Lay down your sword, and I will mine also;

I is ful wight, god waat, as is a raa;
I am as quick, God knows, as a roe;

By goddes herte he sal nat scape us bathe.
By God's heart, he shall not escape us both.

Why nadstow pit the capul in the lathe?   168
Why didn't you put the nag in the barn?

Il-hayl, by god, Aleyn; thou is a fonne!"
Bad cess to you, by God; Alan, you're a fool!"

This sely clerkes had ful faste y-ronne
These poor students ran off quickly

To-ward the fen, bothe Aleyn and eek John.
Toward the fen, both Alan and also John.

And whan the miller saugh that they were gon,   172
And when the miller saw that they were gone,

He half a busshel of hir flour hath take
He took half a bushel of their flour

And bad his wyf go knede it in a cake.
And told his wife to knead it into a cake.

He seyde, "I trowe the clerkes were aferd;
He said, "I imagine the students were frightened;

Yet can a miller make a clerkes berd   176
A miller can still outdo a scholar's beard

For al his art; now lat hem goon hir weye.
For all his learning; now let them go their way.

Lo wher they goon, ye, lat the children pleye;
See where they've gone, sure, let the children play;

They gete him nat so lightly, by my croun."
They won't catch him very easily, by my crown."

Thise sely clerkes rennen up and doun   180
These poor students ran up and down

With "keep, keep, stand, stand, joss, warderere,
With "Look out, look out, whoa, whoa, down here, look out
behind,

Ga whistle thou, and I shall kepe him here!"
You go whistle and I will watch him here!"

But shortly, til that it was verray night,
But in short, until it was really night,

They coude nat, though they do al hir might,   184
They could not, even with their best efforts,

Hir capul cacche, he ran alwey so faste.
Catch their nag, he always ran so fast.

Til in a dich they caughte him atte laste.
Until they finally caught him in a ditch.

Wery and weet, as beste is in the reyn,
Weary and wet, like cattle in the rain,

Comth sely John, and with him comth Aleyn. 188
Returned poor John, and Alan came with him.

"Allas," quod John, "the day that I was born!
"Alas," said John, "the day that I was born!

Now are we drive til hething and til scorn.
Now are we driven to contempt and scorn.

Our corn is stole, men wil us foles calle,
Our corn is stolen, people will call us fools,

Bathe the wardeyn and our felawes alle, 192
Both the warden and all our comrades,

And namely the miller; weylaway!"
And especially the miller; rot it!"

Thus pleyneth John as he goth by the way
So John complained as he went on his way

Toward the mille, and Bayard in his hand.
Toward the mill, leading Bayard with his hand.

The miller sitting by the fyr he fond, 196
He found the miller sitting by the fire,

For it was night, and forther mighte they noght;
For it was night, and they could go no farther;

But, for the love of god, they him bisoght
But, for the love of God, they asked him

Of herberwe and of ese, as for hir peny.
For lodging and comfort, to be paid for.

The miller seyde agayn, "if ther be eny, 200
The miller replied, "If there is any,

Swich as it is, yet shal ye have your part.
Such as it is, you shall have your share.

Myn hous is streit, but ye han lerned art;
My house is cramped, but you have acquired learning;

Ye conne by argumentes make a place
You know how by arguments to make a place

A myle brood of twenty foot of space.   *204*
A mile wide out of a twenty-foot space.

Lat see now if this place may suffyse,
Let's see now if this place will do,

Or make it roum with speche, as is youre gyse."
Or else make it bigger with talking, as your custom is."

"Now, Symond," seyde John, "by seint Cutberd,
"Now, Simon," said John, "by Saint Cuthbert,

Ay is thou mery, and this is faire answerd.   *208*
You are always fooling, and this is a fair answer.

I have herd seyd, man sal taa of twa thinges
I have heard it said, a person must take one of two things,

Slyk as he fyndes, or taa slyk as he bringes.
Such as he finds or such as he brings.[1]

But specially, I pray thee, hoste dere,
But especially, I beg you, dear host,

Get us som mete and drinke, and make us chere,   *212*
Get us some food and drink, and make us comfortable,

And we wil payen trewely atte fulle.
And we will truly pay in full.

With empty hand men may na haukes tulle;
With an empty hand nobody can catch a hawk;

Lo here our silver, redy for to spende."
See, here's our money, ready to be spent."

This miller in-to toun his doghter sende   *216*
The miller sent his daughter to town

For ale and breed, and rosted hem a goos,
For ale and bread, and roasted them a goose,

And bond hir hors, it sholde nat gon loos;
And tied up their horse so it wouldn't get loose;

And in his owne chambre hem made a bed
And made up a bed for them in his own bedroom

With shetes and with chalons faire y-spred,   220
Nicely spread with sheets and blankets,

Noght from his owne bed ten foot or twelve.
Not more than ten or twelve feet from his own bed.

His doghter hadde a bed, al by hir-selve,
His daughter had a bed, all by herself,

Right in the same chambre, by and by;
Right in the same bedroom, very near by;

It mighte be no bet, and cause why,   224
It could be no better, and the reason was

Ther was no roumer herberwe in the place.
There was no other room in the place.

They soupen and they speke, hem to solace,
They ate and they talked, to amuse themselves,

And drinken ever strong ale atte beste.
And continued to drink strong ale steadily.

Aboute midnight wente they to reste.   228
They went to bed about midnight.

Wel hath this miller vernisshed his heed;
The miller had thoroughly varnished his head;

Ful pale he was for-dronken, and nat reed.
He was wanly drunk, and not flushed.

He yexeth, and he speketh thurgh the nose
He hiccupped, and he talked through his nose

As he were on the quakke, or on the pose.   232
As if he were hoarse or had a cold in the head.

To bedde he gooth, and with him goth his wyf.
To bed he went, and with him went his wife.

As any jay she light was and jolyf,
She was as gay and jolly as a jay,

So was hir joly whistle wel y-wet.
Since she had well wet her merry whistle.

The cradel at hir beddes feet is set,   236
The cradle was set at the foot of their bed,

To rokken, and to yeve the child to souke.
To be rocked and to suckle the child.

And whan that drouken al was in the crouke,
And when all that was in the jug had been drunk,

To bedde went the doghter right anon;
The daughter went to bed right away;

To bedde gooth Aleyn and also John;   240
To bed went Alan and John too;

Ther nas na more; hem nedede no dwale.
There was nothing left; they didn't need a sleeping potion.

This miller hath so wisly bibbed ale
This miller had so surely imbibed ale

That as an hors he snorteth in his sleep,
That he snorted in his sleep like a horse,

Ne of his tayl bihinde he took no keep.   244
Nor was he careful of his tail behind.

His wyf bar him a burdon, a ful strong,
His wife accompanied him, in full measure,

Men mighte hir routing here two furlong;
Their snoring could be heard two furlongs away;

The wenche routeth eek *par companye.*
The girl also snored to keep them company.

Aleyn the clerk, that herd this melodye,   248
When Alan the student heard this melody,

He poked John, and seyde, "slepestow?
He poked John and said, "Are you asleep?

Herdestow ever slyk a sang er now?
Did you ever before hear such a song?

Lo, whilk a compline is y-mel hem alle!
What an evening service they are having!

A wilde fyr up-on thair bodyes falle!   252
May erysipelas fall on their bodies!

Wha herkned ever slyk a ferly thing?
Who ever listened to such a weird thing?

Ye, they sal have the flour of il ending.
Yea, they will have the flour of a bad ending.

This lange night ther tydes me na reste;
This long night will see no rest for me;

But yet, na fors, al sal be for the beste.   256
But still, no matter, all will be for the best.

For John," seyde he, "als ever moot I thryve,
For John," said he, "as I ever hope to prosper,

If that I may, yon wenche wil I swyve.
If I can manage it, I will screw that girl.

Som esement has lawe y-shapen us;
Som redress has been provided us by law;

For John, ther is a lawe that says thus,   260
For John, there is a law that says

That gif a man in a point be y-greved,
That if a man be hurt in one point,

That in another he sal be releved.
That he will be relieved in another.

Our corn is stoln, shortly, it is na nay,
Our corn is stolen; in short, that can't be denied,

And we han had an il fit al this day.   264
And we have had a bad time all this day.

And sin I sal have neen amendement,
And since I will get no just treatment,

Agayn my los I will have esement.
I will have compensation against my loss.

By goddes saule, it sal neen other be!”
By God's soul, it won't be otherwise!”

This John answerde, “Alayn, avyse thee;   268
This John replied, “Alan, be careful;

The miller is a perilous man,” he seyde,
The miller is a dangerous man,” he said,

“And gif that he out of his sleep abreyde,
“And if he is suddenly roused out of his sleep,

He mighte doon us bathe a vileinye.”
He might do us both great harm.”

Aleyn answerde, “I count him nat a flye”;   272
Alan replied, “I don't consider him worth a fly”;

And up he rist, and by the wenche he crepte.
And up he rose, and by the girl he crept.

This wenche lay upright, and faste slepte,
This girl lay face up, and slept soundly,

Til he so ny was, er she mighte espye,
Until he was so near, before she could see him,

That it had been to late for to crye,   276
That it was too late for her to cry out,

And shortly for to seyn, they were at on;
And to speak briefly, they were as one;

Now pley, Aleyn! for I wol speke of John.
Now enjoy yourself, Alan! for I will speak of John.

This John lyth stille a furlong-wey or two,
This John lay quietly about a furlong away,

And to him-self he maketh routhe and wo: 280
And pities and commiserates with himself:

“Allas!” quod he, “this is a wikked jape;
“Alas!” he said, “this is a wicked joke;

Now may I seyn that I is but an ape.
Now I can say that I'm no better than a monkey.

Yet has my felawe som-what for his harm;
Yet my friend has something for his bad treatment;

He has the milleris doghter in his arm.   *284*
He has the miller's daughter in his arms.

He auntred him, and has his nedes sped,
He took a chance and has succeeded,

And I lye as a draf-sek in my bed;
And I lie in my bed like a garbage-sack;

And when this jape is tald another day,
And when this trick is told some day,

I sal been halde a daf, a cokenay!   *288*
I shall be considered a fool, a sissy!

I wil aryse, and auntre it, by my fayth!
I will get up and chance it, by my faith!

'Unhardy is unsely,' thus men sayth."
'Timidity is unhappy,' as the saying goes."

And up he roos and softely he went
And up he rose and quietly went

Un-to the cradel, and in his hand it hente,   *292*
Up to the cradle and picked it up

And baar it softe un-to his beddes feet.
And carried it quietly to the foot of his bed.

  Sone after this the wyf hir routing leet,
* Soon after this the wife stopped snoring,*

And gan awake, and wente hir out to pisse,
And woke up, and went out to piss,

And cam agayn, and gan hir cradel misse,   *296*
And came back, and couldn't find her cradle,

And groped heer and ther, but she found noon.
And groped here and there but found nothing.

"Allas!" quod she, "I hadde almost misgoon;
"Alas!" said she, "I almost lost my way;

I hadde almost gon to the clerkes bed.
I nearly went to the students' bed.

Ey, *ben'cite!* thanne hadde I foule y-sped":   *300*
Ah, bless me! then I'd have been in trouble";

And forth she gooth til she the cradel fond.
And off she went until she found the cradle.

She gropeth alwey forther with hir hond
She groped a little farther with her hand

And fond the bed, and thoghte noght but good,
And found the bed, and thought nothing wrong,

By-cause that the cradel by it stood,   *304*
Because the cradle was beside it,

And niste wher she was, for it was derk;
And didn't know where she was, since it was dark;

But faire and wel she creep in to the clerk,
But in all good conscience she crept in beside the student,

And lyth ful stille, and wolde han caught a sleep.
And lay very quiet and would have gone to sleep.

With-inne a whyl this John the clerk up leep,   *308*
In a little while this John the student popped up,

And on this gode wyf he leyth on sore.
And laid this good wife with a vengeance.

So mery a fit ne hadde she nat ful yore;
So merry a bout she hadn't had in ages;

He priketh harde and depe as he were mad.
He pricked hard and deep as if he were mad.

This joly lyf han thise two clerkes lad   *312*
These two students led this jolly life

Til that the thridde cok bigan to singe.
Until the third rooster began to crow.

Aleyn wex wery in the daweninge,
Alan became weary as dawn came,

For he had swonken al the longe night,
For he had labored all night long,

And seyde, "far wel, Malin, swete wight!   *316*
And said, "Farewell, Molly, sweet thing!

The day is come; I may no lenger byde,
Daylight has come; I can stay no longer,

But evermo, wher so I go or ryde,
But evermore, wherever I walk or ride,

I is thy awen clerk, swa have I see!"
I am your own student, as I may have bliss!"

   "Now dere lemman," quod she, "go, far weel!   *320*
   "Now dear sweetheart," said she, "go, farewell!

But er thou go, o thing I wol thee telle,
But before you go, I'll tell you one thing,

Whan that thou wendest homward by the melle,
When you go towards home passing the mill,

Right at the entree of the dore bihinde,
Right behind the entrance of the door,

Thou shalt a cake of half a busshel finde   *324*
You will find a half-bushel cake

That was y-maked of thyn owne mele,
That was made of your own meal,

Which that I heelp my fader for to stele.
Which I helped my father steal.

And, gode lemman, god thee save and kepe!"
And good dearheart, God save and keep you!"

And with that word almost she gan to wepe.   *328*
And with that word she almost began to weep.

   Aleyn up-rist, and thoughte, "er that it dawe,
   Alan got up and thought, "Before it dawns,

I wol go crepen in by my felawe";
I will go crawl in by my friend";

And fond the cradel with his hand anon,
And immediately his hand touched the cradle,

"By god," thoghte he, "al wrang I have misgon;   332
"By God," he thought, "I've come all wrong;

Myn heed is toty of my swink to-night,
My head is reeling from my work tonight;

That maketh me that I go nat ailght.
That's why I couldn't get my bearings.

I woot wel by the cradel, I have misgo;
I can surely tell by the cradle that I have blundered;

Heer lyth the miller and his wyf also."   336
Here lies the miller together with his wife."

And forth he goth, a twenty devel way,
And off he went, by a twenty devils' road,

Un-to the bed ther-as the miller lay.
Over to the bed occupied by the miller.

He wende have cropen by his felawe John;
He expected to creep in by his friend John;

And by the miller in he creep anon,   340
And actually crawled in beside the miller,

And caughte hym by the nekke, and softe he spak:
And pulled his neck over and whispered:

He seyd, "thou, John, thou swynes-heed, awak
He said, "John, you pig's head, wake up

For Cristes saule, and heer a noble game.
For Christ's soul, and hear a noble sport.

For by that lord that called is seint Jame,   344
For by that lord that is called Saint James,

As I have thryes, in this shorte night,
During this short night, I have three times

Swyved the milleres doghter bolt-upright,
Screwed the miller's daughter straight on her back,

Whyl thow hast as a coward been agast."
While you have been fightened like a coward."

"Ye, false harlot," quod the miller, "hast?   348
"Oh, false rascal," said the miller, "you have?

A! false traitour! false clerk!" quod he,
Hah! cheating traitor! cheating student!" said he,

"Thou shalt be deed, by goddes dignitee!
"You will be dead, by God's honor!

Who dorste be so bold to disparage
Who dares to be so bold to dishonor

My doghter, that is come of swich linage?"   352
My daughter, who comes of such lineage?"

And by the throte-bolle he caughte Alayn,
And he seized Alan by the Adam's apple,

And he hente him despitously agayn,
And he grabbed him mercilessly again,

And on the nose he smoot him with his fest.
And he punched him in the nose with his fist.

Doun ran the blody stream up-on his brest;   356
Down ran the bloody stream onto his chest;

And in the floor, with nose and mouth to-broke,
And on the floor, with nose and mouth broken,

They walwe as doon two pigges in a poke.
They wallowed like two pigs in a poke.

And up they goon, and doun agayn anon,
And up they got, and down again right away,

Til that the miller sporned at a stoon,   360
Until the miller tripped on a stone

And doun he fil bakward up-on his wyf,
And fell down backward upon his wife,

That wiste no-thing of this nyce stryf;
Who knew nothing about this foolish strife;

For she was falle aslepe a lyte wight
For she had just fallen asleep

With John the clerk, that waked hadde al night.   364
With John the student, after being awake all night.

And with the fal, out of hir sleep she breyde—
And with the fall, she was startled out of her sleep—

"Help, holy croys of Bromeholm," she seyde,
"Help, holy cross of Bromholm," she cried,

"*In manus tuas!* lord, to thee I calle!
"*Into thy hands! Lord, to thee I call!*

Awak, Symond! the feend is on us falle;   368
Wake up, Simon! The fiend has fallen on us;

Myn herte is broken, help, I nam but deed;
My heart is broken, help, I am but dead;

There lyth oon up my wombe and up myn heed;
Someone's lying on my womb and on my head;

Help, Simkin, for the false clerkes fighte."
Help, Simkin, for the dastardly students are fighting."

This John sterte up as faste as ever he mighte,   372
This John jumped up as fast as ever he could,

And graspeth by the walles to and fro
And grabbed at the walls here and there

To finde a staf; and she sterte up also,
To find a stick, and she jumped up also,

And knew the estres bet than did this John,
And knew the insides better than this John did,

And by the wal a staf she fond anon,   376
And along the wall she soon found a stick

And saugh a litel shimering of a light,
And saw a little shimmering of light,

For at an hole in shoon the none bright;
For the moon shone brightly through a hole;

And by that light she saugh hem bothe two,
And by that light she saw both of them,

But sikerly she niste who was who,   380
But truly she didn't know which was which,

But as she saugh a whyt thing in hir yë,
But when her eye caught a glimpse of a white thing,

And whan she gan the whyte thing espye,
And when she managed to focus on this white thing,

She wende the clerk hadde wered a volupeer.
She thought the student had worn a night-cap.

And with the staf she drough ay neer and neer,   384
And with the stick she drew nearer and nearer,

And wende han hit this Aleyn at the fulle,
And intended to hit this Alan at her hardest,

And smoot the miller on the pyled skulle,
And so struck the miller on his bald skull

That doun he gooth and cryde, "harrow! I dye!"
That down he went and cried, "Help! I'm dying!"

Thise clerkes bete him weel and lete him lye,   388
The students beat him thoroughly and left him lying there,

And greythen hem, and toke hir hors anon,
And got themselves ready and took their horse quickly,

And eek hir mele, and on hir wey they gon.
And also their meal, and on their way they went.

And at the mille yet they toke hir cake
And besides they took their cake at the mill,

Of half a busshel flour ful wel y-bake.   392
Well baked with half a bushel of flour.

Thus is the proude miller wel y-bete,
So was the proud miller well beaten,

And hath y-lost the grinding of the whete,
And lost his fee for grinding the wheat,

And payed for the soper every-deel
And paid every bit for the supper

Of Aleyn and of John, that bette him weel.   396
Of Alan and John, who beat him well.

His wyf is swyved and his doghter als;
His wife was screwed as well as his daughter;

Lo, swich it is a miller to be fals!
See, that's what happens to a cheating miller!

And therefore this proverbe is seyd ful sooth,
And therefore this proverb is truly stated,

"Him thar nat wene wel that yvel dooth;   400
"He who does evil is not well thought of;

A gylour shal him-self bigyled be."
A trickster shall be tricked himself."

And God, that sitteth heighe in magestee,
And God, who sits high in majesty,

Save al this companye grete and smale!
Save all this company, great and small!

Thus have I quit the miller in my tale.   404
So have I paid back the miller in my tale.

Prologue to the Prioress's Tale

"Wel seyd, by *corpus dominus*," quod our hoste,
"Well said, by our Lord's body," said our host,

"Now longe moot thou sayle by the coste,
"Now long may you sail along the coast,

Sir gentil maister, gentil marineer!
Sir noble master, noble mariner![1]

God yeve this monk a thousand last quad yeer!   4
God give this monk a thousand loads of bad years!

A ha! felawes! beth ware of swiche a jape!
Ah ha! comrades! beware of such a trick!

The monk putte in the mannes hood an ape,
The monk put a monkey in the man's hood,

And in his wyves eek, by seint Austin!
And in his wife's too, by Saint Augustine!

Draweth no monkes more un-to your in.   8
Invite no more monks into your house.[2]

   "But now passe over, and lat us seke aboute,
   "But let that pass, and let us look about

Who shal now telle first, of al this route,
And see who shall tell next, of all this group,

Another tale;" and with that word he sayde,
Another tale;" and with that word he said,

As curteisly as it had been a mayde,   12
As courteously as if he had been a maid,

"My lady prioresse, by your leve,
"My lady prioress, by your leave,

So that I wiste I sholde yow nat greve,
If I knew that I would not disturb you,

I wolde demen that ye tellen sholde
I would deem that you should tell

A tale next, if so were that ye wolde.   16
A tale next, if you would be willing.

Now wol ye vouche-sauf, my lady dere?"
Now will you be so kind, my dear lady?"

"Gladly," quod she, and seyde as ye shal here.
"Gladly," she said, and spoke as you shall hear.

The Prioress's Invocation

DOMINE, DOMINUS NOSTER.[1]

O Lord our lord, thy name how marveillous
O Lord our Lord, how marvellously Thy name

Is in this large worlde y-sprad—quod she:—
Is spread throughout this large world—said she:—

For noght only thy laude precious
For not only is Thy sacred praise

Parfourned is by men of dignitee,   4
Performed by men of rank,

But by the mouth of children thy bountee
But by the mouths of children Thy bounty

Parfourned is, for on the brest soukinge
Is celebrated, for, sucking at the breast,

Som tyme shewen they thyn heryinge.
Sometimes they show Thy praise.

Wherfor in laude, as I best can or may,   8
Wherefore in praise, as I best can or may,

Of thee, and of the whyte lily flour
Of Thee, and of the White Lily-Flower'

Which that thee bar, and is a mayde alway,
Who bore Thee, and ever remained a maid,

To telle a storie I wol do my labour;
I will do my best to tell a story;

Not that I may encresen hir honour;   12
Not that I may increase Her honor;

For she hir-self is honour, and the rote
For She Herself is honor, and the root

Of bountee, next hir sone, and soules bote.—
Of bounty and soul's healing, next to Her Son.—

O moder mayde! o mayde moder free!
O Mother Maid! O gracious Maiden Mother!

O bush unbrent, brenninge in Moyses sight,   16
O Bush Unburnt, burning in Moses' sight,

That ravisedest doun fro the deitee,
Who didst ravish from the Deity,

Thurgh thyn humblesse, the goost that in th'alighte,
Through Thy humility, the Spirit that alighted in Thee,

Of whos vertu, whan he thyn herte lighte,
From Whose virtue, when He dwelt in Thy heart,

Conceived was the fadres sapience,   20
Was conceived the Father's Wisdom,[3]

Help me to telle it in thy reverence!
Help me to tell it in Thy glory!

Lady! thy bountee, thy magnificence,
Lady! Thy bounty, Thy graciousness,

Thy vertu, and thy grete humilitee
Thy virtue, and Thy great humility

Ther may no tongue expresse in no science;   24
No tongue, however learned, can express;

For som-tyme, lady, er men praye to thee,
For sometimes, Lady, before men pray to Thee,

Thou goost biforn of thy benignitee,
Thou dost anticipate, out of Thy goodness,

And getest us the light, thurgh thy preyere,
And sendest us the light, through Thy prayer,

To gyden us un-to thy sone so dere.   28
To guide us to Thy Son so dear.

My conning is so wayk, a blisful quene,
My intellect is so weak, O blessed Queen,

For to declare thy grete worthinesse,
For declaring Thy great worth,

That I ne may the weighte nat sustene,
That I cannot sustain the burden.

But as a child of twelf monthe old, or lesse,   32
But as a child of twelve months old, or less,

That can unnethes any word expresse,
Who can scarcely speak a word,

Right so fare I, and therfor I yow preye,
Even so fare I, and therefore I beseech Thee,

Gydeth my song that I shal of yow seye.
Guide my song that I shall say of Thee.

The Prioress's Tale

Ther was in Asie, in a greet citee,
There was in Asia, in a great city,

Amonges Cristen folk, a Jewerye,
Amidst Christian folk, a Jewish quarter,

Sustened by a lord of that contree
Maintained by a lord of that country

For foule usure and lucre of vilanye,
For foul usury and vile gain,

Hateful to Crist and to his companye;
Hateful to Christ and to His Fellowship;[1]

And thurgh the strete men mighte ryde or wende,
And through the street men could ride or walk,

For it was free, and open at either ende.
For it was public, and open at either end.

A litel scole of Cristen folk ther stood   8
A small school of Christian people stood

Doun at the ferther ende, in which ther were
Down at the farther end, in which there were

Children an heep, y-comen of Cristen blood,
Many children, born of Christian blood,

That lerned in that scole yeer by yere
Who studied in that school, year by year,

Swich maner doctrine as men used there,   12
The sort of learning that was in use there,

This is to seyn, to singen and to rede,
That is to say, to sing and to read,

As smale children doon in hir childhede.
As little children do in their childhood.

Among thise children was a widwes sone,
Among these children was a widow's son,

A litel clergeon, seven yeer of age,   16
A little schoolboy, seven years of age,

That day by day to scole was his wone,
Who on the way to school every day,

And eek also, wher-as he saugh th'image
And other times too, whenever he saw the statue

Of Cristes moder, hadde he in usage,
Of Christ's Mother, he was accustomed,

As him was taught, to knele adoun and seye   20
As had been taught him, to kneel down and say

His AVE MARIE, as he goth by the weye.
His AVE MARIA, as he went on his way.

Thus hath this widwe hir litel sone y-taught
So had this widow taught her little son

Our blisful lady, Cristes moder dere,
Our blessed Lady, Christ's Mother dear,

To worshipe ay, and he forgat it naught,   24
To worship ever, and he never forgot it,

For sely child wol alday sone lere;
For an innocent child will always learn quickly,

But ay, whan I remembre on this matere,
But always, when I think of this subject,

Seint Nicholas stant ever in my presence,
Saint Nicholas stands ever in my presence,

For he so yong to Crist did reverence.   28
Because he did reverence to Christ when so young.²

This litel child, his litel book lerninge,
This little child, studying his little book,

As he sat in the scole at his prymer,
As he sat in school at his primer,

He ALMA REDEMPTORIS herde singe,
Heard the ALMA REDEMPTORIS sung,

As children lerned hir antiphoner;   32
As the children practiced their responses;

And, as he dorste, he drough him ner and ner,
And, close as he dared, he drew nearer and nearer,

And herkned ay the wordes and the note,
And listened to the words and the melody,

Til he the firste vers coude al by rote.
Until he knew all the first verse by heart.

Noght wiste he what this Latin was to seye,   *36*
He knew nothing of what this Latin meant,

For he so yong and tendre was of age;
Because he was so young and tender of age;

But on a day his felaw gan he preye
But one day he begged his comrade

T'expounden him this song in his langage,
To translate this song to him in his language,

Or telle him why this song was in usage;   *40*
Or tell him why this song was in use;

This preyde he him to construe and declare
This he begged him construe and explain

Ful ofte tyme upon his knowes bare.
Many a time on his bare knees.

His felaw, which that elder was than he,
His friend, who was older than he,

Answerde him thus: "This song, I have herd seye,   *44*
Answered him thus: "This song, I have heard say,

Was maked of our blisful lady free,
Was composed about Our Blessed Benign Lady,

Hir to salue, and eek hir for to preye
To greet Her, and also to beseech Her

To been our help and socour whan we deye.
To be our help and comfort when we die.

I can no more expounde in this matere;   *48*
I can expound no more of this matter;

I lerne song, I can but smal grammere."
I study singing, but I know little grammar."

"And is this song maked in reverence
"And is this song offered in reverence

Of Cristes moder?" seyde this innocent;
Of Christ's Mother?" said this innocent;

"Now certes, I wol do my diligence   52
"Now truly, I will do my best

To conne it al, er Cristemasse is went;
To learn it all, before Christmas is over;

Though that I for my prymer shal be shent,
Though I be scolded because of my primer,

And shal be beten thryës in an houre,
And be beaten three times in an hour,

I wol it conne, our lady for to honoure."   56
I will memorize it, to honor Our Lady."

His felaw taughte him homward prively,
His comrade taught him privately, going home

Fro day to day, til he coude it by rote,
From day to day, until he knew it by heart,

And than he song it wel and boldely
And then he sang it well and boldly,

Fro word to word, acording with the note;   60
Word for word, in keeping with the notes;

Twyës a day it passed thurgh his throte,
Twice a day it passed through his throat,

To scoleward and homward whan he wente;
As he went to school and on the way home;

On Cristes moder set was his entente.
His thoughts were directed toward Christ's Mother.

As I have seyd, thurgh-out the Jewerye   64
As I have said, through the Jewish quarter

This litel child, as he cam to and fro,
This little child, as he went back and forth,

Ful merily than wolde he singe, and crye
Most joyously then would he sing and chant

"O ALMA REDEMPTORIS" ever-mo.
"O ALMA REDEMPTORIS" constantly.

The swetnes hath his herte perced so   68
The sweetness had so penetrated his heart

Of Cristes moder, that, to hir to preye,
Of Christ's Mother, that, to pray to Her,

He can nat stinte of singing by the weye.
He could not leave off singing along the way.

Our firste fo, the serpent Sathanas,
Our first enemy, the serpent Satan,

That hath in Jewes herte his waspes nest,   72
Who has his wasp's nest in the Jewish heart,

Up swal, and seide, "O Hebraik peple, allas!
Swelled up, and said, "O Hebrew people, alas!

Is this to yow a thing that is honest,
Is this something that seems decent to you,

That swich a boy shal walken as him lest
That such a boy should walk as he pleases

In your despyt, and singe of swich sentence,   76
In scorn of you, and sing of such a theme

Which is agayn your lawes reverence?"
As is opposed to the sanctity of your laws?"

Fro thennes forth the Jewes han conspyred
Thenceforth the Jews conspired

This innocent out of this world to chace;
To drive this innocent out of this world;

An homicyde ther-to han they hyred,   80
A murderer for this purpose they hired,

That in an aley hadde a privee place;
Who in an alley had a secret hiding-place;

And as the child gan for-by to pace,
And as the child began to walk by there,

This cursed Jew him hente and heeld him faste,
This cursed Jew seized him and held him fast,

And kitte his throte, and in a pit him caste.   84
And cut his throat, and threw him in a pit.

I seye that in a wardrobe they him threwe
I say that in a cesspool they threw him

Wher-as these Jewes purgen hir entraille.
Where the Jews relieved their bowels.

O cursed folk of Herodes al newe,
O cursed modern compatriots of Herod,

What may your yvel entente yow availle?   88
What can your evil intentions avail you?

Mordre wol out, certain, it wol nat faille,
Murder will out, in truth it will not fail,

And namely ther th'onour of God shal sprede,
And especially where it redounds to the glory of God,

The blood out cryeth on your cursed dede.
The blood cries out on your cursed deed.

"O martir, souded to virginitee,   92
"O martyr, devoted to virginity,

Now maystou singen, folwing ever in oon
Now mayst thou sing, following ever

The whyte lamb celestial," quod she,
The white celestial Lamb," said the prioress,

"Of which the grete evangelist, seint John,
"Of whom the great evangelist, Saint John,

In Pathmos wroot, which seith that they that goon   96
Wrote in Patmos, saying that they walk

Biforn this lamb, and singe a song al newe,
Before the Lamb, and sing an ever new song,

That never, fleshly, wommen they ne knewe."
Who never had carnal knowledge of women."

This povre widwe awaiteth al that night
This poor widow waited all that night

After hir litel child, but he cam noght;   100
For her little child, but he came not;

For which, as sone as it was dayes light,
Wherefore, as soon as it was daylight,

With face pale of drede and bisy thoght,
With face pale with fear and constant worrying,

She hath at scole and elles-wher him soght,
She looked for him at school and elsewhere,

Til finally she gan so fer espye   104
Until finally she made the discovery

That he last seyn was in the Jewerye.
That he was last seen in the Jewish quarter.

With modres pitee in hir brest enclosed,
With a mother's pity locked in her breast,

She gooth, as she were half out of hir minde,
She went, as if she were half out of her mind,

To every place wher she hath supposed   108
To every place where she imagined

By liklihede hir litel childe to finde;
In likelihood she might find her little child;

And ever on Cristes moder meke and kinde
And ever on Christ's Mother meek and kind

She cryde, and atte laste thus she wroghte,
She called, and at last She brought it about

Among the cursed Jewes she him soghte.   112
That she sought him among the cursed Jews.

She frayneth and she preyeth pitously
She inquired and she piteously begged

To every Jew that dwelte in thilke place
Every Jew who lived in that place

To telle hir, if hir child wente oght for-by.
To tell her if her child had passed by there.

They seyde, "nay;" but Jesu, of his grace,   116
They said, "No;" but Jesus, of His grace,

Yaf in hir thought, inwith a litel space,
Put in her mind, after a short time,

That in that place after hir sone she cryde,
To call to her son in that place

Wher he was casten in a pit bisyde.
Near the pit into which he had been thrust.

O grete God, that parfournest thy laude   *120*
O great God, Who performest Thy praise

By mouth of innocents, lo heer thy might!
In the mouths of innocents, here behold Thy power!

This gemme of chastitee, this emeraude,
This gem of chastity, this emerald,

And eek of martirdom the ruby bright,
And also the bright ruby of martyrdom,

Ther he with throte y-corven lay upright,   *124*
Where he lay face upright with throat slit,

He "ALMA REDEMPTORIS" gan to singe
Began to sing "ALMA REDEMPTORIS"

So loude, that al the place gan to ringe.
So loud, that all the place began to ring.

The Cristen folk, that thurgh the strete wente,
The Christian folk, who were going through the street,

In coomen, for to wondre up-on this thing,   *128*
Came up to wonder about this thing,

And hastily they for the provost sente;
And hastily they sent for the magistrate;

He cam anon with-outen tarying,
He came at once without delay,

And herieth Crist that is of heven king,
And praised Christ Who is King of Heaven,

And eek his moder, honour of mankinde,   *132*
And His Mother too, glory of mankind,

And after that, the Jewes leet he binde.
And after that, he had the Jews bound.

This child with pitous lamentacioun
This child with piteous lamentation

Up-taken was, singing his song alway;
Was taken up, ever singing his song;

And with honour of greet processioun   *136*
And with the honor of a great procession

They carien him un-to the nexte abbay.
They carried him to the nearest abbey.

His moder swowning by the bere lay;
His mother lay by the bier swooning;

Unnethe might the peple that was there
Hardly could the people who were there

This newe Rachel bringe fro his bere.   *140*
Lead this new Rachel from his bier.

With torment and with shamful deth echon
With torment and with shameful death each one

This provost dooth thise Jewes for to sterve
Of those Jews, the magistrate ordered to be executed,

That of this mordre wiste, and that anon;
Who knew of this murder, and that immediately;

He nolde no swich cursednesse observe.   *144*
He would not countenance any such cursedness.

Yvel shal have that yvel wol deserve.
Evil shall be allotted to those who deserve evil.

Therfor with wilde hors he dide hem drawe,
Therefore he had them dragged by wild horses,

And after that he heng hem by the lawe.
And after that he hanged them according to law.

Up-on his bere ay lyth this innocent   148
Upon his bier still lay this innocent

Biforn the chief auter, whyl masse laste,
Before the main altar, while mass continued,

And after that, the abbot with his covent
And after that, the abbot with his convent

Han sped hem for to burien him ful faste;
Hastened to bury him quickly;

And whan they holy water on him caste,   152
And when they cast holy water on him,

Yet spak this child, whan spreynd was holy water,
Still spoke this child, when holy water was sprinkled,

And song—"O ALMA REDEMPTORIS MATER!"
And sang—"O ALMA REDEMPTORIS MATER!"

This abbot, which that was an holy man
This abbot, who was a holy man

As monkes been, or elles oghten be,   156
As monks are, or at least ought to be,

This yonge child to conjure he bigan,
Began to conjure this young child,

And seyde, "O dere child, I halse thee,
And said, "O dear child, I conjure thee,

In vertu of the holy Trinitee,
By the power of the Holy Trinity,

Tel me what is thy cause for to singe,   160
Tell me what enables thee to sing,

Sith that thy throte is cut, to my seminge?"
Since thy throat is cut, to my understanding?"

"My throte is cut un-to my nekke-boon,"
"My throat is cut to my neck-bone,"

Seyde this child, "and, as by wey of kinde,
Said this child, "and, according to nature,

I sholde have deyed, ye, longe tyme agoon;   *164*
I should have died, yes, a long while ago;

But Jesu Crist, as ye in bokes finde,
But Jesus Christ, as you find in books,

Wil that his glorie laste and be in minde;
Wills that His glory endure and be remembered;

And, for the worship of his moder dere,
And, for the majesty of His Mother dear,

Yet may I singe 'o ALMA' loude and clere.   *168*
Yet may I sing 'o ALMA' loud and clear.

"This welle of mercy, Cristes moder swete,
"This Well of Mercy, Christ's Mother sweet,

I lovede alwey, as after my conninge;
I loved always, according to my understanding;

And whan that I my lyf sholde forlete,
And when I had to forsake my life,

To me she cam, and bad me for to singe   *172*
She came to me, and bade me to sing

This antem verraily in my deyinge,
This anthem, verily, in my dying,

As ye han herd; and, whan that I had songe,
As you have heard; and, after I had sung,

Me thoughte, she leyde a greyn up-on my tonge.
I thought She laid a grain upon my tongue.

"Wherfor I singe, and singe I moot certeyn   *176*
"Wherefore I sing, and sing I must indeed

In honour of that blisful mayden free,
In honor of that Blessed Maiden of Grace,

Til fro my tonge of-taken is the greyn.
Until the grain is taken from my tongue.

And afterward thus seyde she to me,
And afterward She spoke thus to me,

'My litel child, now wol I fecche thee   *180*
'My little child, soon will I take thee

Whan that the greyn is fro thy tonge y-take;
When the grain is taken from thy tongue;

Be nat agast, I wol thee nat forsake.' "
Be not afraid, I will not forsake thee.' "

This holy monk, this abbot, him mene I,
This holy monk, this same abbot I mean,

Him tonge out-caughte, and took a-wey the greyn,   *184*
Drew out his tongue, and took away the grain,

And he yaf up the goost ful softely.
And he gave up the ghost most softly.

And whan this abbot had this wonder seyn,
And when this abbot had seen this wonder,

His salte teres trikled doun as reyn,
His salt tears trickled down like rain,

And gruf he fil al plat up-on the grounde,   *188*
And face downward he fell flat on the ground,

And stille he lay as he had been y-bounde.
And lay as still as if he had been bound.

The covent eek lay on the pavement
The monks too lay on the pavement

Weping, and herien Cristes moder dere;
Weeping, and praised Christ's Mother dear;

And after that they ryse, and forth ben went,   *192*
And after that they rose and went forth,

And toke awey this martir fro his bere,
And carried away this martyr from his bier,

And in a tombe of marbul-stones clere
And in a tomb of pure marble

Enclosen they his litel body swete;
They enclosed his little body sweet;

Ther he is now, God leve us for to mete.   *196*
There he lies now, God grant us to meet him.

O yonge Hugh of Lincoln, slayn also
O young Hugh of Lincoln,³ also slain

With cursed Jewes, as it is notable,
By cursed Jews, as is well known,

For it nis but a litel whyle ago;
Since it was but a little while ago;

Preye eek for us, we sinful folk unstable,   *200*
Pray for us too, sinful, fickle people as we are,

That, of his mercy, God so merciable
That, of His mercy, God so merciful

On us his grete mercy multiplye,
Multiply His great mercy on us,

For reverence of his moder Marye. Amen.
In reverence of His Mother Mary. Amen.

The Prologue to the Nun's Priest's Tale

———

"Ho!" quod the knight, "good sir, na-more of this,
"Ho!" said the knight, "Good sir, no more of this,[1]

That ye han seyd is right y-nogh, y-wis,
What you have said is true enough, I know,

And mochel more; for litel hevinesse
And much more, for a little heaviness

Is right y-nogh to mochel folk, I gesse.   4
Is quite enough for most people, I guess.

I seye for me, it is a greet disese
Speaking for myself, it is a great discomfort,

Wher-as men han ben in greet welthe and ese,
When men have been in great wealth and ease,

To heren of hir sodeyn fal, allas!
To hear of their sudden fall, alas!

And the contrarie is joie and greet solas,   8
And the contrary is a joy and great solace,

As whan a man hath been in povre estaat,
As when a man has been in poor estate,

And clymbeth up, and wexeth fortunat,
And climbs up, and waxes fortunate,

And ther abydeth in prosperitee,
And remains there in prosperity,

Swich thing is gladsom, as it thinketh me,   12
Such a thing is gladdening, it seems to me,

And of swich thing were goodly for to telle."
And of such things it were good to talk."

"Ye," quod our hoste, "by seint Poules belle,
"Yes," said our host, "by Saint Paul's bell

Ye seye right sooth; this monk, he clappeth loude,
You speak the truth; this monk, he chatters loud,

He spak how 'Fortune covered with a cloude'   16
He told how 'Fortune covered with a cloud'

I noot never what, and als of a 'Tragedie'
I never knew what, and also of a 'Tragedy'

Right now ye herde, and parde! no remedie
You heard just now, and by God! no remedy

It is for to biwaille, ne compleyne
Is it to bewail or complain

That that is doon, and als it is a peyne,   20
About what is done, and besides it is painful,

As ye han seyd, to here of hevinesse.
As you remarked, to hear of heaviness.

Sir monk, na-more of this, so God yow blesse!
Sir monk, no more of this, so God may bless you!

Your tale anoyeth al this companye;
Your tale annoys all this company;

Swich talking is nat worth a boterflye;   24
Such talking is not worth a butterfly;

For ther-in is ther no desport ne game.
For there is no joy nor pleasure in it.

Wherfor, sir monk, or dan Piers by your name,
Wherefore, sir monk, or Sir Piers by your name,

I preye yow hertely, telle us somwhat elles,
I beg you heartily, tell us something else,

For sikerly, nere clinking of your belles,   28
For truly, except for the clinking of your bells,

That on your brydel hange on every syde,
That hang on every part of your bridle,

By heven king, that for us alle dyde,
By Heaven's King, Who died for us all,

I sholde er this han fallen doun for slepe,
I should have fallen down for sleep before this,

Although the slough had never been so depe;   32
Although the muck had never been so deep;

Than had your tale al be told in vayn.
Then would your tale have all been told in vain.

For certeinly, as that thise clerkes seyn,
For certainly, as the clerks say,

'Wher-as a man may have noon audience,
'Whenever a man can have no audience,

Noght helpeth it to tellen his sentence.'   36
Nothing aids him in delivering his lecture.'

And wel I woot the substance is in me,
And well I know the understanding is in me

If any thing shal wel reported be.
To know if a thing is well told.

Sir, sey somwhat of hunting, I yow preye."
Sir, tell something about hunting, I beg you."

"Nay," quod this monk, "I have no lust to pleye;   40
"Nay," said this monk, "I have no desire to make sport;

Now let another telle, as I have told."
Now let another tell, for I have told."

Than spak our host, with rude speche and bold,
Then spoke our host, with rude speech and bold,

And seyde un-to the nonnes preest anon,
And said to the nun's priest forthwith,

"Com neer, thou preest, com hider, thou sir John, 44
"Come near, you priest, come hither, you Sir John,

Tel us swich thing as may our hertes glade,
Tell us the sort of thing that will gladden our hearts,

Be blythe, though thou ryde up-on a jade.
Be merry, even though you ride on a nag.

What though thyn hors be bothe foule and lene,
What if your horse is both foul and lean,

If he wol serve thee, rekke nat a bene; 48
If he serves you, don't worry worth a bean;

Look that thyn herte be mery evermo."
See that your heart is merry evermore."

"Yis, sir," quod he, "yis, host, so mote I go,
"Yes, sir," said he, "yes, host, so shall I proceed,

But I be mery, y-wis, I wol be blamed:"—
Unless I am merry, I know I will be blamed."

And right anon his tale he hath attamed, 52
And immediately he broached his tale,

And thus he seyde un-to us everichon,
And thus he spoke to every one of us,

This swete preest, this goodly man, sir John.
This sweet priest, this goodly man, Sir John.

The Nun's Priest's Tale of the Cock and Hen, Chanticleer and Pertelote

A povre widwe, somdel stape in age,
A poor widow, somewhat advanced in age,

Was whylom dwelling in a narwe cottage,
Once lived in a small cottage,

Bisyde a grove, stonding in a dale.
Near a grove, standing in a dale.

This widwe, of which I telle yow my tale,   **4**
This widow, of whom I tell you my tale,

Sin thilke day that she was last a wyf,
Since that day when she was last a wife,

In pacience ladde a ful simple lyf,
In patience led an entirely simple life,

For litel was hir catel and hir rente;
For small was her property and her income;

By housbondrye of such as God hir sente   **8**
By economy of such as God sent her

She fond hir-self, and eek hir doghtren two.
She supported herself and her two daughters besides.

Three large sowes hadde she, and namo,
Three large sows she had, and no more,

Three kyn, and eek a sheep that highte Malle.
Three cows, and also a sheep named Moll.

Ful sooty was hir bour, and eek hir halle,   *12*
Very sooty was her bedroom, and her hall too,

In which she eet ful many a sclendre meel.
In which she had eaten many a slender meal.

Of poynaunt sauce hir neded never a deel.
Of spiced sauce she had no need at all.

No deyntee morsel passed thurgh hir throte;
No dainty morsel passed through her throat;

Hir dyete was accordant to hir cote.   *16*
Her diet was in keeping with her coat.

Repleccioun ne made hir never syk;
Gourmandizing never made her sick;

Attempree dyete was al her phisyk,
A temperate diet was all her medicine,

And exercyse, and hertes suffisaunce.
And exercise, and heart's content.

The goute lette hir no-thing for to daunce,   *20*
The gout prevented her not at all from dancing,

N'apoplexye shente nat hir heed;
Nor did apoplexy hurt her head;

No wyn ne drank she, neither whyt ne reed;
She drank no wine, neither white nor red;

Hir bord was served most with why and blak,
Her table was served most with white and black,

Milk and broun breed, in which she fond no lak,   *24*
Milk and brown bread, of which she found no lack,

Seynd bacoun, and somtyme an ey or tweye,
Broiled bacon, and sometimes an egg or two,

For she was as it were a maner deye.
For she was something of a dairy woman.

A yerd she hadde, enclosed al aboute
A yard she had, enclosed all about

With stikkes, and a drye dich with-oute,   28
With sticks, and a dry ditch outside,

In which she hadde a cok, hight Chauntecleer.
In which she had a cock named Chanticleer.

In al the land of crowing nas his peer;
In all the land of crowing was not his equal;

His vois was merier than the mery orgon
His voice was merrier than the merry organ

On messe-dayes that in the chirche gon;   32
That plays in church on mass-days;

Wel sikerer was his crowing in his logge,
More accurate was his crowing in his hut

Than is a clokke, or an abbey orlogge.
Than is a clock, or an abbey timekeeper.

By nature knew he ech ascencioun
By instinct he knew the beginning

Of equinoxial in thilke toun;   36
Of each equinox in that town;

For whan degrees fifteen were ascended,
For when the first hour had been completed,

Thanne crew he that it mighte nat ben amended.
Then he crew beyond possibility of improvement.

His comb was redder than the fyn coral,
His comb was redder than fine coral,

And batailed as it were a castel-wal.   40
And notched as if it were a castle wall.

His bile was blak, and as the jeet is shoon;
His bill was black, and shone like jet;

Lyk asur were his legges, and his toon;
Like azure were his legs and his toes;

His nayles whytter than the lilie flour,
His spurs were whiter than the lily flower,

And lyk the burned gold was his colour.   44
And his color was like burnished gold.

This gentil cok hadde in his governaunce
This noble cook had in his governance

Sevene hennes, for to doon al his plesaunce,
Seven hens, to carry out all his pleasure,

Which were his sustres and his paramours,
Who were his sisters and his mistresses,

And wonder lyk to him, as of colours.   48
And wondrous like him in coloration.

Of whiche the faireste hewed on hir throte
Of whom the fairest hued on her throat

Was cleped faire damoysele Pertelote.
Was named Fair Miss Pertelote.

Curteys she was, discreet, and debonaire,
Courteous she was, discreet and debonaire,

And compaignable, and bar hir-self so faire,   52
And companionable, and bore herself so fairly,

Sin thilke day that she was seven night old,
Since that day when she was seven nights old,

That trewely she hath the herte in hold
That, truly, she possessed the heart

Of Chauntecleer loken in every lith;
Of Chanticleer locked in her every limb;

He loved hir so, that wel was him therewith   56
He loved her so, that all was well with him.

But such a joye was it to here hem singe,
But such a joy it was to hear them sing,

Whan that the brighte sonne gan to springe,
When the bright sun began to rise,

In swete accord, "My lief is faren in londe."
In sweet harmony, "My love steps through the land."

For thilke tyme, as I have understonde,   60
For at that time, as I understand,

Bestes and briddes coude speke and singe.
Beasts and birds could speak and sing.

And so bifel, that in a daweninge,
And it so happened, that at one dawn,

As Chauntecleer among his wyves alle
As Chanticleer among all his wives

Sat on his perche, that was in the halle,   64
Sat on his perch, which was in the hall,

And next him sat this faire Pertelote,
And next to him sat this fair Pertelote,

This Chauntecleer gan gronen in his throte,
This Chanticleer began to groan in his throat,

As man that in his dreem is drecched sore.
As one who is sorely troubled in a dream.

And whan that Pertelote thus herde him rore,   68
And when Pertelote heard him roar so,

She was agast, and seyde, "O herte dere,
She was aghast, and said, "O dear heart,

What eyleth yow, to grone in this manere?
What ails you, to groan this way?

Ye been a verray sleper, fy for shame!"
You are a sleepy-head, fie for shame!"

And he answerde and seyde thus, "Madame,   72
And he answered and spoke thus, "Madam,

I pray yow, that ye take it nat a-grief:
I pray you that you take it not too hard:

By God, me mette I was in swich meschief
By God, I dreamed that I was in such distress

Right now, that yet my herte is sore afright.
Just now, that my heart is still sorely frightened.

Now God," quod he, "my swevene recche aright.   76
Now God," said he, "make my dream mean well,

And keep my body out of foul prisoun!
And keep my body out of foul prison!

Me mette, how that I romed up and doun
I dreamed that as I roamed up and down

Withinne our yerde, wher-as I saugh a beste,
Within our yard, I saw a beast,

Was lyk an hound, and wolde han maad areste   80
Like a hound, who would have seized

Upon my body, and wolde han had me deed.
Upon my body, and would have killed me.

His colour was bitwixe yelwe and reed;
His color was between yellow and red;

And tipped was his tail and bothe his eres,
And his tail and both his ears were tipped

With blak, unlyk the remenant of his heres;   84
With black, unlike the rest of his coat;

His snowte smal, with glowinge eyen tweye.
He had a small snout and two glowing eyes.

Yet of his look for fere almost I deye;
For fear of his looks I am almost dying yet;

This caused me my groning, doutelees."
This caused my groaning, undoubtedly."

  "Avoy!" quod she, "fy on yow, hertelees!   88
  "Shame!" said she, "fie on you, chicken-hearted!

Allas!" quod she, "for, by that God above,
Alas!" said she, "for, by that God above,

Now han ye lost myn herte and al my love;
Now have you lost my heart and all my love;

I can not love a coward, by my feith.
I cannot love a coward, by my faith.

For certes, what so any womman saith,   92
For truly, whatever any woman says,

We alle desyren, if it mighte be,
We all desire, if it is possible,

To han housbondes hardy, wyse, and free,
To have husbands brave, wise, and generous,

And secree, and no nigard, ne no fool,
And trustworthy, and no niggard, and no fool,

Ne him that is agast of every tool,   96
And not one who is afraid of every weapon,

Ne noon avauntour, by that God above!
And not a braggart, by that God above!

How dorste ye seyn for shame unto your love,
How dared you, for shame, say to your love

That any thing mighte make yow aferd?
That anything could make you afraid?

Have ye no mannes herte, and han a berd?   100
Have you no man's heart, when you have a beard?

Allas! and conne ye been agast of swevenis?
Alas! and can you be afraid of dreams?

No-thing, God wot, but vanitee, in sweven is.
Nothing, God knows, but nonsense is in a dream.

Swevenes engendren of replecciouns,
Dreams are born of gourmandizing,

And ofte of fume, and of complecciouns   104
And often of gas, and of disorders

Whan humours been to habundant in a wight.
When the humors are too abundant in a person.¹

Certes this dreem, which ye han met to-night
Surely this dream, which you had tonight

Cometh of the grete superfluitee
Came from the great superfluity

Of youre rede colera, pardee,   *108*
Of your red bile, by the Lord,

Which causeth folk to dreden in here dremes
Which causes people to dread in their dreams

Of arwes, and of fyr with rede lemes;
Arrows, and fire with red flames;

Of grete bestes, that they wol hem byte,
Huge beasts, for fear they will bite them,

Of contek, and of whelpes grete and lyte;   *112*
Conflict, and cubs large and small;

Right as the humour of malencolye
Just as the melancholy humor

Causeth ful many a man, in sleep to crye,
Causes many a man, in sleep, to cry out

For fere of blake beres, or boles blake,
For fear of black bears, or black bulls,

Or elles, blake develes wole hem take.   *116*
Or else, that black devils will take him.

Of othere humours coude I telle also,
I could tell about the other humors too

That werken many a man in sleep ful wo;
That bring heavy woe to many a man in sleep;

But I wol passe as light as I can.
But I will continue as briefly as I can.

"Lo Catoun, which that was so wys a man,   *120*
"Consider Cato,' who was so wise a man,

Seyde he nat thus, 'Ne do no fors of dremes?'
Did he not say, 'Pay no attention to dreams?'

Now, sire," quod she, "whan we flee fro the bemes,
Now, sir," said she, "when we fly down from our roosts,

For Goddes love, as tak som laxatyf;
For the love of God, take a laxative;

Up peril of my soule, and of my lyf,   124
On peril of my soul and of my life,

I counseille yow the beste, I wol nat lye,
I advise you for the best, I do not lie,

That bothe of colere and of malencolye
That of both red and black bile

Ye purge yow, and for ye shul nat tarie,
You purge yourself, and to avoid delay,

Though in this toun is noon apotecarie,   128
Although there is no apothecary in town,

I shal my-self to herbes techen yow
I shall myself direct you to herbs

That shul ben for your hele, and for your prow;
That will be for your health and your welfare;

And in our yerd tho herbes shal I finde,
And in our yard those herbs I shall find,

The whiche han of hir propretee, by kinde,   132
Which contain properties, by nature,

To purgen yow binethe, and eek above.
To purge you below, and also above.

Forget not this, for Goddes owene love!
Forget not this, for God's own love!

Ye been ful colerik of compleccioun.
You are all choleric of temperament.

Ware the sonne in his ascencioun   136
Beware lest the sun in its rising

Ne fynde yow nat repleet of humours hote;
Find you full of hot humors;

And if it do, I dar wel leye a grote,
And if it does, I dare bet a nickel

That ye shul have a fevere terciane,
That you will have a tertian fever,

Or an agu, that may be youre bane.   140
Or an ague that may be your death.

A day or two ye shul have digestyves
For a day or two you shall have digestives

Of wormes, er ye take your laxatyves,
Of worms before you take your laxatives,

Of lauriol, centaure, and fumetere,
Of laurel, centaury, and fumitory,

Or elles of ellebor, that groweth there,   144
Or else of hellebore, that grows there,

Of catapuce, or of gaytres beryis,
Of caper-spurge, or of dogwood berries,

Of erbe yve, growing in our yerd, that mery is;
Of ground-pine, growing in our yard, which is nice;

Pekke hem up right as they growe, and ete hem in.
Peck them right up as they grow, and eat them.

Be mery, housbond, for you fader kin!   148
Be merry, husband, for your-father's kin!

Dredeth no dreem; I can say yow namore."
Be afraid of no dream; I can tell you no more."

"Madame," quod he, "grant mercy of your lore.
"Madam," said he, "thank you for your advice.

But nathelees, as touching daun Catoun,
But nevertheless, in regard to Cato,

That hath of wisdom such a greet renoun,   152
Who is so greatly renowned for wisdom,

Though that he bad no dremes for to drede,
Although he advised to have no fear of dreams,

By God, men may in olde bokes rede
By God, men may read in old books

Of many a man, more of auctoritee
Of many authors, greater authorities

Than ever Catoun was, so mote I thee,   156
Than ever Cato was, if I may say so,

That al the revers seyn of his sentence,
The exact opposite to his opinion,

And han wel founden by experience,
And they have thoroughly found out by experience

That dremes ben significaciouns,
That dreams are portents

As wel of joy as tribulaciouns   160
Both of joy and tribulation

That folk enduren in this lyf present.
That people endure in this present life.

Ther nedeth make of this noon argument;
There is no use arguing about this;

The verray preve sheweth it in dede.
Actual events are sufficient proof.

"Oon of the gretteste auctours that men rede   164
"One of the greatest authors' read by men

Seith thus, that whylom two felawes wente
Speaks thus, that once two friends went

On pilgrimage, in ful good entente;
On a pilgrimage, with entirely good intentions;

And happed so, thay come into a toun,
And it so happened, they came into a town

Wher-as ther was swich congregacioun   168
Where there was such a crowd

Of peple, and eek so streit of herbergage
Of people, and also such a shortage of lodgings

That they ne founde as muche as o cotage
That they couldn't find even a single cottage

In which they bothe mighte y-logged be.
In which they both might be accommodated.

Wherefor thay mosten, of necessitee,   172
Wherefore they were forced by necessity

As for that night, departen compaignye;
To part company for that night;

And ech of hem goth to his hostelrye,
And each of them went to his lodging

And took his logging as it wolde falle.
And took whatever shelter chance assigned him.

That oon of hem was logged in a stalle,   176
Consequently, one of them was lodged in a stall,

Fer in a yerd, with oxen of the plough;
In a remote yard, with oxen of the plow;

That other man was logged wel y-nough,
The other man was lodged well enough,

As was his aventure, or his fortune,
As was his fortune, or his luck,

That us governeth alle as in commune.   180
Which governs all of us in common.

"And so bifel, that, longe er it were day,
"And it so happened, that long before daybreak,

This man mette in his bed, ther-as he lay,
This man dreamed in his bed where he lay

How that his felawe gan up-on him calle,
That his friend called upon him,

And seyde, 'Allas! for in an oxes stalle   184
And said, 'Alas! for in an ox's stall

This night I shal be mordred ther I lye.
This night I shall be murdered where I lie.

Now help me, dere brother, er I dye;
Now help me, dear brother, before I die;

In alle haste com to me,' he sayde.
In all haste come to me,' he said.

This man out of his sleep for fere abrayde;   188
This man started out of his sleep for fear;

But whan that he was wakned of his sleep,
But when he was awakened from his sleep,

He turned him, and took of this no keep;
He rolled over, and took no heed of this;

Him thoughte his dreem nas but a vanitee.
He thought his dream was only illusory.

Thus twyës in his sleping dremed he.   192
Thus twice in his sleep he dreamed.

And atte thridde tyme yet his felawe
And on the third time his friend

Cam, as him thoughte, and seide, 'I am now slawe;
Came, as he imagined, and said, 'I am now slain;

Bihold my blody woundes, depe and wyde!
Behold my bloody wounds, deep and wide!

Arys up erly in the morwe-tyde,   196
Rise up early tomorrow morning,

And at the west gate of the toun,' quod he,
And at the west gate of the town,' said he,

'A carte ful of dong ther shaltow see,
'A cart full of manure you shall see there,

In which my body is hid ful prively;
In which my body is hidden full secretly;

Do thilke carte aresten boldely.   200
Stop that cart boldly.

My gold caused my mordre, sooth to sayn;'
My gold caused my murder, to reveal the truth;'

And tolde him every poynt how he was slayn,
And told him every detail about how he was slain,

With a ful pitous face, pale of hewe.
With an utterly piteous face, pale of hue.

And truste wel, his dreem he fond ful trewe; 204
And be assured, his dream he found precisely true;

For on the morwe, as sone as it was day,
For on the morrow, as soon as it was day,

To his felawes in he took the way;
To his friend's abode he took his way;

And whan that he cam to this oxes stalle,
And when he came to the ox's stall,

After his felawe he bigan to calle. 208
He began to call out after his friend.

"The hostiler answered him anon,
"The innkeeper answered him immedately,

And seyde, 'Sire, your felawe is agon;
And said, 'Sir, your friend has departed;

As sone as day he wente out of the toun.'
At daybreak he went out of the town.'

This man gan fallen in suspecioun, 212
This man began to be suspicious,

Remembring on his dremes that he mette,
Remembering the dreams that he dreamt,

And forth he goth, no lenger wolde he lette,
And forth he went, no longer would he delay,

Unto the west gate of the toun, and fond
To the west gate of the town, and found

A dong-carte, as it were to donge lond, 216
A dung cart, as if about to manure land,

That was arrayed in the same wyse
Which had the same appearance

As ye han herd the dede man devyse;
As you have heard the dead man describe;

And with an hardy herte he gan to crye
And with a bold heart he demanded

Vengeaunce and justice of this felonye:—   220
Vengeance and justice for this felony:—

'My felawe mordred is this same night,
'My friend has been murdered this very night,

And in this carte he lyth gapinge upright.
And in this cart he lies gaping upwards.

I crye out on the ministres,' quod he,
I cry out to the authorities,' said he,

'That sholde kepe and reulen this citee;   224
'Who should protect and rule this city;

Harrow! allas! her lyth my felawe slayn!'
Help! Alas! Here lies my friend murdered!'

What sholde I more un-to this tale sayn?
What more should I add to this tale?

The peple out-sterte, and caste the cart to grounde,
The people crowded around and overturned the cart,

And in the middel of the dong they founde   228
And in the midst of the dung they found

The dede man, that mordred was al newe.
The dead man, who had just been murdered.

   "O blisful God, that art so just and trewe!
   "O blessed God, Who art so just and true!

Lo, how that thou biwreyest mordre alway!
Behold, how Thou always revealest murder!

Mordre wol out, that see we day by day.   232
Murder will out, we see it day by day

Mordre is so wlatsom and abhominable
Murder is so loathsome and abominable

To God, that is so just and resonable,
To God, Who is so just and reasonable,

That he ne wol nat suffre it heled be;
That He will not suffer it to be concealed;

Though it abyde a yeer or two, or three,   *236*
Though it be secret a year, or two, or three,

Mordre wol out, this is my conclusioun.
Murder will out, this is my conclusion.

And right anoon, ministres of that toun
And right away, authorities of that town

Han hent the carter, and so sore him pyned,
Seized the carter, and tortured him so severely,

And eek the hostiler so sore engyned,   *240*
And besides put the innkeeper on the rack,

That they biknewe hir wikkednesse anoon,
That they quickly confessed their wickedness,

And were an-hanged by the nekke-boon.
And were hanged by the neck-bone.

"Here may men seen that dremes been to drede.
"Here men may see that dreams are to be feared.

And certes in the same book I rede,   *244*
And indeed in the same book I read,

Right in the nexte chapitre after this,
In the very next chapter after this,

(I gabbbe nat, so have I joye or blis,)
(I do not lie, so may I have joy or blessedness)

Two men that wolde han passed over see,
Two men who would have crossed the sea,

For certeyn cause, in-to a fer contree,   *248*
For a certain reason, to a far country,

If that the wind ne hadde been contrairie,
If the wind had not been contrary,

That made hem in a citee for to tarie,
Making them tarry in a city

That stood ful mery upon an haven-syde.
Which was situated cheerfully on a harbor.

But on a day, agayn the even-tyde   252
But on a day, toward evening

The wind gan chaunge, and blew right as hem leste.
The wind changed, and blew just as they desired.

Jolif and glad they wente un-to hir reste,
Joyful and glad they went to their rest,

And casten hem ful erly for to saille;
And planned to sail very early;

But to that oo man fil a greet mervaille.   256
Except that to one man a great marvel occurred.

That oon of hem, in sleping as he lay,
That one, as he lay sleeping,

Him mette a wonder dreem, agayn the day;
Dreamed a wondrous dream, toward daybreak;

Him thoughte a man stood by his beddes syde,
He thought a man stood by his bedside,

And him comaunded that he sholde abyde,   260
And commanded him to stay where he was,

And seyde him thus, 'If thou to-morwe wende,
And said to him, 'If you travel tomorrow,

Thou shalt be dreynt; my tale is at an ende.'
You shall be drowned; my tale is at an end.'

He wook, and tolde his felawe what he mette,
He woke, and told his friend what he had dreamed,

And preyde him his viage for to lette;   264
And begged him to postpone his voyage;

As for that day, he preyde him to abyde.
And begged him to remain just for that day.

His felawe, that lay by his beddes syde,
His friend, who lay in bed beside him,

Gan for to laughe, and scorned him ful faste.
Began to laugh, and made fun of him mercilessly.

'No dreem,' quod he, 'may so myn herte agaste,   268
'No dream,' said he, 'may so frighten my heart

That I wol lette for to do my thinges.
That I will refrain from carrying out my plans.

I sette not a straw by thy dreminges,
I don't value your dreams worth a straw,

For swevenes been but vanitees and japes.
For dreams are but illusions and tomfoolery.

Men dreme al-day of owles or of apes,   272
Men are always dreaming of owls or apes,

And eke of many a mase therwithal;
And of many other amazing things;

Men dreme of thing that never was ne shal.
Men dream of what never was nor will be.

But sith I see that thou wolt heer abyde,
But since I see that you will remain here,

And thus for-sleuthen wilfully thy tyde,   276
And thus deliberately idle away your time,

God wot it reweth me; and have good day.'
God knows I regret it; but good day to you.'

And thus he took his leve, and wente his way.
And so he took his leave, and went his way.

But er that he hadde halfe his cours y-seyled,
But before he had completed half his voyage,

Noot I nat why, ne what mischaunce it eyled,   280
I know not why, nor what mischance befell,

But casuelly the shippes botme rente,
But accidentally the ship's hull split,

And ship and man under the water wente
And ship and man went under the water

In sighte of othere shippes it byside,
In sight of other ships nearby,

That with hem seyled at the same tyde.   284
Which had sailed with them on the same tide.

And therefor, faire Pertelote so dere,
And therefore, fair Pertelote so dear,

By swiche ensamples olde maistow lere,
By such old examples you may learn

That no man sholde been to recchelees
That no man should be too thoughtless

Of dremes, for I sey thee, doutelees,   288
About dreams, for I tell you, beyond doubt,

That many a dreem ful sore is for to drede.
That many a dream is to be sorely feared.

"Lo, in the lyf of seint Kenelm, I rede,
"For example, I read in the life of Saint Kenelm,

That was Kenulphus sone, the noble king
Who was Kenelphus' son, the noble king

Of Mercenrike, how Kenelm mette a thing;   292
Of Mercia, how Kenelm had a dream;

A lyte er he was mordred, on a day,
A day or so before he was murdered,

His mordre in his avisioun he say.
He saw his murder in a vision.

His norice him expouned every del
His nurse interpreted to him every detail

His sweven, and bad him for to kepe him wel   296
Of his dream, and told him to be on guard

For traisoun; but he nas but seven yeer old,
Against treachery; but he was only seven years old.

And therfore litel tale hath he told
And therefore he took little heed

Of any dreem, so holy was his herte.
Of any dream, so holy was his heart.

By God, I hadde lever than my sherte   300
By God, I'd prefer it to my shirt

That ye had rad his legende, as have I.
That you might have read his legend, as I have.

Dame Pertelote, I sey yow trewely,
Dame Pertelote, I tell you truly,

Macrobeus, that writ th'avisioun
Macrobius, who wrote up the vision

In Affrike of the worthy Cipioun,   304
Of the worthy Scipio in Africa,'

Affermeth dremes, and seith that they been
Believes in dreams, and says that they are

Warning of thinges that men after seen.
Warnings of things that men see afterward.

   "And forther-more, I pray yow loketh wel
   "And furthermore, I beseech you to look carefully

In the olde testament, of Daniel,   308
In the Old Testament, at Daniel,

If he held dremes any vanitee.
If he considered dreams illusory.

Reed eek of Joseph, and ther shul ye see
Read about Joseph too, and there you will see

Wher dremes ben somtyme (I sey nat alle)
Where dreams are sometimes (I don't say always)

Warning of thinges that shul after falle.   312
Warnings of things that are to happen.

Loke of Egipt the king, daun Pharao,
Observe Lord Pharaoh, the king of Egypt,

His bakere and his boteler also,
And his baker and his butler too,

Wher they ne felte noon effect in dremes.
Whether they found no truth in dreams.

Who-so wol seken actes of sondry remes   316
Whoever examines the history of sundry realms

May rede of dremes many a wonder thing.
May read many wonderful things about dreams.

  "Lo Cresus, which that was of Lyde king,
  "Consider Croesus, who was king of Lydia,

Mette he nat that he sat upon a tree,
Did he not dream that he sat upon a tree,

Which signified he sholde anhanged be?   320
Which signified that he would be hanged?

Lo heer Andromacha, Ectores wyf,
Consider Andromache, Hector's wife,

That day that Ector sholde lese his lyf,
On the day Hector was to lose his life,

She dremed on the same night biforn,
She dreamed on the very night before

How that the lyf of Ector sholde be lorn   324
How the life of Hector would be lost

If thilke day he wente in-to bataille;
If he went to battle that day;

She warned him, but it mighte nat availle;
She warned him, but it was of no use;

He wente for to fighte nathelees,
He went out to fight nevertheless,

But he was slayn anoon of Achilles.   328
But he was soon killed by Achilles.

But thilke tale is al to long to telle,
But this tale is altogether too long to tell,

And eek it is ny day, I may nat dwelle.
And besides it is nearly day, I must not dally.

Shortly I seye, as for conclusioun,
Briefly I say, by way of conclusion.

That I shal han of this avisioun   332
That from this dream I shall suffer

Adversitee; and I seye forther-more,
Adversity; and furthermore I say

That I ne telle of laxatyves no store,
That I set no store by laxatives,

For they ben venimous, I woot it wel;
For they are poisonous, I know it well;

I hem defye, I love hem never a del.   336
I defy them, I love them not one iota.

"Now let us speke of mirthe, and stinte al this.
"Now let us talk of happiness, and stop all this.

Madame Pertelote, so have I blis,
Madame Pertelote, as I hope to be saved,

Of o thing God hath sent me large grace;
In one thing God has sent me rare grace;

For whan I see the beautee of your face,   340
For when I see the beauty of your face,

Ye ben so scarlet-reed about your yën,
You are so scarlet red around your eyes,

It maketh al my drede for to dyen;
It causes all my fear to die;

For, also siker as IN PRINCIPIO,
For true indeed is IN PRINCIPIO,

MULIER EST HOMINIS CONFUSIO.   344
MULIER EST HOMINIS CONFUSIO.'

Madame, the sentence of this Latin is—
Madam, the meaning of this Latin is—

Womman is mannes joye and al his blis.
Woman is man's joy and all his bliss.

For whan I fele a-night your softe syde,
For when I feel by night your soft side,

Al-be-it that I may nat on you ryde,   348
Although I cannot ride on you,

For that our perche is maad so narwe, alas!
Because our perch is made so narrow, alas!

I am so ful of joye and of solas
I am so full of joy and comfort

That I defye bothe sweven and dreem."
That I defy both visions and dreams."

And with that word he fley doun fro the beem,   352
And with that word he flew down from the roost,

For it was day, and eek his hennes alle;
For it was day, and all his hens did likewise;

And with a chuk he gan hem for to calle,
And with a cluck he called them,

For he had founde a corn, lay in the yerd.
For he had found a corn lying in the yard.

Royal he was, he was namore aferd;   356
Regal he was, he was no more afraid;

He fethered Pertelote twenty tyme,
He feathered Pertelote twenty times,

And trad as ofte, er that it was pryme.
And trod her as often, before it was full morning.

He loketh as it were a grim leoun;
He looked as if he were a fierce lion;

And on his toos he rometh up and doun,   360
And on his toes he roamed up and down,

Him deyned not to sette his foot to grounde.
He did not deign to lower his heel to the ground.

He chukketh, whan he hath a corn y-founde,
He clucked whenever he found a grain of corn,

And to him rennen thanne his wyves alle.
Whereat all his wives ran to him.

Thus royal, as a prince is in his halle, 364
Thus regal, as a prince is in his palace,

Leve I this Chauntecleer in his pasture;
I leave this Chantecleer in his pasture;

And after wol I telle his aventure.
And later I will describe his adventure.

Whan that the month in which the world bigan,
When the month in which the world began,

That highte March, whan God first maked man, 368
Which is called March, when God first made man,'

Was complet, and y-passed were also,
Had ended, and there had also passed

Sin March bigan, thritty dayes and two,
Thirty-two days since March began,

Bifel that Chauntecleer, in al his pryde,
It happened that Chanticleer, in all his pride,

His seven wyves walking by his syde, 372
His seven wives walking by his side,

Caste up his eyen to the brighte sonne,
Cast up his eyes to the bright sun,

That in the signe of Taurus hadde y-ronne
Which in the sign of Taurus had run

Twenty degrees and oon, and somwhat more;
Twenty-one degrees, and somewhat more;

And knew by kynde, and by noon other lore, 376
And knew by instinct, and by no other learning,

That it was pryme, and crew with blisful stevene.
That it was nine o'clock, and crew with blissful sound.

"The sonne," he sayde, "is clomben up on hevene
"The sun," he said, "has climbed up in the sky

Fourty degrees and oon, and more, y-wis.
Forty-one and more degrees, I believe.

Madame Pertelote, my worldes blis,   380
Madam Pertelote, my world's bliss,

Herkneth thise blisful briddes how they singe,
Listen to the blissful birds how they sing,

And see the fresshe floures how they springe;
And see the fresh flowers how they bloom;

Ful is myn herte of revel and solas."
My heart is full of joy and satisfaction."

But sodeinly him fil a sorweful cas;   384
But suddenly a sorrowful event befell him;

For ever the latter ende of joye is wo.
For the latter end of joy is always woe.

God woot that worldly joye is sone ago;
God knows that worldly joy is soon departed;

And if a rethor coude faire endyte,
And if an orator could write eloquently,

He in a cronique saufly mighte it wryte,   388
Without hesitancy he might inscribe it in a chronicle

As for a sovereyn nótabilitee.
As a supremely notable truth.

Now every wys man, lat him herkne me;
Now let every wise man listen to me;

This storie is al-so trewe, I undertake,
This story is just as true, I assert,

As is the book of Launcelot de Lake,   392
As is the book of Lancelot of the Lake,'

That wommen holde in ful gret reverence.
Which women hold in very great esteem.

Now wol I torne agayn to my sentence.
Now will I return again to my story.

  A col-fox, ful of sly iniquitee,
  A black fox, full of sly iniquity,

That in the grove hadde woned yeres three,   *396*
Who had lived three years in the grove,

By heigh imaginacioun forn-cast,
As was forvordained by Heavenly plan,

The same night thurgh-out the hegges brast
The same night broke through the hedges

Into the yerd, ther Chauntecleer the faire
Into the yard where the fair Chanticleer

Was wont, and eek his wyves, to repaire;   *400*
Was accustomed, and his wives too, to repair;

And in a bed of wortes stille he lay,
And in a bed of vegetables he lay still

Til it was passed undern of the day,
Until it was past mid-morning,

Wayting his tyme on Chauntecleer to falle,
Biding his time to fall on Chanticleer,

As gladly doon thise homicydes alle,   *404*
As cheerfully as do all homicides

That in awayt liggen to mordre men.
Who lie in wait to murder men.

O false mordrer, lurking in thy den!
O false murderer, lurking in your den!

O newe Scariot, newe Genilon!
O new Iscariot, new Ganelon!

False dissimilour, O Greek Sinon,   *408*
False dissimulator, O Greek Sinon,[8]

That broghtest Troye al outrely to sorwe!
Who brought Troy utterly to grief!

O Chauntecleer, acursed be that morwe,
O Chanticleer, cursed be that morning

That thou into that yerd flough fro the bemes!
When you flew from the roost into that yard!

Thou were ful wel y-warned by thy dremes,   *412*
You were thoroughly warned by your dreams

That thilke day was perilous to thee.
That that day would be perilous to you.

But what that God forwoot mot nedes be,
But whatever God foreknows must be,

After the opinioun of certeyn clerkis.
According to the opinion of certain clerks.

Witnesse on him, that any perfit clerk is,   *416*
Call to witness any perfect clerk

That in scole is gret altercacioun
That in the schools there is great altercation

In this matere, and greet disputisoun,
About this matter, and great disputing,

And hath ben of an hundred thousand men.
And has been among a hundred thousand men.

But I ne can not bulte it to the bren,   *420*
But I cannot sift it to the kernel,

As can the holy doctour Augustyn,
As can the holy doctor Augustine,

Or Boëce, or the bishop Bradwardyn,
Or Boetheus, or the bishop Bradwardine,'

Whether that Goddes worthy forwiting
Whether God's exalted foreknowledge

Streyneth me nedely for to doon a thing,   *424*
Compels me necessarily to do a thing

(Nedely clepe I simple necessitee);
(By 'necessarily' I mean absolute necessity)

Or elles, if free choys be graunted me
Or whether free choice is granted me

To do that same thing, or do it noght,
To do that same thing, or not do it,

Though God forwoot it, er that it was wroght; 428
Though God foreknew it before it was done;

Or if his witing streyneth nevere a del
Or if His knowing constrains not a bit

But by necessitee condicionel.
Except by way of conditional necessity.

I wol not han to do of swich matere;
I will not be concerned with this matter;

My tale is of a cok, as ye may here, 432
My tale is of a cock, as you may hear,

That took his counseil of his wyf, with sorwe,
Who took counsel of his wife, to his sorrow,

To walken in the yerd upon that morwe
To walk in the yard on that morning

That he had met the dreem, that I yow tolde.
When he had had the dream I told you of.

Wommennes counseils been ful ofte colde; 436
Women's counsels are often enough fatal;

Wommannes counseil broghte us first to wo,
Woman's counsel brought us first to grief,

And made Adam fro paradys to go,
And caused Adam to depart from Paradise

Ther-as he was ful mery, and wel at ese.—
Where he was entirely happy and completely at ease.

But for I noot to whom it mighte displese 440
But since I know not whom it might displease

If I counseil of wommen wolde blame,
If I should disparage the counsel of women,

Passe over, for I seyde it in my game.
Pass over this, for I said it for fun.

Rede auctours, wher they trete of swich matere,
Read the authors who treat of such matters,

And what thay seyn of wommen ye may here.   444
And you can learn what they say of women.

Thise ben the cokkes wordes, and nat myne;
These are the cock's words, not mine;

I can noon harm of no womman divyne. —
I can find nothing wrong with any woman.

    Faire in the sond, to bathe hir merily,
    Serenely in the sand, to bathe herself merrily,

Lyth Pertelote, and alle hir sustres by,   448
Lay Pertelote, together with all her sisters,

Agayn the sonne; and Chauntecleer so free
Under the sun; and Chanticleer so lighthearted

Song merier than the mermayde in the see;
Sang more merrily than the mermaid in the sea;

For PHISIOLOGUS seith sikerly,
For PHYSIOLOGUS[10] *says truly*

How that they singen wel and merily.   452
That they sing well and merrily.

And so bifel that, as he caste his yë,
And it so befell that, as he cast his eye

Among the wortes, on a boterflye,
On a butterfly among the vegetables,

He was war of this fox that lay ful lowe.
He became aware of this fox that lay full low.

No-thing ne liste him thanne for to crowe,   456
He knew no better than to crow,

But cryde anon, "cok, cok," and up he sterte,
But cried at once, "cock, cock," and up he jumped

As man that was affrayed in his herte.
Like one frightened to his marrow.

For naturelly a beest desyreth flee
For instinctively a beast wants to flee

Fro his contrarie, if he may it see,   460
From his natural enemy, if he sees it,

Though he never erst had seyn it with his yë.
Though he had never seen it before with his eyes.

   This Chauntecleer, whan he gan him espye,
   This Chanticleer, when he caught a glimpse of him,

He wolde han fled, but that the fox anon
Would have fled, but that the fox immediately

Seyde, "Gentil sire, allas! wher wol ye gon?   464
Said, "Noble sir, alas! where are you going?

Be ye affrayed of me that am your freend?
Are you afraid of me who am your friend?

Now certes, I were worse than a feend,
Now surely, I would be worse than a fiend

If I to yow wolde harm or vileinye.
If I meant harm or evil to you.

I am nat come your counseil for t'espye;   468
I did not come to spy on your secrets;

But trewely, the cause of my cominge
But truly, the reason for my coming

Was only for to herkne how that ye singe.
Was only to listen to you sing.

For trewely ye have as mery a stevene
For truly you have as joyous a voice

As eny aungel hath, that is in hevene: 472
As has any angel that is in Heaven:

Therwith ye han in musik more felinge
And in addition, you have more feeling for music

Than hadde Boëce, or any that can singe.
Than Boetheus had, or any other singer.

My lord your fader (God his soule blesse!)
My lord your father (God bless his soul!)

And eek your moder, of hir gentilesse,   476
And your mother too, by her graciousness,

Han in myn hous y-been, to my gret ese;
Have been in my house, to my great joy;

And certes, sire, ful fayn wolde I yow plese.
And truly, sir, I am very eager to please you.

But for men speke of singing, I wol saye,
But, speaking of singing, I must say,

So mote I brouke wel myn eyen tweye,   480
As I hope to have the use of my eyes,

Save yow, I herde never man so singe,
Except you, I never heard anyone sing

As dide your fader in the morweninge;
As your father did in the morning;

Certes, it was of herte, al that he song.
Surely, it came from the heart, all that he sang.

And for to make his voys the more strong,   484
And to make his voice stronger,

He wolde so peyne him, that with bothe his yën
He would take such pains, that with both his eyes

He moste winke, so loude he wolde cryen,
He had to blink, so loud he would cry,

And stonden on his tiptoon ther-with-al,
And stand on tip-toe besides,

And strecche forth his nekke long and smal.   488
And stretch his neck forth long and slender.

And eek he was of swich discrecioun,
And, besides, he was of such discretion

That ther nas no man in no regioun
That there was no man in any region

That him in song or wisdom mighte passe.
Who could surpass him in singing or wisdom.

I have wel rad in daun Burnel the Asse,   492
I have thoroughly read in SIR BURNEL THE ASS,[11]

Among his vers, how that ther was a cok,
In his verses, how there was a cock

For that a preestes sone yaf him a knok
Who, because a priest's son gave him a rap

Upon his leg, whyl he was yong and nyce,
Upon his leg, being young and foolish,

He made him for to lese his benefyce.   496
Made him in later years lose his benefice.

But certeyn, ther nis no comparisoun
But it is certain there is no comparison here

Bitwix the wisdom and discrecioun
To the wisdom and discretion

Of youre fader, and of his subtiltee.
Of your father, and his subtlety.

Now singeth, sire, for seinte Charitee,   500
Now sing, sir, for blessed charity,

Let see, conne ye your fader countrefete?"
Let us see, can you imitate your father?"

This Chauntecleer his winges gan to bete,
This Chanticleer began to beat his wings

As man that coude his tresoun nat espye,
As one unable to perceive treachery,

So was he ravisshed with his flaterye.   504
So was he ravished by his flattery.

  Allas! ye lordes, many a fals flatour
  Alas! you lords, many a false flatterer

Is in your courtes, and many a losengcour,
Is in your courts, and many a hypocrite,

That plesen yow wel more, by my feith,
Who pleases you much more, by my faith,

Than he that soothfastnesse unto yow seith.   508
Than he who tells you the truth.

Redeth Ecclesiaste of flaterye;
Read ECCLESIASTES *on flattery;*

Beth war, ye lordes, of hir trecherye.
Be wary, you lords, of their treachery.

This Chauntecleer stood hye up-on his toos,
This Chanticleer stood high upon his toes,

Strecching his nekke, and heeld his eyen cloos,   512
Stretching his neck, and held his eyes closed,

And gan to crowe loude for the nones;
And began to crow loudly all at once;

And daun Russel the fox sterte up at ones,
And Sir Russel the fox leaped up at once,

And by the gargat hente Chauntecleer,
And seized Chanticleer by the throat,

And on his bak toward the wode him beer,   516
And carried him on his back toward the wood,

For yet ne was ther no man that him sewed.
For as yet no one pursued him.

O destinee, that mayst nat been eschewed!
O Destiny, that cannot be avoided!

Allas, that Chauntecleer fleigh fro the bemes!
Alas, that Chanticleer flew from the beams!

Allas, his wyf ne roghte nat of dremes!   520
Alas, that his wife gave no heed to dreams!

And on a Friday fil al this meschaunce.
And on a Friday befell all this bad luck.

O Venus, that art goddesse of pleasaunce,
O Venus, who art goddess of delight,

Sin that thy servant was this Chauntecleer,
Since this Chanticleer was thy servant,

And in thy service dide al his poweer,   524
And in thy service used all his strength

More for delyt, than world to multiplye,
More for delight, than to multiply the world,

Why woldestow suffre him on thy day to dye?
Why wouldst thou allow him to die on thy day?

O Gaufred, dere mayster soverayn,
O Geoffrey," dear sovereign master,

That, whan thy worthy king Richard was slayn   528
Who, when thy worthy King Richard was slain

With shot, compleynedest his deth so sore,
By an arrow, lamented his death so sorely,

Why ne hadde I now thy sentence and thy lore,
Why don't I have now your inspiration and technique,

The Friday for to chyde, as diden ye?
To chide the Friday, as you did?

(For on a Friday soothly slayn was he.)   532
(For truly he was slain on a Friday.)

Than wolde I shewe yow how that I coude pleyne
Then I would show you how I could lament

For Chauntecleres drede, and for his peyne.
For Chanticleer's panic and for his suffering.

  Certes, swich cry ne lamentacioun
  Certainly, such outcry and lamentation

Was never of ladies maad, whan Ilioun   536
Was never made by ladies when Troy

Was wonne, and Pirrus with his streite swerd,
Was captured, and Pyrrhus with his extended sword,

Whan he hadde hent king Priam by the berd,
Had seized King Priam by the beard,

And slayn him (as saith us ENEYDOS),
And killed him (as the AENEID tells us),

As maden alle the hennes in the clos,   540
As all the hens made in the coop,

Whan they had seyn of Chauntecleer the sighte.
When they had seen this sight of Chanticleer.

But sovereynly dame Pertelote shrighte,
But above all Dame Pertelote shrieked

Ful louder than dide Hasdrubales wyf,
Much louder than did Hasdrubal's wife,[18]

Whan that hir housbond hadde lost his lyf,   544
When her husband had lost his life,

And that the Romayns hadde brend Cartage;
And the Romans had burned Carthage;

She was so ful of torment and of rage,
She was so full of torment and of rage

That wilfully into the fyr she sterte,
That willfully she leaped into the fire

And brende hir-selven with a stedfast herte.   548
And burned herself with a steadfast heart.

O woful hennes, right so cryden ye,
O woeful hens, even so you cried

As, whan that Nero brende the citee
As, when Nero burned the city

Of Rome, cryden senatoures wyves,
Of Rome, the senators' wives cried

For that hir housbondes losten alle hir lyves;   552
Because all their husbands had lost their lives;

Withouten gilt this Nero hath hem slayn.
Who, guiltless, had been slain by Nero.

Now wol I torne to my tale agayn.
Now will I turn to my tale again.

This sely widwe, and eek hir doghtres two,
The helpless widow and her two daughters

Herden thise hennes crye and maken wo,   556
Heard the hens cry and make lament,

Aud out at dores sterten they anoon,
And out of doors they ran instantly,

And syen the fox toward the grove goon,
And saw the fox going toward the grove

And bar upon his bak the cok away;
And carrying the cock away on his back;

And cryden, "Out! harrow! and weylaway!   560
And cried, "Stop! help! and alas!

Ha, ha, the fox!" and after him they ran,
Ho there, the fox!" and after him they ran,

And eek with staves many another man;
And many another man besides with sticks;

Ran Colle our dogge, and Talbot, and Gerland,
Coll, our dog, ran, and Talbot, and Garland,

And Malkin, with a distaf in hir hand;   564
And Malkin, with a distaff in her hand;

Ran cow and calf, and eek the verray hogges,
Cow and calf ran, and even the very hogs,

So were they fered for berking of the dogges
They were so frightened by the barking of the dogs

And shouting of the men and wimmen eke;
And the shouting of the men and women too;

They ronne so, hem thoughte hir herte breke.   568
They ran so, they thought their hearts would break.

They yelleden as feendes doon in helle;
They yelled as fiends do in hell;

The dokes cryden as men wolde hem quelle;
The ducks cried as if they were being killed;

The gees for fere flowen over the trees;
The geese flew over the trees for fear;

Out of the hyve cam the swarm of bees;   572
Out of the hive came the swarm of bees;

So hidous was the noyse, a! *benedicite!*
So hideous was the noise, ah, bless us!

Certes, he Jakke Straw, and his meynee,
Truly, Jack Straw and his mobs

Ne made never shoutes half so shrille,
Never emitted shouts half so shrill,

Whan that they wolden any Fleming kille,   576
When they were killing a Fleming,"

As thilke day was maad upon the fox.
As were made that day about the fox.

Of bras thay broghten bemes, and of box,
They brought trumpets of brass, of wood,

Of horn, of boon, in whiche they blewe and pouped,
Of horn, of bone, in which they blew and puffed,

And therwithal thay shryked and they houped;   580
And in addition they shrieked and they whooped;

It seemed as that heven sholde falle.
It seemed as if the heavens would fall.

Now, gode men, I pray yow herkneth alle!
Now, good men, I beseech you all to listen!

  Lo, how Fortune turneth sodeinly
  Behold, how Fortune suddenly overturns

The hope and pryde eek of hir enemy!   584
The hope and pride of her enemy!

This cok, that lay upon the foxes bak,
This cock, who lay upon the fox's back,

In al his drede, un-to the fox he spak,
In spite of his fear, spoke to the fox,

And seyde, "Sire, if that I were as ye,
And said, "Sir, if I were in your position,

Yet sholde I seyn (as wis God helpe me),   588
I should say (so may God help me),

'Turneth agayn, ye proude cherles alle!
'Turn back, all you proud churls!

A verray pestilence up-on yow falle!
A very pestilence fall upon you!

Now am I come un-to this wodes syde,
Now have I reached the edge of this wood

Maugree your heed, the cok shal heer abyde;   592
In spite of your efforts, the cock shall stay here;

I wol him ete in feith, and that anon.'"
I will eat him, in faith, and that at once.'"

The fox answerde, "In feith, it shall be don,"—
The fox answered, "In faith, it shall be done,"

And as he spak that word, al sodeinly
And as he spoke that word, all of a sudden

This cok brak from his mouth deliverly,   596
This cock broke deftly from his mouth,

And heighe up-on a tree he fleigh anon.
And flew right up high into a tree.

And whan the fox saugh that he was y-gon,
And when the fox saw that he was gone,

"Allas!" quod he, "O Chauntecleer, allas!
"Alas!" said he, "O Chanticleer, alas!

I have to yow," quod he, "y-doon trespas,   600
I have done a wrong to you," said he,

In-as-muche as I maked yow aferd,
"Inasmuch as I made you afraid,

When I yow hente, and broghte out of the yerd;
When I seized you and brought you out of the yard;

But, sire, I dide it in no wikke entente;
But, sir, I did it with no evil intentions;

Com doun, and I shall telle yow what I mente.   604
Come down, and I shall tell you what I meant.

I shal seye sooth to yow, God help me so."
I shall speak truth to you, so God help me."

"Nay than," quod he, "I shrewe us bothe two,
"O no," said he, "I curse the two of us,

And first I shrewe my-self, bothe blood and boues,
And first I curse myself, both blood and bones,

If thou bigyle me ofter than ones.   608
If you beguile me more than once.

Thou shalt na-more thurgh thy flaterye,
You shall not again, through your flattery,

Do me to singe and winke with myn yë
Get me to sing and blink my eyes.

For he that winketh, whan he sholde see,
For he who blinks when he should see,

Al wilfully, God lat him never thee!"   612
Intentionally, God let him never prosper!"

"Nay," quod the fox, "but God yeve him meschaunce,
"No," said the fox, "but God give him bad luck,

That is so undiscreet of governaunce,
Who is so lacking in self-control

That jangleth whan he sholde holde his pees."
That he jabbers when he should hold his peace."

Lo, swich it is for to be recchelees,   616
Behold, so it goes if one is heedless,

And necligent, and truste on flaterye.
And negligent, and puts faith in flattery.

But ye that holden this tale a folye,
But you who consider this tale foolishness,

As of a fox, or of a cok and hen,
As concerning a fox, or a cock and a hen,

Taketh the moralitee, good men.   620
Consider the moral, good men.

For seint Paul seith, that al that writen is,
For Saint Paul says, that everything that is written

To our doctryne it is y-write, y-wis.
Is written for our benefit, you know.

Taketh the fruyt, and lat the chaf be stille.
Take the fruit, and let the chaff remain.

　Now, gode God, if that it be thy wille,   624
　Now, good God, if it be Thy will,

As seith my lord, so make us alle good men;
As my lord says, make us all good men,

And bringe us to his heighe blisse. Amen.
And bring us to His exalted bliss. Amen.

Epilogue
to the Nun's Priest's Tale

"Sir nonnes preest," our hoste seyde anoon,
"Sir nun's priest," our host said at once,

"Y-blessed be thy breche, and every stoon!
"Blessed be your breech and your balls!

This was a mery tale of Chauntecleer.
This was a merry tale of Chanticleer.

But, by my trouthe, if thou were seculer,   4
But, on my word, if you were a layman,

Thou woldest been a trede-foul a-right.
You would be a foul-treader all right.

For, if thou have corage as thou has might,
For, if you have as much spirit as strength,

Thee were nede of hennes, as I wene,
You would need hens, I should think,

Ya, more than seven tymes seventene.   8
Yes, sir, more than seven times seventeen.

See, whiche braunes hath this gentil preest,
See, what muscles this noble priest has,

So greet a nekke, and swich a large breest!
So thick a neck, and such a large chest!

He loketh as a sperhauk with his yën;
He glares with his eyes like a sparrow-hawk;

Him nedeth nat his colour for to dyen   12
He doesn't need to paint his complexion

With brasil, ne with greyn of Portingale.
With red dye, nor with stain from Portugal.

Now sire, faire falle yow for youre tale!"
Now sir, good luck to you for your tale!"

And after that he, with ful mery chere,
And after that he, with high good spirits,

Seide to another, as ye shullen here.   16
Said to another, as you shall hear.

The Prologue
to the Pardoner's Tale

RADIX MALORUM EST CUPIDITAS:
AD   THIMOTHEUM,   SEXTO.[1]

"Lordings," quod he, "in chirches whan I preche,
"Gentlemen," said he, "in churches when I preach,

I peyne me to han a hauteyn speche,
I take pains to make my voice carry,

And ringe it out as round as gooth a belle,
And ring it out as round as tolls a bell,

For I can al by rote that I telle.   **4**
For I know by heart what I propound.

My theme is alwey oon, and ever was—
My theme is always the same, and ever was—

'RADIX MALOREM EST CUPIDITAS.'
'Avarice is the root of all evil.'

  "First I pronounce whennes that I come,
  "For I announce where I came from,

And than my bulles shewe I, alle and somme.   **8**
And then I exhibit my papal bulls, each and all.

Our lige lordes seel on my patente,
But our liege lord's seal on my license

That shewe I first, my body to warente,
I show first, to guarantee my security,

That no man be so bold, ne preest ne clerk,
Lest any man may be so bold, whether priest or clerk,

Me to destourbe of Cristes holy werk;   12
As to disturb me in Christ's holy work;

And after that than telle I forth my tales,
And after that I deliver my harangue.

Bulles of popes and of cardinales,
Bulls of popes and of cardinals,

Of patriarkes, and bishoppes I shewe;
Of patriarchs and bishops I show;

And in Latyn I speke a wordes fewe,   16
And I speak a few words in Latin

To saffron with my predicacioun,
To add spice to my preachings,

And for to stire men to devocioun.
And to stir men to devotion.

Than shewe I forth my longe cristal stones,
Then I bring out my long crystal boxes,

Y-crammed ful of cloutes and of bones;   20
Crammed full of rags and of bones;

Reliks been they, as wenen they echoon.
Relics they are, as everyone believes.

Than have I in latoun a sholder-boon
Then in a brass box I have a shoulder bone

Which that was of an holy Jewes shepe.
Which came from a holy Jew's sheep.'

'Good men,' seye I, 'tak of my wordes kepe;   24
'Good men,' I say, 'give heed to my words;

If that this boon be wasshe in any welle,
If this bone is dipped in any well,

If cow, or calf, or sheep, or oxe swelle
If cow, or calf, or sheep, or ox swell up

That any worm hath ete, or worm y-stonge,
From eating a snake, or being stung by it,

Tak water of that welle, and wash his tonge,   28
Take water from that well, and wash its tongue,

And it is hool anon; and forthermore,
And it will be cured at once; and furthermore,

Of pokkes and of scabbe, and every sore
Of pox and of scabs, and every sore

Shal every sheep be hool, that of this welle
Shall every sheep be healed, that from this well

Drinketh a draughte; tak kepe eek what I telle.   32
Drinks a draught; take heed to what I say.

If that the good-man, that the bestes oweth,
If the honest man, who owns the beasts,

Wol every wike, er that the cok him croweth,
Will every week, before the cock crows,

Fastinge, drinken of this welle a draughte,
Before breakfast, drink a draught from this well,

As thilke holy Jewe our eldres taughte,   36
As that holy Jew taught our ancestors,

His bestes and his stoor shal multiplye.
His beasts and his goods shall multiply.

And, sirs, also it heleth jalousye;
And, sirs, it also cures jealousy;

For, though a man be falle in jalous rage,
For, though a man has fallen in a jealous rage,

Let maken with this water his potage,   40
Have his soup made with this water,

And never shal he more his wyf mistriste,
And never again shall he mistrust his wife,

Though he the sooth of hir defaute wiste;
Even though he knows the truth of her fault;

Al had she taken preestes two or three.
Even if she had taken two or three priests.

" 'Heer is miteyn eek, that ye may see.   44
" *'Here is also a mitten that you may see.*

He that his hond wol putte in this miteyn,
He that will put his hand in this mitten

He shal have multiplying of his greyn,
Shall have multiplication of his grain,

Whan he hath sowen, be it whete or otes,
When he sows, whether it be wheat or oats,

So that he offre pens, or elles grotes.   48
If he but contributes pennies or groats.

" 'Good men and wommen, o thing warne I yow,
" *'Good men and women, I warn you of one thing,*

If any wight be in this chirche now,
If anyone is now in this church,

That hath doon sinne horrible, that he
Who has done a horrible sin, so that he

Dar nat, for shame, of it y-shriven be,   52
Dare not, for shame, be confessed of it,

Or any womman, be she yong or old,
Or any woman, be she young or old,

That hath y-maad hir housbond cokewold,
Who has made her husband a cuckold,

Swich folk shul have no power ne no grace
Such people shall have neither power nor grace

To offren to my reliks in this place.   56
To make offerings to my relics here.

And who-so findeth him out of swich blame,
And whoever knows himself free of such guilt,

He wol com up and offre in Goddes name,
Let him come up and offer in God's name,

And I assoille him by the auctoritee
And I will pardon him by the authority

Which that by bulle y-graunted was to me.'   60
Which has been granted to me by bull.'

"By this gaude have I wonne, yeer by yeer,
"By this trick I have taken in, year by year,

An hundred mark sith I was pardoner.
A hundred marks since I became a pardoner.

I stonde lyk a clerk in my pulpet
I stand like a clerk in my pulpit,

And whan the lewed peple is doun y-set,   64
And when the common people have sat down,

I preche, so as he han herd bifore,
I preach, as you have just heard,

And telle an hundred false japes more.
And tell a hundred more false yarns.

Than peyne I me to strecche forth the nekke,
Then I take pains to stretch forth my neck

And est and west upon the peple I bekke,   68
And nod east and west over the people,

As doth a dowve sitting on a berne.
Like a dove sitting on a barn.

Myn hondes and my tonge goon so yerne,
My hands and my tongue go so rapidly

That it is joye to see my bisinesse.
That it is a pleasure to watch my efforts.

Of avaryce and of swich cursednesse   72
Of avarice and of such cursedness

Is al my preching, for to make hem free
Is all my preaching, to make them liberal

To yeve her pens, and namely un-to me.
To give their pennies, and especially to me.

For my entente is nat but for to winne,
For my intention is only for profit,

And no-thing for correccioun of sinne.   76
And not at all for correction of sin.

I rekke never, whan that they ben beried,
I am never concerned, when they are buried,

Though that her soules goon a-blake-beried!
Even though their souls go blackberrying!

For certes, many a predicacioun
For in truth, many a sermon

Comth ofte tyme of yvel entencioun;   80
Comes often out of evil intention;

Som for plesaunce of folk and flaterye,
Some for the pleasing and flattery of people,

To been avaunced by ipocrisye,
To have advancement by hypocrisy,

And som for veyne glorie, and som for hate.
And some for worldly fame, and some for hate.

For, whan I dar non other weyes debate,   84
For, when I dare not oppose a man otherwise,

Than wol I stinge him with my tonge smerte
Then I sting him with my sharp tongue

In preching, so that he shal nat asterte
In preaching, so that he cannot escape

To been defamed falsly, if that he
Being falsely slandered, if he

Hath trespased to my brethren or to me.   88
Has wronged my brothers or myself.

For, though I telle noght his propre name,
For, although I do not tell his exact name,

Men shal wel knowe that it is the same
Men can readily guess whom I mean

By signes and by othere circumstances.
By hints and by other devices.

Thus quyte I folk that doon us displesances;   92
Thus I pay back people who do us bad turns;

Thus spitte I out my venim under hewe
Thus I spit out my venom under color

Of holynesse, to seme holy and trewe.
Of holiness, while seeming holy and sincere.

  "But shortly myn entente I wol devyse;
  "But briefly I shall sum up my aim;

I preche of no-thing but for coveityse.   96
I preach of nothing except for gain.

Therfore my theme is yet, and ever was—
Therefore my text is still, and ever was—

'RADIX MALORUM EST CUPIDITAS.'
'Avarice is the root of all evil.'

Thus can I preche agayn that same vyce
Thus can I preach against that same vice

Which that I use, and that is avaryce.   100
Which I practice, and that is avarice.

But, though my-self be gilty in that sinne,
But, although I myself am guilty of that sin,

Yet can I maken other folk to twinne
Yet I can make other people desist

From avaryce, and sore to repente.
From avarice, and sorely repent.

But that is nat my principal entente.   104
But that is not my principal aim.

I preche no-thing but for coveityse;
I preach nothing except for gain;

Of this matere it oughte y-nogh suffyse.
This should suffice to clear up this matter.

"Than telle I hem ensamples many oon
"Then I give them many examples

Of olde stories, longe tyme agoon: *108*
From old stories of long ago:

For lewed peple loven tales olde;
For common people love old tales;

Swich thinges can they wel reporte and holde.
Such things they can easily remember and repeat.

What? trowe ye, the whyles I may preche,
What? Do you think that, when I can preach

And winne gold and silver for I teche,   *112*
And earn gold and silver for my teachings,

That I wol live in povert wilfully?
That I will deliberately live in poverty?

Nay, nay, I thoghte it never trewely!
Oh no, I never seriously considered it!

For I wol preche and begge in sondry londes;
For I will preach and beg in sundry lands;

I wol not do no labour with myn hondes,   *116*
I will not perform labor with my hands,

Ne make baskettes, and live therby,
Nor make baskets and live thereby,

Because I wol nat beggen ydelly.
Because I will not beg without profit.

I wol non of the apostles counterfete;
I will imitate none of the apostles;

I wol have money, wolle, chese, and whete,   *120*
I will have money, wool, cheese, and wheat,

Al were it yeven of the povrest page,
Even if it be given by the poorest page,

Or of the povrest widwe in a village,
Or by the poorest widow in a village,

Al sholde hir children sterve for famyne.
Though her children should die of hunger.

Nay! I wol drinke licour of the vyne,   124
No! I will drink liquor from the vine,

And have a joly wenche in every toun.
And have a jolly wench in every town.

But herkneth, lordings, in conclusioun;
But give ear, gentlemen, in conclusion;

Your lyking is that I shal telle a tale.
Your wish is that I tell a tale.

Now, have I dronke a draughte of corny ale,   128
Now that I have drunk a daught of malty ale,

By God, I hope I shal yow telle a thing
By God, I hope I shall tell you something

That shal, by reasoun, been at your lyking.
That will, with reason, be to your liking.

For, though myself be a ful vicious man,
For, though I myself am an entirely vicious man,

A moral tale yet I yow telle can,   130
Yet I can tell you a moral tale,

Which I am wont to preche, for to winne.
Which I usually preach for profit.

Now holde your pees, my tale I wol beginne."
Now hold your peace, my tale I will begin."

The Pardoner's Tale

—

In Flaundres whylom was a companye
In Flanders once there was a company

Of yonge folk, that haunteden folye,
Of young people, who pursued folly,

As ryot, hasard, stewes, and tavernes,
Such as rioting, gambling, brothels, and taverns,

Wher-as, with harpes, lutes, and giternes,   4
Where, with harps, lutes, and guitars,

They daunce and pleye at dees bothe day and night,
They danced and played dice both day and night,

And ete also and drinken over her might,
And also ate and drank beyond their capacities,

Thurgh which they doon the devel sacrifyse
By which they made sacrifices to the devil

With-in that develes temple, in cursed wyse,   8
Within the devil's temple, in wicked ways,

By superfluitee abhominable;
By abominable excesses;

Hir othes been so grete and so dampnable,
Their oaths were so great and so damnable

That it is grisly for to here hem swere;
That it was horrible to hear them swear;

Our blissed lordes body they to-tere;   12
Our blessed Lord's body they tore apart;[1]

Hem thoughte Jewes rente him noght y-nough;
They thought the Jews had not rent Him enough;

And ech of hem at otheres sinne lough.
And each of them laughed at the sins of the others.

And right anon than comen tombesteres
And very soon there came the dancing-girls

Fetys and smale, and yonge fruytesteres,   16
Shapely and slender, and young girls selling fruit,

Singers with harpes, baudes, wafereres,
Minstrels, whores, women selling cakes,

Whiche been the verray develes officeres
Who are the devil's very lieutenants

To kindle and blowe the fyr of lecherye,
To kindle and blow up the fire of lechery,

That is annexed un-to glotonye;   20
Which is next door to gluttony;

The holy writ take I to my witnesse,
The Holy Writ I take as my witness,

That luxurie is in wyn and dronkenesse.
That lust proceeds from wine and drunkenness.

   Lo, how that dronken Loth, unkindely,
   Consider how drunken Lot pervertedly

Lay by his doghtres two, unwitingly;   24
Slept with his two daughters, unknowingly;

So dronke he was he niste what he wroghte.
So drunk he was he knew not what he did.

   Herodes, (who-so wel the stories soghte),
   Herod (anyone may read the story),

Whan he of wyn was replet at his feste,
When he was full of wine at his feast,

Right at his owene table he yaf his heste 28
Right at his own table gave the command

To sleen the Baptist John ful giltelees,
To slay the entirely innocent John the Baptist,

Senek seith eek a good word doubtelees;
Seneca also says a good word, beyond a doubt;

He seith, he can no difference finde
He says he can find no difference

Bitwix a man that is out of his minde 32
Between a man that is out of his mind

And a man which that is dronkelewe,
And a man who is drunk,

But that woodnesse, y-fallen in a shrewe,
Except that madness, which happens to scoundrels,

Persevereth lenger than doth dronkenesse.
Lasts longer than drunkenness does.

O glotonye, full of cursednesse, 36
O gluttony, full of cursedness,

O cause first of our confusioun,
O first cause of our ruin,

O original of our dampnacioun,
O origin of our damnation

Til Crist had boght us with his blood agayn!
Until Christ redeemed us with His blood!

Lo, how dere, shortly for to sayn, 40
Behold, how dearly, to sum it up briefly,

Aboght was thilke cursed vileinye;
Bought was that cursed sin;

Corrupt was al this world for glotonye!
The whole world was corrupted by gluttony!

Adam our fader, and his wyf also,
Adam, our father, and his wife too,

Fro Paradys to labour and to wo   44
From Paradise to labor and to misery

Were driven for that vyce, it is no drede;
Were driven for that vice, it is undeniable;

For whyl that Adam fasted, as I rede,
For as long as Adam fasted, as I read,

He was in Paradys; and whan that he
He remained in Paradise; and when he

Eet of the fruyt defended on the tree,   48
Ate of the forbidden fruit on the tree,

Anon he was out-cast to wo and peyne.
Instantly he was cast out to woe and pain.

O glotonye, on thee wel oghte us pleyne!
O gluttony, well may we complain of you!

O, wiste a man how many maladyes
O, if a man but knew how many maladies

Folwen of excesse and of glotonyes,   52
Follow from excess and gluttony,

He wolde been the more mesurable
He would be more moderate

Of his diete, sittinge at his table.
In his diet, sitting at his table.

Allas! the shorte throte, the tendre mouth,
Alas! the short throat, the tender mouth,

Maketh that, Est and West, and North and South,   56
Compels, East and West, and North and South,

In erthe, in eir, in water men to-swinke
Men to work on earth, in air, in water,

To gete a glotoun deyntee mete and drinke!
To procure dainty meat and drink for a glutton!

Of this matere, o Paul, wel canstow trete,
This matter, O Paul, you discuss excellently,

"Mete un-to wombe, and wombe eek un-to mete,   60
"Meat unto belly, and belly in turn to meat,

Shal God destroyen bothe," as Paulus seith.
God shall destroy both," as Paul says.

Allas! a foul thing is it, by my feith,
Alas! a foul thing is it, by my faith,

To seye this word, and fouler is the dede,
To speak the word, and fouler is the deed,

Whan man so drinketh of the whyte and rede,   64
When a man so drinks of the white and red wines

That of his throte he maketh his privee,
That he makes a toilet of his throat

Thurgh thilke cursed superfluitee.
Through this cursed excessiveness.

  The apostel weping seith ful pitously,
  The apostle, weeping, says most piteously,

"Ther walken many of whiche yow told have I,   68
"There walk many of whom I have told you,

I sey it now weping with pitous voys,
I say it now weeping with piteous voice,

That they been enemys of Cristes croys,
That they are enemies of Christ's cross,

Of whiche the ende is deeth, wombe is her god."
Whose end is death, whose belly is their god."

O wombe! O bely! O stinking cod,   72
O stomach! O belly! O stinking bag,

Fulfild of donge and of corrupcioun!
Filled with dung and corruption!

At either ende of thee foul is the soun.
The sounds you make are foul at either end.

How greet labour and cost is thee to finde!
What great labor and expense it is to satisfy you!

Thise cokes, how they stampe, and streyne, and grinde,   76
Those cooks, how they pound, and strain, and grind,

And turnen substaunce in-to accident,
And turn substance into accident,'

To fulfille al thy likerous talent!
To fulfill all your greedy appetites!

Out of the harde bones knokke they
Out of the hard bones they knock

The mary, for they caste noght a-wey   80
The marrow, for they throw nothing away

That may go thurgh the golet softe and swote;
That may go through the gullet soft and sweet;

Of spicerye, of leef, and bark, and rote
Of spices, of leaf and bark and root

Shal been his sauce y-maked by delyt,
Shall his delicious sauce be made,

To make him yet a newer appetyt.   84
To provide him with a newer appetite.

But certes, he that haunteth swich delyces
But in truth, he who cultivates such tastes

Is deed, whyl that he liveth in tho vyces.
Is dead while he is living in those vices.

   A lecherous thing is wyn; and dronkenesse
   A lecherous thing is wine; and drunkenness

Is ful of stryving and of wrecchednesse.   88
Is full of quarreling and wretchedness.

O dronke man, disfigured is thy face,
O drunken man, disfigured is your face,

Sour is thy breeth, foul artow to embrace,
Sour is your breath, foul are you to embrace,

And thurgh thy dronke nose semeth the soun
And through your drunken nose it sounds

As though thou seydest ay, "Sampsoun, Sampsoun;"   92
As though you were always saying, "Samsoon, Samsoon;"

And yet, God wot, Sampsoun drank never no wyn.
And yet, God knows, Samson never drank any wine.

Thou fallest, as it were a stiked swyn;
You fall as if you were a stuck pig;

Thy tonge is lost, and al thyn honest cure;
Your tongue is lost, and all your decent appearance;

For dronkenesse is verray sepulture   96
For drunkenness is the very tomb

Of mannes wit and his discrecioun.
Of man's wisdom and his discretion.

In whom that drinke hath dominacioun,
He who is under the dominion of drink

He can no conseil kepe, it is no drede.
Can keep no counsel, it is not denied.

Now kepe yow fro the whyte and fro the rede,   100
Now stay away from the white and from the red,

And namely fro the whyte wyn of Lepe,[4]
And especially from the white wine of Lepe,

That is to selle in Fish-strete or in Chepe.
That is for sale in Fish Street or Cheapside.

This wyn of Spayne crepeth subtilly
This wine of Spain penetrates subtly

In othere wynes, growing faste by,   104
Into other wines, causing them to grow,[5]

Of which ther ryseth swich fumositee,
From which there rise such fumes

That whan a man hath dronken draughtes three,
That when a man has drunk three draughts,

And weneth that he be at hoom in Chepe,
And thinks that he is at home in Cheapside,

He is in Spayne, right at the toune of Lepe,   108
He is in Spain, right at the town of Lepe,

Nat at the Rochel, ne at Burdeux toun;
Not at Rochelle nor at Bordeaux town,[6]

And thanne wol he seye, "Sampsoun, Sampsoun."
And then will he say, "Samsoon, Samsoon."

But herkneth, lordings, o word, I yow preye,
But listen to one word, gentlemen, I beg you,

That alle the sovereyn actes, dar I seye,   112
That all the supreme acts, I dare assert,

Of victories in th'olde testament,
Of victory in the Old Testament,

Thurgh verray God, that is omnipotent,
By the aid of God, Who is omnipotent,

Were doon in abstinence and in preyere;
Were done in abstinence and prayer;

Loketh the Bible, and ther ye may it lere   116
Look in the Bible, and there you may learn this.

Loke, Attila, the grete conquerour,
Observe how Attila, the great conqueror,

Deyde in his sleep, with shame and dishonour,
Died in his sleep, with shame and dishonor,

Bledinge ay at his nose in dronkenesse;
Still bleeding at the nose in drunkenness;

A capitayn shoulde live in sobrenesse.   120
A captain should live in sobriety.

And over al this, avyseth yow right wel
And beyond all this, consider right well

What was comaunded un-to Lamuel—
What was commanded to Lemuel—[7]

Nat Samuel, but Lamuel, seye I—
Not Samuel, I say, but Lemuel—

Redeth the Bible, and finde it expresly 124
Read the Bible, and find what is said

Of wyn-yeving to hem that han justyse.
About giving wine to dispensers of justice,

Na-more of this, for it may wel suffyse.
No more of this, for this may well suffice.

  And now that I have spoke of glotonye,
  And now that I have spoken of gluttony,

Now wol I yow defenden hasardrye. 128
Now I will forbid you gambling.

Hasard is verray moder of lesinges,
Gambling is the very mother of lies,

And of deceite, and cursed forsweringes,
And of deceit, and cursed false swearing,

Blaspheme of Crist, manslaughtre, and wast also
Blasphemy of Christ, manslaughter, and a waste also

Of catel and of tyme; and forthermo, 132
Of property and of time; and furthermore,

It is repreve and contrarie of honour,
It is shameful and dishonorable

For to ben holde a commune hasardour.
To be known as a common gambler.

And ever the hyër he is of estaat,
And always the higher one is of rank,

The more is he holden desolaat. 136
The more is he considered fallen.

If that a prince useth hasardrye,
If a prince is used to gambling,

In alle governaunce and policye
In matters of government and policy

He is, as by commune opinioun,
He is, as by common consent,

Y-hold the lasse in reputacioun.   *140*
Held the lower in reputation.

Stilbon, that was a wys embassadour,
Chilon,ʳ who was a wise ambassador,

Was sent to Corinthe, in ful greet honour,
Was sent to Corinth, with highest ceremony,

Fro Lacidomie, to make her alliaunce.
From Lacedaemon, to make an alliance.

And whan he cam, him happede, par chaunce,   *144*
And when he arrived, it happened, by chance,

That alle the grettest that were of that lond,
That all the greatest of that land

Pleyinge atte hasard he hem fond.
He found playing at games of chance.

For which, as sone as it mighte be,
Wherefore, as soon as possible,

He stal him hoom agayn to his contree,   *148*
He stole home again to his country,

And seyde, "Ther wol I nat lese my name;
And said, "Yonder I will not lose my good name;

Ne I wol nat take on me so greet defame,
Nor will I take upon myself such dishonor

Yow for to allye un-to none hasardours.
As to ally you with any gamblers.

Sendeth othere wyse embassadours.   *152*
Send other wise ambassadors.

For, by my trouthe, me were lever dye,
For, on my honor, I would rather die

Than I yow sholde to hasardours allye.
Than make alliance between you and gamblers.

For ye that been so glorious in honours
For you who are so glorious in honors

Shul nat allyen yow with hasardours   *156*
Shall not ally yourself with gamblers

As by my wil, ne as by my tretee."
By my will nor by my treaty."

This wyse philosophre thus seyde he.
Thus spoke this wise philosopher.

  Loke eek that, to the King Demetrius
  Observe also how to King Demetrius

The king of Parthes, as the book seith us,   *160*
The king of Parthia, as the book tells us,'

Sente him a paire of dees of gold in scorn,
Sent a pair of golden dice in scorn

For he hadde used hasard ther-biforn;
Because he had practiced gambling before that;

For which he heeld his glorie or his renoun
Wherefore he held his glory or his renown

At no value or reputacioun.   *164*
At no value or repute.

Lordes may finden other maner pley
Lords can find other kinds of diversion

Honeste y-nough to dryve the day awey.
Honest enough to while away the day.

  Now wol I speke of othes false and grete
  Now will I speak of oaths false and great,

A word or two, as olde bokes trete.   *168*
In a word or two, as discussed in old books.

Gret swering is a thing abhominable,
Great swearing is an abominable thing,

And false swering is yet more reprevable.
And false swearing is still more reprehensible.

The heighe God forbad swering at al,
The high God forbade swearing at all,

Witnesse on Mathew; but in special   172
As Matthew" bears witness; but particularly

Of swering seith the holy Jeremye,
Concerning swearing the holy Jeremiah says,

"Thou shalt seye sooth thyn othes, and nat lye,
"Thou shalt speak thine oaths in truth, and not lie,

And swere in dome, and eek in rightwisnesse";
And swear with judgment and in righteousness";[11]

But ydel swering is a cursednesse.   176
But idle swearing is wickedness.

Bihold and see, that in the firste table
Behold and see, in the first table

Of highe Goddes hestes honurable,
Of high God's divine commandments,

How that the second heste of him is this—
That the second of the commandments is this—

"Tak nat my name in ydel or amis."   180
"Take not My name idly or amiss."

Lo, rather he forbedeth swich swering
See how He forbids such swearing sooner

Than homicyde or many a cursed thing;
Than homicide or many an evil thing;

I seye that, as by ordre, thus it stondeth;
In the order of the commandments, thus it stands;

This knowen, that his hestes understondeth,   184
Know this, you who understand His commandments,

How that the second heste of God is that.
That this is the second commandment of God.

And forther over, I wol thee telle al plat,
And furthermore, I will tell you flatly

That vengeance shal nat parten from his hous,
That vengeance shall not be separated from his house,

That of his othes is to outrageous.   188
Who is too excessive in his oaths.

"By Goddes precious herte, and by his nayles,
"By God's precious heart and the nails of the cross,

And by the blode of Crist, that it is In Hayles,
And by the blood of Christ, which is in Hailes Abbey,

Seven is my chaunce, and thyn is cink and treye;
Seven is my point, and yours is five and trey;

By Goddes armes, if thou falsly pleye,   192
By God's arms, if you play unfairly,

This dagger shal thurgh-out thyn herte go"—
This dagger shall plunge straight through your heart"—

This fruyt cometh of the bicched bones two,
Such fruit comes from the two bitchy bones,[12]

Forswering, ire, falsnesse, homicyde.
False swearing, wrath, cheating, homicide.

Now, for the love of Crist that for us dyde,   196
Now, for the love of Christ Who died for us,

Leveth your othes, bothe grete and smale.
Give up your oaths, both great and small.

But, sirs, now wol I telle forth my tale.
But, sirs, now will I proceed with my tale.

Thise ryotoures three, of whiche I telle,
These three rioters, of whom I speak,

Longe erst er pryme rong of any belle,   200
Long before any bell tolled nine,

Were set hem in a taverne for to drinke;
Were sitting in a tavern to drink;

And as they satte, they herde a belle clinke
And as they sat, they heard a bell tinkle

Biforn a cors, was caried to his grave;
Before a corpse being carried to the grave;

That oon of hem gan callen to his knave,   **204**
One of the three then called to his boy,

"Go bet," quod he, "and axe redily,
"Go quickly," he said, "and ask instantly

What cors is this that passeth heer forby;
Whose corpse it is that is passing by;

And look that thou reporte his name wel."
And be sure you report his name correctly."

"Sir," quod this boy, "it nedeth never-a-del.   **208**
"Sir," said the boy, "there is no need at all.

It was me told, er ye cam heer, two houres;
It was told me two hours before you came;

He was, pardee, an old felawe of youres;
He was, by heaven, an old companion of yours;

And sodeynly he was y-slayn to-night,
And suddenly he was slain last night,

For-dronke, as he sat on his bench upright;   **212**
Dead drunk, as he sat upright on his bench;

Ther cam a privee theef, men clepeth Deeth,
There came a sneakthief men call Death,

That in this contree al the peple sleeth,
Who kills all the people in this country,

And with his spere he smoot his herte a-two,
And with his spear he smote his heart in two,

And went his wey with-outen wordes mo.   **216**
And went his way without a word.

He hath a thousand slayn this pestilence:
He has killed a thousand this plague-time:

And, maister, er ye come in his presence,
And, master, before you come in his presence,

Me thinketh that it were necessarie
I believe that it is necessary

For to be war of swich an adversarie: 220
To be wary of such an adversary:

Beth redy for to mete him evermore.
Be ready to meet him from now on.

Thus taughte me my dame, I sey na more."
So my mother taught me, I say no more."

"By Seinte Marie," seyde this taverner,
"By Saint Mary," said the innkeeper,

"The child seith sooth, for he hath slayn this yeer,   224
"The child speaks truth, for he has slain this year,

Henne over a myle, with-in a greet village,
Over a mile from here, in a large village,

Both man and womman, child and hyne, and page.
Both man and woman, child and servant, and page.

I trowe his habitacioun be there;
I think his home is there;

To been avysed greet wisdom it were,   228
It is wise to take heed of him

Er that he dide a man a dishonour."
Before he does evil to one."

"Ye, Goddes armes!" quod this ryotour,
"Yah, God's arms!" said this rioter,

"Is it swich peril with him for to mete?
"Is it so perilous to meet with him?

I shal him seke by wey and eek by strete,   232
I shall seek him out in highways and streets,

I make avow to Goddes digne bones!
I make an oath to God's blessed bones!

Herkneth, felawes, we three been al ones;
Listen, friends, we three are as one;

Lat ech of us holde up his hand til other,
Let each of us hold up his hand to the other,

And ech of us bicomen otheres brother,   236
And each of us become each other's brother,

And we wol sleen this false traytour Deeth;
And we will slay this false traitor Death;

He shal be slayn, which that so many sleeth,
He shall be slain, who slays so many,

By Goddes dignitee, er it be night."
By God's dignity, before nightfall."

   Togidres han this three her trouthes plight,   240
Together these three plighted their troth,

To live and dyen ech of hem for other,
To live and die each of them for the other,

As though he were his owene y-boren brother.
As if he were his own blood brother.

And up they sterte al dronken, in this rage,
And up they jumped all drunk in this madness,

And forth they goon towardes that village,   244
And forth they went toward that village

Of which the taverner had spoke biforn,
Of which the innkeeper had just told them,

And many a grisly ooth than han they sworn,
And many a frightful oath they swore,

And Cristes blessed body they to-rent—
And Christ's blessed body they tore apart—

Deeth shal be deed, if that they may him hente.   248
Death shall be dead, if they can catch him.

   Whan they han goon nat fully half a myle,
When they had proceeded less than half a mile,

Right as they wolde han troden over a style,
Just as they were about to climb over a stile,

An old man and a povre with hem mette.
A poor old man met them.

This olde man ful mekely hem grette,   252
This old man greeted them most humbly,

And seyde thus, "Now, lordes, God yow see!"
And spoke thus, "Now, lords, God keep you!"

The proudest of thise ryotoures three
The most arrogant of these three revellers

Answerde agayn, "What? carl, with sory grace,
Answered back, "What? peasant, confound you,

Why artow al forwrapped save thy face?   256
Why are you all wrapped up except your face?

Why livestow so longe in so greet age?"
Why do you live so long in such old age?"

This olde man gan loke in his visage,
This old man began to peer in his face,

And seyde thus, "For I ne can nat finde
And spoke thus, "Because I cannot find

A man, though that I walked in-to Inde,   260
A man, though I walked as far as India,

Neither in citee nor in no village,
Either in a city or in a village,

That wolde chaunge his youthe for myn age;
Who is willing to exchange his youth for my age;

And therfore moot I han myn age stille,
And therefore I must still keep my age

As longe time as it is Goddes wille.   264
For as long a time as it is God's will.

"Ne deeth, allas! ne wol nat han my lyf;
"And death, alas! will not have my life;

Thus walke I, lyk a restelees caityf,
Thus do I walk like a restless captive,

And on the ground, which is my modres gate,
And on the ground, which is my mother's gate,

I knokke with my staf, bothe erly and late,   268
I knock with my staff, both early and late,

And seye, 'Leve moder, leet me in!
And say, 'Dear mother, let me in!

Lo, how I vanish, flesh, and blood, and skin!
See how I vanish, flesh, and blood, and skin!

Allas! whan shul my bones been at reste?
Alas, when shall my bones be at rest?

Moder, with yow wolde I chaunge my cheste,   272
Mother, with you I would exchange my strong-box

That in my chambre longe tyme hath be,
Which has been a long time in my bedroom,

Ye! for an heyre clout to wrappe me!'
Yes, for a shroud to wrap myself in!'

But yet to me she wol nat do that grace,
But yet she will not do that mercy to me,

For which ful pale and welked is my face.   276
Wherefore my face is all pale and withered.

  "But, sirs, to yow it is no curteisye
  "But, sirs, it is not courteous of you

To speken to an old man vileinye,
To speak harshly to an old man

But he trespasse in worde, or elles in dede.
Unless he wrong you in words or deed.

In holy writ ye may your-self wel rede,   280
In Holy Writ you can easily read yourself,

'Agayns an old man, hoor upon his heed,
'Before an old man with white hair,

Ye sholde aryse;' wherfor I yeve yow reed,
You should rise up;'" wherefore I advise you

Ne dooth un-to an old man noon harm now,
Not to do any harm now to an old man,

Na-more than ye wolde men dide to yow   284
Any more that you would have men do to you

In age, if that ye so longe abyde;
In old age, if you live so long;

And God be with yow, wher ye go or ryde.
And God be with you, wherever you walk or ride.

I moot go thider as I have to go."
I must go where I have to go."

   "Nay, olde cherl, by God, thou shalt nat so,"   288
   "Oh no, old man, by God, you shall not so,"

Seyde this other hasardour anon;
Said another of the gamblers instantly;

"Thou partest nat so lightly, by seint John!
"You don't get away so easily, by Saint John!

Thou spak right now of thilke traitour Deeth,
You spoke just now of that traitor Death

That in this contree alle our frendes sleeth.   292
Who is killing all our friends in this country.

Have heer my trouthe, as thou art his aspye,
Take my word for it, as you are his spy,

Tel wher he is, or thou shalt it abye,
Tell where he is, or you shall pay for it,

By God, and by the holy sacrament!
By God, and by the Holy Sacrament!

For soothly thou art oon of his assent,   296
For truly you are in agreement with him

To sleen us yonge folk, thou false theef!"
To kill us young people, you false thief!"

   "Now, sirs," quod he, "if that yow be so leef
   "Now, sirs," said he. "if you are so eager

To finde Deeth, turne up this croked wey,
To find Death, turn up this crooked path,

For in that grove I lafte him, by my fey,   *300*
For in that grove I left him, by my faith,

Under a tree and ther he wol abyde;
Under a tree and there he will remain;

Nat for your boost he wol him no-thing hyde.
He won't go into hiding because of your boast.

See ye that ook? Right ther ye shul him finde,
Do you see that oak? Right there you will find him.

God save yow, that boghte agayn mankinde,   *304*
God save you, Who redeemed mankind,

And yow amende!"—thus seyde this olde man.
And improve you!"—so spoke this old man.

And everich of thise ryotoures ran,
And each of these rioters ran

Til he cam to that tree, and ther they founde
Until he came to that tree, and there they found,

Of florins fyne of golde y-coyned rounde   *308*
Of fine round florins coined of gold,

Wer ny an eighte busshels, as hem thoughte.
Nearly eight bushels, as they estimated.

No lenger thanne after Deeth they soughte,
No longer then did they search for Death,

But ech of hem so glad was of that sighte,
But each of them was so joyous at that sight,

For that the florins been so faire and brighte,   *312*
Because the florins were so beautiful and bright,

That doun they settle hem by this precious hord.
That they sat down by this precious hoard.

The worste of hem he spake the firste word.
The worst of them spoke the first word.

"Brethren," quod he, "tak kepe what I seye;
"Brothers," he said, "take heed to what I say;

My wit is greet, though that I bourde and pleye.   *316*
My wisdom is great, although I joke and fool.

This tresor hath Fortune un-to us yiven,
Fortune has given this treasure to us

In mirthe and jolitee our lyf to liven;
So that we may live our lives in mirth and joy;

And lightly as it comth, so wol we spende.
And as easily as it came, so will we spend it.

Ey! Goddes precious dignitee! who wende   *320*
Hey! God's precious dignity! Who would have thought

To-day, that we sholde han so fair a grace?
Today, that we should have such good luck?

But mighte this gold be carried fro this place
But if this gold could be carried from this place

Hoom to myn hous, or elles un-to youres—
Home to my house, or else to yours—

For wel ye woot that al this gold is oures—   *324*
For you well know that all this gold is ours—

Than were we in heigh felicitee.
Then would we be in the height of happiness.

But trewely, by daye it may nat be;
But surely, it cannot be done by day;

Men wolde seyn that we were theves stronge,
Men would say that we were mighty thieves,

And for our owene tresor doon us honge.   *328*
And hang us for our own treasure.

This tresor moste y-carried be by nighte
This treasure must be carried off by night

As wysly and as slyly as it mighte.
As wisely and as cautiously as possible.

Wherfore I rede that cut among us alle
Therefore I advise that lots among us all

Be drawe, and lat see wher the cut wol falle;   332
Be drawn, and let us see where the lot will fall;

And he that hath the cut with herte blythe
And he who draws the lot with light heart

Shal renne to the toune, and that ful swythe,
Shall run to the town, and that right quickly,

And bringe us breed and wyn ful prively.
And bring us bread and wine most secretly.

And two of us shul kepen subtilly   336
And two of us shall keep close watch

This tresor wel; and, if he wol nat tarie,
Over this treasure; and, if he doesn't delay,

Whan it is night, we wol this tresor carie
When it is night, we will carry this treasure,

By oon assent, wher-as us thinketh best."
By common consent, wherever we think best."

That oon of hem the cut broughte in his fest,   340
One of them brought the lots in his fist,

And bad hem drawe, and loke wher it wol falle;
And bade them draw, and see where it would fall;

And it fil on the yongeste of hem alle;
And it fell on the youngest of them all;

And forth toward the toun he wente anon.
And immediately he went forth toward the town.

And al-so sone as that he was gon,   344
And as soon as he had gone,

That oon of hem spak thus un-to that other,
One of the two spoke thus to the other,

"Thou knowest wel thou art my sworne brother,
"You well know that you are my sworn brother,

Thy profit wol I telle thee anon.
Now I will tell you something profitable.

Thou woost wel that our felawe is agon;   *348*
You well know that our companion is gone;

And heer is gold, and that ful greet plentee,
And here is gold, and a great plenty at that,

That shal departed been among us three.
Which is to be divided among us three.

But natheles, if I can shape it so
But nevertheless, if I can arrange it so

That it departed were among us two,   *352*
That it be divided between us two,

Hadde I nat doon a freendes torn to thee?"
Wouldn't I have done a friendly turn to you?"

  That other answerde, "I noot how that may be;
  The other answered, "I don't know how that can be;

He woot how that the gold is with us tweye;
He knows that the gold is with us two;

What shal we doon, what shal we to him seye?"   *356*
What shall we do, what shall we say to him?"

  "Shal it be conseil?" seyde the first shrewe,
  "Shall it be a secret?" said the first scoundrel,

"And I shal tellen thee, in wordes fewe,
"And I shall tell you, in a few words,

What we shal doon, and bringe it wel aboute."
What we shall do, and accomplish it neatly."

  "I graunte," quod that other, "out of doute,   *360*
  "I agree," said the other, "beyond question,

That, by my trouthe, I wol thee nat biwreye."
That, on my honor, I will not betray you."

  "Now," quod the firste, "thou woost wel we be tweye,
  "Now," said the first, "you well know we are two,

And two of us shul strenger be than oon.
And two of us will be stronger than one.

Look whan that he is set, and right anoon   *364*
Watch when he sits down, and right away

Arys, as though thou woldest with him pleye;
Get up, as though you would fool with him;

And I shal ryve him thurgh the sydes tweye
And I shall stab him through both sides

Whyl that thou strogelest with him as in game,
While you are struggling with him as if in sport,

And with thy dagger look thou do the same;   *368*
And with your dagger see that you do the same;

And than shal al this gold departed be,
And then all this gold shall be divided,

My dere freend, bitwixen me and thee;
My dear friend, between me and you;

Than may we bothe our lustes al fulfille,
Then we can both satisfy all our desires,

And pleye at dees righte at our owene wille."   *372*
And play dice as much as we please."

And thus acorded been thise shrewes tweye
And thus agreed were these two scoundrels

To sleen the thridde, as ye han herd me seye.
To kill the third, as you have heard me say.

This yongest, which that wente un-to the toun,
The youngest, who went to the town,

Ful ofte in herte he rolleth up and doun.   *376*
Often in imagination rolled up and down

The beautee of thise florins newe and brighte.
The beauty of those florins new and bright.

"O lord!" quod he, "if so were that I mighte
"O Lord!" he said, "if only I might

Have al this tresor to my-self allone,
Have all this treasure alone to myself,

Ther is no man that liveth under the trone   380
There is no man living under the throne

Of God, that sholde live so mery as I!"
Of God, who would live as merry as I!"

And atte laste the feend, our enemy,
And at last, the fiend, our enemy,

Putte in his thought that he shold poyson beye,
Put it in his mind to buy poison

With which he mighte sleen his felawes tweye;   384
With which he might kill his two companions;

For-why the feend fond him in swich lyvinge,
Because the fiend found him living such a life

That he had leve him to sorwe bringe,
That he had permission to bring him to destruction,

For this was outrely his fulle entente
For this was entirely his full intention

To sleen hem bothe, and never to repente.   388
To kill them both, and never to repent.

And forth he gooth, no lenger wolde he tarie,
And forth he went, no longer would be delay,

Into tue toun, un-to a pothecarie,
Into the town, to an apothecary,

And preyed him, that he him wolde selle
And asked him to sell him

Som poyson, that he mighte his rattes quelle;   392
Some poison, that he might kill his rats;

And eek ther was a polcat in his hawe,
And besides there was a pole-cat in his yard,

That, as he seyde, his capouns hadde y-slawe,
Which, as he said, had slaughtered his capons,

And fayn he wolde wreke him, if he mighte,
And he would like to revenge himself, if he could,

On vermin, that destroyed him by nighte.   396
On vermin that ruined him by night.

The pothecarie answerde, "And thou shalt have
The apothecary answered, "And you shall have

A thing that, al-so God my soule save,
A drug that, as God may save my soul,

In al this world ther nis no creature,
In all this world there is no creature

That ete or dronke hath of this confiture   400
Who can eat or drink of this preparation

Noght but the mountance of a corn of whete,
Nothing but the amount of a grain of wheat,

That he ne shal his lyf anon forlete;
Without instantly forfeiting his life;

Ye, sterve he shal, and that in lasse whyle
Yes, die he shall, and in a shorter time

Than thou wolt goon a paas nat but a myle;   404
Than you can travel a mile at a walk;

This poyson is so strong and violent."
This poison is so strong and violent."

This cursed man hath in his hond y-hent
This cursed man took in his hand

This poyson in a box, and sith he ran
This poison in a box, and then he ran

In-to the nexte strete, un-to a man,   408
To a man in the next street,

And borwed of him large botels three;
And borrowed three large bottles from him:

And in the two his poyson poured he;
And poured his poison in two of them;

The thridde he kepte clene for his drinke.
The third he kept clean for his own drink.

For al the night he shoop him for to swinke   412
For all night he planned to labor

In caryinge of the gold out of that place.
In lugging the gold out of that place.

And whan this ryotour, with sory grace,
And when this rioter, may he be confounded,

Had filled with wyn his grete botels three,
Had filled his three big bottles with wine,

To his felawes agayn repaireth he.   416
He returned again to his companions.

What nedeth it to sermone of it more?
What needs it to discuss it further?

For right as they had cast his deeth before,
For just as they had planned his death in advance,

Right so they han him slayn, and that anon.
Even so they killed him, and that instantly.

And whan that this was doon, thus spak that oon,   420
And when this was done, one of them thus spoke,

"Now lat us sitte and drinke, and make us merie,
"Now let us sit and drink and make merry,

And afterward we wol his body berie."
And afterward we will bury his body."

And with that word it happed him, par cas,
And with that word it chanced to him

To take the botel ther the poyson was,   424
To take the bottle containing the poison,

And drank, and yaf his felawe drinke also,
And he drank, and offered some to his friend,

For which anon they storven bothe two.
Whereby they both died instantly.

But, certes, I suppose that Avicen
But, truly, I imagine that Avicenna[14]

Wroot never in no canon, ne in no fen,   428
Never wrote in any chapter of any treatise

Mo wonder signes of empoisoning
More wondrous symptoms of poisoning

Than hadde thise wrecches two, er hir ending.
Than these two wretches showed, before they died.

Thus ended been thise homicydes two,
Thus were ended these two homicides,

And eek the false empoysoner also.   432
And in addition the false poisoner too.

O cursed sinne, ful of cursednesse!
O cursed sin, full of cursedness!

O traytours homicyde, o wikkednesse!
O treacherous homicide, O wickedness!

O glotonye, luxurie, and hasardrye!
O gluttony, lust, and gambling!

Thou blasphemour of Crist with vileinye   436
You blasphemer of Christ with vileness

And othes grete, of usage and of pryde!
And great oaths, customary and arrogant!

Allas! mankinde, how may it bityde,
Alas! mankind, how can it be,

That to thy creatour which that thee wroghte,
That to thy Creator Who made you,

And with his precious herte-blood thee boghte,   440
And redeemed you with His precious heart's blood,

Thou art so fals and so unkinde, allas!
You are so false and so unnatural, alas!

Now, goode men, God forgeve yow your trespas,
Now, good men, God forgive you your iniquity,

And ware yow fro the sinne of avaryce.
And avoid the sin of avarice.

Myn holy pardoun may yow alle waryce,   **444**
My holy pardon can save you all,

So that ye offre nobles or sterlinges,
If you offer nobles or other silver coins,

Or elles silver brooches, spones, ringes.
Or else silver brooches, spoons, rings.

Boweth your heed under this holy bulle!
Bow your heads before this holy bull!

Cometh up, ye wyves, offreth of your wolle!   **448**
Come up, you women, make offering of your wool!

Your name I entre heer in my rolle anon;
Your name I enter here in my roll forthwith;

In-to the blisse of hevene shul ye gon;
Into the bliss of heaven you shall go;

I yow assoile, by myn heigh power,
I pardon you, by my high power,

Yow that wol offre, as clene and eek as cleer   **452**
You who make offering, as clean and also as pure

As ye were born; and, lo, sirs, thus I preche.
As you were born; and, observe, sirs, thus I preach.

And Jesu Crist, that is our soules leche,
And Jesus Christ, Who is our soul's physician,

So graunte yow his pardon to receyve;
So grant you to receive His pardon;

For that is best; I wol yow nat deceyve.   **456**
For that is best; I will not deceive you.

    But sirs, o word forgat I in my tale,
    But sirs, one word I forgot in my tale,

I have relikes and pardon in my male,
I have relics and pardons in my bag,

As faire as any man in Engelond,
As fine as has any man in England,

Whiche were me yeven by the popes hond.   460
Which were given to me by the pope's hand.

If any of yow wol, of devocioun,
If any of you is willing, out of devotion,

Offren, and han myn absolucioun,
Make offering, and have my absolution,

Cometh forth anon, and kneleth heer adoun,
Come forth at once, and kneel down here,

And mekely receyveth my pardoun: 464
And meekly receive my pardon:

Or elles, taketh pardon as ye wende,
Or else, take pardons as you travel,

Al newe and fresh, at every tounes ende,
All new and fresh, at every town's end,

So that ye offren alwey newe and newe
So long as you offer again and again

Nobles and pens, which that be gode and trewe.   468
Nobles and pennies that are good and solid.

It is an honour to everich that is heer,
It is an honor to everyone who is here

That ye mowe have a suffisant pardoneer
That you can have a capable pardoner

T'assoille yow, in contree as ye ryde,
To absolve you, as you ride through the country,

For aventures which that may bityde.   472
Because of occurrences which may happen.

Peraventure ther may falle oon or two
Perchance, one or two of you may fall

Doun of his hors, and breke his nekke atwo.
Down from his horse, and break his neck in two.

Look which a seuretee is it to yow alle
See what a security it is to you all

That I am in your felaweship y-falle,   *476*
That I have chanced to be in your company,

That may assoille yow, bothe more and lasse,
Who may absolve you, both great and small,

Whan that the soule shal fro the body passe.
When the soul shall pass from the body.

I rede that our hoste heer shal biginne,
I advise that our host here shall begin,

For he is most envoluped in sinne.   *480*
For he is most enveloped in sin.

Com forth, sir hoste, and offre first anon,
Come forth, sir host, and offer first now,

And thou shalt kisse the reliks everichon,
And you shall kiss the relics every one,

Ye, for a grote! unbokel anon thy purs.
Yes, for a groat! unfasten now your purse.

"Nay, nay," quod he, "than have I Cristes curs!   *484*
"No, no," said he, "then may I have Christ's curse!

Lat be," quod he, "it shal nat be, so thee'ch!
Give over," said he, "it shall not be, as I would thrive!

Thou woldest make me kisse thyn old breech,
You would make me kiss your old breeches,

And swere it were a relik of a seint,
And swear it was a relic of a saint

Thogh it were with thy fundement depeint!   *488*
Even though it were painted with your excrement!

But by the croys which that Seint Eleyne fond,
But by the cross which Saint Helen found,

I wolde I hadde thy coillons in myn hond
I would I had your testicles in my hand

In stede of relikes or of seintuarie;
Instead of relics or holy things;

Lat cutte hem of, I wol thee helpe hem carie;   492
Let them be cut off, I will help you carry them;

They shul be shryned in an hogges tord."
They shall be enshrined in a hog's turd."

   This pardoner answerde nat a word;
   This pardoner answered not a word;

So wrooth he was, no word ne wolde he seye.
So angry he was, not one word would he utter.

   "Now," quod our host, "I wol no lenger pleye   496
   "Now," said our host, "I will no longer fool

With thee, ne with noon other angry man."
With you, or with any other angry man."

But right anon the worthy knight bigan,
But right away the worthy knight began,

Whan that he saugh that al the peple lough,
When he saw all the people laughing,

"Na-more of this, for it is right y-nough;   500
"No more of this, it has gone far enough;

Sir pardoner, be glad and mery of chere;
Sir pardoner, be gay and merry looking;

And ye, sir host, that been to me so dere,
And you, sir host, who are so dear to me,

I prey yow that ye kisse the pardoner.
I beseech you to kiss the pardoner.

And pardoner, I prey thee, drawe thee neer,   504
And, pardoner, I beg you to draw near,

And, as we diden, lat us laughe and pleye."
And, as we did before, let us laugh and jest."

Anon they kiste, and riden forth hir weye.
And so they kissed, and rode forth on their way.

The Prologue
to the Wife of Bath's Tale

━━━━━

"Experience, though noon auctoritee
"Experience, though no authority

Were in this world, were right y-nough to me
Were in this world, would be quite enough for me

To speke of wo that is in mariage;
To speak of the misery that is in marriage;

For, lordinges, sith I twelf yeer was of age,   4
For, gentlemen, since I was twelve years old,

Thonked be God that is eterne on lyve,
Thanks to God Who lives eternally,

Housbondes at chirche-dore I have had fyve;
Husbands at church door I have had five;

For I so ofte have y-wedded be;
For I have been wedded that often;

And alle were worthy men in hir degree.   8
And all were worthy men in their stations.

But me was told certeyn, nat longe agon is,
But it was certainly told me, not long ago,

That sith that Crist ne wente never but onis
That since Christ never went but once

To wedding in the Cane of Galilee,
To a wedding, in Cana of Galilee,

That by the same ensample taughte he me   *12*
By this same example He taught me

That I ne sholde wedded be but ones.
That I should be wedded only once.

Herke eek, lo! which a sharp word for the nones
And listen too, what a sharp word at the time

Besyde a welle Jesus, God and man,
Beside a well, Jesus, God and man,

Spak in repreve of the Samaritan: *16*
Spoke in reproof of the Samaritan:

Thou hast y-had fyve housbondes,' quod he,
Thou hast had five husbands,' said He,[1]

'And thilke man, the which that hath now thee,
'And this man, who hath thee now,

Is noght thyn housbond'; thus seyde he certeyn;
Is not thy husband,' so He certainly spoke;

What that he mente ther-by, I can nat seyn;   *20*
What He meant by it, I cannot say;

But that I axe, why that the fifthe man
But let me ask why the fifth man

Was noon housbond to the Samaritan?
Was not husband to the Samaritan.

How manye mighte she have in mariage?
How many might she have in marriage?

Yet herde I never tellen in myn age   *24*
Yet I have never heard in all my life

Upon this nombre diffinicioun;
An explanation of this number;

Men may devyne and glosen up and doun.
Men may interpret and explain up and down.

But wel I woot expres, with-oute lye,
But this I know precisely, without lying,

God bad us for to wexe and multiplye;   28
God commanded us to wax and multiply;

That gentil text can I wel understonde.
That noble text I can entirely understand.

Eek wel I woot he seyde, myn housbonde
Besides I know well He said, my husband

Sholde lete fader and moder, and take me;
Should leave father and mother, and take me;

But of no nombre mencioun made he,   32
But He made no mention of number,

Of bigamye or of octogamye;
Of bigamy or of octogamy;

Why sholde men speke of it vileinye?
Why should men speak evil of it?

   "Lo, here the wyse king, dan Salomon;
   "Consider here the wise king, Lord Solomon;

I trowe he hadde wyves mo than oon;   36
I believe he had more wives than one;

As, wolde God, it leveful were to me
As, would to God, it were allowable to me

To be refresshed half so ofte as he!
To be refreshed half so often as he!

Which yifte of God hadde he for alle his wyvis!
What a gift of God he had with all his wives!

No man hath swich, that in this world alyve is.   40
No man has such, who is alive in this world.

God woot, this noble king, as to my wit,
God knows, this noble king, as I see it,

The firste night had many a mery fit
The first night had many a merry bout

With ech of hem, so wel was him on lyve!
With each of them, so vital a man was he!

Blessed be God that I have wedded fyve!   44
Blessed be God that I have wedded five!

Welcome the sixte, whan that ever he shal.
Welcome the sixth, whenever he is ready.

For sothe, I wol nat kepe me chast in al;
For indeed, I won't remain altogether chaste;

Whan myn housbond is fro the world y-gon,
When my husband is departed from the world,

Som Cristen man shal wedde me anon;   48
Some Christian man shall wed me soon;

For thanne th'apostle seith, that I am free
For then the apostle says that I am free

To wedde, a Godd's half, wher it lyketh me.
To wed, in God's name, wherever I please.

He seith that to be wedded is no sinne;
He says that to be married is no sin;

Bet is to be wedded than to brinne.   52
It is better to be married than to burn.

What rekketh me, thogh folk seye vileinye
What do I care, though people speak evil

Of shrewed Lameth and his bigamye?
Of wicked Lamech and his bigamy?

I woot wel Abraham was an holy man,
I know well Abraham was a holy man,

And Jacob eek, as ferforth as I can;   56
And Jacob too, as far as I know;

And ech of hem hadde wyves mo than two;
And each of them had more than two wives;

And many another holy man also.
And many another holy man too.

Whan saugh ye ever, in any maner age,
When did you ever see, in any sort of age,

That hye God defended mariage   60
That high God forbade marriage

By expres word? I pray you, telleth me;
By express word? I pray you, tell me;

Or wher comanded he virginitee?
Or where did He command virginity?

I woot as wel as ye, it is no drede,
I know as well as you, without a doubt,

Th'apostel, whan he speketh of maydenhede;   64
The apostle, when he speaks of maidenhood,

He seyde, that precept ther-of hadde he noon.
Says that he has no precept about it.

Men may conseille a womman to been oon,
Men may counsel a woman to be single,

But conseilling is no comandement;
But advice is no commandment;

He putte it in our owene jugement   68
He left it to our own judgment

For hadde God comanded maydenhede,
For if God had commanded maidenhood,

Thanne hadde he dampned wedding with the dede;
Then He would have condemned marriage along with it;

And certes, if ther were no seed y-sowe,
And certainly, if no seed were sown,

Virginitee, wher-of than sholde it growe?   72
Where would virgins come from?

Poul dorste nat comanden atte leste
Paul dared not command, at least,

A thing of which his maister yaf noon hestor
A thing about which his Master specified nothing.

The dart is set up for virginitee;
The prize is set up for virginity;

Cacche who so may, who renneth best lat see.   76
Win it who can, let us see who runs best.

"But this word is nat take of every wight,
"But this word is not intended for everybody,

But ther as God list give it of his might.
But to such as God in His might pleases to give it.

I woot wel, that th'apostel was a mayde;
I know well that the apostle was a virgin;

But natheless, thogh that he wroot and sayde,   80
But nevertheless, though he wrote and preached

He wolde that every wight were swich as he,
That he would that everyone were such as he,

Al nis but conseil to virginitee;
All this merely advised virginity;

And for to been a wyf, he yaf me leve
And he gave me leave to be a wife

Of indulgence; so it is no repreve   84
By special indulgence, so there is no blame

To wedde me, if that my make dye,
In my marrying, if my mate dies,

With-oute excepcioun of bigamye.
Without accusation of bigamy.

Al were it good no womman for to touche,
Altogether, it would be good to touch no woman,

He mente as in his bed or in his couche;   88
He meant as in his bed or on his couch;

For peril is bothe fyr and tow t'assemble;
For it is dangerous to unite fire and hemp;

Ye knowe what this ensample may resemble.
You know what this example may resemble.

This is al and som, he heeld virginitee
This is the sum and substance: he held virginity

More parfit than wedding in freletee.   92
More perfect than the frailty of marriage.

Freeltee clepe I, but-if that he and she
Frailty I call it, unless he and she

Wolde leden al hir lyf in chastitee.
Would lead all their lives in chastity.

"I graunte it wel, I have noon envye,
"I freely grant it, I have no envy,

Thogh maydenhede prefere bigamye;   96
Though maidenhood is preferred to bigamy;

Hem lyketh to be clene, body and goost,
Some like to be pure, body and soul,

Of myn estaat I nil nat make no boost.
Of my condition I will make no boast.

For wel ye knowe, a lord in his houshold,
For you well know, a lord in his household

He hath nat every vessel al of gold;   100
Doesn't have all his vessels of pure gold;

Somme been of tree, and doon hir lord servyse.
Some are wooden, and are serviceable to their lord.

God clepeth folk to him in sondry wyse,
God calls people to Him in various ways,

And everich hath of God a propre yifte,
And each one has from God his own gift,

Som this, som that,—as him lyketh shifte.   104
Some this, some that,—as He pleases to dispense them.

"Virginitee is greet perfeccioun,
"Virginity is a great perfection,

And continence eek with devocioun.
And so is devoted continence.

But Crist, that of perfeccioun is welle,
But Christ, Who is the source of perfection,

Bad nat every wight he sholde go selle   *108*
Commanded not everyone to go and sell

Al that he hadde, and give it to the pore,
All that he had, and give it to the poor,

And in swich wyse folwe him and his fore.
And in such things follow Him and His way.

He spak to hem that wolde live parfitly;
He spoke to those who would live perfectly;

And lordinges, by your leve, that am nat I.   *112*
And gentlemen, by your leave, such am not I.

I wol bistowe the flour of al myn age
I will bestow the flower of all my years

In th'actes and in fruit of mariage.
In the acts and the fruit of marriage.

"Telle me also, to what conclusioun
"Tell me also, for what purpose

Were membres maad of generacioun,   *116*
Were the organs of generation made,

And for what profit was a wight y-wroght?
And for what purpose was a body made?

Trusteth right wel, they wer nat maad for noght.
Trust it right well, they were not made for nothing.

Glose who-so wole, and seye bothe up and doun,
Explain, whoever will, and say it up and down,

That they were maked for purgacioun   *120*
That they were made for the elimination

Of urine, and our bothe thinges smale
Of urine, and that both our little things

Were eek to knowe a female from a male,
Were there to tell a female from a male,

And for noon other cause: sey ye no?
And for no other cause: do you say 'no'?

The experience woot wel it is noght so; 124
Experience fully teaches it is not so;

So that the clerkes be nat with me wrothe,
In order that the clerks be not angry with me,

I sey this, that they maked been for bothe,
I say this, that they are made for both,

This is to seye, for office, and for ese
That is to say, for function, and for pleasure

Of engendrure, ther we nat God displese. 128
Of begetting, where we do not displease God.

Why sholde men elles in hir bokes sette,
Why otherwise should men state in their books

That man shal yelde to his wyf hir dette?
That man shall pay his debt to his wife?

Now wher-with sholde he make his payement,
Now with what should he make his payment,

If he ne used his sely instrument? 132
If he does not use his blessed instrument?

Than were they maad up-on a creature,
So they were created on a creature

To purge uryne, and eek for engendrure.
To purge urine, and also for generation.

  "But I seye noght that every wight is holde,
  "But I do not say that every person is bound,

That hath swich harneys as I to yow tolde, 136
Who possesses such equipment as I have mentioned,

To goon and use hem in engendrure;
To go and use it for begetting;

Than sholde men take of chastitee no cure.
Then would men take no heed of chastity.

Crist was a mayde, and shapen, as a man,
Christ was a virgin, and formed as a man,

And many a seint, sith that the world bigan,   *140*
And many a saint, since the world began,

Yet lived they ever in parfit chastitee.
Yet they lived always in perfect chastity.

I nil envye no virginitee;
I do not envy any virginity;

Lat hem be breed of pured whete-seed,
Let them be bread of pure wheat,

And lat us wyves hoten barly-breed;   *144*
And let us wives be known as barley bread.

And yet with barly-breed, Mark telle can,
And yet with barley bread, Mark can tell,

Our lord Jesu refresshed many a man.
Our Lord Jesus refreshed many a man.

In swich estaat as God hath cleped us
In such estate as God has called us to,

I wol persevere, I nam nat precious.   *148*
I will persevere, I am not finicky.

In wyfhode I wol use myn instrument
In wifehood I will use my instrument

As frely as my maker hath it sent.
As freely as my Maker has bestowed it.

If I be daungerous, God yeve me sorwe!
If I be grudging, God give me sorrow!

Myn housbond shal it have both eve and morwe,   *152*
My husband shall have it both night and morning,

Whan that him list com forth and paye his dette.
Whenever he wants to come forth and pay his debt.

An housbonde I wol have, I nil nat lette,
A husband I will have, I will not desist,

Which shal be both my dettour and my thral,
Who shall be both my debtor and my slave,

And have his tribulacioun with-al   156
And have his troubles along with it

Up-on his flessh, whyl that I am hiu wyf.
Upon his flush, while I am his wife.

I have the power duringe al my lyf
I have the authority during all my life

Up-on his propre body, and noght he.
Over his own body, and not he.

Right thus th'apostel tolde it un-to me;   160
Just so the apostle told it to me,

And bad our housbondes for to love us weel.
And bade our husbands to love us well.

Al this sentence me lyketh every-deel"—
I like every bit of all this statement"—

Up sterte the pardoner, and that anon,
Up jumped the pardoner, and that instantly,

"Now dame," quod he, "by God and by seint John,   164
"Now madam," said he, "by God and by Saint John,

Ye been a noble prechour in this cas!
You are a noble preacher in this matter!

I was aboute to wedde a wyf; allas!
I was about to wed a wife, alas!

What sholde I bye it on my flesh so dere?
Why should I pay for it so dearly with my flesh?

Yet hadde I lever wedde no wyf to-yere!"   168
Now I would rather wed no wife this year!"

  "Abyde!" quod she, "my tale is nat bigonne;
  "Wait!" she said, "my story is not begun;

Nay, thou shalt drinken of another tonne
No, you shall drink from another cask

Er that I go, shal savoure wors than ale.
Before I go, that will taste worse than ale.

And whan that I have told thee forth my tale   172
And when I have told you my story

Of tribulacioun in mariage,
Of tribulation in marriage,

Of which I am expert in al myn age,
On which I am an expert at my age,

This is to seyn, my-self have been the whippe;—
That is to say, I myself have been the whip;—

Thou maystow chese whether thou wolt sippe   176
You may choose whether you care to sip

Of thilke tonne that I shal abroche.
Of this cask that I shall tap.

Be war of it, er thou to ny approche;
Be careful of it, before you approach too closely;

For I shal telle ensamples mo than ten.
For I shall tell examples more than ten.

Who-so that nil be war by othere men,   180
Whoso will not be warned by other men,

By him shul othere men corrected be.
By him shall other men be warned.

The same wordes wryteth Ptholomee;
These same words Ptolemy writes;

Rede in his ALMAGESTE, and take it there."
Read in his ALMAGEST,² *and find it there."*

"Dame, I wolde praye yow, if your wil it were,"   184
"Madam, I would beg you, if you are willing,"

Seyde this pardoner, "as ye bigan,
Said this pardoner, "as you began,

Telle forth your tale, spareth for no man,
Tell forth your tale, be sparing of no man,

And teche us yonge men of your praktike."
And teach us young men from your experience."

"Gladly," quod she, "sith it may yow lyke.   188
"Glady," said she, "since you may enjoy it.

But yet I praye to al this companye,
But yet I beseech all this company,

If that I speke after my fantasye,
If I speak according to my fancy,

As taketh not a-grief of that I seye;
Not to take grievously what I say;

For myn entente nis but for to pleye.   192
For my intention is only to give pleasure.

"Now sires, now wol I telle forth my tale.—
"Now sirs, now I will tell my story.—

As ever mote I drinken wyn or ale,
As ever I may drink wine or ale,

I shal seye sooth, tho housbondes that I hadde,
I shall speak truth, of the husbands I had,

As three of hem were gode and two were badde.   196
Three of them were good and two were bad.

The three men were gode, and riche, and olde;
The three men were good, and rich, and old;

Unnethe mighte they the statut holde
With difficulty could they hold the bond

In which that they were bounden un-to me.
By which they were bound to me.

Ye woot wel what I mene of this, pardee!   200
You know well what I mean by this, by heaven!

As help me God, I laughe whan I thinke
So help me God, I laugh when I remember

How pitously a-night I made hem swinke;
How pitifully by night I made them work;

And by my fey, I tolde of it no stoor.
And by my faith, I set no store by it.

They had me yeven hir gold and hir tresoor;   204
They had given me their gold and their treasure;

Me neded nat do lenger diligence
I had no need to make further effort

To winne hir love, or doon hem reverence.
To win their love, or pay them any respect.

They loved me so wel, by God above,
They loved me so well, by God above,

That I ne tolde no deyntee of hir love!   208
That I set no value on their love!

A wys womman wol sette hir ever in oon
A wise woman will make every effort

To gete hir love, ther as she hath noon.
To win love, when she hasn't any.

But sith I hadde hem hoolly in myn hond,
But since I had them completely in hand,

And sith they hadde me yeven all hir lond,   212
And since they had given me all their estates,

What sholde I taken hede hem for to plese,
Why should I be zealous to please them,

But it were for my profit and myn ese?
Unless it were for my profit and pleasure?

I sette hem so a-werke, by my fey,
I put them so to work, by my faith,

That many a night they songen 'weilawey!'   216
That many a night they sang, 'Woe is me!'

The bacoun was nat fet for hem, I trowe,
The bacon was not fetched for them, I warrant,

That som men han in Essex at Dunmowe.
*That some men win in Essex at Dunmow.*³

I governed hem so wel, after my lawe,
I governed them so well, according to my law,

That ech of hem ful blisful was and fawe   220
That each of them was very happy and eager

To bringe me gaye thinges fro the fayre.
To bring me gay things from the fair.

They were ful glad whan I spak to hem fayre;
They were most happy when I spoke fairly to them;

For God it woot, I chidde hem spitously.
For God knows, I nagged them spitefully.

"Now herkneth, how I bar me proprely,   224
"Now listen, how I bore myself properly,

Ye wyse wyves, that can understonde.
You wise wives, that can understand.

"Thus shul ye speke and bere hem wrong on honde;
"Thus shall you speak and put them in the wrong;

For half so boldely can there no man
For half so boldly can no man

Swere and lyen as a womman can.   228
Swear and lie as a woman can.

I say nat this by wyves that ben wyse,
I do not say this for wives who are wise,

But-if it be whan they hem misavyse.
Unless it be when they act ill-advisedly.

A wys wyf, if that she can hir good,
A wise wife, if she knows her own good,

Shal beren him on hond the cow is wood,   232
*Will convince her husband the crow is mad,*⁴

And take witnesse of hir owene mayde
And call to witness her own maid

Of hir assent; but herkneth how I sayde.
For her statement; listen to what I used to say:

  " 'Sir olde kaynard, is this thyn array?
  " 'Sir old dotard, is this your way?

Why is my neighebores wyf so gay   236
Why is my neighbor's wife so well dressed?

She is honoured over-al ther she goth;
She is honored wherever she goes;

I sitte at hoom, I have no thrifty cloth.
I sit at home, I have no good clothes.

What dostow at my neighebores hous?
What do you do at my neighbor's house?

Is she so fair? artow so amorous?   240
Is she so fair? are you so amorous?

What rowne ye with our mayde? *ben'cite!*
What do you whisper to our maid? Bless us!

Sir olde lechour, lat thy japes be!
Old Sir Lecher, stop your foolishness!

And if I have a gossib or a freend,
And if I have a comrade or a friend,

With-outen gilt, thou chydest as a feend,   244
Without guilt, you chide like a fiend

If that I walke or pleye un-to his hous!
If I walk to his house for amusement!

Thou comest hoom as dronken as a mous,
You come home as drunk as a mouse,

And prechest on thy bench, with yvel preef!
And preach on your bench, bad luck to you!

Thou seist to me, it is a greet meschief   248
You tell me it is a great misfortune

To wedde a povre womman, for costage;
To wed a poor woman, because of the expense;

And if that she be riche, of heigh parage,
And if she be rich, or of noble birth,

Than seistow that it is a tormentrye
Then you say it is a torment

To suffre hir pryde and hir malencolye.   252
To put up with her pride and her whims.

And if that she be fair, thou verray knave,
And if she be fair, you utter peasant,

Thou seyst that every holour wol hir have;
You say that every lecher will have her;

She may no whyle in chastitee abyde,
That she will not long remain chaste,

That is assailed up-on ech a syde.   256
Who is assailed on every side.

" 'Thou seyst, som folk desyre us for richesse,
" 'You say, some men desire us for our money,

Som for our shap, and som for our fairnesse;
Some for our figure, and some for our beauty;

And som, for she can outher singe or daunce,
And some for talent in singing or dancing,

And som, for gentillesse and daliaunce;   260
And some for manners and sociability;

Som, for hir handes and hir armes smale;
Some for slender hands and arms;

Thus goth al to the devel by thy tale.
But all goes to the devil, according to you.

Thou seyst, men may nat kepe a castel-wal;
You say men cannot keep a castle wall

It may so longe assailled been over-al.   264
Which is constantly assailed on all sides.

" 'And if that she be foul, thou seist that she
" 'And if she be ugly, you say that she

Coveiteth every man that she may see;
Covets every man that she sees;

For as a spaynel she wol on him lepe,
For she will leap on him like a spaniel

Til that she finde som man hir to chepe;   268
Until she finds some man to woo her;

Ne noon so grey goos goth ther in the lake,
Nor does any grey goose swim there in the lake

As, seistow, that wol been with-oute make.
That, as you see, will be without a mate.

And seyst, it is an hard thing for to welde
And you say, it is a hard thing to bind

A thing that no man wol, his thankes, helde.   272
A thing that no man wants to hold.

Thus seistow, lorel, whan thow goost to bedde;
Thus you speak, wretch, when you go to bed;

And that no wys man nedeth for to wedde,
Adding that no wise man need wed,

Ne no man that entendeth un-to hevene.
Nor any man who intends to go to heaven.

With wilde thonder-dint and firy levene   276
With wild thunder-clap and fiery lightning

Mote thy welked nekke be to-broke!
May your wrinkled neck be broken!

 " 'Thow seyst that dropping houses, and eek smoke,
 " *'You say that leaking houses, and also smoke,*

And chyding wyves, maken men to flee
And nagging wives, make men flee

Out of hir owene house; a! *ben'cite!*   280
Out of their own homes; ah, bless us!

What eyleth swich an old man for to chyde?
What ails such an old man to chide so?

" 'Thou seyst, we wyves wol our vyces hyde
" *You say we women hide our vices*

Til we be fast, and than we wol hem shewe;
Until we are tied, and then we exhibit them;

Wel may that be a proverbe of a shrewe!   284
That is certainly a scoundrel's proverb!

" 'Thou seist, that oxen, asses, hors, and houndes,
" *You say that oxen, asses, horses, and hounds*

They been assayed at diverse stoundes;
Are tried out at various times,

Bacins, lavours, er that men hem bye,
As well as basins and bowls, before men buy them,

Spones and stoles, and all swich housbondrye,   288
Spoons and stools too, and all such furnishings,

And so been pottes, clothes, and array;
And so are pots, materials, and clothes;

But folk of wyves maken noon assay
But men make no tests of wives

Til they be wedded; old dotard shrewe!
Until they are married; you evil old dotard!

And than, seistow, we wol oure vices shewe.   292
And then, you say, we show our vices.

" 'Thou seist also, that it displeseth me
" *You also say, that it displeases me*

But-if that thou wolt preyse my beautee,
Unless you praise my beauty,

And but thou poure alwey up-on my face,
And that unless you constantly gaze on my face,

And clepe me "faire dame" in every place;   296
And call me "fair lady" in every place;

And but thou make a feste on thilke day
And unless you arrange a feast on that day

That I was born, and make me fresh and gay,
When I was born, and dress me fresh and gay,

And but thou do to my norice honour,
And unless you honor my nurse

And to my chamberere with-inne my bour,   *300*
And my chambermaid in my dressing room,

And to my fadres folk and his allyes;—
And my father's relatives and friends;—

Thus seistow, olde barel ful of lyes!
So you speak, old barrel full of lies!

  "'And yet of our apprentice Janekyn,
  "'*And yet of our apprentice Jenkin,*

For his crisp heer, shyninge as gold so fyn,   *304*
Because of his crisp hair, shining like gold so fine,

And for he squiereth me bothe up and doun,
And because he squires me up and down,

Yet hastow caught a fals suspecioun;
You have caught a false suspicion;

I wol hym noght, thogh thou were deed to-morwe.
I wouldn't have him even if you died tomorrow.

  "'But tel me this, why hydestow, with sorwe,   *308*
  "'*But tell me this, why do you hide (woe to you!)*

The keyes of thy cheste awey fro me?
The keys of your strongbox from me?

It is my good as wel as thyn, pardee.
They are my goods as well as yours, by heaven!

What wenestow make an idiot of our dame?
Why would you make a fool of your wife?

Now by that lord, that called is seint Jame,   *312*
Now by that lord who is called Saint James,

Thou shalt nat bothe, thogh that thou were wood,
You shall not, rage as much as you please,

Be maister of my body and of my good;
Be master of both my body and my property;

That oon thou shalt forgo, maugree thyne yën;
One of them you shall forego, in spite of your eyes;

What nedeth thee of me to enquere or spyën?   *316*
Why do you need to question or spy on me?

I trowe, thou woldest loke me in thy cheste!
I believe you would like to lock me in your box!

Thou sholdest seye, "wyf, go where thee leste,
You should say, "Wife, go wherever you please,

Tak your disport, I wol nat leve no talis;
Take your pleasure, I will believe no tales;

I knowe yow for a trewe wyf, dame Alis."   *320*
I know you for a faithful wife, Dame Alice."

We love no man that taketh keep or charge
We love no man who supervises or takes note of

Wher that we goon, we wol ben at our large.
Where we go, we want to have our freedom.

  "'Of alle men y-blessed moot he be,
  "'Of all men, may he be blessed,

The wyse astrologien dan Ptholome,   *324*
The wise astrologer, Lord Ptolemy,

That seith this proverbe in his ALMAGESTE,
Who speaks this proverb in his ALMAGEST,

"Of alle men his wisdom is the hyeste,
"Of all men his wisdom is the highest,

That rekketh never who hath the world in honde."
Who never considers who has the world in hand."

By this proverbe thou shalt understonde,   *328*
By this proverb you are to understand,

Have thou y-nogh, what thar thee recche or care
If you have enough, why be concerned or care

How merily that othere folkes fare?
How merrily other people fare?

For certeyn, olde dotard, by your leve,
For in truth, old dotard, by your leave,

Ye shul have queynte right y-nough at eve.   332
You shall have quite enough tail at night.

He is to greet a nigard that wol werne
He is too great a miser who will forbid

A man to lighte his candle at his lanterne;
A man to light his candle at his lantern;

He shal have never the lasse light, pardee;
He won't have any the less light, by heaven;

Have thou y-nough, thee thar nat pleyne thee.   336
If you have enough, you have no complaints there.

  " 'Thou seyst also, that if we make us gay
  " 'You also say, that if we make ourselves gay

With clothing and with precious array,
With clothes and precious ornaments,

That it is peril of our chastitee;
That it endangers our chastity;

And yet, with sorwe, thou most enforce thee,   340
And yet, bad luck to you, you must reinforce yourself,

And seye thise wordes in the apostles name,
And add these words in the apostle's name,[5]

"In habit, maad with chastitee and shame,
"In clothing, made chastely and modestly,

Ye wommen shul apparaille yow," quod he,
You women shall dress yourselves," he said.

"And noght in tressed heer and gay perree,   344
"And not in braided hair and gay jewelry,

As perles, ne with gold, ne clothes riche;"
Such as pearls or gold, nor rich clothes;"

After thy text, ne after thy rubriche
For your text and for your saying

I wol nat wirche a muchel as a gnat.
I will not perform as much as a gnat.

Thou seydest this, that I was lyk a cat;   *348*
You said this, that I was like a cat;

For who-so wolde senge a cattes skin,
For whoever would singe a cat's fur

Thanne wolde the cat wel dwellen in his in;
Would have the cat live happily in his home;

And if the cattes skin be slyk and gay,
And if the cat's fur be sleek and gay,

She wol nat dwelle in house half a day,   *352*
She will not stay in the house half a day,

But forth she wole, er any day be dawed,
But out she will go, before daybreak,

To shewe hir skin, and goon a-caterwawed
To show off her fur, and go caterwauling.

This is to seye, if I be gay, sir shrewe,
That is to say, if I am gay, Sir Scoundrel,

I wol renne out, my borel for to shewe.   *356*
I will run out to show off my clothes.

   " 'Sire old fool, what eyleth thee to spyën?
   " 'Sir Old Fool, what ails you to spy so?

Thogh thou preye Argus, with his hundred yën,
Though you beg Argus, with his hundred eyes,[6]

To be my warde-cors, as he can best,
To be my guardian, as best he can,

In feith, he shal nat kepe me but me lest;   *360*
In faith, he shall not guard me unless I am willing;

Yet coude I make his berd, so moot I thee.
For I could delude him, so can I you.

" 'Thou seydest eek, that ther ben thinges three,
" *You also said, that there are three things*

The whiche thinges troublen al this erthe,
That trouble all this earth,

And that no wight ne may endure the ferthe;   364
And that nobody can endure the fourth;'

O leve sir shrewe, Jesu shorte thy lyf!
O dear Sir Scoundrel, Jesus shorten your life!

Yet prechestow, and seyst, an hateful wyf
So do you preach, and say that a hateful wife

Y-rekened is for oon of thise meschances.
Is considered one of these misfortunes.

Been ther none other maner resemblances   368
Are there no other kind of similitudes

That he may lykne your parables to,
That you can compare your parables to,

But-if a sely wyf be oon of tho?
Unless a helpless wife be one of them?

" 'Thou lykenest wommanes love to helle,
" *You compare woman's love to hell,*

To bareyne lond, ther water may not dwelle.   372
To barren land, where water cannot remain.

Thou lyknest it also to wilde fyr;
You compare it also to wildfire;

The more it brenneth, the more it hath desyr
The more it burns, the more it is desirous

To consume every thing that brent wol be.
To consume everything that can be burned.

They seyst, that right as wormes shende a tree,   376
You say, that just as worms destroy a tree,

Right so a wyf destroyeth hir housbonde;
Even so a wife destroys her husband;

This knowe they that been to wyves bonde.'
Those who have been bound to wives know this.'

"Lordinges, right thus, as ye have understonde,
"Gentlemen, just so, as you have understood it,

Bar I stifly myne olde housbondes on honde, 380
I insisted firmly to my aged husbands,

That thus they seyden in hir dronkenesse;
That they said these things in their drunkenness;

And al was fals, but that I took witnesse
And it was all false, but I called to witness

On Janekin and on my nece also.
Jenkin and my niece too.

O lord, the peyne I dide hem and the wo, 384
O Lord, the pain I caused them and the woe,

Ful giltlees, by Goddes swete pyne!
Entirely innocent, by God's sweet sufferings!

For as an hors I coude byte and whyne.
For I could bite and whinny like a horse.

I coude pleyne, thogh I were in the gilt,
I could wail, even though I was in the wrong,

Or elles often tyme hadde I ben spilt. 388
Or else many a time I would have been killed.

Who-so that first to mille comth, first grint;
He who comes first to the mill, grinds first;

I pleyned first, so was our werre y-stint.
I complained first, so our war was ended.

They were ful glad t'excusen hem ful blyve
They were very glad to excuse themselves quickly

Of thing of which they never agilte hir lyve. 392
For things they were never guilty of in their lives.

"Of wenches wolde I beren him on honde,
"I would accuse my husband of women

Whan that for syk unnethes might he stonde.
When he could scarcely stand up for sickness.

Yet tikled it his herte, for that he
Yet it tickled his heart, because he

Wende that I hadde of him so greet chiertee.   396
Believed that I held so much fondness for him.

I swoor that al my walkinge out by nighte
I swore that all my walking out at night

Was for t'esype wenches that he dighte;
Was to spy on women that he slept with;

Under that colour hadde I many a mirthe.
Under color of that I had many a laugh.

For al swich wit is yeven us in our birthe;   400
For all such cleverness is given to us at birth;

Deceite, weping, spinning God hath yive
Deceit, weeping, spinning, God has given

To wommen kindely, whyl they may live.
As natural gifts to women, as long as they live.

And thus of o thing I avaunte me,
And so of one thing I boast,

Atte ende I hadde the bettre in ech degree,   404
In the end I had the better in every way,

By sleighte, or force, or by som maner thing,
By trickery, or force, or by some kind of device,

As by continuel murmur or grucching;
Such as by continual whining or grumbling;

Namely a-bedde hadden they meschaunce,
Especially in bed they had a bad time,

Ther wolde I chyde and do hem no plesaunce;   408
There I would nag and give them no pleasure;

I wolde no lenger in the bed abyde,
I would no longer remain in bed,

If that I felte his arm over my syde,
If I felt my husband's arm over my side,

Til he had maad his raunson un-to me;
Until he had paid his ransom to me;

Than wolde I suffre him do his nycetee.　　　　412
Then I would allow him to do his foolishness.

And ther-fore every man this tale I telle,
And therefore I tell every man this truth,

Winne who-so may, for al is for to selle.
Let whoever can, win, for everything is for sale.

With empty hand men may none haukes lure;
With empty hand men cannot lure hawks;

For winning wolde I al his lust endure,　　　　416
For a price I would endure all his lust,

And make me a feyned appetyt;
And make myself a pretended appetite;

And yet in bacon hadde I never delyt;
And yet I never found any pleasure in old meat;

That made me that ever I wolde hem chyde.
That is what made me forever nag them.

For thogh the pope had seten hem bisyde,　　　　420
For though the pope had sat beside them,

I wolde nat spare hem at hir owene bord.
I would not spare them at their own table.

For by my trouthe, I quitte hem word for word.
For on my honor, I repaid them word for word.

As help me verray God omnipotent,
So help me omnipotent God Himself,

Thogh I right now sholde make my testament,　　　　424
Though I should make my testament right now,

I ne owe hem nat a word that it nis quit,
I owe them not a word that is not paid up,

I broghte it so aboute by my wit,
I so brought it about by my cleverness

That they moste yeve it up, as for the beste;
That they had to give up, as for the best,

Or elles hadde we never been in reste.   428
Or else we would never have been at peace.

For thogh he loked as a wood leoun,
For though he looked mad as a lion,

Yet sholde he faille of his conclusioun.
Yet he would fail to attain his end.

"Thanne wolde I seye, 'gode lief, tak keep
"Then I would say, 'My dear, take notice

How mekely loketh Wilken oure sheep;   432
How meek our sheep Wilken looks;

Com neer, my spouse, lat me ba thy cheke!
Come near, my spouse, let me kiss your cheek!

Ye sholde ben al pacient and meke,
You should be entirely patient and meek,

And han a swete spyced conscience,
And have a sweetly spiced conscience,

Sith ye so preche of Jobes pacience.   436
Since you preach so about Job's patience.

Suffreth alwey, sin ye so wel can preche;
Suffer always, since you can preach so well;

And but ye do, certein we shal yow teche
And unless you do, we shall certainly teach you

That it is fair to have a wyf in pees.
That it is pleasant to have a wife in peace.

Oon of us two moste bowen, doutelees;   440
One of us two must give in, without a doubt;

And sith a man is more resonable
And since a man is more reasonable

Than womman is, ye moste been suffrable.
Than woman is, you must be patient.

What eyleth yow to grucche thus and grone?
What ails you to grouch so and groan?

Is it for ye wolde have my quente allone?   *444*
Is it that all you want is my tail?

Why taak it al, lo have it overy-deel;
Why take it all, here, have every bit of it;

Peter! I shrewe yow but ye love it weel!
Peter! Curse you but you love it well!

For if I wolde selle my *bele chose,*
For if I wanted to sell my pretty thing,

I could walke as fresh as is a rose;   *448*
I could go walking as fresh as a rose;

But I wol kepe it for your owene tooth.
But I will keep it for your own tooth.

Ye be to blame, by God, I sey yow sooth.'
You are to blame, by God, I tell you the truth.'

"Swiche maner wordes hadde we on honde.
"Words such as these we had on and off.

Now wol I speken of my fourthe housbonde.   *452*
Now I will talk about my fourth husband.

"My fourthe housbonde was a revelour,
"My fourth husband was a playboy,

This is to seyn, he hadde a paramour;
That is to say, he had a mistress;

And I was yong and ful of ragerye,
And I was young and full of passion,

Stiborn and strong, and joly as a pye.   *456*
Stubborn and strong, and pretty as a pie.

Wel coude I daunce to an harpe smale,
Well could I dance to a little harp,

And singe, y-wis, as any nightingale,
And sing, I can tell you, like a nightingale,

Whan I had dronke a draughte of swete wyn.
When I had drunk a draught of sweet wine.

Metellius, the foule cherl, the swyn,   460
Metellius, the foul peasant, the swine,

That with a staf birafte his wyf hir lyf,
Who with a stick beat his wife to death,

For she drank wyn, thogh I hadde been his wyf,
Because she drank wine; if I had been his wife,

He sholde nat han daunted me fro drinke;
He would not have frightened me from drink;[8]

And, after wyn, on Venus moste I thinke: 464
And, after wine, I think of Venus most:

For al so siker as cold engendreth hayl,
For just as sure as cold begets hail,

A likerous mouthe moste han a likerous tayl.
A licentious mouth must have a licentious tail.

In womman vinolent is no defence,
Wine drinking in women is no hindrance,

This knowen lechours by experience.   468
Lechers know this by experience.

"But lord Crist! whan that it remembreth me
"But Lord Christ! when I think back

Up-on my yowth, and on my jolitee,
Upon my youth, and on my gaiety,

It tikleth me aboute myn herte rote.
It tickles me to the bottom of my heart.

Unto this day it dooth myn herte bote   472
To this day it does my heart good

That I have had my world as in my tyme.
That I have had my day in my time.

But age, allas! that al wol envenyme,
But age, alas! that poisons everything,

Hath me biraft my beautee and my pith;
Has robbed me of my beauty and my vigor;

Lat go, fare-wel, the devil go therwith! 476
Let it go, farewell, the devil go with it!

The flour is goon, thur is na-more to telle,
The flour is gone, there is no more to say,

The bren, as I best can, now moste I selle;
The chaff, as best I can, I must sell now;

But yet to be right mery wol I fonde.
But still I will attempt to be right merry.

Now wol I tellen of my fourthe housbonde. 480
Now I will tell about my fourth husband.

   "I seye, I hadde in herte greet despyt
   "As I said, I held great malice in my heart

That he of any other had delyt.
That he should have delight of any other.

But he was quit, by God and by seint Joce!
But he was paid back, by God and by Saint Joce!

I made him of the same wode a croce; 484
I made him a cross of the same wood;

Nat of my body in no foul manere,
Not of my body in any foul manner,

But certeinly, I made folk swich chere,
But truly, I appeared so gay to people

That in his owene grece I made him frye
That I made him fry in his own grease

For angre, and for verray jalousye. 488
For anger, and for very jealousy.

By God, in erthe I was his purgatorie,
By God, on earth I was his purgatory,

For which I hope his soule be in glorie.
For which I hope his soul is in glory.

For God it woot, he sat ful ofte and song
For God knows he sat often enough and sang

Whan that his shoo ful bitterly him wrong.   *492*
When his shoe pinched him most bitterly.

Ther was no wight, save God and he, that wiste,
There was no one, except God and he, that knew,

In many wyse, how sore I him twiste.
In many ways, how sorely I tortured him.

He deyde whan I cam fro Jerusalem,
He died when I came back from Jerusalem,

And lyth y-grave under the rode-beem,   *496*
And lies buried under the cross,

Al is his tombe noght so curious
Although his tomb is not so unique

As was the sepulcre of him, Darius,
As was the sepulchre of Darius,

Which that Appelles wroghte subtilly;
Which Apelles made cleverly;

It nis but wast to burie him preciously.   *500*
It was but a waste to bury him preciously.

Lat him fare-wel, God yeve his soule reste,
May he fare well, God give rest to his soul,

He is now in the grave and in his cheste.
He is now in the grave and in his coffin.

"Now of my fifthe housbond wol I telle.
"Now I will tell of my fifth husband.

God lete his soule never come in helle!   *504*
God save his soul from ever going to hell!

And yet was he to me the moste shrewe;
And yet he was to me the most scoundrelly;

That fele I on my ribbes al by rewe,
I can still feel the pain on my ribs,

And ever shal, un-to myn ending-day.
And ever shall, unto my dying day.

But in our bed he was so fresh and gay,   508
But in our bed he was so fresh and gay,

And ther-with-al so wel coude he me glose,
And, besides, he could cajole me so well,

Whan that he would han my *bele chose,*
When he would have my pretty thing,

That thogh he hadde me bet on every boon,
That even though he had beaten me on every bone,

He coude winne agayn my love anoon.   512
He could very quickly win my love again.

I trowe I loved him beste, for that he
I guess I loved him best because he

Was of his love daungerous to me.
Was miserly of his love to me.

We wommen han, if that I shal nat lye,
We women have, if I do not lie,

In this matere a queynte fantasye;   516
A curious notion in this matter;

Wayte what thing we may nat lightly have,
Pick out whatever thing we cannot easily have,

Ther-after wol we crye al-day and crave.
That we will crave and cry for all day.

Forbede us thing, and that desyren we;
Forbid us something and that we desire;

Prees on us faste, and thanne wol we flee.   520
Press on us hard, and then we will flee.

With daunger oute we al our chaffare;
Sparingly we show all our merchandise;

Greet prees at market maketh dere ware,
Great crowds at market make for expensive goods,

And to greet cheep is holde at litel prys;
And too small a price is held at little value;

This knoweth every womman that is wys.   524
Every woman who is wise knows this.

"My fifthe housbonde, God his soule blesse!
"My fifth husband, God bless his soul!

Which that I took for love and no richesse,
Whom I took for love and not for money,

He som-tyme was a clerk at Oxenford,
Had been formerly a clerk at Oxford,

And had left scole, and wente at hoom to bord   528
And had left school, and went to board at the home

With my gossib, dwellinge in oure toun,
Of my girl friend, who lived in our town,

God have hir soule! hir name was Alisoun.
God rest her soul! Her name was Alice.

She knew myn herte and eek my privetee
She knew my heart and all my secrets

Bet than our parisshe-preest, so moot I thee!   532
Better than our parish priest, so help me!

To hir biwreyed I my conseil al.
To her I gave my complete confidence.

For had myn husbonde pissed on a wal,
For if my husband had pissed on a wall,

Or doon a thing that sholde han cost his lyf,
Or done something that would have cost his life,

To hir, and to another worthy wyf,   536
To her, and to another worthy woman,

And to my nece, which that I loved weel,
And to my niece, whom I loved well,

I wolde han told his conseil every-deel.
I would have told every bit of his secret.

And so I dide ful often, God it woot,
And so I very often did, God knows it,

That made his face ful often reed and hoot   540
Which made his face very often red and hot

For verray shame, and blamed him-self for he
For very shame, and he blamed himself because he

Had told to me so greet a privetee.
Had told me so great a secret.

"And so bifel that onces, in a Lente,
"And it so happened that once, in Lent,

(So often tymes I to my gossib wente,   544
(I often went so to my girl friend's,

For ever yet I loved to be gay,
For I always loved to be gay,

And for to walke, in March, Averille, and May,
And to walk, in March, April, and May,

Fro hous to hous, to here sondry talis),
From house to house, to hear sundry stories)

That Jankin clerk, and my gossib dame Alis,   548
That Clerk Jenkin, and my girl friend, Dame Alice,

And I my-self, in-to the feldes wente.
And I myself went into the fields.

Myn housbond was at London al that Lente;
My husband was in London all that Lent;

I hadde the bettre leyser for to pleye,
I had the more leisure to play,

And for to see, and eek for to be seye   552
And to see, and also to be seen

Of lusty folk; what wiste I wher my grace
By lively people; what did I know where my favor

Was shapen for to be, or in what place?
Was destined to be, or in what place?

Therefore I made my visitaciouns,
Therefore I made my appearances

To vigilies and to processiouns,   556
At vigils and at processions,

To preching eek and to thise pilgrimages,
At preachings too and on pilgrimages like this,

To pleyes of miracles and mariages,
At miracle plays and weddings,

And wered upon my gay scarlet gytes.
And wore my gay scarlet gown.

Thise wormes, ne thise motthes, ne this mytes,   560
The worms and moths and mites,

Upon my peril, frete hem never a deel;
On my peril, ate them never a bit;

And wostow why? for they were used weel.
And do you know why? because they were well used.

"Now wol I tellen forth what happed me.
"Now I will tell what happened to me.

I seye, that in the feeldes walked we,   564
I was saying that we were walking in the fields,

Til trewely we hadde swich daliance,
Until, truly, we had caressed so much,

This clerk and I, that of my purveyance
This clerk and I, that in my foresight

I spak to him, and seyde him, how that he,
I spoke to him, and told him that he,

If I were widwe, sholde wedde me.   568
If I were a widow, could marry me.

For certeinly, I sey for no bobance,
For indeed, I say it without boasting,

Yet was I never with-outen purveyance
I was never yet without foresight

Of mariage, n'of othere thinges eek.
Regarding marriage, nor about other things, too.

I holde a mouses herte nat worth a leek,   572
I hold a mouse's life not worth a leek,

That hath but oon hole for to sterte to,
That has but one hole to run to,

And if that faille, thanne is al y-do.
And if that fails, then that is the end.

  "I bar him on honde, he hadde enchanted me;
"I made him believe he had enchanted me;

My dame taughte me that soutiltee.   576
My mother taught me that procedure.

And eek I seyde, I mette of him al night;
And I told him also that I dreamed of him all night;

He wolde han slayn me as I lay up-right,
That he would have slain me as I lay on my back,

And al my bed was ful of verray blood,
And that my bed was all full of blood,

But yet I hope that he shal do me good;   580
But that I still hoped he would do me good;

For blood bitokeneth gold, as me was taught.
For blood betokens gold, as it was taught me.

And al was fals, I dremed of it right naught,
And it was all a lie, I dreamed no such thing,

But as I folwed ay my dames lore,
Only I followed my mother's teaching,

As wel of this as of other thinges more.   584
On this as well as on many other things.

  "But now sir, lat me see, what I shal seyn?
"But now sir, let me see, what was I saying?

A! ha! by God, I have my tale ageyn.
Oh yes! By God, I have my story again.

"Whan that my fourthe housbond was on bere,
"When my fourth husband was on his bier,

I weep algate, and made sory chere,   588
I wept continually, and put on a sad face,

As wyves moten, for it is usage,
As wives must, for it is customary,

And with my coverchief covered my visage;
And with my kerchief covered my face;

But for that I was purveyed of a make,
But since I was provided with a new mate,

I weep but smal, and that I undertake.   592
I wept but little, I can assure you.

"To chirche was myn housbond born a-morwe
"In the morning my husband was borne to the church

With neighbores, that for him maden sorwe;
By neighbors who mourned for him;

And Jankin oure clerk was oon of tho.
And Jenkin our clerk was one of them.

As help me God, whan that I saugh him go   596
So help me God, when I watched him walk

After the bere, me thoughte he hadde a paire
Following the bier, I thought he had a pair

Of legges and of feet so clene and faire,
Of legs and feet so clean-cut and beautiful,

That al myn herte I yaf un-to his hold.
That all my heart I gave to his keeping.

He was, I trowe, a twenty winter old,   600
He was, I believe, about twenty winters old,

And I was fourty, if I shal seye sooth;
And I was forty, if I speak the truth;

But yet I hadde alwey a coltes tooth.
But yet I always had a colt's tooth.

Gat-tothed I was, and that bicam me weel;
Widely-spaced teeth I had, and that became me well;

I hadde the prente of sëynt Venus seel.   604
I had on me the print of Saint Venus' birthmark.

As help me God, I was a lusty oon,
So help me God, I was a lively one,

And faire and riche, and yong, and well bigoon,
And fair and rich, and young, and well provided for,

And trewely, as myne housbondes tolde me,
And truthfully, as my husbands told me,

I had the beste *quoniam* mighte be.   608
I had the best pudendum there could be.

For certes, I am al Venerien
For certainly, I am entirely Venus-like

In felinge, and myn herte is Marcien.
In feeling, and my heart is Mars-like.

Venus me yaf my lust, my likerousnesse,
Venus gave me my lust, my lecherousness,

And Mars yaf me my sturdy hardinesse.   612
And Mars gave me my robust hardiness.

Myn ascendent was Taur, and Mars ther-inne.
My astrological sign was Mars in Taurus.

Allas! allas! that ever love was sinne!
Alas! alas! That ever love was sin!

I folwed ay myn inclinacioun
I always followed my inclination

By vertu of my constellacioun;   616
By virtue of my constellation;

That made me I coude noght withdrawe
That made me so that I could not withhold

My chambre of Venus from a good felawe.
My chamber of Venus from a good fellow.

Yet have I Martes mark up-on my face,
Yet I have the mark of Mars on my face,

And also in another privee place.   620
And also in another private place.

For God so wis be my savacioun,
For, God in His wisdom be my salvation.

I ne loved never by no discrecioun,
I never loved with discretion,

But ever folwede myn appetyt,
But always followed my appetite,

Al were he short or long, or blak or whyt;   624
Whether he were short or tall, or black or white;

I took no kepe, so that he lyked me,
I took no heed, so that he pleased me,

How pore he was, ne eek of what degree.
How poor he was, nor of what rank either.

"What sholde I seye, but, at the monthes ende,
"What may I say, but, at the month's end,

This joly clerk Jankin, that was so hende,   628
This handsome clerk Jenkin, who was so handy,

Hath wedded me with great solempnitee,
Married me with great ceremony,

And to him yaf I al the lond and fee
And I gave him all the land and capital

That ever was me yeven ther-bifore;
That had ever been given to me before;

But afterward repented me ful sore.   632
But afterwards I bitterly repented.

He nolde suffre nothing of my list.
He would not allow any of my desires.

By God, he smoot me ones on the list,
By God, he struck me once on the ear,

For that I rente out of his book a leef,
Because I tore a leaf out of his book,

That of the strook myn ere wex al deef.   636
That my ear became entirely deaf from the blow.

Stiborn I was as is a lconesse,
I was as stubborn as a lioness,

And of my tonge a verray jangleresse,
And of my tongue a very jabberer,

And walke I wolde, as I had doon biforn,
And walk I would, as I had done before,

From hous to hous, al-though he had it sworn.   640
From house to house, although he had forbidden it.

For which he often tymes wolde preche,
Wherefore he would preach many a time,

And me of olde Romayn gestes teche,
And teach me about ancient Roman history,

How he, Simplicius Gallus, lefte his wyf,
How Simplicius Gallus left his wife

And hir forsook for terme of al his lyf,   644
And forsook her for the rest of his life,

Noght but for open-heeded he hir say
For nothing except that he saw her bareheaded

Lokinge out at his dore upon a day.
Looking out of his door one day.

"Another Romayn tolde he me by name,
"Another Roman he told me about by name,

That, for his wyf was at a someres game   648
Who, because his wife was at a summer game

With-oute his witing, he forsook hir eke.
Without his knowledge, he forsook her, too.

And than wolde he up-on his Bible seke
And then he would look up in his Bible

That ilke proverbe of Ecclesiaste,
That proverb in ECCLESIASTES,

Wher he comandeth and forbedeth faste,   652
Where the preacher commands and strictly forbids,

Man shal nat suffre his wyf go roule aboute;
Man shall not allow his wife to go roaming about;

Than wolde he seye right thus, withouten doute,
Then he would undoubtedly say just this:

'Who-so that buildeth his hous al of salwes,
'Whoso builds his house entirely of twigs,

And priketh his blinde hors over the falwes,   656
And spurs his blind horse over the ditches,

And suffreth his wyf to go seken halwes,
And allows his wife to go visiting shrines,

Is worthy to been hanged on the galwes!'
Is worthy to be hanged on the gallows!'

But al for noght, I sette noght an hawe
But all for nothing, I didn't care a fig

Of his proverbes n'of his olde sawe,   660
For his proverbs or his old sayings,

Ne I wolde nat of him corrected be.
Nor would I be corrected by him.

I hate him that my vices telleth me,
I hate him who tells me about my errors,

And so do mo, God woot! of us than I.
And so, God knows, do more of us than I.

This made him with me wood al outrely;   664
This made him violently angry with me;

I nolde noght forbere him in no cas.
I could not endure him in any case.

"Now wol I seye yow sooth, by seint Thomas,
"Now will I tell you the truth, by Saint Thomas,

Why that I rente out of his book a leef,
About why I tore a leaf out of his book,

For which he smoot me so that I was deef.   668
For which he struck me so hard I became deaf.

"He hadde a book that gladly, night und day,
"He had a book which happily, night and day,

For his desport he wolde rede alway.
He would always read for his amusement.

He cleped it VALERIE AND THEOFRASTE,
He called it VALERIUS AND THEOPHRASTUS,'

At whiche book he lough alway ful faste.   672
At which book he always laughed uproariously.

And eek ther was som-tyme a clerk at Rome,
And besides there was once a clerk at Rome,

A cardinal, that highte seint Jerome,
A cardinal named Saint Jerome,

That made a book agayn Jovinian;
Who wrote a book against Jovinian;

In whiche book eek ther was Tertulan,   676
In which book there was also Tertullian,

Crisippus, Trotula, and Helowys,
Chrysippus, Trotula, and Heloise,

That was abbesse nat fer fro Parys;
Who was an abbess not far from Paris,

And eek the PARABLES OF SALAMON,
And also the PROVERBS OF SOLOMON,

Ovydes ART, and bokes many on,   680
Ovid's ART OF LOVE *and many other books,*

And alle thise wer bounden in o volume.
And all these were bound in one volume.

And every night and day was his custume,
And every night and day it was his habit,

Whan he had leyser and vacacioun
When he had leisure and spare time

From other worldly occupacioun,   684
From other worldly occupations,

To reden on this book of wikked wyves.
To read in this book of wicked women.

He knew of hem mo legendes and lyves
He knew more biographies and legends about them

Than been of gode wyves in the Bible.
Than there are of good women in the Bible.

For trusteth wel, it is an impossible   688
For trust it well, it is an impossibility

That any clerk wol speke good of wyves,
For any clerk to speak well of women,

But-if it be of holy seintes lyves,
Unless it be of the life of a holy saint,

Ne of noon other womman never the mo.
But not a bit of any other woman.

Who peynted the leoun, tel me who?   692
Who depicted Aesop's lion, tell me who?

By God, if wommen hadde writen stories,
By God, if women had written stories,

As clerkes han with-inne hir oratories,
As clerks have in their oratories,

They wolde han writen of men more wikkednesse
They would have written more wickedness about men

Than all the mark of Adam may redresse.   696
Than all the progeny of Adam can redress.

The children of Mercurie and of Venus
The children of Mercury and those of Venus

Been in hir wirking ful contrarious;
Are entirely opposite in their doings;

Mercurie loveth wisdom and science,
Mercury loves wisdom and knowledge,

And Venus loveth ryot and dispence.   *700*
And Venus loves revelry and lavishness.

And, for hir diverse disposicioun,
And, because of their different temperaments,

Ech falleth in otheres exaltacioun;
Each drops when the other is exalted;

And thus, God woot! Mercurie is desolat
And thus, God knows! Mercury is desolate

In Pisces, wher Venus is exaltat;   *704*
In the Sign of the Fish, where Venus is exalted;

And Venus falleth ther Mercurie is reysed;
And Venus falls where Mercury is raised up;

Therefore no womman of no clerk is preysed.
Therefore no woman is praised by any clerk.

The clerk, whan he is old, and may noght do
The clerk, when he is old, and cannot perform

Of Venus werkes worth his olde sho,   *708*
The works of Venus worth his old shoe,

Than sit he doun, and writ in his dotage
Then sits down, and writes in his dotage

That wommen can nat kepe hir mariage!
That women cannot be faithful in marriage!

"But now to purpos, why I tolde thee
"But now for the reason why, as I told you,

That I was beten for a book, pardee.   *712*
I was beaten because of a book, by heaven.

Up-on a night, Jankin, that was our syre,
One night, Jenkin, who was head of the house,

Redde on his book, as he sat by the fyre,
Read in his book, as he sat by the fire,

Of Eva first, that, for hir wikkednesse,
Of Eve first, that, because of her wickedness,

Was al mankinde broght to wrecchednesse,   716
All mankind was brought to misery,

For which that Jesu Crist him-self was slayn,
For which Jesus Christ Himself was slain,

That boghte us with his herte-blood agayn.
Who redeemed us again with His heart's blood.

Lo, here expres of womman may ye finde,
Behold, here you may read expressly about woman,

That womman was the los of al mankinde.   720
That woman was the ruin of all mankind.

"Tho redde he me how Sampson loste his heres,
"Then he read me how Samson lost his hair,

Slepinge, his lemman kitte hem with hir sheres;
Sleeping; his sweetheart cut it with her shears;

Thurgh whiche tresoun loste he bothe his yën.
Through which treachery he lost both his eyes.

Tho redde he me, if that I shal nat lyen,   724
Then he read me, unless I am lying,

Of Hercules and of his Dianyre,
About Hercules and his Dejanira,

That caused him to sette himself a-fyre.
Who caused him to set himself on fire.

"No-thing forgat he the penaunce and wo
"Not at all did he forget the sorrow and woe

That Socrates had with hise wyves two;   728
That Socrates had with his two wives;

How Xantippa cast pisse up-on his heed;
How Xantippe threw piss on his head;

This sely man sat stille, as he were deed;
That good man sat as still as if he were dead;

He wyped his heed, namore dorste he seyn
He wiped his head, no more dared he say

But 'er that thonder stinte, comth a reyn.'   732
But 'Before the thunder stops, the rain comes.'

"Of Phasipha, that was the quene of Crete,
"Of Pasiphaë, who was queen of Crete,

For shrewednesse, him thoughte the tale swete;
For cleverness, he thought the tale sweet;

Fy! spek na-more—it is a grisly thing—
Fie! say no more—it is a ghastly story—

Of hir horrible lust and hir lyking.   736
About her horrible lust and its object."

"Of Clitemistra, for hir lecherye,
"Of Clytemnestra, whose lechery

That falsly made hir housbond for to dye,
Caused the treacherous death of her husband,

He redde it with ful good devocioun.
He read with great devotion.

"He tolde me eek for what occasioun   740
"He also told me for what reason

Amphiorax at Thebes loste his lyf;
Amphiaraus lost his life at Thebes;

Myn housbond hadde a legende of his wyt
My husband had a legend about his wife

Eriphilem, that for an ouche of gold
Eriphyle, who for a gold clasp

Hath prively un-to the Grekes told   744
Secretly told the Greeks

Wher that hir housbonde hidde him in a place,
Where her husband's hiding place was,

For which he hadde at Thebes sory grace.
Wherefore he had a sad fortune at Thebes.

"Of Lyma tolde he me, and of Lucye,
"Of Livia he told me, and of Lucilia,

They bothe made hir housbondes for to dye;　　　748
They both caused their husbands to die;

That oon for love, that other was for hate;
The one for love, the other out of hate;

Lyma hir housbond, on an even late,
Livia her husband late one evening

Empoysoned hath, for that she was his fo.
Poisoned, because she was his enemy.

Lucyna, likerous, loved hir housbond so,　　　752
Lucilia, lecherous, loved her husband so,

That, for he sholde alwey up-on hir thinke,
That, so that he would think of her always,

She yaf him swich a maner love-drinke,
She gave him a love drink of such a sort

That he was deed, er it were by the morwe;
That he was dead before the next morning;

And thus algates housbondes han sorwe.　　　756
And thus eternally husbands have sorrow.

"Than tolde he me, how oon Latumius
"Then he told me how one Latumius

Compleyned to his felawe Arrius,
Complained to his friend Arrius

That in his gardin growed swich a tree,
That in his garden there grew a certain tree,

On which, he seyde, how that his wyves three　　　760
On which, he said, his three wives

Hanged hem-self for herte dispitous.
Hanged themselves for heartsickness.

O leve brother,' quod this Arrius,
'O dear brother,' said this Arrius,

'Yif me a plante of thilke blissed tree,
'Give me a shoot of that blessed tree,

And in my gardin planted shal it be!'   764
And it shall be planted in my garden!'

  "Of latter date, of wyves hath he red,
  "He read of wives of a later time,

That somme han slayn hir housbondes in hir bed,
That some had slain their husbands in their beds,

And let hir lechour dighte hir al the night
And allowed their lovers to sleep with them all night

Whyl that the corps lay in the floor up-right.   768
While the corpse lay on its back on the floor.

And somme han drive nayles in hir brayn
And some drove nails into their brains

Whyl that they slepte, and thus they han hem slayn.
While they slept, and thus they killed them.

Somme han yeve poysoun in hir drinke.
Some gave them poison in their drink.

He spak more harm than herte may bithinke.   772
He spoke more evil than the mind can conceive.

And ther-with-al, he knew of mo proverbes
And in addition, he knew more proverbs

Than in this world ther growen gras or herbes.
Than there grows grass or greenery in this world.

'Bet is,' quod he, 'thyn habitacioun
'It is better,' he said, 'to live

Be with a leoun or a foul dragoun,   776
With a lion or a foul dragon

Than with a womman usinge for to chyde.
Than with a nagging woman.

Bet is,' quod he, 'hye in the roof abyde
It is better,' he said, 'to live up in the attic

Than with an angry wyf doun in the hous;
Than down in the house with an angry wife;

They been so wikked and contrarious;   780
They are so wicked and contrary;

They haten that hir housbondes loveth ay.'
They always hate whatever their husbands love.'

He seyde, 'a womman cast hir shame away,
He said, 'A woman casts off her modesty

Whan she cast of hir smok;' and forthermo,
When she takes off her dress;' and furthermore,

'A fair womman, but she be chaast also,   784
'A beautiful woman, unless she is chaste too,

Is lyk a gold ring in a sowes nose.'
Is like a gold ring in a sow's nose.'

Who wolde wenen, or who wolde suppose
Who can understand, or who can imagine

The wo that in myn herte was, and pyne?
The grief and woe that was in my heart?

"And whan I saugh he wolde never fyne   788
"And when I saw that he would never finish

To reden on this cursed book al night,
Reading in this cursed book all night,

Al sodeynly three leves have I plight
All of a sudden I ripped three leaves

Out of his book, right as he radde, and eke,
Out of his book, right while he read, and besides,

I with my fist so took him on the cheke,   792
I so struck him on the cheek with my fist

That in our fyr he fil bakward adoun.
That he fell down backward in our fire.

And he up-stirte as dooth a wood leoun,
And he jumped up like a raging lion,

And with his fist he smoot me on the heed,
And with his fist he so smote me on the head

That in the floor I lay as I were deed.   796
That on the floor I lay as if I were dead.

And when he saugh how stille that I lay,
And when he saw how still I lay,

He was agast, and wolde han fled his way,
He was aghast, and would have run away,

Til atte laste out of my swogh I breyde:
Until at last I came out of my swoon:

'O! hastow slayn me, false theef?' I seyde,   800
'O! Have you killed me, false thief?' I said,

'And for my land thus hastow mordred me?
'And have you murdered me thus for my land?

Er I be deed, yet wol I kisse thee.'
Yet I would kiss you before I die.'

   "And neer he cam, and kneled faire adoun,
   "And near he came, and kneeled gently down,

And seyde, 'dere suster Alisoun,   804
And said, 'Dear sister Alice,

As help me God, I shal thee never smyte;
So help me God, I shall never strike you again;

That I have doon, it is thy-self to wyte.
For what I have done, you have yourself to blame.

Foryeve it me, and that I thee biseke'—
Forgive me for it, I beseech you'—

And yet eft-sones I hitte him on the cheke,   808
And yet again I hit him on the cheek,

And seyde, 'theef, thus muchel I am wreke;
And said, 'Thief, this much I am revenged;

Now wol I dye, I may no lenger speke.'
Now will I die, I can talk no longer.'

But atte laste, with muchel care and wo,
But at last, with much effort and grief,

We fille acorded, by us selven two.   812
We came to an agreement between ourselves.

He yaf me al the brydel in myn hond
He gave me the bridle entirely in my hand

To han the governance of hous and land,
To have charge of the house and property,

And of his tonge and of his hond also,
And also of his tongue and his hand,

And made him brenne his book anon right tho.   816
And I made him burn his book right then at once.

And whan that I hade geten un-to me,
And when I had gotten for myself,

By maistrie, al the soveraynetee,
By my skill, complete sovereignty,

And that he seyde, 'myn owene trewe wyf,
And when he said, 'My own true wife,

Do as thee lust the terme of al thy lyf,   820
Do as you please all the rest of your life,

Keep thyn honour, and keep eek myn estaat'—
Supervise your own honor and my estate as well'—

After that day we hadden never debaat.
After that day we never had an argument.

God help me so, I was to him as kinde·
So God help me, I was to him as kind

As any wyf from Denmark un-to Inde,   824
As any wife from Denmark to India,

And also trewe, and so was he to me.
And faithful too, and so was he to me.

I prey to God that sit in magestee,
I pray to God Who sits in majesty,

So blesse his soule, for his mercy dere!
To bless his soul, out of His dear mercy!

Now wol I seye my tale, if ye wol here."   828
Now I will tell my tale, if you will listen."

WORDS BETWEEN THE SUMMONER AND THE FRIAR

The frere lough, whan he hadde herd al this,
The friar laughed, when he had heard all this,

"Now dame," quod he, "so have I joye or blis,
"Now, madam," said he, "so I may have joy or bliss,

This is a long preamble of a tale!"
This is a long preamble to a tale!"

And whan the somnour herde the frere gale,   832
And when the summoner heard the friar exclaim,

"Lo!" quod the somnour, "Goddes armes two!
"Observe!" said the summoner, "by God's two arms!

A frere wol entremette him ever-mo.
A friar will butt in every time.

Lo, gode men, a flye and eek a frere
Behold, good men, a fly and also a friar

Wol falle in every dish and eek matere.   836
Will fall in every dish and subject too.

What spekestow of preambulacioun?
Why do you talk of preambulation?

What! amble, or trotte, or pees, or go sit doun;
Why! amble, or trot, or keep quiet, or go sit down;

Thou lettest our disport in this manere."
You spoil our pleasure in this way."

"Ye, woltow so, sir somnour?" quod the frere,   840
"Yes? Will you so, sir summoner?" said the friar,

"Now, by my feith, I shal, er that I go,
"Now, by my faith, I shall, before I leave,

Telle of a somnour swich a tale or two,
Tell such a tale or two about a summoner

That alle the folk shal laughen in this place."
That all the people here will laugh."

"Now elles, frere, I bishrewe thy face,"   844
"Now, besides, friar, I curse your face,"

Quod this somnour, "and I bishrewe me,
Said this summoner, "and I curse myself,

But-if I telle tales two or three
If I don't tell two or three tales

Of freres er I come to Sidingborne,
About friars before I get to Sittingbourne,

That I shal make thyn herte for to morne;   848
That I shall make your heart grieve;

For wel I woot thy pacience is goon."
For I well know your patience is exhausted."

Our hoste cryde, "pees! and that anoon!"
Our host cried, "Quiet! and that at once!"

And seyde, "lat the womman telle hir tale.
And said, "Let the woman tell her tale.

Ye fare as folk that dronken been of ale.   852
You act like people who are drunk with ale.

Do, dame, tel forth your tale, and that is best."
Proceed, madam, tell your tale. That is best."

"Al redy, sir," quod she, "right as yow lest,
"All ready, sir," said she, "just as you please,

If I have licence of this worthy frere."
If I have the permission of this worthy friar."

"Yis, dame," quod he, "tel forth, and I wol here."   856
"Yes, madam," said he, "tell on, and I will listen."

The Wife of Bath's Tale

In th'olde dayes of the king Arthour,
In the old days of King Arthur,

Of which that Britons speken greet honour,
Whom Britons hold in high esteem,

Al was this land fulfild of fayerye.
All this land was filled with fairies.

The elf-queen, with hir joly companye,   4
The elf-queen, with her lovely company,

Daunced ful ofte in many a grene mede;
Very often danced in many a green meadow;

This was the olde opinion, as I rede.
This was the ancient belief, as I read.

I speke of manye hundred yeres ago;
I speak of many hundred years ago;

But now can no man see none elves mo.   8
But now no man can see elves any more.

For now the grete charitee and prayeres
For now the great charity and prayers

Of limitours and other holy freres,
Of limiters¹ and other holy friars,

That serchen every lond and every streem,
That seek out every land and every stream,

As thikke as motes in the sonne-beem,   12
As thick as motes in the sunbeam,

Blessinge halles, chambres, kitchenes, boures,
Blessing halls, chambers, kitchens, boudoirs,

Citees, burghes, castels, hy toures,
Cities, towns, castles, high towers,

Thropes, bernes, shipnes, dayeryes,
Villages, barns, stables, dairies,

This maketh that ther been no fayeryes.   16
This makes it that there are no fairies.

For ther as wont to walken was an elf,
For where an elf used to walk,

Ther walketh now the limitour himself
There walks now the limiter himself

In undermeles and in morweninges,
During afternoons and mornings,

And seyth his matins and his holy thinges   20
And says his matins and his holy things

As he goth in his limitacioun.
As he goes on his rounds.

Wommen may go saufly up and doun;
Women may go safely up and down;

In every bush, or under every tree,
In every bush, or under every tree,

Ther is noon other incubus but he,   24
There is no other seducing spirit but he,

And he ne wol doon hem but dishonour.
And he won't do anything to them but dishonor.

And so bifel it, that this king Arthour
And it so happened, that this King Arthur

Hadde in his hous a lusty bacheler,
Had in his house a lively young knight,

That on a day cam rydinge fro river;   28
Who one day came riding from the river;

And happed that, allone as she was born,
And it chanced that, alone as she was born,

He saugh a mayde walkinge him biforn,
He saw a maid walking ahead of him,

Of which mayde anon, maugree hir heed,
From which maid at once, in spite of her protests,

By verray force he rafte hir maydenheed;   32
By sheer force he stole her maidenhood;

For which oppressioun was swich clamour
For which violation there was such clamor

And swich pursute un-to the king Arthour,
And such running to King Arthur,

That dampned was this knight for to be deed
That this knight was doomed to be executed

By cours of lawe, and sholde han lost his heed   36
By course of law, and would have lost his head

Paraventure, swich was the statut tho;
Since such happened to be the law then;

But that the quene and othere ladies mo
But that the queen and other ladies besides

So longe preyeden the king of grace,
So long begged the king for mercy,

Til he his lyf him granted in the place,   40
Until he there granted him his life,

And yaf him to the quene al at hir wille,
And turned him over to the queen, at her disposal,

To chese, whether she wolde him save or spille.
To chose, whether she would save or kill him.

   The quene thanketh the king with al hir might,
   The queen thanked the king with all her might,

And after this thus spak she to the knight,   44
And after that she spoke thus to the knight,

Whan that she saugh hir tyme, up-on a day:
When she found a good time one day:

"Thou standest yet," quod she, "in swich array,
"You still remain," she said, "in such a situation

That of thy lyf yet hastow no suretee.
That you still have no certainty of living.

I grante thee lyf, if thou canst tellen me   48
I grant you life, if you can tell me

What thing is it that wommen most desyren?
What thing it is that women most desire.

Be war, and keep thy nekke-boon from yren.
Be careful, and keep your neck-bone from the blade.

And if thou canst nat tellen it anon,
And if you cannot tell it at once,

Yet wol I yeve thee leve for to gon   52
Even so I will give you leave to go

A twelf-month and a day, to seche and lere
A twelvemonth and a day, to search out and learn

An answere suffisant in this matere.
A satisfactory answer to this problem.

And suretee wol I han, er that thou pace,
And security I will have, before you leave,

Thy body for to yelden in this place."   56
That you will yield up your body in this place."

   Wo was this knight and sorwefully he syketh;
   Woebegone was this knight and sorrowfully he sighed;

But what! he may nat do al as him lyketh.
What of it? he couldn't do just as he pleased.

And at the laste, he chees him for to wende,
And at last, he chose to journey forth,

And come agayn, right at the yeres ende,   60
And return again, exactly at the year's end,

With swich answere as god wolde him purveye;
With whatever answer God might grant him;

And taketh his leve, and wendeth forth his weye.
And so he took his leave, and went on his way.

He seketh every hous and every place,
He sought out every house and every place,

Wher-as he hopeth for to finde grace,   64
Wherever he hoped to find a clue,

To lerne, what thing wommen loven most;
To learn what thing women love most;

But he ne coude arryven in no cost,
But he never came to any place

Wher-as he might finde in this matere
Where he could find, on this subject,

Two creatures accordinge in-fere.   68
Two persons in agreement.

Somme seyde, wommen loven best richesse,
Some said, women loved money best.

Somme seyde, honour, somme seyde, jolynesse;
Some said, reputation; some said, beauty;

Somme, riche array, somme seyden, lust abedde,
Some, fine clothes; some said, lust abed,

And ofte tyme to be widwe and wedde.   72
And frequently to be widowed and married.

Somme seyde, that our hertes been most esed,
Some said, that our spirits are most soothed,

Whan that we been y-flatered and y-plesed.
When we are flattered and spoiled.

He gooth ful ny the sothe, I wol nat lye;
That comes very close to the truth, I will not lie;

A man shal winne us best with flaterye;   76
A man shall win us best with flattery;

And with attendance, and with bisinesse,
And with attentions, and with thoughtful acts,

Been we y-lymed, bothe more and lesse.
Are we caught, both the strong and the weak.

  And somme seyn, how that we loven best
  And some said, that we love best

For to be free, and do right as us lest,   80
To be free and do just as we please,

And that no man repreve us of our vyce,
And have no man reprove us for our sins,

But seye that we be wyse, and no-thing nyce.
But say that we are wise and not at all foolish.

For trewely, ther is noon of us alle,
For truly, there is not one of us all,

If any wight wol clawe us on the galle,   84
If any man rubs us on a sore spot,

That we nil kike, for he seith us sooth;
Who will not kick because he tells the truth;

Assay, and he shal finde it that so dooth.
Try it, and he who does will find out.

For be we never so vicious with-inne,
For however wicked we may be within,

We wol been holden wyse, and clene of sinne.   88
We would be considered wise, and pure of sin.

  And somme seyn, that greet delyt han we
  And some said, that we take great delight

For to ben holden stable and eek secree,
In being considered dependable and trustworthy,

And in o purpos stedefastly to dwelle,
And able to hold steadfastly to one purpose,

And nat biwreye thing that men us telle.   92
And not betray things men tell us.

But that tale is nat worth a rake-stole,
But that idea is not worth a rake handle;

Pardee, we wommen conne no-thing hele;
By heaven, we women can conceal nothing;

Witnesse on Myda; wol ye here the tale?
Take Midas to witness; will you hear the tale?

Ovyde, amonges othere thinges smale,   96
Ovid, among other brief writings,

Seyde, Myda hadde, under his longe heres,
Said that Midas had, under his long hair,

Growinge up-on his heed two asses eres,
Two ass's ears growing on his head,

The whiche vyce he hidde, as he best mighte,
Which deformity he hid, as best he could,

Ful subtilly from every mannes sighte,   100
Most cleverly from every man's sight,

That, save his wyf, ther wiste of it namo.
So that, except for his wife, no one knew of it.

He loved hir most, and trusted hir also;
He loved her most, and trusted her as well;

He preyede hir, that to no creature
He begged her, that to no creature

She sholde tellen of his disfigure.   104
She would tell of his disfigurement.

She swoor him "nay, for al this world to winne,
She swore to him that, to gain all this world,

She nolde do that vileinye or sinne,
She would not commit that wickedness or sin,

To make hir housbond han so foul a name;
To make her husband have so foul a name;

She nolde nat telle it for hir owene shame."   *108*
She would not tell it for her own reputation.

But nathelees, hir thoughte that she dyde,
But nevertheless, she thought she would die

That she so longe sholde a conseil hyde;
From having to keep a secret so long;

Hir thoughte it swal so sore aboute hir herte,
She thought it pressed so sorely on her heart

That nedely som word hir moste asterte;   *112*
That some word must necessarily escape her;

And sith she dorste telle it to no man,
And since she did not dare tell it to any man,

Doun to a mareys faste by she ran;
She ran down to a nearby marsh;

Til she came there, hir herte was a-fyre,
Until she got there, her heart was on fire,

And, as a bitore bombleth in the myre,   *116*
And, just as a bittern bumbles in the mire,

She leyde hir mouth unto the water doun:
She laid her mouth down to the water:

"Biwreye me nat, thou water, with thy soun,"
"Betray me not, thou water, with thy sound,"

Quod she, "to thee I telle it, and namo;
Said she, "to thee I tell it, and to no one else;

Myn housbond hath longe asses eres two!   *120*
My husband has two long ass's ears!

Now is myn herte all hool, now is it oute;
Now is my heart all healed, now it is out;

I mighte no lenger kepe it, out of doute."
I could no longer hold it, beyond a doubt."

Heer may ye se, thogh we a tyme abyde,
Here you may see, though we hold on awhile,

Yet out it moot, we can no conseil hyde;   *124*
Yet out it must, we can keep no secret;

The remenant of the tale if ye wol here,
The rest of the tale, if you want to hear it,

Redeth Ovyde, and ther ye may it lere.
Read Ovid, you can find it there.'

　This knight, of which my tale is specially,
　This knight, whom my tale especially concerns,

Whan that he saugh he mighte nat come therby,   *128*
When he saw he could not come by it,

This is to seye, what wommen loven moost,
That is to say, what women love most,

With-inne his brest ful sorweful was the goost;
Within his breast most sorrowful was his spirit;

But hoom he gooth, he mighte nat sojourne.
But home he went, he could not loiter.

The day was come, that hoomward moste he tourne,   *132*
The day had come when he had to turn homeward,

And in his wey it happed him to ryde,
And on his way it chanced that he rode,

In al this care, under a forest-syde,
In all this worry, beneath a forest's side,

Wher-as he saugh up-on a daunce go
Where he saw, joined in a dance,

Of ladies foure and twenty, and yet mo;   *136*
Four and twenty and yet more ladies;

Toward the whiche daunce he drow ful yerne,
Toward which dance he drew most eagerly,

In hope that som wisdom sholde he lerne.
In hopes that he might learn some wisdom.

But certeinly, er he came fully there,
But indeed, before he quite reached there,

Vanisshed was this daunce, he niste where.   140
Vanished was this dance, he knew not where.

No creature saugh he that bar lyf,
No living creature saw he,

Save on the grene he saugh sittinge a wyf;
Except a woman sitting on the grass;

A fouler wight ther may no man devyse
A fouler creature no man can imagine.

Agayn the knight this olde wyf gan ryse,   144
To meet the knight this old woman stood up

And seyde, "sir knight, heer-forth ne lyth no wey.
And said, "Sir knight, no road goes through here.

Tel me, what that ye seken, by your fey?
Tell me, what do you seek, by your faith?

Paraventure it may the bettre be;
Perchance it will be of use to you;

Thise olde folk can muchel thing," quod she.   148
These old people know many a thing," said she.

"My leve mooder," quod this knight, "certeyn
"My dear mother," said this knight, "surely

I nam but deed, but-if I can seyn
I am but dead, unless I can tell

What thing it is that wommen most desyre;
What thing it is that women most desire;

Coude ye me wisse, I wolde wel quyte your hyre."   152
If you could inform me, I would well repay your trouble."

"Plight me thy trouthe, heer in myn hand," quod she,
"Pledge me your honor, here on my hand," said she,

"The nexte thing that I requere thee,
"That the next thing I require of you,

Thou shalt it do, if it lye in thy might;
You will perform, if it lies in your power;

And I wol telle it yow er it be night."   156
And I will tell it to you before night."

"Have heer my trouthe," quod the knight, "I graunte."
"Take here my pledge," said the knight, "I grant it."

"Thanne," quod she, "I dar me wel avante,
"Then," said she, "I dare confidently boast,

Thy lyf is sauf for I wol stonde therby,
Your life is safe, for I will guarantee,

Up-on my lyf, the queen wol seye as I.   160
On my life, the queen will say as I do.

Lat see which is the proudeste of hem alle,
Let us see if the proudest of all of them

That wereth on a coverchief or a calle,
That wear coverchiefs or bonnets

That dar seye nay, of that I shal thee teche;
Will dare deny what I shall teach you;

Lat us go forth with-outen lenger speche."   164
Let us go forth without further speech."

Tho rouned she a pistel in his ere,
Then she whispered a message in his ear,

And bad him to be glad, and have no fere.
And bade him be at ease, and have no fear.

Whan they be comen to the court, this knight
When they had arrived at the court, this knight

Seyde, he had holde his day, as he hadde hight,   168
Said he had held to his day, as he had promised,

And redy was his answere, as he sayde.
And his answer was ready, as he said.

Ful many a noble wyf, and many a mayde,
Many a noble wife, and many a maid,

And many a widwe, for they ben wyse,
And many a widow, for they are the wise ones,

And the quene hir-self sittinge as a justyse,   172
And the queen herself sitting as a judge,

Assembled been, his answere for to here;
Were assembled to hear his answer;

And afterward this knight was bode appere.
Whereupon this knight was ordered to appear.

To every wight comanded was silence,
Everybody was commanded to be silent,

And that the knight sholde telle in audience   176
And the knight was ordered to tell the assembly

What thing that worldly wommen loven best.
What thing mortal women love best.

This knight ne stood nat stille as doth a best,
This knight stood not dumb as a beast,

But to his questioun anon answerde
But answered his question at once.

With manly voys, that al the court it herde: 180
With manly voice, so that all the court heard it:

"My lige lady, generally," quod he,
"My liege lady, — generally speaking," said he,

"Wommen desyren to have sovereyntee
"Women desire to have sovereignty

As wel over hir housbond as hir love,
Over their husbands as much as over their lovers,

And to been in maistrie him above;   184
And to be the masters of them;

This is your moste desyr, thogh ye me kille,
This is your greatest desire, though you kill me;

Doth as yow list, I am heer at your wille."
Do as you please, I am here at your mercy."

In al the court ne was ther wyf ne mayde,
In all the court there was not wife nor maid

Ne widwe, that contraried that he sayde,   *188*
Nor widow that contradicted what he said,

But seyden, "he was worthy han his lyf"
But said that he deserved to have his life.

And with that word up stirte the olde wyf,
And with that word up jumped the old woman,

Which that the knight saugh sittinge in the grene:
Whom the knight had seen sitting on the grass:

"Mercy," quod she, "my sovereyn lady quene!   *192*
"Thank you," she said, "my sovereign lady queen!

Er that your court departe, do me right.
Before your court adjourns, grant me justice.

I taughte this answere un-to the knight;
I taught this answer to the knight;

For which he plighte me his trouthe there,
For which he pledged me then his honor,

The firste thing I wolde of him requere,   *196*
That the first thing I should require of him,

He wolde it do, if it lay in his might.
He would perform, if it lay in his power.

Bifore the court than preye I thee, sir knight,"
So before the court I ask you, sir knight,"

Quod she, "that thou me take un-to thy wyf;
Said she, "that you take me as your wife;

For wel thou wost that I have kept thy lyf.   *200*
For well you know that I have saved your life.

If I sey fals, sey nay, up-on thy fey!"
If I speak falsely, refuse me, on your faith!"

This knight answerde, "allas! and weylawey!
This knight replied, "Alas! and woe is me!

I woot right wel that swich was my biheste.
I know all too well that such was my pledge;

For goddes love, as chees a new requeste;   204
But, for God's love, choose another request;

Tak al my good, and lat my body go."
Take all my goods, and let my body go."

   "Nay than," quod she, "I shrewe us bothe two!
*   "Oh no," said she, "I curse both of us if I do!*

For thogh that I be foul, and old, and pore,
For though I be foul, and old, and poor,

I nolde for al the metal, ne for ore,   208
I would not have all the metal or ore

That under erthe is grave, or lyth above,
That is buried in the earth or lies above,

But-if thy wyf I were, and eek thy love."
Unless I were your wife, and your love too."

   "My love?" quod he; "nay, my dampnacioun!
*   "My love?" said he, "No, my damnation!*

Allas! that any of my nacioun   212
Alas! that any of my family

Sholde ever so foule disparaged be!"
Should ever be so foully dishonored!"

But al for noght, the ende is this, that he
But all for nothing, the result was that he

Constreyned was, he nedes moste hir wedde;
Was compelled, he had to marry her;

And taketh his olde wyf, and gooth to bedde.   216
And so he took his old wife and went to bed.

   Now wolden som men seye, paraventure,
*   Now some men might possibly say*

That, for my necligence, I do no cure
That, out of negligence, I take no pains

To tellen yow the joye and al th'array
To tell you about the joy and all the festivities

That at the feste was that ilke day.   220
Which were at the feast that same day.

To whiche thing shortly answere I shal;
To which accusation I make a brief answer;

I seye, ther nas no joye ne feste at al,
I say, there was no joy nor feast at all,

Ther nas but hevinesse and muche sorwe;
There was nothing but heaviness and much sorrow;

For prively he wedded hir on a morwe,   224
For he married her privately on a morning,

And al day after hidde him as an oule;
And all the rest of the day hid like an owl;

So wo was him, his wyf looked so foule.
So woeful was he, his wife looked so foul.

   Greet was the wo the knight hadde in his thoght,
   Great was the despair the knight had in his thoughts

When he was with his wyf a-bedde y-broght;   228
When he was brought to go to bed with his wife;

He walweth, and he turneth to and fro.
He rolled about, and he turned to and fro.

His olde wyf lay smilinge evermo,
His old wife lay smiling all the time,

And seyde, "o dere housbond, ben'cite!
And said, "O dear husband, bless you!

Fareth every knight thus with his wyf as ye?   232
Does every knight behave thus with his wife as you do?

Is this the lawe of king Arthoures hous?
Is this the custom of King Arthur's court?

Is every knight of his so dangerous?
Is every knight of his so timid?

I am your owene love and eek your wyf;
I am your own love and also your wife;

I am she, which that saved hath your lyf;   *236*
I am the one who saved your life;

And certes, yet dide I yow never unright;
And truly, I have never yet done you any wrong;

Why fare ye thus with me this firste night?
Why do you act this way with me this first night?

Ye faren lyk a man had lost his wit;
You act like a man who has lost his mind;

What is my gilt? for Goddes love, tel me it,   *240*
What is my guilt? For God's love, tell me,

And it shal been amended, if I may."
And it shall be amended, if I can."

"Amended?" quod this knight, "allas! nay, nay!
"Amended?" said this knight, "Alas! no, no!

It wol nat been amended never mo!
It cannot be amended forevermore!

Thou art so loothly, and so old also,   *244*
You are so loathsome, and so old besides,

And ther-to comen of so lowe a kinde,
And, in addition, come from such a low class,

That litel wonder is, thogh I walwe and winde.
That it is little wonder that I toss and turn.

So wolde God myn herte wolde breste!"
I would to God my heart would break!"

"Is this," quod she, "the cause of your unreste?"   *248*
"Is this," said she, "the cause of your restlessness?"

"Ye, certainly," quod he, "no wonder is."
"Yes, indeed," said he, "and no wonder."

"Now, sire," quod she, "I coude amende al this,
"Now, my lord," said she, "I could amend all this,

If that me liste, er it were dayes three,
If I cared to, before the end of three days.

So wel ye mighte bere yow un-to me.   *252*
If you behave nicely to me.

   "But for ye speken of swich gentillesse
   "But as for your talk of such nobility

As is descended out of old richesse,
As is descended from ancient wealth,

That therfore sholden ye be gentil men,
And that therefore you are noblemen,

Swich arrogance is nat worth an hen.   *256*
Such arrogance is not worth a hen.

Loke who that is most vertuous alway,
Observe the one who is always most virtuous,

Privee and apert, and most entendeth ay
Secretly and openly, and is always most concern

To do the gentil dedes that he can,
To do whatever noble deeds he can,

And tak him for the grettest gentil man.   *260*
And take him for the greatest noble man.

Crist wol, we clayme of him our gentillesse,
Christ wills that we claim our nobility from Him,

Nat of our eldres for hir old richesse.
Not from our ancestors because of their wealth.

For thogh they yeve us al hir heritage,
For though they give us all their heritage,

For which we clayme to been of heigh parage,   *264*
Wherefore we claim to be of high birth,

Yet may they nat biquethe, for no-thing,
Yet they cannot bequeath, for anything,

To noon of us hir vertuous living,
To any of us their virtuous living,

That made hem gentil men y-called be;
Which made them known as noble men;

And bad us folwen hem in swich degree.   268
And they bade us follow the same pattern

   "Wel can the wyse poete of Florence,
   "Well can the wise poet of Florence,

That highte Dant, speken in this sentence;
Named Dante, speak in this passage;

Lo in swich maner rym is Dantes tale:
Here in verse something like this is Dante's saying:

'Ful selde up ryseth by his branches smale   272
'Seldom rises from root to branches

Prowesse of man; for God, of his goodnesse,
The worth of man; for God, of His goodness,

Wol that of him we clayme our gentillesse;'
Wills that from Him we derive our nobility;'

For of our eldres may we no-thing clayme
For from our ancestors we can derive nothing

But temporel thing, that man may hurte and mayme.   276
But temporal things, which man can hurt and injure.

   "Eek every wight wot this as wel as I,
   "Besides, everyone knows this as well as I,

If gentillesse were planted naturelly
If nobility were given by nature

Un-to a certeyn linage, doun the lyne,
To a certain lineage, down the line,

Privee ne apert, than wolde they never fyne   280
Then, secretly or openly, they would never fail

To doon of gentillesse the faire offyce;
To do the good deeds of nobility;

They mighte do no vileinye or vyce.
They could not commit any sin or evil.

"Tak fyr, and ber it in the derkeste hous
"Take fire, and carry it into the darkest house

Bitwix this and the mount of Caucasus,   284
Between here and the mount of Caucasus,

And lat men shette the dores and go thenne;
And let men shut the doors and go away;

Yet wol the fyr as faire lye and brenne,
Yet will the fire as brightly stay and burn

As twenty thousand men mighte it biholde;
As if twenty thousand men were watching it;

His office naturel ay wol it holde,   288
It will always preserve its true nature,

Up peril of my lyf, til that it dye.
On peril of my life, until it dies.

"Heer may ye see wel, how that genterye
"Here you can well see that gentility

Is nat annexed to possessioun,
Is not connected with possessions,

Sith folk ne doon hir operacioun   292
Since people do not perform their deeds

Alwey, as dooth the fyr, lo! in his kinde.
Always, as the fire does, take note, after its nature.

For, God it woot, men may wel often finde
For God knows, men well may often see

A lordes sone do shame and vileinye;
A lord's son do shameful and low deeds;

And he that wol han prys of his gentrye   296
And he who would have esteem for his rank

For he was boren of a gentil hous,
Because he was born of a noble house,

And hadde hise eldres noble and vertuous,
And had noble and virtuous ancestors,

And nil him-selven do no gentil dedis,
And will not himself do any noble deeds,

Ne folwe his gentil auncestre that deed is,   300
Nor imitate his noble ancestor who is dead,

He nis nat gentil, be he duk or erl;
He is not noble, be he duke or earl;

For vileyns sinful dedes make a cherl.
For low sinful deeds make a man common.

For gentillesse nis but renomee
For gentility is not only the renown

Of thyne auncestres, for hir heigh bountee,   304
Of your ancestors, because of their high excellence,

Which is a strange thing to thy persone.
Which is something unconnected with yourself.

Thy gentillesse cometh fro God allone;
Your gentility comes from God alone;

Than cometh our verray gentillesse of grace,
So our true nobility comes by grace,

It was no-thing biquethe us with our place.   308
It was not bequeathed to us with our rank.

"Thenketh how noble, as seith Valerius,
"Consider how noble, as Valerius says,

Was thilke Tullius Hostilius,
Was that Tullius Hostilius,

That out of povert roos to heigh noblesse.
Who out of poverty rose to high nobility.

Redeth Senek, and redeth eek Boëce,   312
Read Seneca, and read Boethius too,

Ther shul ye seen expres that it no drede is,
There you shall see so clearly that it leaves no doubt,

That he is gentil that doth gentil dedis;
That he is noble who does noble deeds;

And therfore, leve housbond, I thus conclude,
And therefore, dear husband, I thus conclude,

Al were it that myne auncestres were rude,   *316*
Even though my ancestors might have been common,

Yet may the hye God, and so hope I,
Yet may the high God, and I hope so too,

Grante me grace to liven vertuously.
Grant me grace to live virtuously.

Thanne am I gentil, whan that I biginne
Then will I be noble, when I begin

To liven vertuously and weyve sinne.   *320*
To live virtuously and avoid sin.

"And ther-as ye of povert me repreve,
"And as for your reproving me of poverty,

The hye God, on whom that we bileve,
The high God, in Whom we believe,

In wilful povert chees to live his lyf.
In deliberate poverty chose to live His life.

And certes every man, mayden, or wyf,   *324*
And certainly every man, maid, or wife,

May understonde that Jesus, hevene king,
Can understand that Jesus, Heavenly King,

Ne wolde nat chese a vicious living.
Would not choose an evil way of life.

Glad povert is an honest thing, certyn;
Contented poverty is an honest thing indeed;

This wol Senek and other clerkes seyn.   *328*
To this Seneca and other clerks will testify.

Who-so that halt him payd of his poverte,
Whoso holds himself satisfied with his poverty,

I holde him riche, al hadde he nat a sherte.
I consider him rich, even if he hasn't a shirt.

He that coveyteth is a povre wight,
He who covets is a poor man,

For he wolde han that is nat in his might.   332
For he would have what is not in his power.

But he that noght hath, ne coveyteth have,
But he that has nothing, and wants nothing,

Is riche, al-though ye hold him but a knave.
Is rich, although you consider him only a peasant.

"Verray povert, it singeth proprely;
"True poverty sings by nature;

Juvenal seith of povert merily: 336
Juvenal cheerfully says of poverty:

'The povre man, whan he goth by the weye,
'The poor man, when he goes along the way,

Bifore the theves he may singe and pleye.'
In front of thieves may sing and play.'

Povert is hateful good, and, as I gesse,
Poverty is a hateful good, and, as I imagine,

A ful greet bringer out of bisinesse,   340
A very great incentive to work;

A greet amender eek of sapience
A great stimulant too of wisdom

To him that taketh it in pacience.
To him who takes it patiently.

Povert is this, al-though it seme elenge:
Poverty is this, although it may seem wretched:

Possessioun, that no wight wol chalenge.   344
A possession that no man will challenge.

Povert ful ofte, whan a man is lowe,
Poverty very often, when a man is brought low,

Maketh his God and eek him-self to knowe.
Brings him to know his God and himself as well.

Povert a spectacle is, as thinketh me,
Poverty is a lens, as it seems to me,

Thurgh which he may his verray frendes see.   348
Through which one may see his real friends.

And therefore, sire, sin that I noght yow greve,
And therefore, my lord, since I do not disturb you

Of my povert, na-more ye me repreve.
By my poverty, reprove me no longer.

"Now, sire, of elde ye repreve me;
"Now, my lord, you blamed me for my age;

And certes, sire, thogh noon auctoritee   352
And truly, my lord, though no authority

Were in no book, ye gentils of honour
Were in any book, you honorable gentlemen

Seyn that men sholde an old wight doon favour,
Say that men should be courteous to an old person,

And clepe him fader, for your gentillesse;
And call him 'father,' out of your gentility;

And auctours shal I finden, as I gesse.   356
And I could find authorities for that I imagine.

"Now ther ye seye, that I am foul and old,
"Now when you say that I am foul and old,

Than drede you noght to been a cokewold;
Then you need not fear to be made a cuckold;

For filthe and elde, al-so mote I thee,
For filth and old age, I can tell you,

Been grete wardeyns up-on chastitee.   360
Are great guardians over chastity.

But nathelees, sin I knowe your delyt,
But nevertheless, since I know your desires,

I shal fulfille your worldly appetyt.
I shall fulfill your worldly appetite.

"Chees now," quod she, "oon of thise thinges tweye,
"Choose now," said she, "one of these two things,

To han me foul and old til that I deye,   364
To have me foul and old until I die,

And be to yow a trewe humble wyf,
And be to you a faithful humble wife,

And never yow displese in al my lyf,
And never displease you in all my life,

Or elles ye wol han me yong and fair,
Or else to have me young and beautiful,

And take your aventure of the repair   368
And take your chances on the visitors

That shal be to your hous, by-cause of me,
Who will come to your house because of me,

Or in som other place, may wel be.
Or meet me somewhere else, as well may be.

Now chees your-selven, whether that yow lyketh."
Now choose yourself which you prefer."

This knight avyseth him and sore syketh,   372
This knight pondered and sighed wretchedly,

But atte laste he seyde in this manere,
But at last he spoke in this manner,

"My lady and my love, and wyf so dere,
"My lady and my love, and wife so dear,

I put me in your governance;
I place myself under your management;

Cheseth your-self, which may be most pleasance,   376
Choose yourself whichever may bring most pleasure

And most honour to yow and me also.
And most honor to you as well as me.

I do no fors the whether of the two;
I make no choice of either of the two;

For as yow lyketh, it suffiseth me."
For whichever pleases you suffices me."

"Thanne have I gete of yow maistrye," quod she,   380
"Then I have won mastery over you," said she,

"Sin I may chese, and governe as me lest?"
"Since I may choose, and run things as I please?"

"Ye, certes, wyf," quod he, "I holde it best."
"Yes, certainly, wife," said he, "I think it best."

"Kis me," quod she, "we be no lenger wrothe;
"Kiss me," said she, "we are no longer enemies;

For, by my trouthe, I wol be to yow bothe,   384
For, on my honor, I will be both to you,

This is to seyn, ye, bothe fair and good.
That is to say, yes, both beautiful and good.

I prey to God that I mot sterven wood,
I pray to God that I may die insane

But I to yow be al-so good and trewe
Unless I am as good and faithful to you

As ever was wyf, sin that the world was newe.   388
As ever wife was, since the world was young.

And, but I be to-morn as fair to sene
And, unless I am in the morning as fair to see

As any lady, emperyce, or quene,
As any lady, empress, or queen,

That is bitwixe the est and eke the west,
Who exists anywhere between east and west,

Doth with my lyf and deeth right as yow lest.   392
Do with my life and death whatever you please.

Cast up the curtin, loke how that it is."
Open the curtain, see how it is."

And whan the knight saugh verraily al this,
And when the knight really saw all this,

That she so fair was, and so yong ther-to,
That she was so beautiful, and so young too,

For joye he hente hir in his armes two,   396
For joy he took her in his arms,

His herte bathed in a bath of blisse;
His heart bathed in a bath of bliss;

A thousand tyme a-rewe he gan hir kisse.
A thousand times in succession he kissed her.

And she obeyed him in every thing
And she obeyed him in every thing

That mighte doon him pleasance or lyking.   400
That might give him pleasure or enjoyment.

And thus they live, un-to hir lyves ende,
And so they lived to the end of their lives

In parfit joye; and Jesu Crist us sende
In perfect joy; and may Jesus Christ send us

Housbondes meke, yonge, and fresshe a-bedde,
Husbands meek, young, and fresh in bed,

And grace t'overbyde hem that we wedde.   404
And grace to outlive those we wed.

And eek I preye Jesu shorte hir lyves
And also I pray Jesus to cut short their lives

That wol nat be governed by hir wyves;
Who will not be ruled by their wives;

And olde and angry nigardes of dispence,
And as for old and mean tightwads in spending,

God sende hem sone verray pestilence.   408
God send them quickly the plague itself.

The Prologue
to the Franklin's Tale

"Thise olde gentil Britons in hir dayes
"Those old noble Bretons in their day

Of diverse aventures maden layes,
Made lays about various events,

Rymeyed in hir firste Briton tonge;
Rhymed in their early Breton tongue;

Which layes with hir instruments they songe,   4
Which lays they sang to their instruments,

Or elles redden hem for hir pleasaunce;
Or else read them for their pleasure;

And oon of hem have I in remembraunce,
And one of them I have in my memory,

Which I shal seyn with good wil as I can.
Which I shall tell with good will as well as I can.

   "But, sires, by-cause I am a burel man,   8
*   "But, gentlemen, because I am an uneducated man,*

At my biginning first I yow biseche
Before I begin I beg you

Have me excused of my rude speche;
To excuse me for my unpolished language;

I lerned never rethoryk certeyn;
I certainly never studied rhetoric;

Thing that I speke, it moot be bare and pleyn.   *12*
Whatever I say must be bare and simple.

I sleep never on the mount of Pernaso,
I never slept on Mount Parnassus,

Ne lerned Marcus Tullius Cithero.
Nor studied Marcus Tullius Cicero.

Colours ne knowe I none, with-outen drede,
Colorfulness I know nothing about, beyond a doubt,

But swich colours as growen in the mede,   *16*
Except such colors as grow in the meadow,

Or elles swich as men dye or peynte.
Or else such as men dye or paint.

Colours of rethoryk ben to me to queynte;
Colorful language is too artistic for me;

My spirit feleth noght of swich matere.
My spirit has no feeling for such matters.

But if yow list, my tale shul ye here."   *20*
But if you are willing, you shall hear my tale."

The Franklin's Tale

In Armorik, that called is Britayne,
In Armorica, which is called Brittany,

Ther was a knight that loved and dide his payne
There was a knight that loved and did his best

To serve a lady in his beste wyse;
To serve a lady with his best talents;

And many a labour, many a greet empryse   4
And many an adventure, many a great enterprise

He for his lady wroghte, er she were wonne.
He carried out for his lady, before she was won.

For she was oon, the faireste under sonne,
For she was one of the fairest under the sun,

And eek therto come of so heigh kinrede,
And in addition came from such an exalted family,

That wel unnethes dorste this knight, for drede,   8
That this knight scarcely dared, for fear,

Telle hir his wo, his peyne, and his distresse.
Tell her of his woe, his pain, and his suffering.

But atte laste, she, for his worthinesse,
But at last, she, because of his worthiness,

And namely for his meke obeysaunce,
And especially because of his respectful bearing,

Hath swich a pitee caught of his penunce,   *12*
Took such pity on his lovesickness,

That prively she fil of his accord
That secretly she was won over

To take him for hir housbonde and hir lord,
To take him as her husband and lord,

Of swich lordshipe as men han over hir wyves;
Of such lordship as men have over their wives;

And for to lede the more in blisse hir lyves,   *16*
And in order to lead their lives in greater bliss,

Of his free wil he swoor hir as a knight,
Of his free will he swore to her as a knight,

That never in al his lyf he, day ne night,
That never in all his life, day or night,

Ne sholde up-on him take no maistrye
Would he take upon himself any authority

Agayn hir wil, ne kythe hir jalousye,   *20*
Against her will, or be jealous of her,

But hir obeye, and folwe hir wil in al
But would obey her, and always follow her wishes,

As any lovere to his lady shal;
As any lover behaves to his lady;

Save that the name of soveraynetee,
Except that the appearance of sovereignty

That wolde he have for shame of his degree.   *24*
He would keep for the reputation of his rank.

  She thanked him, and with ful greet humblesse
  She thanked him, and with very great humility

She seyde, "sire, sith of your gentillesse
She said, "My lord, since out of your nobility

Ye profre me to have so large a reyne,
You offer me so free a rein,

Ne wolde never God bitwixe us tweyne,   28
May God never allow between us two,

As in my gilt, were outher werre or stryf.
For fault of mine, either conflict or disagreement.

Sir, I wol be your humble trewe wyf,
Sir, I will be your humble faithful wife,

Have heer my trouthe, til that myn herte breste."
Take here my word, until my heart breaks."

Thus been they bothe in quiete and in reste.   32
Thus were they both at peace and at rest.

For o thing, sires, saufly dar I seye,
For one thing, gentlemen, I dare safely say,

That frendes everich other moot obeye,
That friends must obey each other,

If they wol longe holden companye.
If they would long keep company.

Love wol nat ben constreyned by maistrye;   36
Love will not be bound by master

Whan maistrie comth, the god of love anon
When mastery enters, the god of love at once

Beteth hise winges, and farewel! he is gon!
Beats his wings, and farewell! he is gone!

Love is a thing as any spirit free;
Love is a thing as free as any spirit;

Wommen of kinde desiren libertee,   40
Women by nature desire liberty,

And nat to ben constreyned as a thral;
Ana not to be held down like slaves;

And so don men, if soth seyen shal.
And so do men, if I speak the truth.

Loke who that is most pacient in love,
Observe him who is most patient in love,

He is at his avantage al above.   44
He has the advantage over all others.

Pacience is an heigh vertu certeyn;
Patience is truly a lofty virtue;

For it venquisseth, as thise clerkes seyn,
For it vanquishes, as the clerks say,

Thinges that rigour sholde never atteyne
Things that violence could never manage.

For every word men may nat chyde or pleyne.   48
Men must not chide or complain about every word.

Lerneth to suffre, or elles, so moot I goon,
Learn to suffer, or else, I assure you,

Ye shul it lerne, wher-so ye wole or noon.
You shall learn it, whether you will or not.

For in this world, certein, ther no wight is,
For in this world, for certain, there is no one

That he ne dooth or seith som-tyme amis.   52
Who does not do or say wrong at some time.

Ire, siknesse, or constellacioun,
Anger, sickness, or the stars,

Wyn, wo, or chaunginge of complexioun
Wine, sorrow, or change of temperament

Causeth ful ofte to doon amis or speken.
Very often causes mistaken speech or action.

On every wrong a man may nat be wreken;   56
For every wrong a man cannot be revenged;

After the tyme, moste be temperaunce
According to the circumstances, care must be taken,

To every wight that can on governaunce.
By every person who can control himself.

And therfore hath this wyse worthy knight,
And therefore this wise worthy knight,

To live in ese, suffrance hir bihight,   *60*
To live contentedly, pledged tolerance to her,

And she to him ful wisly gan to swere
And she very wisely gave her promise

That never sholde ther be defaute in here.
That there should never be lack of it in her.

Heer may men seen an humble wys accord;
Here may men see a humble wise agreement;

Thus hath she take hir servant and hir lord,   *64*
Thus she took her servant and her lord,

Servant in love, and lord in mariage;
Servant in love, and lord in marriage;

Than was he both in lordship and servage;
Then he was both in lordship and stewardship;

Servage? nay, but in lordshipe above,
Stewardship? no, but rather above lordship,

Sith he hath bothe his lady and his love;   *68*
Since he had both his lady and his love;

His lady, certes, and his wyf also,
His lady indeed, and his wife too,

The which that lawe of love acordeth to.
Who was in agreement with that law of love.

And what he was in this prosperitee,
And when he had attained this good fortune,

Hoom with his wyf he gooth to his contree,   *72*
He went home with his wife to his own country,

Nat fer fro Penmark, ther his dwelling was,
Not far from Penmark, where his dwelling was,

Wher-as he liveth in blisse and in solas.
And there he lived in joy and happiness.

Who coude telle, but he had wedded be,
Who can tell, unless he has been married,

The joye, the ese, and the prosperitee 76
The joy, the pleasantness, and the contentment

That is bitwixe an housbonde and his wyf?
Which exists between a husband and his wife?

A yeer and more lasted this blisful lyf,
A year and more this blissful life lasted,

Til that the knight of which I speke of thus,
Until the knight, of whom I have been speaking,

That of Kayrrud was cleped Arveragus, 80
Who was called Arveragus of Kayrrud,

Shoop him to goon, and dwelle a year or tweyne
Planned to go and live a year or two

In Engelond, that cleped was eek Briteyne,
In England, which was also called Britain,

To seke in armes worship and honour;
To seek in arms fame and honor;

For al his lust he sette in swich labour; 84
For his interest was entirely in such pursuits;

And dwelled ther two yeer, the book seith thus.
And he lived there two years, so the book says.

Now wol I stinte of this Arveragus,
Now will I leave this Arveragus,

And speken I wole of Dorigene his wyf,
And I will tell of Dorigen his wife,

That loveth hir housbonde as hir hertes lyf. 88
Who loved her husband as the beating of her heart.

For his absence wepeth she and syketh,
For his absence she wept and sighed,

As doon thise noble wyves whan hem lyketh.
As these noble wives do when it pleases them.

She moorneth, waketh, wayleth, fasteth, pleyneth;
She mourned, watched, wailed, fasted, lamented;

Desyr of his presence hir so distreyneth, 92
Longing for his presence so distracted her

That al this wyde world she sette at noght.
That all this wide world she counted as nothing.

Hir frendes, whiche that knewe hir hevy thoght,
Her friends, who knew of her heavy heart,

Conforten hir in al that ever they may;
Comforted her in every way they could;

They prechen hir, they telle hir night and day, 96
They lectured her, they told her night and day,

That causelees she sleeth hir-self, allas!
That she was killing herself without reason, alas!

And every confort possible in this cas
And every possible comfort in such circumstances

They doon to hir with al hir bisinesse,
They gave to the best of their abilities,

Al for to make hir leve hir hevinesse. 100
All to make her leave off her heaviness.

By proces, as ye knowen everichoon,
By persistence, as you all know,

Men may so longe graven in a stoon,
Men may so long chisel on a stone

Til som figure ther-inne emprented be.
Until some figure is engraved on it.

So longe han they conforted hir, til she 104
So long they comforted her, until she

Receyveth hath, by hope and by resoun,
Received, through hope and reasoning,

Th'emprenting of hir consolacioun,
The impression of their consolation,

Thurgh which hir grete sorwe gan aswage;
Through which her deep sorrow began to abate;

She may nat alwey duren in swich rage.   *108*
She could not remain forever in such a state.

And eek Arveragus, in al this care,
And, besides, Arveragus, during all this trial,

Hath sent hir lettres hoom of his welfare,
Sent home letters to her about his welfare,

And that he wol come hastily agayn;
And said that he would return soon;

Or elles hadde this sorwe hir herte slayn.   *112*
Or otherwise this grief would have slain her heart.

Hir freendes sawe hir sorwe gan to slake,
Her friends saw that her sorrow began to wane,

And preyede hir on knees, for Goddes sake,
And begged her on their knees, for God's sake,

To come and romen hir in companye,
To come and partake of their company

Awey to dryve hir derke fantasye.   *116*
To drive her dark fancies away.

And finally, she graunted that requeste;
And finally, she granted their request,

For wel she saugh that it was for the beste.
For well she saw that it was for the best.

Now stood hir castel faste by the see,
Now her castle stood close to the sea,

And often with hir freendes walketh she   *120*
And she often walked with her friends

Hir to disporte up-on the bank an heigh,
To take pleasure on the high cliff

Wher-as she many a ship and barge seigh
Where she saw many a ship and barge

Seilinge hir cours, wher-as hem liste go;
Sailing on its course to wherever it was going;

But than was that a parcel of hir wo.   124
But then that became a part of her grief.

For to hir-self ful ofte "allas!" seith she,
For to herself she often said, "Alas!

"Is ther no ship, of so manye as I see,
Is there no ship of the many that I see

Wol bringen hom my lord? than were myn herte
That brings home my lord? Then would my heart

Al warisshed of his bittre peynes smerte."   128
Be entirely cured of its bitter sharp pain."

Another tyme ther wolde she sitte and thinke,
At other times she would sit there and think,

And caste hir eyen dounward fro the brinke.
And cast her eyes downward from the precipice,

But whan she saugh the grisly rokkes blake,
But when she saw the horrible black rocks,

For verray fere so wolde hir herte quake,   132
For very fear so would her heart quake

That on hir feet she mighte hir noght sustene.
That she could not stand up on her feet.

Than wolde she sitte adoun upon the grene,
Then she would sit down on the grass,

And pitously into the see biholde,
And gaze piteously into the sea,

And seyn right thus, with sorweful sykes colde: 136
And speak even so, with sorrowful, cold sighs:

"Eterne God, that thurgh thy purveyaunce
"Eternal God, Who through Thy guidance

Ledest the world by certein governaunce,
Leadest the world by sure government,

In ydel, as men seyn, ye no-thing make;
Thou makest, as men say, no useless thing;

But, lord, thise grisly feendly rokkes blake,   140
But, Lord, these horrible, fiendish, black rocks,

That semen rather a foul confusioun
Which seem like rather a foul disorder

Of werk than any fair creacioun
Of work than any fair creation

Of swich a parfit wys God and a stable,
Of such a perfect, wise, and unchanging God,

Why han ye wroght this werk unresonable?   144
Why hast Thou wrought this meaningless work?

For by this werk, south, north, ne west, ne eest,
For by this work, south, north, or west, or east,

Ther nis y-fostred man, nor brid, nor beest;
There is nourished neither man, nor bird, nor beast;

It dooth no good, to my wit, but anoyeth.
It does no good, to my mind, but vexes instead.

See ye nat, lord, how mankinde it destroyeth?   148
Seest Thou not, Lord, how it destroys mankind?

An hundred thousand bodies of mankinde
A hundred thousand bodies of mankind

Han rokkes slayn, al be they nat in minde,
Have rocks slain, though I don't know of them all,

Which mankinde is so fair part of thy werk
Of mankind which is so fair a part of Thy work

That thou it madest lyk to thyn owene merk.   152
That Thou didst make it after Thine own image.

Than semed it ye hadde a greet chiertee
It seemed then that Thou didst have great charity

Toward mankinde; but how than may it be
Toward mankind; but how, then,.can it be

That ye swiche menes make it to destroyen,
That Thou makest such means to destroy it,

Whiche menes do no good, but ever anoyen?   156
Means that do no good, but are always harmful?

I woot wel clerkes wol seyn, as hem leste,
I know well the clerks will say, as it pleases them,

By arguments, that al is for the beste,
By arguments, that all is for the best,

Though I ne can the causes nat y-knowe.
Though I cannot understand the reasons.

But thilke God, that made wind to blowe,   160
But may that God Who made the wind to blow

As kepe my lord! this my conclusioun;
Protect my lord! This is my conclusion;

To clerkes lete I al disputisoun.
To clerks I leave all disputation.

But wolde God that all thise rokkes blake
But would to God that all these black rocks

Were sonken in-to helle for his sake!   164
Were sunk into hell for his sake!

Thise rokkes sleen myn herte for the fere."
These rocks slay my heart for fear."

Thus wolde she seyn, with many a pitous tere.
Thus would she speak, with many a piteous tear.

    Hir freendes sawe that it was no disport
    Her friends saw that it was no diversion

To romen by the see, but disconfort;   168
To wander by the sea, but rather anguish;

And shopen for to pleyen somwher elles.
And planned to find pastime somewhere else.

They leden hir by riveres and by welles,
They led her by rivers and by streams,

And eek in other places delitables;
And to other delightful places as well;

They dauncen, and they pleyen at ches and tables.   172
They danced, and they played chess and backgammon.

  So on a day, right in the morwe-tyde,
  So one day, during the morning,

Un-to a gardin that was ther bisyde,
To a garden that was near by,

In which that they had maad hir ordinaunce
In which they had made preparations

Of vitaille and of other purveyaunce,   176
Of food and other articles,

They goon and pleye hem al the longe day.
They went and diverted themselves all day long.

And this was on the sixte morwe of May,
And this was on the sixth morning of May,

Which May had peynted with his softe shoures
And May had painted with his soft showers

This gardin ful of leves and of floures;   180
This garden full of leaves and flowers;

And craft of mannes hand so curiously
And human handiwork so deftly

Arrayed hadde this gardin, trewely,
Had arranged this garden, truly,

That never was ther gardin of swich prys,
That there never was a garden of such beauty,

But-if it were the verray paradys.   184
Unless it were paradise itself.

Th'odour of floures and the fresshe sighte
The odor of flowers and the fresh sight

Wolde han maad any herte for to lighte
Would have made any heart lighten

That ever was born, but-if to gret siknesse,
That was ever born, unless too great sickness

Or to gret sorwe helde it in distresse;   *188*
Or too great sorrow held it in distress;

So ful it was of beautee with plesaunce.
So full it was of soothing beauty.

At-after diner gonne they to daunce
After dinner they proceeded to dance

And singe also, save Dorigen allone,
And also sing, save Dorigen alone,

Which made alwey hir compleint and hir mone;   *192*
Who continually moaned and lamented;

For she ne saugh him on the daunce go,
For in the dance she did not see him

That was hir housbonde and hir love also.
Who was her husband as well as her lover.

But natheless she moste a tyme abyde,
But nevertheless she had to remain awhile,

And with good hope lete hir sorwe slyde.   *196*
And with good hope let her sorrow wane.

   Up-on this daunce, amonges othere men,
   In this dance, among other men,

Daunced a squyer beforen Dorigen,
A squire danced in front of Dorigen,

That fressher was and jolyer of array,
Who was fresher and more gaily clothed,

As to my doom, than is the monthe of May.   *200*
In my judgment, than is the month of May.

He singeth, daunceth, passinge any man
He sang, danced, surpassing any man

That is, or was, sith that the world bigan.
Who is, or was, since the world began.

Ther-with he was, if men sholde him discryve,
Along with that he was, if men should describe him,

Oon of the beste faringe man on-lyve;   204
One of the best endowed men alive;

Yong, strong, right vertuous, and riche and wys,
Young, strong, entirely virtuous, and rich and wise,

And wel biloved, and holden in gret prys.
And well liked, and held in great esteem.

And shortly, if the sothe I tellen shal,
And in brief, if I am telling the truth,

Unwiting of this Dorigen at al,   208
Without Dorigen's slightest awareness of it,

This lusty squyer, servant to Venus,
This lively squire, this servant to Venus,

Which that y-cleped was Aurelius,
Who was called Aurelius,

Had loved hir best of any creature
Had loved her best of any creature

Two yeer and more, as was his aventure,   212
For two years and more, as was his fate,

But never dorste he telle hir his grevaunce;
But never dared he tell her his predicament;

With-outen coppe he drank al his penaunce.
Not by cupfuls he drank all his meed of woe.

He was despeyred, no-thing dorste he seye,
He was in despair, he dared say nothing,

Save in his songes somwhat wolde he wreye   216
Except that in his songs he somewhat revealed

His wo, as in a general compleyning;
His woe, as in a general lament;

He seyde he loved, and was biloved nothing.
He said he loved, but was not at all beloved.

Of swich matere made he manye layes,
Of such substance he made many lays,

Songs, compleintes, roundels, virelayes,   220
Songs, complaints, rondels, virelays,

How that he dorste nat his sorwe telle,
About how he dared not tell his sorrow,

But languissheth, as a furie dooth in helle;
But languished, as a monster does in hell;

And dye he moste, he seyde, as did Ekko
And he must die, he said, as Echo did

For Narcisus, that dorste nat telle hir wo.   224
For Narcissus, when she dared not tell her woe.

In other manere than ye here me seye,
In any other way than I have told you,

Ne dorste he nat to hir his wo biwreye;
He dared not reveal his woe to her;

Save that, paraventure, som-tyme at daunces,
Except that, by chance, sometimes at dances,

Ther yonge folk kepen hir observaunces,   228
Where young people have customs of their own,

It may wel be he loked on hir face
It may well be he looked into her face

In swich a wyse, as man that asketh grace;
In such a way as would a man begging for favor;

But no-thing wiste she of his entente.
But she suspected nothing of his intent.

Nathelees, it happed, er they thennes wente,   232
Nevertheless, it happened, before they departed,

By-cause that he was hir neighebour,
Because he was her neighbor,

And was a man of worship and honour,
And was a man of esteem and honor,

And hadde y-knowen him of tyme yore,
And she had known him from of old,

They fille in speche; and forth more and more   236
They fell into conversation; and more and more near

Un-to his purpos drough Aurelius,
Aurelius drew to his purpose,

And whan he saugh his tyme, he seyde thus:
And when he saw his opportunity, he spoke thus:

"Madame," quod he, "by God that this world made,
"Madam," said he, "by God Who made this world,

So that I wiste it mighte your herte glade,   240
If I knew that it would gladden your heart,

I wolde, that day that your Arveragus
I would, on that day when your Arveragus

Wente over the see, that I, Aurelius,
Went overseas, that I, Aurelius,

Had went ther never I sholde have come agayn;
Had gone whence I would never have returned;

For wel I woot my service is in vayn.   244
For well I know my service is in vain.

My guerdon is but bresting of myn herte;
My reward is but the breaking of my heart;

Madame, reweth upon my peynes smerte;
Madam, have pity on my sharp pains;

For with a word ye may me sleen or save,
For with a word you may slay or save me,

Heer at your feet God wolde that I were grave!   248
Here at your feet, would to God that I were buried!

I ne have as now no leyser more to seye;
I have now no time to say more;

Have mercy, swete, or ye wol do me deye!"
Have mercy, sweet, or you will cause my death!"

She gan to loke up-on Aurelius:
She turned to look upon Aurelius:

"Is this your wil," quod she, "and sey ye thus?   252
"Is this your desire," said she, "and say you so?

Never erst," quod she, "ne wiste I what ye mente.
Never before," said she, "did I know what you meant.

But now, Aurelie, I knowe your entente,
But now, Aurelius, I know your intent,

By thilke God that yaf me soule and lyf,
By that God Who gave me soul and life,

Ne shal I never been untrewe wyf   256
I shall never be an unfaithful wife

In word ne werk, as fer as I have wit:
In word or deed, as far as I have my wits:

I wol ben his to whom that I am knit;
I will be his to whom I am joined;

Tak this for fynal answer as of me."
Take this for my final answer."

And after that in pley thus seyde she: 260
And after that in fun she spoke thus:

"Aurelie," quod she, "by heighe God above,
"Aurelius," said she, "by the high God above,

Yet wolde I graunte yow to been your love,
Yet would I agree to be your love,

Sin I yow see so pitously complayne;
Since I see you complain so piteously,

Loke what day that, endelong Britayne,   264
On that day when, the length of Brittany,

Ye remoeve alle the rokkes, stoon by stoon,
You remove all the rocks, stone by stone,

That they ne lette ship ne boot to goon—
So that they hinder neither ship nor boat—

I seye, whan ye han maad the coost so clene
I say, when you have made the coast so free

Of rokkes, that ther nis no stoon y-sene,   *268*
Of rocks, that there is no stone seen,

Than wol I love yow best of any man;
Then will I love you best of any man;

Have heer my trouthe in al that ever I can."
Take here my pledge for anything I can give."

"Is ther non other grace in yow?" quod he.
"Is there no other grace in you?" said he.

"No, by that lord," quod she, "that maked me!   *272*
"No, by that Lord," said she, "Who made me!

For wel I woot that it shal never bityde.
For well I know that it shall never happen.

Lat swiche folies out of your herte slyde.
Let such folly disappear from your heart.

What deyntee sholde a man han in his lyf
What pleasure would a man have in his life

For to go love another mannes wyf,   *276*
To go love another man's wife,

That hath hir body whan so that him lyketh?"
Who has her body whenever he pleases?"

   Aurelius ful ofte sore syketh;
   Aurelius sighed bitterly again and again;

Wo was Aurelie, whan that he this herde,
Woe was Aurelius, when he heard this,

And with a sorweful herte he thus answerde: *280*
And with a sorrowful heart he answered thus:

   "Madame," quod he, "this were an inpossible!
   "Madam," said he, "this is impossible!

Than moot I dye of sodein deth horrible."
Then must I die a sudden horrible death."

And with that word he turned him anoon.
And with that word he turned away at once.

Tho come hir othere freendes many oon,   *284*
Then came many of her other friends,

And in the aleyes romeden up and doun,
And wandered up and down the paths,

And no-thing wiste of this conclusioun,
And knew nothing of this affair,

But sodeinly bigonne revel newe
But quickly resumed their merrymaking

Til that the brighte sonne loste his hewe;   *288*
Until the bright sun lost his brilliance;

For th'orisonte hath reft the sonne his light;
For the horizon had robbed the sun of his light;

This is as muche to seye as it was night.
This is as much as to say that it was night.

And hoom they goon in joye and in solas,
And home they went in joy and contentment,

Save only wrecche Aurelius, allas!   *292*
Except only wretched Aurelius, alas!

He to his hous is goon with sorweful herte;
He went to his house with sorrowful heart;

He seeth he may nat fro his deeth asterte.
He saw that he could not avoid his death.

Him semed that he felte his herte colde;
He fancied that he felt his heart grow cold;

Up to the hevene his handes he gan holde,   *296*
He held up his hands to the heavens,

And on his knowes bare he sette him doun,
And fell down on his bare knees,

And in his raving seyde his orisoun.
And in his frenzy spoke his prayer.

For verray wo out of his wit he breyde.
For very grief he went out of his mind.

He niste what he spak, but thus he seyde;   300
He knew not what he was saying, but thus he spoke;

With pitous herte his pleynt hath he bigonne
With piteous heart he began his plea

Un-to the goddes, and first un-to the sonne:
To the gods, and first to the sun:

  He seyde, "Appollo, god and governour
  He said, "Apollo, god and ruler

Of every plaunte, herbe, tree and flour,   304
Of every plant, herb, tree, and flower,

That yevest, after thy declinacioun,
Who givest, according to thy revolutions,

To ech of hem his tyme and his sesoun,
To each of them his time and his season,

As thyn herberwe chaungeth lowe or hye,
As thy dwelling changes low or high,

Lord Phebus, cast thy merciable yë   308
Lord Phoebus, cast thy merciful eye

On wrecche Aurelie, which that am but lorn.
On wretched Aurelius, who am but lost.

Lo, lord! my lady hath my deeth y-sworn
See, lord! my lady has sworn my death

With-oute gilt, but thy benignitee
Without guilt, unless thy goodness

Upon my dedly herte have som pitee!   312
Have some pity on my dying heart!

For wel I woot, Lord Phebus, if yow lest,
For well I know, Lord Phoebus, if it pleases thee,

Ye may me helpen, save my lady, best.
Thou mayst help me best of anyone except my lady.

Now voucheth sauf that I may yow devyse
Now vouchsafe that I may tell thee

How that I may been holpe and in what wyse.　　　　316
How I can be helped and in what way.

"Your blisful suster, Lucina the shene,
"Thy blessed sister, Lucina the bright,

That of the see is chief goddesse and quene,
Who is chief goddess and queen of the sea,

Though Neptunus have deitee in the see,
Though Neptune hath lordship over the sea,

Yet emperesse aboven him is she:　　　　320
Yet is she empress above him:

Ye knowen wel, lord, that right as hir desyr
Thou knowest well, lord, that just as her desire

Is to be quiked and lightned of your fyr,
Is to be quickened and lighted by your fire,

For which she folweth yow ful bisily,
Wherefore she follows you most earnestly,

Right so the see desyreth naturelly　　　　324
Even so the sea desires naturally

To folwen hir, as she that is goddesse
To follow her, since she is goddess

Bothe in the see and riveres more and lesse.
Both of the sea and rivers large and small.

Wherefore, lord Phebus, this is my requeste—
Wherefore, Lord Phoebus, this is my request—

Do this miracle, or do myn herte breste—　　　　328
Perform this miracle, or break my heart—

That now, next at this opposicioun,
That in your next opposition,'

Which in the signe shal be of the Leoun,
Which will be in the sign of the Lion,

As preyeth hir so greet a flood to bringe,
Do thou beseech her to bring so great a flood

That fyve fadme at the leest it overspringe   332
That it will cover by at least five fathoms

The hyeste rokke in Armorik Briteyne;
The highest rock in Armorican Brittany;

And lat this flood endure yeres tweyne;
And let this flood last for two years;

Than certes to my lady may I seye:
Then indeed I may say to my lady:

'Holdeth your heste, the rokkes been aweye.'   336
'Keep your promise, the rocks are gone.'

"Lord Phebus, dooth this miracle for me;
"Lord Phoebus, perform this miracle for me;

Preye hir she go no faster cours than ye;
Ask her to go at no faster rate than you;

I seye, preyeth your suster that she go
I say, beseech your sister to go

No faster cours than ye thise yeres two.   340
No faster than you for these two years.

Than shal she been evene atte fulle always,
Then will she be always just at the full,

And spring-flood laste bothe night and day.
And spring flood will last both night and day.

And, but she vouch-sauf in swiche manere
And, if she will not grant in this way

To graunte me my sovereyn lady dere,   344
To give me my sovereign lady dear,

Prey hir to sinken every rok adoun
Pray her to sink every rock down

In-to hir owene derke regioun
Into her own dark realm

Under the ground, ther Pluto dwelleth inne,
Under the ground, wherein Pluto dwells,

Or never-mo shal I my lady winne.   348
Or nevermore shall I win my lady.

Thy temple in Delphos wol I barefoot seke;
Thy temple in Delphi will I seek barefoot;

Lord Phebus, see the teres on my cheke,
Lord Phoebus, see the tears on my cheek,

And of my peyne have som compassioun."
And have compassion on my suffering."

And with that word in swowne he fil adoun,   352
And with that word he fell down in a swoon,

And longe tyme he lay forth in a traunce.
And for a long time he lay in a trance.

His brother, which that knew of his penaunce,
His brother, who knew of his trouble,

Up caughte him and to bedde he hath him broght.
Picked him up and carried him to bed.

Dispeyred in this torment and this thoght   356
Despairing in this torment and this brooding,

Lete I this woful creature lye;
I leave this woebegone creature lying;

Chese he, for me, whether he wol live or dye.
Let him choose, for all of me, whether to live or die.

Arveragus, with hele and greet honour,
Arveragus, with health and great honor,

As he that was of chivalrye the flour,   360
As one who was the flower of chivalry,

Is comen hoom, and othere worthy men.
Came home along with other worthy men.

O blisful artow now, thou, Dorigen,
O happy are you now, Dorigen,

That hast thy lusty housbonde in thyne armes,
Who have your lusty husband in your arms,

The fresshe knight, the worthy man of armes,   364
The fresh knight, the worthy man of arms,

That loveth thee, as his owene hertes lyf.
Who loves you as his own heartbeat.

No-thing list him to been imaginatyf
It never occurred to him to be inquisitive

If any wight had spoke, whyl he was oute,
If any man had spoken, while he was away,

To hire of love; he hadde of it no doute.   368
To her of love; he had no suspicion of it.

He noght entendeth to no swich matere,
He was not concerned with any such matter,

But daunceth, justeth, maketh hir good chere;
But danced, jousted, and made her good cheer;

And thus in joye and blisse I lete hem dwelle,
And thus I leave them living in joy and bliss,

And of the syke Aurelius wol I telle.   372
And I will speak of the sick Aurelius.

In langour and in torment furious
In languor and in frantic torment

Two yeer and more lay wrecche Aurelius,
Two years and more lay wretched Aurelius

Er any foot he mighte on erthe goon;
Before he could set foot on earth;

Ne confort in this tyme hadde he noon,   376
Nor did he have any comfort during this time

Save of his brother, which that was a clerk;
Except from his brother, who was a clerk;

He knew of al this wo and al this werk.
He knew of all this woe and all this labor.

For to non other creature certeyn
For surely to no other creature

Of this matere he dorste no word seyn.   *380*
Dared he speak a word of this matter.

Under his brest he bar it more secree
Within his heart he bore it more secretly

Than ever dide Pamphilus for Galathee.
Than did Pamphilius for Galatea.'

His brest was hool, with-oute for to sene,
His breast was unscarred, to see it from without,

But in his herte ay was the arwe kene.   *384*
But ever in his heart was the pointed arrow.

And wel ye knowe that of a sursanure
And you well know that a surface healing

In surgerye is perilous the cure,
In surgery is perilous to recovery,

But men mighte touche the arwe, or come therby.
Unless men can touch the arrow, or get at it.

His brother weep and wayled prively,   *388*
His brother wept and wailed secretly,

Til atte laste him fil in remembraunce,
Until at last he happened to remember

That whyl he was at Orliens in Fraunce,
That when he was at Orleans in France,

As yonge clerkes, that been likerous
Just as young clerks, who are eager

To reden artes that been curious,   *392*
To study exotic arts,

Seken in every halke and every herne
Search in every nook and cranny

Particuler sciences for to lerne,
To learn special sciences,

He him remembred that, upon a day,
It occurred to him that, one day,

At Orliens in studie a book he say   396
At Orleans in a study he saw a book

Of magik naturel, which his felawe,
Of natural magic, which his friend,

That was that tyme a bacheler of lawe,
Who was at that time a law student,

Al were he ther to lerne another craft,
Although he was there to study another art,

Had prively upon his desk y-laft;   400
Had left unwittingly on his desk;

Which book spak muchel of the operaciouns,
Which book told much of the operations

Touchinge the eighte and twenty mansiouns
Concerning the twenty-eight mansions'.

That longen to the mone, and swich folye,
That belong to the moon, and such nonsense,

As in our dayes is nat worth a flye;   404
As in our day is not worth a fly;

For holy chirches feith in our bileve
For Holy Church's faith in our belief

Ne suffreth noon illusion us to greve.
Does not allow any illusion to hurt us.

And whan this book was in his remembraunce,
And when this book came to his mind,

Anon for joye his herte gan to daunce,   408
At once for joy his heart began to dance,

And to him-self he seyde prively:
And to himself he said secretly:

"My brother shal be warisshed hastily;
"My brother shall be quickly cured;

For I am siker that ther be sciences,
For I am sure that there are sciences

By whiche men make diverse apparences   *412*
By which men create various apparitions

Swiche as thise subtile tregetoures pleye.
Such as these clever magicians put on.

For ofte at festes have I wel herd seye,
For often at banquets, I have heard told,

That tregetours, with-inne an halle large,
That magicians, within a large hall,

Have maad come in a water and a barge,   *416*
Have made appear water and a barge,

And in the halle rowen up and doun.
And made it sail up and down in the hall.

Somtyme hath semed come a grim leoun;
Sometimes there seemed to appear a fierce lion;

And somtyme floures springe as in a mede;
And sometimes flowers sprang up as in a meadow;

Somtyme a vyne, and grapes whyte and rede;   *420*
Sometimes a vine and white and red grapes;

Somtyme a castel, al of lym and stoon;
Sometimes a castle made of stone and mortar;

And whan hem lyked, voyded it anoon.
And when they pleased, made it disappear.

Thus semed it to every mannes sighte.
Thus it seemed to every man's sight.

"Now than conclude I thus, that if I mighte   *424*
"Now then I so conclude, that if I could

At Orliens som old felawe y-finde,
Find at Orleans some old friend,

That hadde this mones mansions in minde,
Who had these moon's mansions in mind,

Or other magik naturel above,
Or other natural magic besides,

He sholde wel make my brother han his love.   428
He would easily make my brother have his love.

For with an apparence a clerk may make
For with an apparition a clerk can make it seem

To mannes sighte, that alle the rokkes blake
To man's sight, that all the black rocks

Of Britaigne weren y-voyded everichon,
Of Brittany have vanished,

And shippes by the brinke comen and gon,   432
And that ships come and go near the shore,

And in swich forme endure a day or two;
And that this illusion remain a day or two;

Than were my brother warisshed of his wo.
Then would my brother be cured of his grief.

Than moste she nedes holden hir biheste,
Then she must needs keep her promise,

Or elles he shal shame hir atte leste."   436
Or else he shall shame her at least."

What sholde I make a lenger tale of this?
Why should I make a longer tale of this?

Un-to his brotheres bed he comen is,
He came to his brother's bed,

And swich confort he yaf him for to gon
And gave him such encouragement to go

To Orliens, that he up stirte anon,   440
To Orleans, that he jumped up at once,

And on his wey forthward thanne is he fare,
And then pursued his way onward,

In hope to ben lissed of his care.
In hope of being eased of his trouble.

Whan they were come almost to that citee,
When they had almost arrived at that city,

But-if it were a two furlong or three,   44
All but perhaps two or three furlongs,

A yong clerk rominge by him-self they mette,
They met a young clerk wandering by himself,

Which that in Latin thriftily hem grette,
Who greeted them circumspectly in Latin,

And after that he seyde a wonder thing:
And after that he said a wondrous thing:

"I knowe," quod he, "the cause of your coming;"   448
"I know," said he, "the reason for your coming;"

And er they ferther any fote wente,
And before they went a step farther,

He tole hem al that was in hir entente.
He told them all their intentions.

This Briton clerk him asked of felawes
This Breton clerk asked him about his friends

The whiche that he had knowe in olde dawes;   452
Whom he had known in the old days;

And he answerde him that they dede were,
And he replied to him that they were dead,

For which he weep ful ofte many a tere.
Wherefore he wept many a tear.

Doun of his hors Aurelius lighte anon,
Down from his horse Aurelius alighted at once,

And forth with this magicien is he gon   456
And went forth with this magician

Hoom to his hous, and made hem wel at ese.
Home to his house, where they were made comfortable.

Hem lakked no vitaille that mighte hem plese;
They lacked no food that might please them;

So wel arrayed hous as ther was oon
So well furnished a house as that one

Aurelius in his lyf saugh never noon.   *460*
Aurelius never saw in his life.

He shewed him, er he wente to sopeer,
He showed him, before he went to supper,

Forestes, parkes ful of wilde deer;
Forests, parks full of wild deer;

Ther saugh he hertes with hir hornes hye,
There he saw harts with their lofty antlers,

The gretteste that ever were seyn with yë.   *464*
The largest that were ever seen by the eye.

He saugh of hem an hondred slayn with houndes,
He saw a hundred of them slain by hounds,

And somme with arwes blede of bittre woundes.
And some bleeding with bitter arrow wounds.

He saugh, whan voided were thise wilde deer,
He saw, when these wild deer vanished,

Thise fauconers upon a fair river,   *468*
Some falconers on a fair river,

That with hir haukes han the heron slayn.
Who slew the heron with their hawks.

Tho saugh he knightes justing in a playn;
Then he saw knights jousting on a plain;

And after this, he dide him swich plesaunce,
And after that, he gave him such pleasure

That he him shewed his lady on a daunce   *472*
That he showed him his lady in a dance

On which him-self he daunced, as him thoughte.
In which he himself joined, as it seemed to him.

And whan this maister, that this magik wroughte,
And when this master, who performed this magic,

Saugh it was tyme, he clapte his handes two,
Saw it was time, he clapped his two hands,

And farewell al our revel was ago.   476
And farewell! all our revel was gone.

And yet remoeved they never out of the hous,
And yet they never moved out of the house,

Whyl they saugh al this sighte merveillous,
While they saw all these marvellous sights,

But in his studie, ther-as his bookes be,
But in his study, where his books were,

They seten stille, and no wight but they three.   480
They sat still, and the three of them alone.

　To him this maister called his squyer,
　This master called his squire to him,

And seyde him thus: "is redy our soper?
And said to him thus: "Is our supper ready?

Almost an houre it is, I undertake,
It is almost an hour, I warrant,

Sith I yow bad our soper for to make,   484
Since I told you to prepare our supper,

Whan that thise worthy men wenten with me
When these worthy men went with me

In-to my studie, ther-as my bookes be."
Into my study, where my books are."

　"Sire," quod this squyer, "whan it lyketh yow,
　"Sir," said this squire, "when it pleases you,

It is al redy, though ye wol right now."   488
It is all ready, though you wish it right now."

"Go we than soupe," quod he, "as for the beste;
"Let us go sup then," said he, "for that is best;

This amorous folk som-tyme mote han reste."
These amorous people must rest sometime."

At-after soper fille they in tretee,
After supper they fell into discussion

What somme sholde this maistres guerdon be,   492
About how much this master should be paid

To remoeven alle the rokkes of Britayne,
To remove all the rocks of Brittany,

And eek from Gerounde to the mouth of Sayne.
From the Gironde to the mouth of the Seine.

He made it straunge, and swoor, so God him save,
He made it difficult, and swore, as God might save him,

Lasse than a thousand pound he wolde nat have,   496
He would not take less than a thousand pounds,

Ne gladly for that somme he wolde nat goon.
And that he wasn't anxious to do it for that.

Aurelius, with blisful herte anoon,
Aurelius, at once with happy heart,

Answerde thus, "fy on a thousand pound!
Answered thus, "Fie on a thousand pounds!

This wyde world, which that men seye is round,   500
This wide world, which men say is round,

I woulde it yeve, if I were lord of it.
I would give, if I were lord of it.

This bargayn if ful drive, for we ben knit.
This bargain is fully driven, for we are agreed.

Ye shal be payed trewely, by my trouthe!
You shall be faithfully paid, on my honor!

But loketh now, for no necligence or slouthe,   504
But take care that, from neglectfulness or sloth,

Ye tarie us heer no lenger than to-morwe."
You keep us here no longer than tomorrow."

"Nay," quod this clerk, "have heer my feith to borwe."
"No," said this clerk, "take my word as a pledge."

To bedde is goon Aurelius whan him leste,
Aurelius went to bed when he was ready,

And wel ny al that night he hadde his reste;   508
And slept well nearly all that night;

What for his labour and his hope of blisse,
Since of his tribulation and hope of bliss

His woful herte of penaunce hadde a lisse.
His woeful heart had relief from grieving.

Upon the morwe, whan that it was day,
In the morning, when it was light,

To Britaigne toke they the righte way,   512
To Brittany they took the shortest way,

Aurelius, and this magicien bisyde,
Aurelius, and this magician with him,

And been descended ther they wolde abyde;
And they alighted where they planned to stay;

And this was, as the bokes me remembre,
And this was, as the books remind me,

The colde frosty seson of Decembre.   516
The cold frosty season of December.

Phebus wex old, and hewed lyk latoun,
Phoebus waxed old and copper-colored,

That in his hote declinacioun
Who in his hot summit

Shoon as the burned gold with stremes brighte;
Had shone like burnished gold with bright beams;

But now in Capricorn adoun he lighte,   520
But now he had settled down in Capricorn

Wher-as he shoon ful pale, I dar wel seyn.
Where he shone most pale, I dare well assert.

The bittre frostes, with the sleet and reyn,
The bitter frosts, with the sleet and rain,

Destroyed hath the grene in every yerd.
Had killed the greenery in every yard.

Janus sit by the fyr, with double berd,   524
January sat by the fire, with twin beard,

And drinketh of his bugle-horn the wyn.
And drank wine from his ox-horn.

Biforn him stant braun of the tusked swyn,
Before him was the flesh of the tusked boar,

And "Nowel" cryeth every lusty man.
And "Noël" shouted every lusty man.

Aurelius, in al that ever he can,   528
Aurelius, in everything that lay in his power,

Doth to his maister chere and reverence,
Made cheer and comfort for his master,

And preyeth him to doon his diligence
And begged him to perform his services

To bringen him out of his peynes smerte,
To bring him out of his sharp pains,

Or with a swerd that he wolde slitte his herte.   532
Or else he would slice his heart with a sword.

This subtil clerk swich routhe had of this man,
This clever clerk had such pity for this man,

That night and day he spedde him that he can,
That night and day he hastened as much as possible

To wayte a tyme of his conclusioun;
To find an auspicious time for his operations;

This is to seye, to make illusioun,   536
That is to say, to create an apparition,

By swich an apparence or jogelrye,
By such an illusion or sleight-of-hand,

I ne can no termes of astrologye,
(I don't know the astrological terms)

That she and every wight sholde wene and seye,
So that she and everybody would believe and say

That of Britaigne the rokkes were aweye,   540
That the rocks of Brittany had vanished,

Or elles they were sonken under grounde.
Or else that they had sunk beneath the earth.

So atte laste he hath his tyme y-founde
So at last he found the right time

To maken his japes and his wrecchednesse
To work his tricks and his skulduggery

Of swich a supersticious cursednesse.   544
Of that sort of superstitious cursedness.

His tables Toletanes forth he broght,
He produced his Arabic tables,

Ful wel corrected, ne ther lakked noght,
Perfectly corrected, so that nothing was lacking,

Neither his collect ne his expans yeres,
Neither his data on single years or long periods,

Ne his rotes ne his othere geres,   548
Nor his root-numbers nor his other accessories,

As been his centres and his arguments,
Such as his focal points and his base figures,

And his proporcionels convenients
And his suitable proportionals

For his equacions in every thing.
For his equations for each operation.

And, by his eighte spere in his wirking,   552
And, by the eighth sphere in his calculations,

He knew ful wel how fer Alnath was shove
He knew exactly how far the star Alnath had moved

Fro the heed of thilke fixe Aries above
From the head of that fixed Aries in the sky,

That in the ninthe speere considered is;
Which is held to be in the ninth sphere;

Ful subtilly he calculed al this.   556
Most cleverly he calculated all this.

   Whan he had founde his firste mansioun,
   When he had located his first mansion,

He knew the remenant by proporcioun;
He knew the rest by proportion;

And knew the arysing of his mone weel,
And well understood the rising of the moon,

And in whos face, and terme, and everydeel;   560
And in what planet's face, and its period, and the rest;

And knew ful weel the mones mansioun
And knew very well that the moon's mansion

Acordaunt to his operacioun,
Was right for his operations,

And knew also his othere observaunces
And knew also his other devices

For swiche illusiouns and swiche meschaunces   564
For such illusions and such evil practices

As hethen folk used in thilke dayes;
As heathens used in those days;

For which no lenger maked he delayes,
Wherefore he made no further delay,

But thurgh his magik, for a wyke or tweye,
But through his magic, for a week or two,

It semed that alle the rokkes were aweye.   568
It seemed that all the rocks had disappeared.

   Aurelius, which that yet despeired is
   Aurelius, who was still in despair

Wher he shal han his love or fare amis,
Whether he would have his love or fare badly,

Awaiteth night and day on this miracle;
Waited night and day for this miracle;

And whan he knew that ther was noon obstacle,   572
And when he knew that there was no obstacle,

That voided were thise rokkes everichon,
And that all the rocks had disappeared,

Doun to his maistres feet he fil anon,
Down at his master's feet he fell at once,

And seyde, "I woful wrecche, Aurelius,
And said, "I, woebegone wretch, Aurelius,

Thanke yow, lord, and lady myn Venus,   576
Thank you, lord, and my lady Venus,

That me han holpen fro my cares colde:"
Who have relieved me from my bitter cares;"

And to the temple his wey forth hath he holde,
And he made his way toward the temple

Wher-as he knew he sholde his lady see.
Where he knew he would see his lady.

And whan he saugh his tyme, anon-right he,   580
And when he saw an opportunity, instantly he,

With dredful herte and with ful humble chere,
With fearful heart and most humble looks,

Salewed hath his sovereyn lady dere:
Greeted his sovereign lady dear:

"My righte lady," quod this woful man,
"My true lady," said this miserable man,

"Whom I most drede and love as I best can,   584
"Whom I most fear and love as best I can,

And lothest were of al this world displese,
And whom of all this world I would least displease,

Nere it that I for yow have swich disese,
Were it not that for you I have such a malady

That I moste dyen heer at your foot anon,
That I must die at once here at your feet,

Noght wolde I telle how me is wo bigon;   588
I would not tell you how wretched I am;

But certes outher moste I dye or pleyne;
But truly either I must die or complain;

Ye slee me giltelees for verray peyne.
You kill me, guiltless, for very pain.

But of my deeth, thogh that ye have no routhe,
But if you have no pity for my death,

Avyseth yow, er that ye breke your trouthe.   592
Consider well, before you break your pledge.

Repenteth yow, for thilke God above,
Repent, by that God above,

Er ye me sleen by-cause that I yow love.
Before you slay me because I love you.

For, madame, wel ye woot what ye han hight;
For, madam, you well know what you promised;

Nat that I chalange any thing of right,   596
Not that I enforce anything, as by right,

Of yow my sovereyn lady, but your grace;
Of you, my sovereign lady, except your mercy;

But in a gardin yond, at swich a place,
But in a garden yonder, in a certain place,

Ye woot right wel what ye bihighten me;
You know right well what you promised me;

And in myn hand your trouthe plighten ye   600
And in my hand you made your pledge

To love me best, God woot, ye seyde so,
To love me best, God knows you said so

Al be that I unworthy be therto.
Although I am unworthy of your love.

Madame, I speke it for the honour of yow,
Madam, I say this more for your honor,

More than to save myn hertes lyf right now: 604
Than to save the beating of my heart right now:

I have do so as ye comanded me;
I have done as you commanded me;

And if ye vouche-sauf, ye may go see.
And if you will be so good, you may go and see.

Doth as yow list, have your biheste in minde,
Do as you please, keep your promise in mind,

For quik or deed, right ther ye shul me finde;   608
For quick or dead, you shall find me right there;

In yow lyth al, to do me live or deye;—
On you everything depends, to let me live or die;—

But wel I woot the rokkes been aweye!"
But well I know the rocks are gone!"

  He taketh his leve, and she astonied stood,
  He took his leave, and she stood astounded.

In al hir face nas a drope of blood;   612
In all her face was not a drop of blood;

She wende never han come in swich a trappe:
She never thought to have come into such a trap:

"Allas!" quod she, "that ever this sholde happe!
"Alas!" said she, "that ever this should happen!

For wende I never, by possibilitee,
For I never dreamed, by any possibility,

That swich a monstre or merveille might be!   616
That such a monstrosity or miracle could occur!

It is agayns the proces of nature;"
It is against the laws of nature;"

And hoom she gooth a sorweful creature.
And home she went a sorrowful creature.

For verray fere unnethe may she go,
For very fear she could hardly walk,

She wepeth, wailleth, al a day or two,　　　　　　620
She wept and wailed all of a day or two,

And swowneth, that it routhe was to see;
And swooned, so that it was pitiful to see;

But why it was, to no wight tolde she;
But the reason for it she told no one;

For out of toune was goon Arveragus.
For Arveragus had gone out of town.

But to hir-self she spak, and seyde thus,　　　　　624
But she consulted with herself, and said thus,

With face pale and with ful sorweful chere,
With pale face and most sorrowful appearance,

In hir compleynt, as ye shul after here:
In her lament, as you shall soon hear:

"Allas," quod she, "on thee, Fortune, I pleyne,
"Alas," said she, "of thee, Fortune, I complain,

That unwar wrapped hast me in thy cheyne;　　　628
Who hast wrapped me unwittingly in thy chains;

For which, t'escape, woot I no socour
To escape from which, I know of no salvation

Save only deeth or elles dishonour;
Save only death or else dishonor;

Oon of thise two bihoveth me to chese.
One of these two I am forced to choose.

But nathelees, yet have I lever lese　　　　　　632
But nevertheless, yet I would rather lose

My lyf than of my body have a shame,
My life than endure the shaming of my body,

Or knowe my-selven fals, or lese my name,
Or know myself false, or lose my good name,

And with my deth I may be quit, y-wis.
And with my death I may be free, I know.

Hath ther nat many a noble wyf, er this,   636
Has not many a noble wife, before this,

And many a mayde y-slayn hir-self, allas!
And many a maiden slain herself, alas!

Rather than with hir body doon trespas?
Rather than do wrong with her body?

"Yis, certes, lo, thise stories beren witnesse;
"Yes, of a truth, see, these stories bear witness;

Whan thretty tyraunts, ful of cursednesse,   640
When thirty tyrants, full of wickedness,

Had slayn Phidoun in Athenes, atte feste,
Had slain Phidon at a feast in Athens,

They comanded his doghtres for t'areste,
They commanded his daughters to be seized,

And bringen hem biforn hem in despyt,
And brought before them, out of spite,

Al naked, to fulfille hir foul delyt,   644
All naked, to fulfill their foul pleasure,

And in hir fadres blood they made hem daunce
And they made them dance in their father's blood

Upon the pavement, God yeve hem mischaunce!
Upon the pavement, God send them misfortune!

For which thise woful maydens, ful of drede,
Wherefore these miserable maidens, full of fear,

Rather than they wolde lese hir maydenhede,   648
Rather than lose their maidenhood,

They prively ben stirt in-to a welle,
Secretly jumped into a well,

And dreynte hem-selven, as the bokes telle.
And drowned themselves, as the books say.

"They of Messene lete enquere and seke
"They of Messina caused to be sought out

Of Lacedomie fifty maydens eke,   652
Fifty maidens from Lacedaemon, also,

On whiche they wolden doon hir lecherye;
On whom they would do their lechery;

But was ther noon of al that companye
But there was none of all that company

That she nas slayn, and with a good entente
Who was not killed, and with good intent

Chees rather for to dye than assente   656
Choosing rather to die than consent

To been oppressed of hir maydenhede.
To be ravished of her maidenhood.

Why sholde I thanne to dye been in drede?
Why then should I be afraid to die?

"Lo, eek, the tiraunt Aristoclides
"Consider too the tyrant Aristoclides,

That loved a mayden, heet Stimphalides,   660
Who loved a maiden named Stymphalis,

Whan that hir fader slayn was on a night,
When her father was slain one night,

Un-to Dianes temple goth she right,
She went directly to Diana's temple,

And hente the image in hir handes two,
And grasped the statue in her two hands,

Fro which image wolde she never go.   664
And would never leave the statue.

No wight ne mighte hir handes of it arace,
No one could tear her hands from it,

Til she was slayn right in the selve place.
Until she was slain right on that very spot.

Now sith that maydens hadden swich despyt
Now since maidens had such scorn

To been defouled with mannes foul delyt,   668
Of being defiled with man's foul pleasure,

Wel oghte a wyf rather hir-selven slee
Well ought a wife rather kill herself

Than be defouled, as it thinketh me.
Than be defiled, as it seems to me.

   "What shal I seyn of Hasdrubales wyf,
   "What shall I say of Hasdrubal's wife,

That at Cartage birafte hir-self hir lyf?   672
Who at Carthage took her life?

For whan she saugh that Romayns wan the toun,
For when she saw that the Romans had won the town,

She took hir children alle, and skipte adoun
She took all her children, and leaped down

In-to the fyr, and chees rather to dye
Into the fire, and chose rather to die

Than any Romayn dide hir vileinye.   676
Than allow any Roman to harm her.

   "Hath nat Lucresse y-slayn hir-self, allas!
   "Did not Lucrece slay herself, alas!

At Rome, whanne she oppressed was
At Rome, when she was violated

Of Tarquin, for hir thoughte it was a shame
By Tarquin, for she thought it was shameful

To liven whan she hadde lost hir name?   680
To live when she had lost her good name?

   "The sevene maydens of Milesie also
   "The seven maidens of Miletus also

Han slayn hem-self, for verray drede and wo,
Killed themselves, for very fear and misery,

Rather than folk of Gaule hem sholde oppresse.
Rather than be violated by men of Gaul.

Mo than a thousand stories, as I gesse,   684
More than a thousand stories, as I imagine,

Coude I now telle as touchinge this matere.
Could I now tell concerning this subject.

"Whan Habradate was slayn, his wyf so dere
"When Abradates was slain, his wife so dear

Hirselven slow, and leet hir blood to glyde
Killed herself, and let her blood flow

In Habradates woundes depe and wyde,   688
Into Abradates' deep and broad wounds,

And seyde, 'my body, at the leeste way,
And said, 'My body, in the slightest way,

Ther shal no wight defoulen, if I may.'
No man shall defile, if I can prevent it.'

"What sholde I mo ensamples heer-of sayn,
"Why should I speak of more examples of this,

Sith that so manye han hem-selven slayn   692
Since so many have slain themselves

Wel rather than they wolde defouled be?
Rather than allow themselves to be defiled?

I wol conclude, that it is bet for me
I will conclude, that it is better for me

To sleen my-self, than been defouled thus.
To slay myself, than to be thus defiled.

I wol be trewe un-to Arveragus,   696
I will be faithful to Arveragus,

Or rather sleen my-self in som manere,
Or else slay myself in some way,

As dide Demociones doghter dere,
As Demotion's dear daughter did,

By-cause that she wolde nat defouled be.
Because she would not be defiled.

   "O Cedasus! it is ful greet pitee,   700
   "O Scedasus! it is a most great pity

To reden how thy doghtren deyde, allas!
To read how your daughtors died, alas!

That slowe hem-selven for swich maner cas.
Who killed themselves for the same reason.

   "As greet a pitee was it, or wel more,
   "As great a pity was it, or even more,

The Theban mayden, that for Nichanore   704
The Theban maiden, who for Nicanor

Hir-selven slow, right for swich maner wo.
Killed herself, for exactly the same kind of woe.

   "Another Theban mayden dide right so;
   "Another Theban maiden did the same;

For oon of Macedoine hadde hir oppressed,
Because one of Macedonia had violated her,

She with hir deeth hir maydenhede redressed.   708
She with her death redressed her maidenhood.

   "What shal I seye of Nicerates wyf,
   "What shall I say of the wife of Niceratus,

That for swich cas birafte hir-self hir lyf?
Who took her life for this reason?

   "How trewe eek was to Alcebiades
   "How true too to Alcibiades was

His love, that rather for to dyen chees   712
His love, who chose rather to die

Than for to suffre his body unburied be!
Than to suffer his body to remain unburied!

Lo which a wyf was Alceste," quod she.
See what a wife Alcestis was," said she.

"What seith Omer of gode Penalopee?
"What does Homer say of good Penelope?

Al Grece knoweth of hir chastitee. 716
All Greece knows of her chastity.

"Pardee, of Laodomya is writen thus,
"By heaven, of Laodamia it is so written,

That whan at Troye was slayn Protheselaus,
That when Protesilaus was slain at Troy,

No lenger wolde she live after his day.
No longer would she live beyond his day.

"The same of noble Porcia telle I may; 720
"The same of noble Portia I may narrate;

With-oute Brutus coude she nat live,
She could not live without Brutus,

To whom she hadde al hool hir herte yive.
To whom she had given her whole heart.

"The parfit wyfhod of Arthemesye
"The perfect wifehood of Artemisia

Honoured is thurgh al the Barbarye. 724
Is honored throughout all barbarian lands.

"O Teuta, queen! thy wyfly chastitee
"O Queen Teuta! Your wifely chastity

To alle wyves may a mirour be.
To all wives may be a mirror.

The same thing I seye of Bilia,
The same thing I say of Bilia,

Of Rodogone, and eek Valeria." 728
Of Rhodogune, and Valeria too."

Thus pleyned Dorigene a day or tweye,
So Dorigen bewailed a day or two,

Purposinge ever that she wolde deye.
Intending always that she would die.

But nathelees, upon the thriddle night,
But nevertheless, upon the third night,

Hom cam Arveragus, this worthy knight,   732
Arveragus came home, that worthy knight,

And asked hir, why that she weep so sore?
And asked her why she wept so bitterly?

And she gan wepen ever lenger the more,
And she began to weep all the more.

"Allas!" quod she, "that ever was I born!
"Alas!" said she, "that I was ever born!

Thus have I seyd," quod she, "thus have I sworn"—   736
This have I said," said she, "this have I sworn"—

And told him al as ye han herd bifore;
And told him everything as you have heard;

It nedeth nat reherce it yow na-more.
There is no need to repeat it to you again.

This housbond with glad chere, in freendly wyse,
This husband with cheerful looks, in a friendly way,

Answerede and seyde as I shal yow devyse   740
Answered and said as I shall recount to you:

"Is ther oght elles, Dorigen, but this?"
"Is there anything else, Dorigen, except this?"

"Nay, nay," quod she, "God help me so, as wis;
"No, no," said she, "so God help me, since I know

This is to muche, and it were Goddes wille."
This is too much even though it were God's will."

"Ye, wyf," quod he, "lat slepen that is stille: 744
"Yes, wife," said he, "let sleep what is at rest:

It may be wel, paraventure, yet to-day.
All may yet be well today, perchance.

Ye shul your trouthe holden, by my fay!
You shall keep your promise, by my faith!

For God so wisly have mercy on me,
For may God so wisely have mercy on me,

I hadde wel lever y-stiked for to be,   748
I would much rather be stabbed,

For verray love which that I to yow have,
For the true love which I have for you,

But-if ye sholde your trouth kepe and save.
Than that you should not keep and honor your pledge.

Trouthe is the hyeste thing that man may kepe:"—
Honor is the highest thing that man may possess:"—

But with that word he brast anon to wepe,   752
But with that word at once he burst out crying,

And seyde, "I yow forbede, up peyne of deeth,
And said, "I forbid you, on pain of death,

That never, whyl thee lasteth lyf ne breeth,
Never, while you have life or breath,

To no wight tel thou of this aventure.
To tell anyone of this thing.

As I may best, I wol my wo endure,   756
As best I can, I will endure my suffering,

Ne make no contenance of hevinesse,
And give no appearance of heaviness,

That folk of yow may demen harm or gesse."
Lest people think or suspect evil of you."

And forth he cleped a squyer and a mayde:
And he called forth a squire and a maid:

"Goth forth anon with Dorigen," he sayde,   760
"Go forth at once with Dorigen," he said,

"And bringeth hir to swich a place anon."
"And take her to such and such a place at once."

They take hir leve, and on hir wey they gon;
They took their leave, and went on their way;

But they ne wiste why she thider wente.
But they did not know why she was going there.

He nolde no wight tellen his entente.   764
He would tell his intentions to no one.

   Paraventure an heep of yow, y-wis,
   Perhaps a lot of you, I imagine,

Wol holden him a lewed man in this,
Will consider him a wanton man in this,

That he wol putte his wyf in jupartye;
That he would put his wife in jeopardy;

Herkneth the tale, er ye up-on hir crye.   768
Listen to the tale, before you cry out upon her.

She may have bettre fortune than yow semeth;
She may have better fortune than you think;

And whan that ye han herd the tale, demeth.
And when you have heard the tale, make judgment.

   This squyer, which that highte Aurelius,
   This squire, who was called Aurelus,

On Dorigen that was so amorous,   772
Who was so in love with Dorigen,

Of aventure happed hir to mete
By chance happened to meet her

Amidde the toun, right in the quikkest strete,
In the middle of town, right in the busiest street,

As she was boun to goon the wey forthright
As she was going on her way directly

Toward the gardin ther-as she had hight.   776
Toward the garden as she had promised.

And he was to the gardinward also;
And he was going to the garden too;

For wel he spyed, whan she wolde go
For he kept close watch whenever she would go

Out of hir hous to any maner place.
Out of her house to any sort of place.

But thus they mette, of aventure or grace;   780
But so they met, by chance or good fortune;

And he saleweth hir with glad entente,
And he greeted her with happy heart,

And asked of hir whiderward she wente?
And asked her where she was going.

And she answerde, half as she were mad,
And she replied, half as if she were mad,

"Un-to the gardin, as myn housbond bad,   784
"To the garden, as my husband commanded,

My trouthe for to holde, allas! allas!"
To keep my promise, alas! alas!"

Aurelius gan wondren on this cas,
Aurelius wondered about this matter,

And in his herte had greet compassioun
And in his heart had great compassion

Of hir and of hir lamentacioun,   788
For her and for her lamentation,

And of Arveragus, the worthy knight,
And for Arveragus, the worthy knight,

That bad hir holden al that she had hight,
Who bade her keep all that she had promised,

So looth him was his wyf sholde breke hir trouthe;
So loath was he that his wife should break her word;

And in his herte he caughte of this greet routhe,   792
And in his heart he found great pity for this,

Consideringe the beste on every syde,
Thinking it for the best on all sides,

That fro his lust yet were him lever abyde
That he would rather refrain from his desire

Than doon so heigh a cherlish wrecchednesse
Than do so low a deed to one so noble,

Agayns franchyse and alle gentillesse;
Against liberality and all gentility;
796

For which in fewe wordes seyde he thus:
Wherefore in few words he spoke thus:

"Madame, seyth to your lord Arveragus,
"Madam, say to your lord Arveragus,

That sith I see his grete gentillesse
That since I behold his great nobility

To yow, and eek I see wel your distresse,
To you, and also well perceive your own distress,
800

That him were lever han shame (and that were routhe)
That he would rather have shame (and that were pity)

Than ye to me sholde breke thus your trouthe,
Than that you should thus break your pledge to me,

I have wel lever ever to suffre wo
I would much rather suffer eternal misery

Than I departe the love bitwix yow two.
Than sever the love between you two.
804

I yow relesse, madame, in-to your hond
I release you, madam; into your hand

Quit every surement and every bond,
I return every assurance and every bond

That he yan maad to me as heer-biforn,
That you gave me in the past

Sith thilke tyme which that ye were born.
Since the day you were born.
808

My trouthe I plighte, I shal yow never repreve
My word I pledge, I shall never reproach you

Of no biheste, and here I take my leve,
Concerning any promise, and I take here my leave,

As of the treweste and the beste wyf
As of the truest and the best wife

That ever yet I knew in al my lyf.   *812*
That I ever knew in all my life.

But every wyf be-war of hir biheste,
But let every wife be wary of her promises,

On Dorigene remembreth atte leste.
Or at least keep Dorigen in mind.

Thus can a squyer doon a gentil dede,
Thus a squire can do a noble deed

As well as can a knight, with-outen drede."   *816*
As well as a knight, beyond a doubt."

She thonketh him up-on hir knees al bare,
She thanked him on her knees all bare,

And hoom un-to hir housbond is she fare,
And went home to her husband,

And tolde him al as ye han herd me sayd;
And told him everything as you have heard me relate;

And be ye siker, he was so weel apayd,   *820*
And you may be sure, he was so well satisfied

That it were inpossible me to wryte;
That it were impossible for me to describe it;

What sholde I lenger of this cas endyte?
Why should I continue further on this subject?

Arveragus and Dorigene his wyf
Arveragus and his wife Dorigen

In sovereyn blisse leden forth hir lyf.   *824*
In perfect bliss continued to lead their lives.

Never efte ne was ther angre hem bitwene;
Never again was there trouble between them;

He cherisseth hir as though she were a quene;
He cherished her as though she were a queen;

And she was to him trewe for evermore.
And she was true to him for evermore.

Of thise two folk ye gete of me na-more.   828
Of these two people you get no more from me.

Aurelius, that his cost hath al forlorn,
Aurelius, who had lost all the expense,

Curseth the tyme that ever he was born:
Cursed the day that he was ever born:

"Allas," quod he, "allas! that I bihighte
"Alas," said he, "alas! that I promised

Of pured gold a thousand pound of wighte   832
A thousand pounds in weight of pure gold

Un-to this philosophre! how shal I do?
To that philosopher! What shall I do?

I see na-more but that I am fordo.
I see nothing except that I am ruined.

Myn heritage moot I nedes selle,
I shall have to sell my heritage

And been a begger; heer may I nat dwelle,   836
And be a beggar; I cannot live here,

And shamen al my kinrede in this place,
And shame all my kindred in this place,

But I of him may gete bettre grace.
Unless I obtain more kindness from him.

But nathelees, I wol of him assaye,
But nevertheless, I will try to arrange with him

At certeyn dayes, yeer by yeer, to paye,   840
To pay on certain days, year by year,

And thanke him of his grete curteisye;
And thank him for his great courtesy;

My trouthe wol I kepe, I wol nat lye."
My pledge I will keep, I will not be a liar."

With herte soor he gooth un-to his cofre,
With aching heart he went to his coffer,

And broghte gold un-to this philosophre,   *844*
And brought gold to this philosopher,

The value of fyve hundred pound, I gesse,
Of the value of five hundred pounds, I think,

And him bisecheth, of his gentillesse,
And besought him, by his honorableness,

To graunte him dayes of the remenaunt,
To grant him time for the remainder,

And seyde, "maister, I dar wel make avaunt,   *848*
And said, "Master, I dare well boast

I failled never of my trouthe as yit;
I have never yet failed of my promise;

For sikerly my dette shal be quit
For certainly my debt shall be paid

Towardes yow, how-ever that I fare
To you, even though I am forced

To goon a-begged in my kirtle bare.   *852*
To go begging in my bare jacket.

But wolde ye vouche-sauf, up-on seurtee,
But if you would grant, on security,

Two yeer or three for to respyten me,
Two years or three to give me respite,

Than were I wel; for elles moot I selle
It would be well for me; otherwise I must sell

Myn heritage; ther is na-more to telle."   *856*
My heritage; there is nothing more to say."

This philosophre sobrely answerde,
This philosopher soberly replied,

And seyde thus, whan he thise wordes herde:
And spoke thus, when he heard these words:

"Have I nat holden covenant un-to thee?"
"Have I not kept my agreement with you?"

"Yes, certes, wel and trewely," quod he.　　　　　860
"Yes, indeed, well and truly," said he.

"Hastow nat had thy lady as thee lyketh?"
"Have you not had your lady, as you desired?"

"No, no," quod he, and sorwefully he syketh.
"No, no," said he, and sighed sorrowfully.

"What was the cause? tel me if thou can."
"What was the reason? Tell me if you can."

Aurelius his tale anon bigan,　　　　　864
Aurelius at once began his story,

And tolde him al, as ye han herd bifore;
And told him all, as you have already heard;

It nedeth nat to yow reherce it more.
It is not necessary to repeat it again.

He seide, "Arveragus, of gentillesse,
He said, "Arveragus, out of his nobility,

Had lever dye in sorwe and in distresse　　　　　868
Would rather have died in sorrow and distress

Than that his wyf were of hir trouthe fals."
Than that his wife should be false to her pledge."

The sorwe of Dorigen he tolde him als,
The sorrow of Dorigen he told him besides,

How looth hir was to been a wikked wyf,
How loath she was to be a wicked wife,

And that she lever had lost that day hir lyf,　　　　　872
And that she would rather have lost her life that day,

And that hir trouthe she swoor, thurgh innocence:
And that she had sworn her oath through innocence:

"She never erst herde speke of apparence;
"She had never before heard tell of apparitions;

That made me han of hir so greet pitee.
That made me take so much pity on her.

And right as frely as he sente hir me,   876
And just as freely as he sent her to me,

As frely sente I hir to him ageyn.
As freely I sent her to him again.

This al and som, ther is na-more to seyn."
This is the sum and substance, there is no more to say."

   This philosophre answerde, "leve brother,
   This philosopher answered, "Dear brother,

Everich of yow dide gentilly til other.   880
Each of you behaved nobly to the other.

Thou art a squyer, and he is a knight;
You are a squire, and he is a knight;

But God forbede, for his blisful might,
But God forbid, by His blessed power,

But-if a clerk coude doon a gentil dede
That a clerk cannot do a noble deed

As wel as any of yow, it is no drede!   884
As well as any of you, beyond a doubt!

   "Sire, I relesse thee thy thousand pound,
   "Sir, I release you of your thousand pounds,

As thou right now were cropen out of the ground,
As if you had just this minute crept out of the earth,

Ne never er now ne haddest knowen me.
Or had never known me before this.

For sire, I wol nat take a peny of thee   888
For sir, I will not take a penny of you

For al my craft, ne noght for my travaille.
For all my science, nor anything for my work.

Thou hast y-payed wel for my vitaille;
You have paid well for my meals;

It is y-nogh, and farewel, have good day:"
It is enough, and farewell, good luck to you:"

And took his hors, and forth he gooth his way.   892
And he took his horse and went forth on his way.

Lordinges, this question wolde I aske now,
Gentlemen, I would now ask this question,

Which was the moste free, as thinketh yow?
Which was the most generous, as it seems to you?

Now telleth me, er that ye ferther wende.
Now tell me, before you travel farther.

I can na-more, my tale is at an ende.   896
I know no more, my tale is at an end.

Notes

1. The west wind.
2. The sun had passed half-way through the sign of the Ram (Aries) in the zodiac.
3. Pilgrims who had brought palm leaves from the Holy Land.
4. A section of London.
5. The name of the inn.
6. The Mediterranean. The Knight's battles had led him to remote sections of the medieval world. Algeciras is near Cape Trafalgar; Benmarin and Tremeyen are in northern Africa; Ayas, Adalia, and Palatia are in Asia Minor.
7. A medallion of St. Christopher, patron saint of travellers.
8. An oath by Saint Loy was the mildest possible kind of swearing.
9. A Benedictine nunnery near London. The French taught here was probably Anglo-Norman French, not the pure French of Paris.
10. A kind of bonnet, gathered round the head and pleated under the chin.
11. A monk permitted to travel on business of his order.
12. A friar licensed to beg within a specified territory.
13. Dominicans, Franciscans, Carmelites, and Augustinians comprised the four great mendicant orders.
14. The opening words of the gospel of St. John, containing the basis of the Christian mystery: "In the beginning was the Word, and the Word was with God, and the Word was God."
15. Special days appointed for the settling of disputes out of court, generally presided over by the clergy.
16. Middleburg in the Netherlands is opposite the mouth of the English river Orwell.
17. The term *philosopher* was in current use as a synonym for *alchemist*.
18. The porch of St. Paul's Church in London was a favorite meeting place for lawyers.
19. A wealthy landowner.
20. Patron saint of hospitality.

21. He made them walk the plank.
22. The proportion of the four qualities (hot, cold, moist, dry) in the human body was believed to be connected with a man's health and temperament. Sickness resulted from an excess of one of these. Most of medieval medical practice revolved around these and the four humors, red bile, black bile, phlegm, and blood, which were also responsible for producing respectively choleric, bilious, phlegmatic, and sanguine temperaments.
23. An imposing list of famous medical men from ancient to medieval times.
24. A subordinate manager on a feudal estate.
25. One whose function was to summon culprits to appear before an ecclesiastical court.
26. A seller of papal indulgences.
27. A purchaser of provisions for a college or similar institution. This manciple is a buyer for an Inn-of-Court, an organization of lawyers.
28. A reference to the proverb, "An honest miller has a golden thumb," implying that this miller was as honest as others of his trade.
29. "The question is what is the law?" This phrase was apparently in constant use in court.
30. A copy of the handkerchief which received the imprint of Christ's face when St. Veronica loaned it to Him on the way to the crucifixion.

THE KNIGHT'S TALE

1. Statius, *Thebaid*, XII, 519 f. *The Knight's Tale* is adapted from Boccaccio's *Teseide* which, in turn, was derived from the *Thebaid* by the Roman poet Statius.
2. Argus was the hundred-eyed watchman of the gods whom Hera (Juno) had commissioned to guard Io, her husband's paramour. At the request of Zeus (Jupiter), Hermes (Mercury) lulled all the eyes to sleep and made Io's escape possible.
3. Puella and Rubeus are figures in the art known as geomancy. In this branch of divination they appear to have been associated with Mars.
4. The reference is probably to the story in Ovid's *Metamor-*

phoses (III, 156) which recounts how Actaeon was turned into a stag.
5. As Diana (1. 1439), Luna (1. 1440), and Proserpina (1. 1441).
6. In northern Africa. Cf. *Prologue,* note 6.

THE MILLER'S PROLOGUE
1. Pilate was a stage villain in medieval mystery plays. The Miller swears by the arms and blood and bones of Christ.

THE REEVE'S TALE
1. There is no sensible way of translating the several passages where the students speak in their northern dialect.

THE PRIORESS'S PROLOGUE
1. This prologue follows immediately after *The Sailor's Tale.*
2. The sailor had just recounted the story of a monk who was invited to a merchant's house where he became friendly with the merchant's wife. When the merchant was about to depart on a business trip, his wife asked the monk for a hundred francs for which she had become indebted without having dared tell her husband. Just before the merchant left, the monk asked for and received from him a loan of a hundred francs. The monk then gave the money to the merchant's wife during her husband's absence in return for her bodily favors. Upon the merchant's return, the monk informed him that he had already repaid the loan to his wife.

THE PRIORESS'S INVOCATION
1. This is the Latin of the opening lines of the *Invocation,* the first stanza of which paraphrases the opening psalm of Matins in the Office of the Blessed Virgin. The remainder of the *Invocation* recalls other passages in that Office.
2. A common symbol for the Virgin Mary, as was the burning bush in the following stanza.
3. Wisdom was held to be the special attribute of Christ, the Son.

THE PRIORESS'S TALE

1. Medieval Christianity forbade the loaning of money at interest. Hence, the Jews in Europe became the professional "usurers" or money-lenders and, as such, received the opprobrium customarily accorded bankers (those other "robbers of widows and orphans") in nineteenth century melodramas. In addition to this, they were infidels in a Church-dominated world. In consequence, completely unfounded stories like this one grew up in the imaginations of people who were as eager to invent devils as to make use of charms against them. This legend remains as beautiful as it is because all the emphasis is placed on the child's martyrdom, leaving the Jew to play the role of the conventional villain.

2. The infant St. Nicholas, according to legend, sucked only once on Wednesdays and Fridays.

3. Hugh of Lincoln was murdered in 1255. A ballad recorded the story.

THE NUN'S PRIEST'S PROLOGUE

1. The monk has just regaled the company with a series of seventeen "tragedies" concerning the downfalls of famous men and women, all lamentable and designed to produce the heavy-heartedness to which the knight refers in line 3.

THE NUN'S PRIEST'S TALE

1. In medieval medicine good health was held to result from a balance of the four humors in the body. Red and black bile were two of the humors. Cf. *Prologue*, note 22.

2. The medieval Dionysius Cato, to whom was assigned the authorship of a collection of maxims.

3. Either Cicero or Valerius, both of whom tell the story.

4. Macrobius' Commentary on Cicero's *Dream of Scipio* (*De Republica*, VI) was one of the most popular medieval treatises on the subject of dreams.

5. "In the beginning, woman is man's ruin."

6. The Creation was popularly believed to have taken place in the Spring.

7. The version of the Arthurian legend here referred to was compiled by Walter Map who was notable for untruthfulness.

8. Judas Iscariot betrayed Christ, Ganelon betrayed the French hero Roland, Sinon invented the Trojan horse.
9. An English theologian (d. 1349).
10. A medieval bestiary containing moralized descriptions of animals.
11. An Anglo-Latin satirical poem, subtitled *Speculum Stultorum* (*The Mirror of Fools*), composed around 1190 by Nigellus Wireker.
12. Geoffrey de Vinsauf (c. 1200) included a specimen lament for Richard I. in his *Nova Poetria*, a handbook for poets.
13. The wife of the King of Carthage killed herself when the Romans captured the city in 146 B. C.
14. In the London insurrection of 1381 many Flemings were killed.

THE PARDONER'S PROLOGUE
1. "Avarice is the root of all evil," 2 *Timothy*, III, 16.
2. Possibly Jacob is intended.
3. Another way of saying, "go afield."

THE PARDONER'S TALE
1. It was a medieval belief that Christ was pained in whatever part of his body a person swore by profanely.
2. *Philippians*, III, 19: "Whose end is destruction whose God is their belly, and whose glory is in their shame, who mind earthly things."
3. A distinction of scholastic logic. Substance is the basic nature of a thing; accident describes the outward attributes such as color, taste, etc.
4. A town near Cadiz noted for its strong wines.
5. Implying the dilution of better or more delicate wines.
6. Wines from La Rochelle and Bordeaux were milder.
7. *Proverbs*, XXXI, 4-5: "It is not for kings, O Lemuel, it is not for kings to drink strong wine . . . lest they drink, and forget the law . . ."
8. The story is told in John of Salisbury's *Policraticus*, I, 5.
9. This story follows the preceding one in the *Policraticus*.
10. *Matthew* V, 34: "But I say unto you, swear not at all."
11. *Jeremiah*, IV, 2.
12. The same as current slang for dice.

13. *Leviticus*, XIX, 32.

14. The Arabian physician and commentator on Aristotle (980-1037?)

THE WIFE OF BATH'S PROLOGUE

1. *John* IV, 7-18.
2. It wouldn't be found there, nor would the later supposed quotation (1. 326). Both sayings were published in a sixteenth century collection of maxims attributed to Ptolemy.
3. A side of bacon was there awarded to any married couple who had lived together a year without quarreling.
4. The crow, literally chough, was known as the telltale bird because it traditionally revealed the love affairs of wives to their husbands.
5. I *Timothy*, II, 9.
6. See *The Knight's Tale*, note 2.
7. From *Proverbs*, XXX, 21-23: "For three things the earth is disquieted, and for four which it cannot bear: For a servant when he reigneth; and a fool when he is filled with meat; For an odious woman when she is married; and an handmaid that is heir to her mistress."
8. The story appears in Valerius Maximus, VI, 3, 9, and in Pliny's *Natural History*, XIV, 13. The same chapter in Valerius is referred to in lines 642 and 647.
9. This and the following are all books about women.
10. Pasiphaë gave birth to the Minotaur as a result of her unnatural passion for a bull.

THE WIFE OF BATH'S TALE

1. A friar licensed to beg in a limited territory.
2. *Metamorphoses*, XI, 174, where the story is of Midas' hairdresser rather than his wife. The reeds in the marsh grew up and whispered the story whenever they were rustled by a breeze.

THE FRANKLIN'S TALE

1. Aurelius explains that the moon depends on the sun and the tides on the moon. The highest tides occur when the sun and moon are in conjunction or opposition. Aurelius therefore prays that, when the sun and moon are next in opposition, which will occur when the sun is in the zodiacal

sign of Leo or the lion, the sun and moon will move at the same rate for two years, thus maintaining the Spring flood-tide at its height during that period.

2. *Pamphilus de Amore* was a medieval Latin poem.

3. The twenty-eight mansions of the moon, corresponding to the twenty-eight days of a lunation, were very significant in astrology and other magic arts such as the creation of "illusions" referred to in line 406 and explained in the ensuing passage.

Books on Chaucer and His England

Marchette Chute, *Geoffrey Chaucer of England*. New York: Dutton, 1946.

Nevill Coghill, *The Poet Chaucer*. London: Oxford University Press, 1010.

G. G. Coulton, *Chaucer and his England*, 3d ed. New York: Barnes and Noble, 1963 *Medieval Panorama*. New York: Meridian, 1955.

G. L. Kittredge, *Chaucer and his Poetry*. Cambridge, Mass: Harvard University Press, 1915.

W. W. Laurence, *Chaucer and the Canterbury Tales*. New York: Columbia University Press, 1950.

Emile Legouis, *Geoffroy Chaucer*. London: Russell, 1913.

J. L. Lowes, *The Art of Geoffrey Chaucer*. Indiana: Indiana University Press, 1958.

Kemp Malone, *Chapters on Chaucer*. Baltimore: Johns Hopkins University Press, 1951.

R. K. Root, *The Poetry of Chaucer*, rev. ed. Boston: Smith, Peter, 1922.

J. S. P. Tatlock, *The Mind and Art of Chaucer*. Syracuse, N. Y.: Gordian, 1950.